Staying at Home

Integration and Conflict Studies
Published in association with the Max Planck Institute for Social Anthropology, Halle/Saale

Series Editor: Günther Schlee, Director of the Department of Integration and Conflict at the Max Planck Institute for Social Anthropology

Editorial Board: Brian Donahoe (Max Planck Institute for Social Anthropology), John Eidson (Max Planck Institute for Social Anthropology), Peter Finke (University of Zurich), Joachim Görlich (Max Planck Institute for Social Anthropology), Jacqueline Knörr (Max Planck Institute for Social Anthropology), Bettina Mann (Max Planck Institute for Social Anthropology), Stephen Reyna (Max Planck Institute for Social Anthropology)

Assisted by: Cornelia Schnepel and Viktoria Zeng (Max Planck Institute for Social Anthropology)

The objective of the Max Planck Institute for Social Anthropology is to advance anthropological fieldwork and enhance theory building. "Integration" and "conflict", the central themes of this series, are major concerns of the contemporary social sciences and of significant interest to the general public. They have also been among the main research areas of the institute since its foundation. Bringing together international experts, *Integration and Conflict Studies* includes both monographs and edited volumes, and offers a forum for studies that contribute to a better understanding of processes of identification and inter-group relations.

Volume 1
How Enemies are Made: Towards a Theory of Ethnic and Religious Conflict
Günther Schlee

Volume 2
Changing Identifications and Alliances in North-East Africa
Vol.I: Ethiopia and Kenya
Edited by Günther Schlee and Elizabeth E. Watson

Volume 3
Changing Identifications and Alliances in North-East Africa
Vol.II: Sudan, Uganda and the Ethiopia-Sudan Borderlands
Edited by Günther Schlee and Elizabeth E. Watson

Volume 4
Playing Different Games: The Paradox of Anywaa and Nuer Identification Strategies in the Gambella Region, Ethiopia
Dereje Feyissa

Volume 5
Who Owns the Stock? Collective and Multiple Forms of Property in Animals
Edited by Anatoly M. Khazanov and Günther Schlee

Volume 6
Irish/ness Is All Around Us: Language Revivalism and the Culture of Ethnic Identity in Northern Ireland
Olaf Zenker

Volume 7
Variations on Uzbek Identity: Strategic Choices, Cognitive Schemas and Political Constraints in Identification Processes
Peter Finke

Volume 8
Domesticating Youth: Youth Bulges and their Socio-Political Implications in Tajikistan
Sophie Roche

Volume 9
Creole Identity in Postcolonial Indonesia
Jacqueline Knörr

Volume 10
Friendship, Descent and Alliance in Africa: Anthropological Perspectives
Edited by Martine Guichard, Tilo Grätz and Youssouf Diallo

Volume 11
Masks and Staffs: Identity Politics in the Cameroon Grassfields
Michaela Pelican

Volume 12
The Upper Guinea Coast in Global Perspective
Edited by Jacqueline Knörr and Christoph Kohl

Volume 13
Staying at Home: Identities, Memories and Social Networks of Kazakhstani Germans
Rita Sanders

Staying at Home
Identities, Memories and Social Networks of Kazakhstani Germans

Rita Sanders

berghahn
NEW YORK · OXFORD
www.berghahnbooks.com

First published in 2016 by
Berghahn Books
www.berghahnbooks.com

© 2016, 2021 Rita Sanders
First paperback edition published in 2021

All rights reserved. Except for the quotation of short passages for the purposes of criticism and review, no part of this book may be reproduced in any form or by any means, electronic or mechanical, including photocopying, recording, or any information storage and retrieval system now known or to be invented, without written permission of the publisher.

Library of Congress Cataloging-in-Publication Data

Names: Sanders, Rita, author.
Title: Staying at home : identities, memories and social networks of Kazakhstani Germans / Rita Sanders.
Description: First edition. | New York : Berghahn Books, [2016] | Series: Integration and conflict studies ; volume 13 | Includes bibliographical references and index.
Identifiers: LCCN 2016024964| ISBN 9781785331923 (hardback) | ISBN 9781785331930 (ebook)
Subjects: LCSH: Germans—Kazakhstan—Ethnic identity. | Germans—Kazakhstan—Social conditions. | Collective Memory—Kazakhstan. | Transnationalism—Social aspects—Kazakhstan. | Social networks—Kazakhstan. | Social networks—Germany. | Kazakhstan—Ethnic relations. | Kazakhstan—Emigration and immigration. | Kazakhstan—Relations—Germany. | Germany—Relations—Kazakhstan.
Classification: LCC DK907.15.G47 S36 2016 | DDC 305.83/10584—dc23
LC record available at http://lccn.loc.gov/2016024964

British Library Cataloguing in Publication Data

A catalogue record for this book is available from the British Library

ISBN 978-1-78533-192-3 hardback
ISBN 978-1-80073-004-5 paperback
ISBN 978-1-78533-193-0 ebook

for Agnes and Josef Sanders

Table of Contents

List of Maps, Figures and Tables	x
Acknowledgements	xii
Note on Transliteration	xiv
Introduction	1
Kazakhstani Germans and the Study of Nationalities in Central Asia	4
Concepts of Ethnicity	6

Based on Cultural Grounds – Ethnicity as a Resource – Categorization and Power – A Product of Individual Life Experience – Ethnic Boundaries as Cultural Schemas

Fieldwork in Taldykorgan	15

Part I: Memories, Histories and Life Stories

Chapter 1: Memories and Histories	23
Shifting Memories of the Past	23

The Deportation of 1941 – Discrimination against Germans – Transition and Continuity – The Hard-Working German

The Russian Empire: Colonization of the Kazakh Steppe	30
The Russian Empire: The Settlers from the German States	33
The Soviet Union: Concepts of Nation and Nationality	35
The Soviet Union: Its Formation and Nationality Policies	37

National Delineation – Collectivization – Facing the Menace of the German Reich: The Passport System and Deportations – The Kazakh SSR after 1945

Kazakhstan: The Formation of a Nation State and the Role of Nationality	45

'Kazakhization' – Language Policies – Kazakhstani Identity – Kazakhstani Germans

Chapter 2: The Enmeshment of Identities and Life Stories	60
The Truth of Life Stories	61
Four Life Stories, Four Identity Types	62

Soviet Identity – Kazakhstani Identity – Russian-German Identity – Kazakhstani-German Identity

Summary	87

Part II: Nationality, Power and Change

Chapter 3: Assessing Nationality ... 95
Nationality as a Unifier of Territorial Belonging, Language,
  Religion and 'Mentality' ... 97
  Common Ancestry – Language – Religion – 'Mentality'
National Dichotomies ... 106
Kazakh Primordialism vs. Russian Constructionism ... 110
  Kazakhs' Esteem – Russians' Inclusiveness
Normative Entanglements ... 116
Summary ... 119

Chapter 4: Everyday Nationality in the Kazakh Nation State ... 123
'The Friendship of Peoples – Is Our Wealth!' ... 124
Losing Language Hegemony ... 130
Identification: Strategies and Emotions ... 133
Kazakhstan as a Homeland ... 137
Summary ... 140

Part III: Non-Migrants' Social Ties

Chapter 5: Relations in the Locality: Ethnic Mixing and Missing Kazakhs ... 147
The Relevance of Nationality in Personal Networks ... 147
The Relevance of Nationality in Marriages ... 155
Is There a 'German Community' in Taldykorgan? ... 157
Summary ... 159

Chapter 6: Disruption in the Transnational Social Field ... 162
Relatives and Friends Abroad ... 163
Exodus to an 'Historic Homeland' ... 166
Views on Germany ... 173
Networks and Identity ... 178
Summary ... 181

Part IV: The Effect of Two States' Policies of 'Germanness'
on Kazakhstani Germans

Chapter 7: Changing Transnational Institutions ... 189
The 'German House' ... 189
Support from Germany ... 192
Socializing with Other Germans ... 195
A Parish in Transition from 'German' to 'Lutheran' ... 198
The German House in Transition ... 202
Summary ... 204

Chapter 8: The Divergent Ethnic Policies of Kazakhstan and Germany 207
   The Kazakh State's Official Promotion of Interethnic Harmony 208
   The German State's Contradictory Policies 216
   Summary 222

Conclusion: Germans at Home in Kazakhstan 225
   Identity and Memories 226
   Identities and Identifications 226
   Friendship of the Peoples? 228
   Exclusion through Inclusion: The Role of Personal and Institutional
      Links to Germany 231

References 235

Appendix 250

Index 251

List of Maps, Figures and Tables

Maps

I.1	Field site in Kazakhstan	16

Figures

I.1	Surrounding landscape of Taldykorgan	17
I.2	The main *bazar* in Taldykorgan	18
3.1	Pile sort and free list of Anna (left) and Tanya	107
3.2	Yulia's pile sort and free list	108
4.1	When people enter Taldykorgan they read: 'The friendship of peoples – is our wealth!'	125
6.1	Genealogy of Tamara	167
6.2	Letters and parcels are no longer delivered home	169
6.3	Almost as in Germany: new houses in Taldykorgan	172
7.1	The German House in Taldykorgan	190
7.2	The Sunday school in the German House in Taldykorgan	191
7.3	Sunday mass in the 'German parish'	199
8.1	The *Jugendclub* of the German House presenting a polka during *Nauriz*	209
8.2	The German stand serving 'traditional' food at the 'day of the town'	213

Tables

5.1	Nationality of respondents' relations	149
5.2	Nationality and social roles	150
5.3	Nationality and kind of support	151
5.4	Number of relationships	152
5.5	Number of relationships to Kazakhs	152
5.6	Relatives' nationalities	155
5.7	Spouses' nationalities	156

5.8	Number of relationships to Germans	157
6.1	Residence of kin	163
6.2	Residence of supporting persons	164
6.3	Role of supporting persons and place of residence	165
6.4	Place of residence and kind of support	165
6.5	Number of relationships to Germany	166

Acknowledgements

I would like to thank the many people who have helped to make this research project possible. First of all, I feel very grateful for the openness and cooperation of people in Kazakhstan who took care of my well-being and who were willing to share their ideas and life stories with me. I feel particularly indebted to the Head of the German minority centre in Taldykorgan, Vladimir Molodtsov, and to Eleonora Frisen, Irina Voronina, and Ludmilla Iterman. Their enthusiasm for my work, their warmth and hospitality, and their enormous practical and intellectual support made my research in Taldykorgan a pleasure. Furthermore, I want to thank Vladimir Kraisman and his family, Anna Fabritsius, Erina, Galina Antonovna, Bilimtay Tumenbaev, Roza Shtoppel, Natalya Shenknecht, Shinara Abdulina, Olevtin, Bibitgul, Anna Klaus, and many more people not mentioned by name for their support, hospitality, and ideas. Similarly, I want to thank Irina Erofeeva, Elvira Pak from the Friedrich-Ebert-Stiftung, and Cornelia Riedel from the *Deutsche Allgemeine Zeitung* for sharing their insights with me and for providing me with information.

In Germany, I would like to thank my first supervisor Günther Schlee, director of the Max Planck Institute for Social Anthropology in Halle, for his commitment and his intellectual contributions. I also feel indebted to Peter Finke, head of the Department of Social and Cultural Anthropology at the University of Zürich, who inspired my interest in Kazakhstan years ago. This research benefited substantially from his encouragement, his sharp comments and his expertise in the field. Furthermore, I would like to thank Wolfgang Holzwarth from the Oriental Studies Centre, Martin Luther University Halle-Wittenberg and Irene Hilgers, recently deceased, Svetlana Jacquesson, Philipp Schröder, Aksana Ismailbekova, Sophie Roche, Mateusz Laszczkowski, Joachim Görlich, John Eidson, Mathijs Pelkmans, Florian Mühlfried and many more colleagues at the Max Planck Institute for Social Anthropology for their contributions and critical insights, and also for their encouragement and companionship.

For the logistical and practical support of my work, I thank especially Bettina Mann, Jutta Turner and Oliver Weihmann who dealt carefully and efficiently with all upcoming concerns. Moreover, I express my appreciation to Paul Tyler for his excellent stylistic corrections and for his patience. I also thank the editorial staff at Berghahn Books for their professionalism. Warm thanks go to Cornelia Schnepel for expertly guiding the manuscript through the review and production process. Furthermore, I am particularly indebted to four anonymous reviewers who helped me to improve the final version of the manuscript. Finally, I want to thank the Max Planck Society for providing me with the necessary financial means to conduct this research study and to write this book.

My deepest appreciation goes to those friends and family members whose encouragement and friendship have sustained me through writing this book. In particular, I want to thank my partner, Björn Pecina, for his enthusiasm for the project, for his intellectual insights and for his sense of humour. Our daughter Sontje was born in the middle of writing this book in 2012. I thank her for teaching me all the fundamentals of life and for making me laugh at times when I was stressed out. Finally, I thank my parents, Agnes and Josef Sanders, who have always believed in me and supported my life plans, although those took me thousands of kilometres away from them. It is to them that I dedicate this book.

Note on Transliteration

Transliteration is a difficult matter since there is no standard system of transliteration from the Kazakh language. In this book, I use a simplified version of the BGN (United States Board on Geographic Names) system for transliterating Kazakh and Russian words. For the sake of readability, I have omitted apostrophes for the Russian soft and hard signs and converted 'ë' to 'yo'. Secondly, with regard to Kazakh words, I have removed diacritical marks. Thirdly, I have used the most common form for place names well known beyond Central Asia, though this leads to certain inconsistencies. In Kazakhstan, the old Soviet-era Russian designations for names and places are still very widespread, which is why I sometimes use them instead of the official Kazakh designations.

Introduction

My first encounter with Kazakhstan's Germans took place, rather by chance, in a small village in the south-eastern corner of Kazakhstan in 1999, where I had been living for about two months. While I was researching the significance of Kazakh kinship categories, my Kazakh host father happened to mention the 'village's German family'. By the time I had finally arranged to meet them, it was the last day before their emigration, and they were extremely excited about their new life in Germany. For me it was quite unsettling to realize, after talking with them, that they had little clue about the country in which they had longed to live for so many years and to which they were now heading. Not to mention my disorientation as I sat eating the same apple pie my mother bakes, while in a garden full of flowers, the likes of which I had never seen before in a Kazakh village.

Those Kazakhstani Germans, as many others before them, desired to live among Germans, and had therefore sold everything to leave for an unknown land, often precluding any possibility of coming back. Three years later, I decided to write my MA thesis about homeland conceptions of Russian Germans living in Cologne. I understood that the vision of 'returning to the historic homeland' had been for many a strong motivator, fuelling high expectations, but at the same time those feelings worked against them because this vision of an 'historic homeland' was not accepted by local Germans. The fact that people born thousands of kilometres from Germany claim 'Germanness' on the grounds of common blood simply reminds most people in Germany of times they hoped had long passed.

In 2006, I returned to Kazakhstan, this time to learn what being German meant to Kazakhstani Germans and how it affected their behaviour. I met Germans who, above all, considered themselves more punctual, organized and hard-working than those around them, which they proudly attributed to their ethnic belonging. For me, this was hard to accept since the attribution of 'mentality' to ethnic groups contradicts my very personal viewpoint and experience. The fact that I am a German researcher has impacted this work. My presence often disturbed the well-established mechanisms of inclusion and exclusion since I was perceived as a different kind of German. Furthermore, some Kazakhstani Germans were aware that many Germans dislike the category 'German', and this was particularly troubling to so-called ethno-activists who held positions in one of the German minority's institutions and whose reservations towards me were sometimes difficult to dispel. But also encounters with non-officials were often affected by the contradictory expectations of each other's concept of a German identity. This either resulted in people trying their best to prove that they were 'real, pure' Germans by, for instance, showing me how well they kept their house, or – not solely but sometimes depending on their knowledge of Germany's Germans – by doing their best to make it clear that they were not 'nationalists'. Fortunately most people realized I was not an official representative of the German state, and only a few times was I approached under the mistaken notion that I could provide assistance in pursuing immigration to Germany.

My research has profited greatly from the fact that I spent an extended period of time with my subjects. I was able to experience many encounters and conversations in which my presence became increasingly insignificant over the months, and divergent findings between interview statements and everyday conversation contributed to my insights into the significance of a German identity in present-day Kazakhstan. But above all people allowed me to be part of their community and to attain intimate knowledge of who they were and how they viewed their paths in life.

This book explores the lives, perceptions and actions of those who chose to stay in Kazakhstan and those who did not necessarily choose to stay but who stayed nevertheless. Why did they stay? Was it not important for them to live 'among their own kind'? Or did they fear that they would be regarded as Russian in their 'historic homeland' Germany? What, then, does a German identity mean to people? When is it important? For whom is it important? What constitutes a German identity in Kazakhstan, and has it been changing?

Kazakhstan is often characterized as the most prosperous and 'international' of all Central Asian states. According to official statistics, present-day Kazakhstan is home to more than one hundred different ethnic groups; however, the two major groups – Kazakhs and Russians – comprise more than eighty per cent of the country's population. After the Soviet Union's dissolution, many of its long-term observers predicted ethnic turmoil, but in Kazakhstan this largely failed to materialize. Nor was there any intense aspiration to independence in 1991, which is why the country's existence has been referred to as 'accidental' (Olcott 2002). Kazakhstan's first and – as of this writing – only president, Nursultan Nazarbayev, is said to have successfully unified a Kazakh 'national and cultural regeneration' with a policy of 'ethnic harmony' and economic reforms (Dave 2007: 3). However, despite economic growth and ethnic stability, a vast number of people have opted to leave the country since 1991.

By 1997 alone, approximately 1.5 million people had left Kazakhstan, or roughly ten per cent of the country's population. This huge migratory outflow had the largest impact on Kazakhstan's Germans, of whom more than eighty per cent have emigrated. Between 1989 and 1999, the German population in Kazakhstan dropped from about one million to about 350,000 (or from 5.8 to 2.4 per cent of the total population) and was, according to official statistics, estimated at about 180,000 in 2012. Germany's constitutional guarantee of citizenship and generous benefits for immigrants from the former USSR during the late 1980s and early 1990s, in support of the *Ruf der Heimat* ('call of the homeland'), had laid the groundwork for this massive immigration (Römhild 1998: 130f).

Kazakhstani-German history is marked by several turning points, and ethnic belonging has had varying impacts on the lives of Kazakhstani Germans and their ancestors. At the time when most German settlers came to Russia – towards the end of the eighteenth century – they were considered more 'developed' simply because they had come from a Western country. For about a century they enjoyed more freedom and greater rights than their Russian neighbours, who were mostly bound to serfdom during that time. But as the twentieth century unfolded, the situation gradually reversed. Russia's Germans had always been affected by the mutual relations of the two states, which, for obvious reasons, worsened during the First World War, and which, after the attack of the German Wehrmacht on the Soviet Union in 1941, brought about the catastrophe of deportation. All Soviet Germans were forced to leave their settlements in the Volga region and in Ukraine, and to begin a new life in Siberia or Central Asia. Many lost most or all of their relatives after the Second World War and faced discrimination because of their link to a Soviet 'enemy nation'. However, once more, in the 1980s and 1990s, the situation reversed. Being German turned into an asset, for it permitted immigration to Germany.

Kazakhstani Germans are usually referred to as a diaspora (Akiner 2005; Brown 2005; Diener 2004), which presumes an ethnically distinct group that is characterized by its attachment to an 'historic homeland'. More recent studies operate additionally within the framework of transnationalism (Sienkiewicz 2015; Stoll 2007); thus they account for the numerous ties between those Kazakhstani Germans who left and those who stayed, which are assumed to build a social field that transgresses national borders. This book critically reflects on the concepts of diaspora and transnationalism by elaborating on social (transnational) networks, the flows of support, the meanings transmitted by such networks and support, and how both impact the lives of Kazakhstani Germans and the role that ethnicity plays in them. I will explore how transnationally transmitted meanings are reinterpreted by people in Kazakhstan to meet their predominantly locally defined needs. Along these lines, it will be investigated how views about Germany interact with Kazakhstani Germans' memories of 'their past' and their views of a German identity. Further, I will elaborate on the role of the two states' policies – the effect of Germany's immigration and minority policies on Kazakhstani Germans' perception of a German identity, and how Kazakhstan's nationality policies are viewed and used. Thus I will explore the interplay of memories, networks and state policies and how they constrain and enable people in the 'construction' of a (Kazakhstani) German identity. In doing so, my study adds to research on migratory processes and transnationalism that have so far focused on labour migrants and refugees after immigration. Firstly, only by equally investigating those who did not leave a place that is deeply affected by emigration are the effects of transnational ties to be fully understood. Secondly, a predominantly ethnically triggered out-migration raises the question of how a significant reduction in numbers affects the process of ethnic identification in the place that has been abandoned. To this end, I will discuss when, how and why people identify themselves as Germans in present-day Kazakhstan, and those aspects that influence this process of identification.

I will argue that German identity in Kazakhstan has been transformed during the last decades. Memories of the past, which had been built upon unjust treatment received during Soviet times, have been partially replaced with 'German success stories', due both to the diminishing Soviet notion of the 'German enemy nation' and to increasing contact with Germany, which has also resulted in the influx of 'good German products' into the Kazakhstani market, which is particularly appreciated by Kazakhs. However, a growing knowledge of Germany's Germans, personally transmitted by relatives who sometimes face a range of difficulties in Germany, is reflected in negative attitudes towards Germany and its Germans, and has ultimately contributed to a reformation of the German category, namely by excluding Germany's Germans and by partly dismissing the idea of an 'historic German homeland'. More locally defined identities appear to be 'under construction', and may increasingly become bound up in the newly established Kazakh nation state and find expression in a Kazakhstani German or Kazakhstani identity.

My research contributes to the anthropological study of ethnicity in present-day Kazakhstan. At the same time, it deals with a largely ethnically triggered migratory process by focusing on those who did not migrate. Neither of these issues has been extensively investigated thus far, and to do so this research project will need to engage with a diverse field of studies and research both within and outside of anthropology.

Kazakhstani Germans and the Study of Nationalities in Central Asia

The process of ethnic identification with regard to Kazakhstani Germans has not been extensively investigated. What few studies exist (Brown 2005; Diener 2004, 2009a; Moore 2000) primarily deal with the impact of Kazakh state policies on Kazakhstani Germans as a minority nationality 'inherited' from the Soviet

Union.[1] Though some of them are based in part on fieldwork in Kazakhstan, their findings are largely a contribution to the body of literature on the 'nationality question' in the former Soviet Union and its successor states (Abashin 2007; Bremmer and Taras 1993; Brubaker 1999; Chinn and Kaiser 1996; Hirsch 2005; Kolstø 1999; Martin 2001; Slezkine 1994; G. Smith 1996; Tishkov 1997; Weitz 2002; for Kazakhstan see Akiner 2005; Dave 2007; Gumppenberg 2004; Olcott 2002). Most of the authors are political scientists who are concerned with the 'transition process' within societies in the context of a post-Soviet framework. In doing so, most studies touch on the notion of identity, but identity formation is conceptualized – at least implicitly – only as a 'top-down' process and conceived of as identity politics. Thus, very often, people are placed into categories and ethnic belonging is assumed rather than analysed. This is one of the reasons why most studies, until the end of the 1990s, tended to predict ethnic turmoil and large-scale ethnic uprisings in the Soviet Union successor states. Furthermore, many of those analyses were mistaken in that they conceived of ethnicity itself as a source of potential conflicts, thus arguing that once the Soviet Union as an oppressive force had faded away, ethnic differences would trigger various kinds of (ethnic) conflicts (cf. Finke, Sanders and Zanca 2013: 133). Since most countries of the former Soviet Union followed a different course from what was predicted by the nationality experts, the study of nationalities in Central Asia almost ground to a halt.

The formation of new Central Asian nation states and its effects on ethnic boundary drawing have not attracted much attention in anthropology circles (Finke 2014 and Schoeberlein 1994 among the exceptions). Since fieldwork in Central Asia has only recently become possible, there are few anthropological research studies on Central Asia, and they are scattered between such diverse fields as household economy and economic strategies in an 'economy in transition' (Finke 2004; Werner 1997; Yessenova and Dobson 2000; Zanca 1999), the role of religious belonging, conversion and everyday Islam (Kehl-Bodrogi 2008; McBrien 2006; Pelkmans 2007; Roberts 2007), gender relations (Finke and Sancak 2007; Reeves 2010), state borders (Reeves 2007, 2014) and local-level state administration (Alexander 2007; Jones Luong 2004a, 2004b; cf. also Wolfe 2000 for anthropological research on Eastern Europe and the former Soviet Union). However, features and effects of migratory processes, from an anthropological point of view, remain understudied. Exceptions are several projects on labour migration from Kyrgyzstan and Uzbekistan to Russia and the United States (Ilkhamov 2013; Isabaeva 2011; Reeves 2011a; Schröder 2013), which also capture the concerns of those who stayed behind.[2] Their work is insightful insofar as they shift attention to the unfinished outcomes of place making by multiple movements and (power) relations in a field of analysis that appears to be determined by fixed ethnic and spatial categories. Furthermore, several studies investigate the politics and effects of the repatriation of the Kazakh diaspora

(Bonnenfant 2012; Diener 2009b; Dubuisson and Genina 2011; Finke 2004, 2013; Finke and Sancak 2005; Sancak 2007).

The history of Russian Germans has attracted more academic attention. Historians and *Volkskundler* have presented a Russian-German history largely in terms of 'sovietology', and thus Germans are primarily perceived as victims of the Soviet regime (Brandes 1996, 1997; Eisfeld 1999; Krieger 2006; but cf. also Oltmer 2006). In this regard, Eisfeld (1999: 7) states that 'their [Russian Germans'] fate is among the worst that was done to the Germans before, during and after the Second World War'.[3] This victimizing stance, as well as the search for a German essence by investigating *Wolgadeutschtum* or *Sibiriendeutschtum*, which is described by Brake (1998: 42) as a search for a *Reliktkultur*, has been rightly critiqued as a continuation of Nazi ideology (e.g., by Bausinger 1987).

Furthermore, the fact that the field of *Vertriebenenvolkskunde* has been for the most part non-academic and pursued by several independent institutes implies that insights of social theory have been largely ignored (cf. Brake 1998: 42).[4] This has gradually changed due to a shift in focus to the present-day situation of Russian/Kazakhstani Germans in Germany, and several studies explicitly draw on a biographical approach (Brake 1998; Pfister-Heckmann 1998; Römhild 1998). These studies, like several others (Boll 1996; Dietz 1996, 2006; Eder, Rauer and Schmidtke 2004; Graudenz and Römhild 1996; Ingenhorst 1997; Kühnel and Strobl 2000; Radenbach and Rosenthal 2015), elaborate on Russian-German history, in order to understand why it is often so complicated to integrate Russian Germans into German society. As of late, research on Russian/Kazakhstani Germans takes into account questions of transnational social networks and identity, but research remains mostly focused on the migrants' situation in Germany (Savoskul 2015; Schönhuth and Kaiser 2015; Sienkiewicz 2015; among the few exceptions are Stoll 2007 who has investigated the migration decisions of Germans in Kazakhstan and Tauschwitz 2015 who has analysed why some Russian Germans have stayed in Russia).

Concepts of Ethnicity

Ethnicity refers to one particular type of social or collective identity, and thus shares features with the broader concept of identity, so it is helpful to begin here with a general discussion on identity. The notion of identity is contested; for instance, Stuart Hall (1998: 1) asks, 'Who needs it?' In the same vein, Rogers Brubaker (2004: 41–48) suggests abandoning the notion of identity as an analytical concept and instead looking separately at identification and categorization, at self-understanding and at commonality, connectedness and groupness. I find all aspects – and their separate consideration – useful, but because the notion of identity brings them together, I will employ it as an analytical tool.

The critique of identity as an analytical category is argued largely on the same grounds as the critique of structuralism and structural functionalism in general. Thus the notion of identification, which implies investigating processes instead of representations and structures, is seen as superior (Schlee et al. 2009: 7). I, however, follow Schlee (ibid.: 7f) in that both identity/structure and identification/process have to be explored since 'the latter cannot be understood without the former. Just as there can be no identities without identification, so can there be no identification without identities'. Thus, existing identities establish the frameworks for people's identifications, but though they imply 'normative appeals to potentially interconnected actors' (ibid.: 2), they certainly do not determine how actors respond to such appeals. In order to explain processes of identification it is, therefore, not enough to study prevalent identities; rather, both the wider context (socially, economically, politically and historically) and individual motivations and choices have to be taken into consideration. The next sections will outline the theoretical aspects that are most relevant for a discussion of Kazakhstani-German identity.

Based on Cultural Grounds

Almost every statement on ethnicity or ethnic group starts with a reference to Barth's seminal 'introduction' to *Ethnic Groups and Boundaries: The Social Organization of Culture Difference*, originally written in 1969. Barth (1996 [1969]: 78) states: 'To the extent that actors use ethnic identities to categorize themselves and others for purposes of interaction, they form ethnic groups in this organizational sense'. Thus, according to Barth, people build groups in order to interact with others; only for this purpose do they differentiate themselves from others on the basis of cultural differences. But those differences in culture are not the reason for building groups, and, therefore, 'the critical focus of investigation from this point of view becomes the ethnic boundary that defines the group, not the cultural stuff that it encloses' (ibid.: 79). Logically then, ethnic groups only persist as long as the boundary is maintained and interaction with others takes place (ibid.: 78f).

Barth's ideas challenged essentialist notions of ethnicity, asserting that ethnicity is an ongoing construction process, in which cultural attributes are secondary. However, there is no similar controversy in terms of boundary making, which is always based on making distinctions with regard to language, religion, customs, shared norms and the like. Barth took his basic idea from Weber (1996 [1922]: 35), who states that 'the political community inspires the belief in common ethnicity' and not the other way round, but Weber (and also Barth in his later writings) also made clear that such a presumed identity may last, once the *Gemeinschaft*, the political community, has dissolved. Furthermore, particular cultural attributes – such as language, religion, a conception of what is correct and proper or a sense of honour – can play a decisive role in the continuity of a group (cf. ibid.: 37).

Ethnicity, therefore, has a cultural basis and, precisely for that reason, differs from class, gender or age (Brass 1996: 85; May 2001: 41). But any common cultural trait can provide a basis for ethnic group formation. Hence a description and analysis limited to differences in language and religion, customs and habits does not reveal how, when and why ethnic belonging matters and when and why it does not because ethnicity 'is produced and reproduced in social interaction' (Jenkins 1997: 40). Moreover, ethnic identification depends on the particular situation and the particular interlocutor, i.e., people might situationally switch between different identities (cf. Elwert 2002; Schlee 1989, 2006).

In present-day social science, it is widely accepted that every facet of an ethnic identity is constructed,[5] but how the often observed significance and persistence of ethnicity is to be explained is a controversial matter. Explanations draw on the power of categorization, emotion and memories as well as the aspiration of individuals to achieve their aims. These explanations will be discussed in the following sections.

Ethnicity as a Resource

According to Abner Cohen, who takes up Weber's ideas, ethnicity is largely a political phenomenon. Cohen (1996 [1969]: 84) states: 'people do not kill each other because their customs are different', but because 'these cultural differences are associated with serious political cleavages'. In particular the context of colonialism catalysed people to organize themselves against the colonial rulers, often by emphasizing parts of their 'traditional culture' and, on that basis, building 'ethnic groups' (ibid.: 83). Seen this way, ethnically captured cultural traits are instrumental in instigating action to pursue political objectives and, therefore, are used as a resource.

The view of ethnicity as an instrument and resource is taken furthest by rational choice theorists. According to Hechter (1996: 90), 'rational choice considers individual behaviour to be a function of the interaction of structural constraints and the sovereign preferences of individuals' and, thus, intends to bridge the micro and macro levels of analysis. Acknowledging that individual preferences vary and are difficult to assess, rational choice theorists hold that the aggregate of many individuals' reactions to structural constraints is predictable. This is feasible because individuals' behaviour is assumed ultimately to seek to optimize cost-benefit calculations (Hechter 1996).

Any kind of group activity, therefore, only occurs when people expect a net benefit for themselves. However, how people make such calculations depends on their knowledge and their experience. In order to be able to predict someone else's behaviour (which is of course decisive) people are geared to share norms or institutions. In general, the more norms or institutions people share, the better they are able to predict each other's behaviour, which in turn engenders trust, and is why some rational choice theorists argue – in particular against the background of weak states and legal uncertainty – that trade or business activities are most likely to occur in ethnically homogeneous networks (Landa 1998).

Schlee (2008: 26) underlines the relevance of the size of a particular group. For any kind of group activity, the ideal number of members is desired in order to perform collective action as efficiently as possible. There should be a sufficient number of members to perform the action or to fulfil certain criteria, but any additional member also means another person with whom benefits must be shared. Striving for the ideal number of group members, then, has its effects on the process of identification itself, since the group would be motivated to opt for a wider or narrower interpretation of certain identities in order to constitute the ideal number of potential members (cf. also Hechter 1988).

The ideal size of a particular group is, however, only one explanatory component in Schlee's decision theory of identification (2008). The two other components are the identities' cognitive representations and the politics of inclusion and exclusion. That is, identities must match up with a shared category system since they must be plausible to others, and only certain actors have the power to actively engage and/or manipulate identity discourses. Both aspects will be detailed in the next section.

Generally speaking, all 'instrumentalists', not only rational choice advocates, interpret ethnicity as something principally positive that people use (and 'construct' in the first place) to organize their common activities and to predict the behaviour of others. However, many social anthropologists observe that the individual's agency is much more constrained than is generally assumed by instrumentalists.

Categorization and Power
Anthony P. Cohen argues against viewing ethnicity as merely a matter of tactics and strategy. Cohen (2000a: 5) criticizes 'Goffman's legacy to identity studies':

> [It] overstated the gamelike character of social interaction, and the extent to which individuals and groups can control their own destinies. It understates culture. It ignores self-consciousness, and the commitment made by individuals and, perhaps, groups to views of themselves which, contrary to another horrendously overused term in identity studies, they do not regard as 'negotiable'.

Thus, people often do not have a choice in deciding who they are or who they wish to pretend they are, for they are classified by powerful others (cf. Cohen 2000a: 10; cf. Verdery 2000: 36).

Jenkins (1996) views social identities as the result of a dialectical process of self-identification and categorization, and he (1997: 54–56) criticizes social anthropologists, in particular the postmodern ones, for having overly focused on group identification. Such one-sided observance advanced the perception of ethnicity as a social resource at the expense of neglecting the possible negative aspects of social categorizations.[6] Negative consequences of social categorizing are often attributed to racism and nationalism instead of ethnicism (cf. May 2001: 33–35).[7] One might view both nationalism and racism as 'historically specific manifestations of ethnicity', but both are ideologies and, therefore, 'bodies of knowledge which make claims about the way the social world is and crucially about the way it ought to be' (Jenkins 1997: 84).

According to Jenkins (1997: 56–59), categorizations take place at three different layers: the individual, the interactional and the institutional. Thus, even the 'sense of self', the individual layer, is the result of social interaction.[8] Furthermore, Jenkins (ibid.: 63–69) sees a gradual distinction between formal and informal ways of classifying others, ranging from state classifications to employment to public interaction.

The state holds a prominent position with respect to the categorizing of people (e.g., Brass 1985). Verdery (2000: 37) asserts that state-makers tend to fix social identities by classifying their subjects according to clear-cut categories, with an aim to maintain better control over them. Therefore, 'identity categories become mandatory elements of people's existence within the state' (ibid.: 39), though, according to Verdery, there is still some room for the manipulation of identities in 'micro-interaction'. But different states, at different times, vary in their efforts to keep track of and classify people, thus the 'imperativeness of identities has its own historicity', which is why 'the conditions that make identities more or less imperative, according to the organization and histories of the states that contain them' (ibid.) shall be the focus of investigation.

The modernist assumption, above all associated with the writings of Anderson (1983), Hobsbawm and Ranger (1983), Hobsbawm (1990) and Gellner (1983), is that the state came first, and it was the state that 'constructed' the ethnicity of its subjects. Modernists view the rise of the nation state, as well as of nationalism – i.e., viewing nations (each with its own distinct identity) as the crucial source of political power (A.D. Smith 1994) – in connection with modernity. The building of nations, which eventually entails a process of cultural homogenization, also brought about the category of 'ethnic minority' for those who, for various reasons, could not become part of the nation (cf. Sökefeld 2007: 46; cf. Verdery 2000: 45–47). May (2001: 25f) hints at the paradox that modernists, although they rejected the 'pre-modern' notion of ethnicity and saw it replaced by the nation, ultimately provoked the postmodern celebration of ethnic minorities in a plural society (cf. also Herzfeld 2005: 114f).

One potent way in which states can shape their subjects' actions is through the forming of stereotypes, which are seen by Herzfeld (2005: 202) as a 'discursive weapon of power'. Local actors are affected by state actors since 'the categorical systems of local communities absorb (or are forced to swallow) increasingly regimented typifications of "others" emanating from above and authorized as the weapons of a locally reproduced form of power' (ibid.). At the same time, stereotypes entail the 'possibility of subversion' (ibid.). Herzfeld (ibid.: 26, 203, 209) raises the question of how stereotypes fit into his advocacy to look at actions, since stereotypes are generally associated with the static analysis of classificatory systems; he still stresses their importance, however, by placing the emphasis on investigating how, by whom and under what circumstances they are used. Herzfeld (ibid.: 207) points out that an actor refers to 'stereotypes of a dominant discourse and deploys them in the pursuit of personal interests'; thus he stresses people's agency and does not primarily view people as the victims of powerful states.

My study takes up Herzfeld's idea that states are able to exert power by means of coining stereotypes which, however, might be used otherwise by local actors. With regard to Kazakhstani Germans, the power of several states – the Russian Empire, the Soviet Union, Kazakhstan and Germany – in the shaping of people's identities and the influencing of their behaviour will be explored. State actors affect their subjects' lives and behaviour, but this is not a one-way process, and even when state policies aim to fully control people, they certainly never determine behaviour. Therefore, Brubaker (2004: 53) is right when he states with respect to the USSR: 'Categorical group denominations – however authoritative, however pervasively institutionalized – cannot serve as indicators of real "groups" or robust "identities"'.

Beyond the role of states in categorizing people, this study explores other processes of categorization. The starting point of this investigation will be the individual person and her or his life experience. Thus it will be necessary to consider how someone has been categorized throughout his/her life in order to understand how present-day identities are perceived, lived and used.

A Product of Individual Life Experience

Ethnic identities, like any other identities, are not grasped comprehensively solely by viewing them as products of categorizing others, and/or by seeing in them potential resources for action. On the contrary, ethnicity may under certain circumstances appear as an obstacle, and may cause one to question why in such circumstances people continue to hold to their ethnic belonging. T.H. Eriksen (1993), for instance, indicates that ethnicity might even be reproduced, though this rather limits the prosperity and power of those who 'belong' to the group.

Ethnicity can only be fully understood by looking at how people identify themselves, which implies looking at individual persons because 'any social identity … must mean something to individuals before it can be said to "exist" in the social world' (Jenkins 1997: 166). In this vein, Anthony P. Cohen (2000b: 61) highlights that by paying attention to people's consciousness, to the question of 'the person I believe myself to be', social anthropologists are also better equipped to avoid any kind of 'groupism'. Cohen (ibid.: 76) states: 'The ethnic group is an aggregate of selves each of whom produces ethnicity for itself. What these various productions have in common may well be more a matter of formal appearance than of meaningful reality'. Thus, people might have very different things in mind when they, for instance, refer to a German identity.

If one takes into account what social identities mean to people, such identities may not be as flexible, shifting and negotiable as often assumed because social identities are an aspect of each individual's emotional and psychological constitution. In early socialization human beings develop a sense of self that may prove extremely resistant to change (Jenkins 1997: 47, 58; cf. E.H. Erikson 1959). Emotional attachments to social identities might, therefore, be seen as constraining forces to the 'free usage' of ethnic belonging. Emotions might also help to explain why 'ethnic attachments do not have the same salience and force everywhere' (Jenkins 1997: 77). But the salience of ethnic belonging, can, logically, only be identified for individual persons, and not attached to any given group.

How such an emotional bond is constituted and what people precisely attach to certain identities is, therefore, fundamental and brings us back to the 'cultural grounds', to the 'ethnic memories, values, symbols, myths and tradition' (A.D. Smith 1996: 189) that are seen as crucial for 'ethnic survival'. Likewise, how ethnic belonging is constructed by people – e.g., whether or not in primordial terms – is part of culture, too (cf. Barth 2000). This knowledge of 'who someone is', and how the categories to which people belong are defined, is transmitted from generation to generation. To be sure, this is not to say that the knowledge of ethnicity is unlikely to be highly contradictory. Exactly for this reason, it offers a great range of alternative belongings, at certain times and under certain circumstances. But what people 'have in their minds' while acting has to be considered. Thus, in order to systematically investigate people's minds, this research study also draws on insights from cognitive anthropology.

Ethnic Boundaries as Cultural Schemas

Cognitive approaches investigate the relation between human society and human thought by seeking to understand how people organize and use knowledge (D'Andrade 1996: xiv, 1). Cognitive anthropology stems from a long-standing anthropological interest in classification and categorization (Durkheim and Mauss 1970; Lévi-Strauss 1969). From the beginning it has additionally been concerned with developing appropriate methods through which to study the structures and forms of idea systems. This is also why the writings of Lounsbury (1968) and Goodenough (1968) were so authoritative since they – using the example of kinship terminology – presented a method for identifying 'idea units' and comprehending the structure of these units which, then, became known as componential (or feature) analysis (D'Andrade 1996: 17, 21). During the 1960s, feature analysis expanded to other areas – e.g., colour terms or classification of animals – and turned away from 'structuralist thinking'; its emphasis shifted from dichotomous features to more continuous dimensional types of representation (cf. ibid.: 58–91).

A decade later, in the mid-1970s, with a further shift in research interest to 'on the ground discourses', it became apparent that human cognition relies on more complex structures than previously analysed through feature analysis. The new concept that was developed in order to better grasp complex human thinking became popularly known as 'schema' (D'Andrade 1996: 122). A schema can be defined as 'an organized framework of objects and relations which has yet to be filled with concrete detail' (ibid.: 124). Thus a schema is not a 'picture' or representation that is stored in one's mind but rather a processor or 'a kind of mental recognition "device" which *creates* a complex interpretation from minimal inputs' (ibid.: 136). The concept of schema was further developed by connectionists (e.g., Strauss and Quinn 1997) who use a neural (rather than a lingual) metaphor for knowledge in order to better illustrate that 'a schema is not a set of sentences but rather a pattern of interaction among strongly interconnected units' (ibid.: 52). An event, for instance, activates all units that respond to features of similar events. In this daily process, mental networks are constantly modified (ibid.: 51–53). But 'networks can range from very easy to very hard to change with experience and from very biased towards one interpretation to very balanced in choice' (D'Andrade 1996: 142). Generally, mental networks develop through encounters with a structured environment and, hence, they are shaped by someone's life experience, or they can be described as 'an abstract organization of experience' (ibid.: 150).[9]

A further step, then, is to ask when and how schemas and networks affect perception or memory, and how they influence behaviour. D'Andrade (1996: 239) states that 'schemas do not by themselves have any force or power'. It is only through linkage with the emotional or motivational system of individuals that cultural schemas affect human action (ibid.: 218).[10] Feelings and motivations are incorporated into schemas; for example, someone might associate Christmas with pleasant feelings. Thus, motivations are mediated by the inner experience of feeling, which stems, in part, from the approval and disapproval of those who are important to us. But experiences also produce conflicting goals and, therefore, never stimulate behaviour unambiguously (Strauss and Quinn 1997: 101–10). Generally, 'not all cultural schemas acquire affective and motivational force for people; to understand which do and which do not, we need to learn the particularities of a person's experience' (ibid.: 110). For instance, to the extent that evaluations (like 'good girl') become aspects of someone's self-identity, they can act as stable goals towards which people strive throughout their lives in order to remain true to their self-images.

Few studies on ethnicity have explicitly drawn on insights from the field of cognitive science (an exception is Finke 2014), even though many studies elaborate on the power of categorization in general (cf. Brubaker 2004: 69). Brubaker

(2004), who advocates for the integration of cognitive approaches into the study of ethnicity, points to the 'clash with the positivist, experimentalist, individualist and reductionist commitment of cognitive science' (ibid.: 69) and the epistemological assumptions of those who investigate ethnicity in a usually 'humanistic, interpretive, holistic and antireductionist' manner (ibid.).[11]

With regard to research on the former USSR and the nation states that gained independence after its dissolution, Brubaker (2004: 66) suggests that most related studies on ethnicity are almost exclusively concerned with 'official, codified, formalized categorization practices employed by powerful and authoritative institutions, above all the state', whereas 'unofficial informal "everyday" classification and categorization of ordinary people' are rather understudied. This is all the more problematic since 'the connection between official categories and popular self-understanding is seldom demonstrated in detail' (ibid.: 68). Those 'everyday classifications' might, however, significantly deviate from official ones, because the former leave 'considerable room for maneuver' and people are 'often able to deploy such categories strategically' (ibid.). Since, as mentioned above, schemas are built up in relation to engagement with the 'real world', Brubaker (ibid.: 79) is correct when he asserts that cognitive approaches connect 'what goes on in people's heads with our analysis of what goes on in public'.

Furthermore, the concept of schema allows for the consideration of more complex knowledge structures than the notion of category does (Brubaker 2004: 76). For instance, it is not only about how people are classified but 'about how gestures, utterances, situations, events, states of affairs, actions, and sequences of actions get classified (and thereby interpreted and experienced)' (ibid.: 77). Hence, it is about the daily reproduction of ethnicity. One key aspect of processes of ethnicization is, then, to investigate the degree to which ethnic schemas are accessible; in some contexts they might become hyperaccessible and in effect outdo other interpretive schemas.

It is not my intention to advocate for a single concept of ethnicity; instead, I wish to combine the above-presented ideas and theoretical thoughts. Ethnicity is based on cultural grounds. Self-identification and categorization are carried out on the basis of language, religion, a shared memory of the past, common customs, norms, habits and/or other features. Through interaction people build groups and categories, and thus they create identities that are linked to those dimensions. Those identities are at a given time already available, which is why their features and how they relate to one another has to be investigated: they set the framework for future action. People in principle strive to pursue their goals or life projects, and since they have agency they both use and alter those given identities. However, differences in power among people have to be kept in mind, along with state identity policy and its history. Finally, emotional attachments to language, religion and other identity dimensions, as well as to identity categories, have an impact on how people identify themselves and classify others.

This book addresses the core questions of when, how and why people identify themselves as Germans and when and why not. To discuss when people stress their ethnic belonging, it is necessary to elaborate upon the situational linking of ethnicity. To discuss how people identify themselves as Germans, one must refer to the elements that comprise the cultural basis. Why people identify themselves as Germans is, on one level, dependent upon an individual's situation; but in a larger sense the answer also lies in instrumental uses, emotional bonds and performative expressions.

In particular, this book seeks to combine the ideas and concepts of Schlee, D'Andrade and Herzfeld and to investigate structure and process in equal measure to account for how it is that identities exert power. In this endeavour, I treat ethnic belonging both as a mental representation and as a discursive expression, as a motor for deliberate action and as performance, as an instrument of the state to control its people and as a weapon of power of its citizens. In order to investigate such diverse aspects of identity my research study applies various methods from the social sciences and combines them in a novel manner. Next to methods stemming from cognitive approaches, this research is inspired by network analysis and by life story interviews. However, my main insights derive from the intimate knowledge that people were willing to share with me during informal interviews and participant observation (Spradley 2005). In the city of Taldykorgan, I conducted twelve months of fieldwork in 2006 and 2007. In the following section, I will briefly introduce my research site.

Fieldwork in Taldykorgan

Taldykorgan is a medium-sized city of about 135,000 inhabitants, situated approximately 300 kilometres north-east of Almaty. According to official statistics, about sixty per cent of the city's inhabitants are Kazakh and thirty per cent are Russian; the German population was estimated at 1,500 in 2007. Taldykorgan became the centre of the Almaty oblast in 2001,[12] which resulted in a rapid increase in population that 'brought money to the city', created large-scale building activities and gave many people hope for a prosperous future. This contrasts sharply with the disastrous living circumstances prevalent during the second half of the 1990s, when the city's infrastructure, as in many other areas of Kazakhstan, was on the verge of collapse, not to mention the widespread failure of former state enterprises. In present-day Taldykorgan, there is only one large factory (which produces batteries), and thus most people are engaged in small business ventures. Jobs in administration, however, have rapidly increased since 2001, as well as in other parts of the public sector such as for teachers and hospital employees. The soil of the surrounding area is comparatively good, and the amount of water available for farming exceptional by Kazakhstani standards. During the Soviet era, the region was famous for growing sugar beet. However,

Map I.1 Field site in Kazakhstan. Reproduced with kind permission of the Max Planck Institute for Social Anthropology, Halle.

at present most of the previous agricultural crop land lies fallow because farming is not considered to be particularly profitable.

Taldykorgan is situated in the *Zhetisu* (seven rivers) region; its Karatal River is one of the seven rivers flowing into Lake Balkhash. Before Russian colonization, the area was used as a winter camp by nomadic Kazakhs. Russians and Ukrainians came to the region mainly after the 1860s, and by 1880 there were more than three thousand primarily Russian families who settled in the region and built thirty-six settlements. One such settlement was Gavrilovka, with about twenty-five farmyards, which was renamed Taldykorgan in 1920. Most Germans were deported to the city, or to nearby villages, in 1941. Other Germans moved from various places in Siberia to Taldykorgan after the abolition of *komandatura* in the second half of the 1950s,[13] basically because of the better climatic conditions in southern Kazakhstan. Shortly after the Second World War, the city had about twenty thousand inhabitants. In the following decades the population rapidly increased, and from the 1950s onwards, five suburbs spread out from the city centre which – aside from the bigger shopping areas in the very centre of the town – is still composed of single-family dwellings.

The city of Taldykorgan was chosen as a field site because it has a sizable German population but is itself relatively small, which allowed me to contact people more easily and to become more integrated into the city's social life. In terms of the Russian-Kazakh dynamics the city of Taldykorgan sits between the 'Kazakh cities' of the south and west and the 'Russian cities' of the north.

Figure I.1 Surrounding landscape of Taldykorgan (photo: R. Sanders, 2007)

This book is divided into four parts. Part I reflects on history and memory, detailing people's memories of 'their past' and contrasting these with official histories. In this vein, it points to the role ethnicity has played within the changing political frameworks of Russia, the Soviet Union and Kazakhstan. Furthermore, this part's second chapter explores the interplay of individual life experience and history by presenting four personal stories reflecting on the past and present situations of Kazakhstani Germans. Using these stories as a springboard, I elaborate on diverse interpretations of a German identity, and different attitudes as to how significant an ethnic identity is for individuals.

Part II deals with the interconnectedness of identities and identifications. Chapter 3 examines the dominant discourse on nationality and analyses stereotypes as a social practice. Additionally, schema theory allows me to investigate categories and to understand when and why people use them and to what effect. Chapter 4 explores how people relate nationality to their lives in the Kazakh nation state. It is shown how concepts such as the 'friendship of the peoples' (*druzhba narodov*) and a 'Kazakhstani identity' are perceived, transformed and lived.

Part III explores the interplay of social relations and identity. It refers back to the different identity types presented in Chapter 2 and proceeds to explore

Figure I.2 The main *bazar* in Taldykorgan (photo: R. Sanders, 2007)

the interconnectedness of mental schemas of the nationality category and actual interethnic relationships. This focus on social ties also leads beyond the city of Taldykorgan and Kazakhstan. Thus in Chapter 6 I show how transnational and local networks are interwoven, and I identify central persons and their role in transmitting information about Germany and how such information impacts on the construction of identities in Kazakhstan. In this context, the motives for people's self-identification as Germans in the city of Taldykorgan are seen as decisive with regard to how the flow of information and support from Germany are evaluated and how they contribute to establishing a Kazakhstani-German identity.

Part IV elaborates on the minority nationality policies of the German and the Kazakh states by focusing on the work of the German minority centre in Taldykorgan and its effects. It is shown how people deal with the often conflicting intentions of the policies of the two states, how those policies impact on the conceptualization and on performative expressions of a German identity, and how they stimulate the process of ethnic identification. I point out that people also transgress the prescribed role of the minority centre in order to use the institution and its economic, symbolic and social potential to their own advantage.

Notes

1. Furthermore, there are Kazakhstani-German studies that focus mainly on 'German culture', namely literature, theatre and music (Kalshev 1998; Sakenova 1998; Seifert 2006; Wensel 1998, 2006; see also Dorlin 2005). These studies often aim to show the value of particular cultural traits for which the German language is generally seen as a prerequisite.

2. The articles by Ilkhamov and Schröder are part of a special issue of *Zeitschrift für Ethnologie* that brings together various types of socio-spatial mobility in and beyond Central Asia. The articles by Isabaeva and Reeves are part of a special issue of *Central Asian Survey* that focuses on movement, place and power by advocating a dynamic approach to place that explores its habitual production (Beyer 2011; Bunn 2011; Féaux de la Croix 2011; Reeves 2011b).
3. This translation is provided by the author; the original text in German is as follows: '*Ihr Schicksal [das der Russlanddeutschen] aber gehört zu dem Schlimmsten, was Deutschen vor, in und nach dem Zweiten Weltkrieg angetan wurde*'.
4. Among others: Institut für Deutschland- und Osteuropaforschung des Göttinger Arbeitskreises e.V., Volkskundliche Forschungsstelle Berlin, Institut für Kultur- und Sozialforschung München e.V., Ostdeutsches Volkskundearchiv NRW.
5. The distinction between 'primordial' and 'instrumental' and/or 'constructivist' approaches to ethnicity has been comprehensively depicted and, as far as possible, resolved (among many others, Jenkins 1997; Finke 2014; May 2004). The fundamental agreement among social scientists, including Geertz (who is misleadingly considered the grandfather of primordialism) – and apart from sociobiological accounts, above all associated with the writings of van den Berghe (1981) – is that the ties of blood and culture themselves are not natural but that they might be viewed as such by actors. On the other hand, the constructivist Barth did not deny that ethnic identity might have meaning for an individual person which, then, aids in understanding why ethnic belonging becomes so crucial under certain circumstances (cf. Jenkins 1997: 44–48). However, this does not hold true for all Soviet, Russian and German historians and ethnographers who have dealt with Russian Germans. Their search for the peoples' *Volksgeist* will be explored in Chapter 1.
6. In contrast to Anthony P. Cohen, Jenkins (1997: 58f), however, holds that Goffman's view of social selfhood as performative and processual perfectly supplements Barth's model of ethnicity as transactional.
7. The absence of an ideological model of ethnicity supports the contention that ethnicity is mostly perceived as a 'good thing', while, as mentioned above, negative aspects are encompassed within the terms 'racism' and 'nationalism' (cf. Jenkins 1997: 86).
8. Jenkins (1997: 57) refers to G.H. Mead's concept of embodied selfhood and his distinction between the 'I', 'the active aspect of the self which responds to others', and the 'me' that 'comprises the attitudes and responses of significant others, as they are incorporated into the self'.
9. This challenges the assumption that one might study a culture by learning its rules or other types of 'verbal declarative knowledge' (D'Andrade 1996: 145). Hence, 'there may be regularity in behaviour but no direct representation of the rules in symbols' (ibid.) (cf. also Bloch 1998).
10. D'Andrade (1996: 182) generally advocates for an interactionist approach which asserts that culture and psyche mutually affect each other; thus, only by the integration of psychological insights can anthropological thinking advance: 'This seesaw between culture as completely and unproblematically internalized and culture as entirely negotiable and contested results from an attempt to have a cultural theory without any psychology – a cultural theory with empty people' (ibid.: 234).
11. Interpretative and postmodern approaches tend to stress the publicness of meanings and their performative aspects, and argue for a de-essentializing turn by stating that discourses do not represent realities but that they create them (cf. Strauss and Quinn 1997: 27f). Strauss and Quinn (ibid.: 28–33) advocate for maintaining the difference between the inner world of subjects and the outer world of objects because discourses about desire,

for instance, are not the same as desire since social discourses do not directly construct psychological realities.
12. An oblast is an administrative unit that had its origins in the Soviet era and most resembles what would be referred to in English as a 'province'.
13. The *komandatura* demanded registration (first weekly, then monthly) at the local administration and thus ensured that Germans did not remigrate to their former homelands in Ukraine or the previous Volga Republic, which was forbidden after the Second World War. The *komandatura* was not abolished until 1956 (Brake 1998: 66–68; Römhild 1998: 118f).

Part I
Memories, Histories and Life Stories

In the current public discourse within Germany, those Germans who live in the independent states that arose after the dissolution of the Soviet Union are mostly perceived to have been plagued by misfortune throughout their history. This is assumed to have fostered a common identity based on a shared memory of victimhood. Keeping this in mind, I began to collect life story interviews during the first weeks of my fieldwork. Therefore, I was rather astonished when one of my first interviewees, Valentina, reported on her life. As is true of many Germans in Taldykorgan, she was born in the Volga Republic and was deported to Siberia during her childhood, but then she spoke of another specific moment of sorrow in her life. She depicted how she and her classmates mourned when they learned from their teacher the news of Stalin's death. Valentina's narrative surprised me because I had not anticipated that the collective Kazakhstani-German memory is not primarily a memory of victimhood but also a memory built in part upon identification as a Soviet – and later a Kazakhstani – citizen.

Chapter 1

Memories and Histories

This chapter focuses on the most relevant incidents in the history of Kazakhstani/Russian Germans by examining the nationality policies of Russia, the Soviet Union and Kazakhstan and how they have affected the lives of their subjects. State institutions, legislation and public statements by politicians will be explored since they establish frameworks for behaviour and impact attitudes in various ways. However, I begin this chapter by exploring how Kazakhstani Germans remember 'their history' and elaborating on how different generations draw upon this history.

Shifting Memories of the Past

In this study memories are traced through life stories. I focus on shared interpretations of the history of Kazakhstani Germans, instead of concentrating on the individual peculiarities of a person's distinct biography, which is the topic of the next chapter. A life story is first of all an individual account, but in telling his or her story a person invariably also draws upon shared knowledge. Hence, a life story develops not only in response to other individuals or groups in everyday interaction but also in relation to discourses and practices on a variety of levels extending as far up as the state itself (and beyond). The notion of memory encompasses this complex relationship of interlinked fields of knowledge. Thereby, memory is mostly used in order to distinguish the predominantly orally transmitted knowledge of a particular group of people from (official) written accounts that constitute the 'history'.[1] Therefore, life stories are shaped by memories (and historiography) while at the same time constituting and reformulating those memories. Thus the notion of memory can be described as follows: 'Memory is both individual and collective, it is highly selective, it is both part of each individual's life story and simultaneously a flexible and shifting resource drawn on, and continually reformed through relationships in groups and collectivities' (Pine et al. 2004: 20).

What holds true for a life story is certainly also valid for memories of the past in general: they do not provide a pure account of historical events, nor even a single perspective of a certain event, since memories are always shaped by the layered knowledge and experiences that have followed the remembered incident. Here I investigate the memory of Kazakhstani Germans with respect to four major themes: the experience of deportation, feelings of discrimination after the Second World War, experiences of transition and, finally, how memory constitutes identity.

The Deportation of 1941

The deportation of 1941 is always mentioned in the course of the life story of a Kazakhstani German, irrespective of a person's age. Those who experienced the deportation first-hand recall with much emotion and great detail leaving their hometown or village and the painful beginning of a new life in Siberia or Central Asia. Since those who talked with me in 2006/07 were young in 1941, they focus less on the loss of their home in the Volga Republic or in Ukraine and more on the stress of the terrible conditions they endured in what was meant to be their new home. They describe how they lived in shacks or other kinds of provisional housing, eating what others gave them or had left behind. The famine in the winter of 1941/42, the death of close relatives and the unknown fate of lost relatives are the central subjects driving their narratives. Their deportation stories thus dwell upon the theme of basic survival.

It is certainly also due to their age at that time that the wider context of the Second World War, though present, is not elaborated on. Interestingly, the question of who should be blamed is rarely, if ever, addressed. In most cases, Stalin's policies of deportation are not clearly regarded as systematic efforts to inflict damage on Russian Germans. Also, official persons with whom they dealt directly are rarely blamed; most often they are excused for having done no more than follow orders. Consequently, the deportation of Russian Germans is attributed to a kind of inexplicable fate, which nonetheless deeply affected their lives.

I do not intend to assert, however, that Kazakhstani Germans are generally indifferent towards politics and history. When asked directly, most of them come across as well informed about Nazi Germany and the course of events during the Second World War, and none of my informants demonstrated any sort of sympathy with the policies of Nazi Germany. On the contrary, it is generally held that it was Germany's Germans who brought about the Russian Germans' catastrophe (among many other catastrophes).

At first it might be considered surprising that the life stories do not usually take a political stance, but the narratives are generally regarded as personal and intimate; for example, Valentina's recollection of how they all cried at school upon hearing of Stalin's death. Even today, she describes this incident as a moment of mourning, not even mentioning that his policies brought about the death of many of her relatives and countless others. Her narrative is an extreme example, but it demonstrates the complicated situation in which Russian Germans found themselves after the Second World War. Being regarded as enemies of the Russian people, they had to prove the opposite, namely that they were reliable Soviet citizens. To a certain extent, this also involved the denial – at least with regard to its significance – of their own tragic history, and it certainly forbade them from blaming others for what they themselves were blamed, not only officially but also by many people in their immediate environment.[2] Even today, dwelling on the fate of the Russian Germans as a deported people continues to evoke in them the feeling of being considered the cause for the deportation (and, furthermore, for the war itself), which is why it is usually avoided in life stories. However, I do not intend to assert that a German identity in general could not become stronger over time; rather, the ambiguous memory of deportation is in fact not well suited to building an affirmative ethnic identity.[3]

Those born after 1941 always mention the experience of their parents' or grandparents' deportation, although my initial request was that they should tell me only their own life story.[4] Not surprisingly, the narratives about their parents or grandparents are less detailed and more circumspect than their own stories. While the younger Germans mostly mentioned that their parents suffered, hardly any of them attempted to evoke their parents' or grandparents' feelings of fear or despair. Simultaneously, there are no accusations made. This emotional distance and lack of detailed knowledge is reflected in the following:

> They lived at the Volga. Then, they were somehow deported, here, to Kazakhstan, uh no to Kiselyovsk, a beautiful town. My father was born there. My grandmother spoke only German, and so did I with her. Then, a year later, they came to Kazakhstan, to Tekeli. My grandmother worked in Tekeli. To be honest, she wrote with many mistakes. She went to school for only four years, during the war. With the family, she spoke German, and my father knew it, and his sister, too. (Anna, 22 years old)[5]

The memory of deportation is an essential element of Russian-German identity,[6] considering that everyone, as if prefacing their own lives, mentions it. But one may find that the memories of the catastrophe rarely go beneath the surface. Rather, it appears that several generations of Germans have tried to suppress their experiences of ethnic discrimination, simply in order to make living more manageable. In this context, they often regarded it as unadvisable to pass on to their children all the details of their suffering caused by their German identity, and at the same time underemphasizing their ethnic origin. Even if they did not explicitly try to become Russian, they at least strove to become less German, namely, by not speaking German and not often alluding to their destiny as

Germans. Therefore, narratives of younger generations often appear somewhat flat and lacking in affect, even when recounting the circumstances surrounding the survival or death of relatives.[7]

Nevertheless, the fate of their ancestors is remembered and serves as a feature that distinguishes them from Russians. Furthermore, in many life stories Russian-German history is moved to the foreground in order to stress one's distinctive identity. However, it is usually not the negative aspect of deportation but instead the golden age of the Volga Republic that is put forth as evidence of the Russian Germans as a successful and hard-working people. Moreover, the memory of the tragedy is above all placed in an individual context; it is not used in order to assert any kind of claim with regard to identity, nor used to promote a sense of group solidarity.[8]

Stoll (2007: 171f), however, remarks that official representatives of the German minority usually refer to hardship and discrimination during and after the Second World War when they seek to explain their lack of German language proficiency in present-day Kazakhstan. Thus, in official statements by Kazakhstani-German representatives, memories of the past are used to claim a German identity, but individual narratives, as indicated above, only rarely draw upon a common fate of Russian/Kazakhstani Germans.

Discrimination against Germans

Another theme that arises in each life story is the experience of discrimination against Germans. Though this is certainly related to the memory of deportation, it has its own characteristics and, therefore, requires separate consideration. First of all, in contrast to the memory of deportation, hostility in the years after Stalinism was mostly experienced on a personal level. Therefore, these stories are more emotionally charged. Equally important is the fact that the discriminatory behaviour of others towards Germans is clearly perceived by the Germans as being unjustified.

It is often mentioned in the life stories that Germans were insulted as 'fascists'. Moreover, many Germans said that as children they were excluded from playing with other children, and described how they then quarrelled with the other children and tried to defend themselves. Rarely did Germans describe being subjected to serious physical assault. Many, however, highlighted that they were institutionally discriminated against as Germans in that, above all, they were denied the chance to pursue an education.

Explicitly or implicitly many narratives indicate that it was primarily Russians, not Kazakhs, who discriminated against Germans, as suggested here:

> I was born in 1951 in Kazakhstan, here in the Taldykorgan oblast. Then, I went to school, then to a technical secondary school, then to university. I suffered like all Germans had to suffer. Well, and now you see

me sitting here.⁹ ... When we went to school in the post-war time, the fact that I'm German made everything very difficult. We received all the offenses and indignities of the Russian people for this war – although, in general, we were born after it.¹⁰ Today, however, I can be proud of being a German. (Olga, 55 years old)

The experience of discrimination is recognized by Olga as a consequence of the Second World War and, thus, perceived as being grounded in the Russian-German relationship. Very often, Kazakhs are not even mentioned when experiences of indignity are described. The narrative of the 'war game' that was often told in similar ways is illustrative:

A long time ago when I was still a little boy, something like eight to ten years old, we often played different kinds of children's games in the courtyard. And one of these games was the 'war game'. And we separated into Russians and Germans. And I always had to be the head of the German army. Well, of course, this was always unfavourable. This was – because the Russians, anyhow, always won. And that we were not only Germans but directly fascists, not a nationality but fascists. This was associated with Germans, with the German people. This was always unpleasant for me. I always felt uncomfortable with it. But time passed, and I began to understand all these things in life, that how and where from and where to. ... Today, we are producing in our factory – well, in general, I really like wood, and there the covers for rifles are produced – made out of wood. ... And I do everything myself, what concerns these covers, and he and his wife [the owners of this factory], they say that only a German can do things like this: So accurate, with such strictness and cleanliness everywhere. Well, everything that concerns the German people is also a characteristic of mine. (Sasha, 50 years old)

The incident described above by Sasha took place in Taldykorgan in the 1960s or 1970s, but the 'war game' divided the group only into Russians and Germans; Kazakhs were not present. Often it is even stressed that it was only Russians who insulted Germans, or it is explicitly stated that Kazakhs did not insult Germans.

Both narratives reveal another important feature: they conclude by highlighting that there is no such discrimination in present-day Kazakhstan. Instead, they describe how Kazakhs generally appreciate Germans and that they, therefore, feel encouraged to express their pride in being German. This change in self-esteem is central to many narratives. Three distinctive incidents mark this gradual change: the end of the Second World War, Stalin's death and the collapse of the Soviet Union. The first two incidents are only elaborated by those who themselves experienced this period and are referred to with a sense of relief. The fall of the Soviet Union, however, is widely seen as the definite endpoint of discrimination, as elaborated by Kolya:

> Since Kazakhstan became independent, anyhow, it became better. Well, probably, the president, the government; certain kinds of policies are made in this respect. And that's why the relationship [between different ethnic groups] has become much better than in the Soviet Union. If you were German, they didn't choose you for a leading position, you could not study at a good university, or at a college of the army. Well, I tried to study there, at an army college for pilots. I was not chosen, just because I'm German. But those with worse marks could study there, Russians.[11] Well, those things happened. This was during Soviet times. But now, thanks to Kazakhstan, I think so, thanks to Kazakhstan, yes, it has become much better. I see it this way. (Kolya, 47 years old)

Transition and Continuity

In the context of the Soviet Union, biographical research could in effect only be carried out after its collapse. Therefore, many studies deal with the issue of continuity: How did people experience large-scale change? How did they attempt to preserve their identity? Or how did they change it? Furthermore, it is hoped that research on such transitional phases will provide insights into the general functioning of identity formation. Working with the concept of 'habitus',[12] Humphrey, Miller and Zdravomyslova (2003: 12f) propose that during a phase of profound transformation, an individual's choices become more transparent since they have to be adapted to suit the new circumstances and altered symbolic values.

Certainly, it is difficult to judge from a life story, narrated in a specific moment in time, whether someone would have articulated the same identity twenty years earlier. Nevertheless, the narratives of Kazakhstani Germans do tell us something about the continuity of an individual's identity. At the beginning of my research, I directly addressed the question of continuity. By asking my informants whether they had always openly presented themselves as German (in other words, had always openly admitted they were German), I sought to find out how people presented themselves before 1991. Oleg gave the following answer:

> I could not be a Russian! They would say to me, 'What? You have changed your nationality?' How is this to be understood, hey? Women, of course, they can change their family names, and she says: 'Yes, yes, I'm Russian!' And you don't find it out. But in my case, how could

I change it? I'm not this kind. How I was born I will always be, and I will die like this. Anyhow, a German remains a German. I buried my parents as Germans and so I – so I don't know, crap. It was not necessary to ask me that question! (Oleg, 60 years old)

Oleg became angry with me because in effect I had questioned the strength of his identity, which I understood to be a very sensitive issue.[13] Virtually no one told me directly that he or she had ever pretended to be Russian. On the contrary, many highlighted how they resisted being pressured by others to change their ethnic identity:

Nobody changed his nationality. I married a Russian husband. And he asked me, don't say to anybody – you don't look like a German, you look more like a Ukrainian. But you – when you meet somebody – you tell everybody directly 'I'm German'. But he didn't like that. He wanted me to be a Russian. But I said, 'I'm not uncomfortable with my nationality'. … Then, they built the factory in Zhansugurov and my husband and I moved to Zhansugurov in 1969. And he was saying to me: 'At least now, don't say that you're German'. But I told him: 'Don't tell me that. Anyhow, I will say that I'm German. I'm not uncomfortable with my nationality. Maybe you're uncomfortable with the fact that you've married a German, but I'm not uncomfortable with it'. (Ilona, 68 years old)

This story is often told in similar ways. In particular, marrying Russians raises the issue of ethnic continuity. As presented by Oleg's statement, it is commonly held that many women tried to marry Russians in order to rid themselves of their German surnames and pretend to be Russian. I do not want to speculate about the particular case of Ilona, but it is obvious that, against this background of a general discourse of ethnic denial, it is all the more necessary to stress how one acted differently. In general, many life stories refer to the issue of continuity. Most of them aim to prove that one has always been the person he or she is today, while simultaneously criticizing others for having denied their ethnic identity at times when it was difficult to be a German.

The Hard-Working German
Almost all of the Kazakhstani Germans' life stories refer to 'typical German characteristics'. Nearly everyone characterized their grandparents, parents and themselves as always having been hard-working. Irrespective of age, sex, profession or educational background, 'working' is a recurrent theme. Along these lines they describe how their parents told them to be assiduous in transmitting such virtues to their children.

When listening to the life stories, one may perceive Kazakhstani-German history first of all as a history of hard workers. It often starts with the beautiful houses, orderly gardens and the general wealth (due to hard work) of their parents or grandparents before the war. During the war, their ancestors basically did nothing but work. The experience of the labour camp is often communicated by emphasizing the contribution of their ancestors to the building of socialism. Some narratives give the impression that most of the infrastructure (e.g., streets and railways) of the entire Soviet Union was built by Germans during and after the war. The *kolkhozes* that were predominantly German are described as the most efficient. Moreover, once Germans regained the opportunity in the late 1950s, they built the best houses and again had the most orderly gardens. After independence, everybody was upset that the best workers (that is, the Germans) were leaving Kazakhstan, but on the other hand, at that same time the best cars and other products (again, German) were flowing into the country. Each of which further validates the image of the hard-working German.

Of course, no one related to me such a condensed and explicit version of the hard-working German, but the above represents the 'working meta-narrative' many refer to when telling their individual life story. Therefore, I hold that the Russian/Kazakhstani-German history told in Kazakhstan in 2006/07 is not primarily a history of victims but rather a history of a decisive people. Thus, their stories aim at recounting success, not victimhood. Furthermore, the success they always had – when viewed in this way – and the final reward for their hard work is the basis for their pride in being German in present-day Kazakhstan.

Not everybody, however, asserts the 'working meta-narrative'. Generation is the decisive factor. Only those born long after the incidents of the Second World War rely on this reduced one-sided abstraction of this memory of the Kazakhstani-German past; furthermore, hardly anyone from the oldest generation mentioned that they were proud of being German. But their silence, and their avoidance of telling the younger generations about their experiences during and after the Second World War, have both contributed to the 'German success memory'.[14]

In the subsequent section, I will elaborate on Kazakhstani Germans' history as written by historians and other social scientists. The section is divided according to the three political systems under which Kazakhstani Germans have lived: the Russian Empire, the Soviet Union and the state of Kazakhstan.

The Russian Empire: Colonization of the Kazakh Steppe

The history of Russia, remarked the noted nineteenth-century historian Vasilii Kliuchevskii,[15] 'is the history of a country undergoing colonization. Migration and colonization constituted the basic feature of our history, to which all other features were more or less related' (cited in Sabol 2003: 25). Indeed, with the expansion of the Russian Empire, millions of people migrated eastwards. In the last century of Tsarist Russia alone, more than two million peasants settled in the Kazakh steppe region or Turkestan (ibid.: 26). Furthermore, as the Russian Empire expanded southwards to the Black Sea after two successful wars of conquest against the Ottoman Empire (1768–74 and 1787–92), hundreds of thousands of settlers, mostly from the German states and Switzerland, were drawn there (Römhild 1998: 37). In particular the policies of Peter the Great (1682–1725) and Catherine the Great (1762–96) pushed for colonization to the east and south and the recruitment of new subjects from the west.

Until the sovereignty of Peter the Great, there were only sporadic relations between Russians and Kazakhs, though trade was increasing during the seventeenth century. In order to enhance trade and security, Peter sent several missions into the steppe region, finally resulting in the construction of a line of forts manned by Siberian Cossacks,[16] and therewith establishing Russia's presence in the Kazakh steppe (Sabol 2003: 26f). It is often stated (e.g., Svanberg 1996: 319), and sometimes with astonishment, that Kazakh rulers very easily submitted to their Russian conquerors, which is generally explained by their need for support against the Jungars. Sabol (2003: 28f), however, questions this view, contending that Abulkhair, the Khan of the *Kishi Zhuz* (Little Horde) in 1734, was not in truth the 'Khan of all Kazakhs' and that while he sought Russian assistance he did not seek incorporation into the Russian Empire. Nonetheless, the Russian rulers were simply in a better position to assert their interpretation of the alliance.

It was during the sovereignty of Catherine the Great that the notion of *inorodtsy* (allogenes or 'the others') became codified, which in the beginning was largely meant to comprise only nomads (cf. Slocum 1998: 178). In this vein, she considered the conquered territories in the Upper Volga, where the Germans were to be settled, as 'empty',[17] since nomads were not regarded as ordinary inhabitants (Römhild 1998: 37). The notion of *inorodtsy*, until fairly recently, drew a firm line between the civilized and 'the others' (Dave 2007) and was responsible in part for a wide range of activities at different times. In accordance with Catherine's 'enlightened', paternalistic worldview, nomadic people ought to be settled and civilized, which also meant that they were deprived of their land.[18] In this way, it was hoped to improve trade throughout the Kazakh steppe, since nomadism was seen as a hindrance to the expansion of Russian business (Crowe 1998: 400; Römhild 1998: 49). However, the increase in Russian trade and the expansion of Russian settlements worsened Kazakh-Russian relations during the second half of the eighteenth century, which led to several violent revolts against the Russian conquerors (Sabol 2003: 30f).

Throughout the nineteenth century the situation in the Kazakh steppe was characterized by colonization and the influx of Russian and Cossack settlers. The actual seizure of land caused several revolts. In 1822, Russia officially annexed the territories that had belonged to the Little and Middle Hordes; in 1824 the institution of the Khan was formally abolished. According to Sabol (2003: 35) some of the rebellions in the 1830s were also motivated by political resistance and aimed at restoring the titles of Sultan and Khan. In 1865, Russia conquered Turkestan, and in 1868 the steppe territories were divided into three separate Russian administrative entities of governance: Orenburg, West Siberia and Turkestan. The associated imposition of taxes and restrictions on pastoral migration incited uprisings in some areas of the Kazakh steppe (Dave 2007: 32–36; Sabol 2003: 32–37).

The liberation from serfdom facilitated a mass migration of Russian settlers from 1861 onwards. For many settlers Siberia and the Kazakh steppe represented freedom from government and onerous regulations, whereas the Russian government considered the movement as a useful measure to fortify control in Central Asia and, secondly, as a needed solution to agrarian problems in Russia itself. However, the often chaotic allotment of land and the fact that many Russians settled on land that was actually allocated for use by Kazakhs caused further tension and conflicts between Kazakhs and the newly arriving settlers (Sabol 2003: 39–42).[19]

But migration increased even more dramatically at the beginning of the twentieth century; between 1896 and 1914 approximately 1.5 million Russian settlers came to the Kazakh steppe. In 1900, the regions of Semirechie and Syr-Darya were also opened to settlers. The revolution in 1905, the completed train line between Orenburg and Taschkent in 1906, and the so-called Stolypin reforms (1906–12)[20] brought about this vast influx of migrants (Sabol 2003: 47–52). It is often stated that this huge immigration wave, which resulted in the massive seizure of Kazakh land, and which deeply altered life on the Kazakh steppe, triggered a national consciousness among the Kazakhs which, then, also led to the revolts in Russian Central Asia in 1916 (cf. Chinn and Kaiser 1996; Sabol 2003: 51f; Svanberg 1996: 320).[21] But it is debatable to what extent Kazakhs thought and acted as a homogeneous community or whether a sense of national consciousness was limited to the Kazakh intelligentsia,[22] which was moreover trained and deeply influenced by Tsarist Russia's ideas, though they, at the same time, blamed Russia for the imminent loss of Kazakh life (Dave 2007; Sabol 2003).

It was never the objective of Tsarist Russia to Russify Kazakhs, however, and any attempt to impose a sedentary way of life on them was primarily intended to improve their control over the 'uncivilized'. Russification was in fact regarded as impossible by Russia's elite since Kazakhs were considered *inorodtsy*, 'the others', who therefore could never become Russians (cf. Dave 2007: 34–36). Such a primordial view of the nation had developed only gradually during the nineteenth century, freed from the more elitist definition set forth by Peter the Great and Catherine the Great, which excluded all – i.e., also Russians – who were uncivilized, and moving towards an ethno-national understanding that excluded only non-Russians, or at least those who were considered unable to become Russian (cf. Chinn and Kaiser 1996: 51–53).

The Russian Empire: The Settlers from the German States

German settlers came in several waves to Russia. Many Russian rulers felt the need to lure whom they considered to be more advanced 'Western people' (Nolte 1996). In particular Peter the Great initiated the recruitment of Western specialists (craftsmen but also officers), who were meant to support the Empire with their sophisticated skills (Römhild 1998: 50f). By the middle of the eighteenth century, half of the higher officers in the Russian army were non-Russians, mostly Germans and Baltic Germans (ibid.: 38).[23] But Russian-German history is above all associated with Catherine the Great and her manifest of 1763,[24] which attracted about twenty-five thousand German settlers (ibid.: 51).

The immigration measures enforced by Catherine the Great facilitated large-scale expansion policies, in large part because Russian subjects were, until the abolition of serfdom in 1861, not allowed to leave their lord. Therefore, the territories newly conquered by Catherine in the south had to be settled by foreigners,[25] who were supposed to cultivate and secure those territories against their previous (nomadic) inhabitants, and generally to increase the number of her subjects (Römhild 1998: 37–40).

Alexander I (1801–25), whose policies initiated a second wave of immigration comprising about fifty thousand Germans to the Black Sea Coast from 1804 onwards, did not want to repeat the mistakes of Catherine the Great. The settlers recruited by Catherine were largely unable to cultivate the land, because most of them were either not farmers or were unfamiliar with how to grow successfully in the region, which led to widespread famine and terrible difficulties for the first two generations of settlers. Alexander instead aimed at hiring wealthier and more qualified families,[26] who were furthermore granted double the amount of farming land (sixty *desiatyn*, instead of thirty *desiatyn* for the Volga settlers).[27] The Black Sea Coast settlements prospered from the outset, and many Germans soon became much wealthier than their Russian neighbours with whom, however, contacts were rather poorly developed (Pfister-Heckmann 1998: 24–26; Römhild 1998: 40–56).

It is not only that Germans had little contact with their non-German neighbours;[28] contact was also rare between different segments of the German community (which community as such was actually non-existent). First and foremost religious affiliation, and secondarily the very different German dialects, formed the basis for the composition of villages,[29] whereby intermarriage between Catholic and Protestant Germans was unusual (Römhild 1998: 60). The different situations of Baltic, Volga and Black Sea Germans, the significance of distinct religious and dialect affiliations, and the fact that a German state would not be established until 1871, meant that an ethnic German identity was of minor importance.

It is also due to the worldviews and policies of Peter and Catherine – each of whom was inspired by the European Enlightenment and favoured the idea of an elite civilization of the West – that the relative positions of Kazakhs and Germans differed remarkably in the Russian Empire. Though Catherine's immigration policies varied from Peter's in that they were not designed to hire Western specialists, the privileges that those newcomers were guaranteed ensured them a beneficial position, not only compared to the 'backward Kazakhs', but also compared to the vast majority of Russians who were not released from serfdom until nearly a century after the German settlers arrived. Therefore, it does not come as a surprise that German settlements are mostly described as 'flourishing' and praised for their 'sobriety, efficiency, and greater productivity' (Hyman 1996: 463), particularly with regard to German settlements along the Black Sea Coast.

Over the course of the nineteenth century, the position of Russians generally rose to the level of the rights and status accorded to the Germans. Towards the end of that century, the pressure began to increase on non-Russians to learn Russian and to eventually assimilate as Russians (cf. Römhild 1998: 45f). In 1871, privileges initially given to German settlers (e.g., with respect to taxpaying) were abolished. Furthermore, in 1874 Germans were no longer exempt from military service,[30] and the school system was brought under Russian administration (apart from religious education). In 1887, a law was passed that forbade all non-Russians living in the western and southern regions to buy or rent land outside of towns (ibid.: 45–75). Though most of the legislation concerned all European non-Russians living in Russia, Römhild states (ibid.: 72–74) that there arose a distinct anti-German stance at the end of the nineteenth century. In particular the German *Reichsgründung* in 1871 and the possible threat of a 'strong state' made Russian nationalists aware of how deeply their country was influenced by Germans, who at that time held important positions in almost every public sphere: the military, the economy and politics. Moreover, due to ongoing German immigration into previously Polish territories – especially Wolhynien – larger parts of Russia's western territories were predominantly inhabited by Germans.[31]

But despite growing anti-German sentiment, ethno-national awareness remained weakly developed among most Russian Germans, whereas belonging to different denominations and class groups seemed to be more important. By the beginning of the twentieth century, some of Russia's Germans had begun to deplore the policies of Russification and the loss of their 'traditional German life'. However, efforts by Baltic Germans and Germans from the Black Sea Coast, following the revolution in 1905 and in the run-up to the first *Duma* elections, to form a united pan-Russian-German movement failed, largely because most Volga Germans supported the movements representing poor Russian subjects in the Baltic provinces, with whom they obviously identified more than with their

German rulers. Overall it appeared that many perceived themselves as Germans but not as *Deutschländer*, meaning that they did not feel an association with the German Reich and, furthermore, resisted anyone who questioned their loyalty to the Russian tsar (cf. Casteel 2008: 119; Römhild 1998: 76–84).

The First World War confirmed Russian nationalists' fears of a German military expansion. Not surprisingly, thereafter anti-German sentiment strengthened: German schools and newspapers were shut down and the use of the German language in public was prohibited. During that war, however, Russian Germans fought against the German Reich, and in doing so demonstrated their loyalty to the tsar (cf. Ingenhorst 1997: 35–42; cf. Römhild 1998: 82f).

The Soviet Union: Concepts of Nation and Nationality

About half a year after the revolution in February 1917, in October, the Bolsheviks, under the leadership of Lenin, finally established themselves, and won the subsequent civil war. The relevance that the Bolsheviks attached to the concepts of nation and nationality has been comprehensively discussed (e.g., Abashin 2007; Brubaker 1999; Chinn and Kaiser 1996; Dave 2007; Hirsch 2005; Jones Luong 2004a; Martin 2001; Slezkine 1994; G. Smith 1996; Szporluk 1994; Weitz 2002). While nations and nationalities contradicted Marxism, since they were fundamentally bourgeois phenomena and therefore had to be overcome, those concepts nonetheless were accorded 'a key role in organizing and controlling the Soviet people' (Sanders 2013b: 79). Notwithstanding, at once, nations and nationalities were widely depoliticized identities that were seen by Lenin solely as a necessary transitional phase on the way to socialism. By means of organizing people first into nationalities and subsequently into nations, it was thought to give them the possibility to 'develop' and, thus, to overcome the oppressive Russian rulers and their 'Great Russian Chauvinism'. Seen in this way, the formation of the Soviet Union was also meant to be a wide-ranging decolonizing endeavour.

Though 'nationality' became a crucial classificatory concept during the formation of the USSR, its definition had never been agreed upon, and 'on the eve of the revolution, Russia had census nationalities, national parties and national "questions", but it had no official view of what constituted nationality' (Slezkine 1994: 427). Already in 1913, Stalin, in his article 'Marxism and the National Question', provided the often-cited definition of a nation as 'a historically constituted, stable community of people, formed on the basis of a common language, territory, economic life, and psychological make-up manifested in a common culture' (Stalin 1913: 307, cited in Weitz 2002: 21).[32] The contradiction between the Marxist-Leninist constructivist assumption of nations and the ascription of fixed features such as language and customs to the nation marked the ensuing controversies over the concept of nationality (cf. Weitz 2002: 21).

Likewise, the adjunctive notions of *nationalnost* and *narodnost* were far from clear; they had various interpretations at different times, which partly contradicted each other and the very concept of nationality.[33] Inspired by Herder's idea of *Volksgeist*, Nadezhdin argued in 1846 that Russia's ethnographers should use the term *narodnost* as their primary category of investigation. By so doing, ethnographers could study the 'essence' of the Russian people, its *Volksgeist*, which is expressed in language, culture and customs (Hirsch 2005: 36f). Already in 1836, Nadezhdin wrote in 'Europeanism and *Narodnost* in Relation to Russian Literature' that *narodnost* was the 'totality of all traits' (cited in Knight 2000: 55) and thus 'was the essence of distinctiveness, the well-spring of identity, from which all people, regardless of social standing, derived a consciousness of uniqueness and belonging' (ibid.). During the early twentieth century, Russian ethnography largely remained the science of *narodnost*. However, the Bolsheviks used the terms *natsiya* and *natsionalnost* – derived from the French words *nation* and *nationalité* – at first often synonymously, whereas the term *narodnost* – which derives from the Russian word *narod* for 'people' – was used by them to connote 'backwardness' (cf. Hirsch 2005: 38, 41–44).

Already in the 1840s, Vissarion Belinskii argued that *narodnost* and *nationalnost* represented two different levels of national development,[34] the latter with national consciousness, the former without it, while both had in common that they refer to a group of people who share language and culture (Hirsch 2005: 44). Russia's ethnographers, as well as Marx and Engels, were inspired by the evolutionary schemes of Lewis Henry Morgan and Edward B. Tylor. But Russia's ethnographers focused on cultural-evolutionary development, seeking to understand the process of tribes uniting into *narodnosti*. Lenin and other Bolsheviks argued that different stages in socioeconomic development correspond to the different nationality concepts of *narodnost*, *nationalnost* and *natsiya*; 'but it was not until the 1920s and 1930s that these terms came to systematically connote specific stages on the Marxist timeline' (ibid.: 45). For post-war Soviet ethnographers the term of choice became *ethnos* which, then, served as the basic unit for ethnic classification (Abashin 2007: 5–7; Hirsch 2005: 313–19). The introduction of a single term did not abolish the other nationality terms, however, nor did it challenge the fundamental assumption of 'ethnic development', against the continually postponed objective of communism and the merging (*sliyanie*) of all ethnic groups into the Soviet people.

The merging of nationality groups in the post-war period took more time than Stalin had expected,[35] while exerting pressure to accelerate this process was regarded as impermissible. Various experts were put in charge of writing nationality histories and promoting their research results on languages and customs of the different nationalities to a broad audience; thereby 'narratives about the formation of the socialist nations proved far more popular than narratives about their future disappearance or merger' (Hirsch 2005: 318). Hence, the very idea of equal nationalities that, moreover, could and should learn from one another had obviously become popular, and the thing that could be learned from one another was each nationality's distinct *kultura* (culture), which became a crucial concept. Furthermore, Soviet culture became understood as the result of the development of all individual nationalities.[36] Consequently, it was each nationality's duty to celebrate its own language and customs in order to be able to contribute to Soviet culture (ibid.: 316).

The branch of Soviet science chiefly entrusted with analysing and developing the cultures of nationalities was Soviet folklore, which started up in the 1930s. However, at that time, the promotion of socialism was still the foremost priority, and it was hoped that such things as national folk songs about the glorious benefits of the revolution would lead to its speedier implementation. To such ends, the folkloric scientists sometimes had to 'help' local poets to write such songs. Therefore, the cultural product that was envisioned is best described by the oft-cited 'national in form, socialist in content' (Hirsch 2005: 269–71; cf. Martin 2001: 12f).

Language played a crucial role with regard to the culture of nationalities; as Slezkine (1994: 418) states: 'Insofar as national culture was a reality, it was about language and a few "domestic arrangements"'. In the writings of Stalin, language gained in importance over the years. In his 1950 article 'Marxism and Language Questions', Stalin interpreted language as neither belonging to the economic 'basis' nor to political, cultural, religious and social 'superstructures'; as to the latter, Stalin regarded language as more enduring than 'superstructures' (Abashin 2008). The Soviet concept of culture, as well as the contradictory discussion of nationality categories, had fundamental consequences for the lives of the people concerned. But the very fact that national belonging became a crucial category in organizing Soviet citizens was anything but self-evident.

The Soviet Union: Its Formation and Nationality Policies

When the Bolsheviks seized power in 1917, they promoted the right of nations to self-determination,[37] which was, however, 'designed to recruit ethnic support for the revolution' and not to govern a Soviet state (Martin 2001: 2). Against the background of the fading Habsburg and Ottoman empires, as well as in light of several nationality-based movements and parties demanding more political and cultural autonomy after the revolution in 1917, the Bolsheviks needed to take action. Ukrainian and Georgian nationalists claimed the creation of a federation with autonomous national rights, and Polish and Finnish leaders also aimed at national independence (Hirsch 2005: 54; cf. Martin 2001: 19). Likewise, Kazakhs formed a semi-independent state in the aftermath of the February revolution, which, however, proved short-lived; it was incorporated as the Kirghiz Autonomous Soviet Socialist Republic in August 1920 (cf. Svanberg 1996: 320).

In March 1917 some of Russia's Germans founded the 'Allrussischer Verband' (all-Russian union) with the aim of guaranteeing religious freedom, protecting property and strengthening the position of the German language. To this end, Alexander Baron Meyendorf from Petrograd, Karl Lindemann from Moscow and Pastor Winkler from Odessa strove for a superregional consortium, but failed to develop an integrated party programme and, ultimately, to unite the Germans (cf. Römhild 1998: 108).

National Delineation
Although the provisional government was unwilling to grant autonomous status to nationalities, 'the Bolsheviks proclaimed the right of nationalities to secede from the state' (Hirsch 2005: 55). However, national self-determination was a disputed issue among the Bolsheviks in 1917, and some of them regarded it as betrayal of Marxist internationalism (Hirsch 2005: 64f; Martin 2001: 20f; Slezkine 1994: 421).[38] All in all, 'the new nationalities policy was widely seen as a "temporary, if necessary, evil"' (Martin 2001: 20).

In 1918, the Communist Party chose in its constitution a federal form of state organization and proclaimed the Russian Soviet Federation of Socialist Republics (RSFSR). According to Martin (2001: 3), the period from 1919 to 1923 was devoted to establishing what exactly was meant by non-Russian national self-determination, which resulted in an 'affirmative action empire'.[39] On 31 January 1924 the All-Union Congress of Soviets ratified the Constitution of the USSR. Consequently, a huge number of nationality-based administrative units were established. Those units were organized as a 'nationality pyramid', which comprised ten distinct levels.[40] The idea was to allow a maximum number of people to reside in a district of one's own nationality (cf. ibid.: 10), which also resulted in a maximum number of national cadres working in their own national territories (Brubaker 1999: 29).

Brubaker (1999) hints at the conceptual contradiction between nationality and nationhood: a person's nationality does not depend as much on place of residence as on descent. The result – that nationality was often inconsistent with nationhood – was, according to Brubaker (ibid.: 31f), due to 'ad hoc regime policies'. A solution for this 'Soviet nationalities policy dilemma' was attempted through the hierarchically nested arrangement of nationality-based territories (Martin 2001: 72).

The Volga German Autonomous Soviet Socialist Republic,[41] which was established in 1924, was one of the first autonomous republics.[42] The territory, which measured about 250 square kilometres, had Russian, Estonian and Tatar settlements as well, but it did not include Saratov, the urban centre of the previous German *Arbeiterkommune*. Instead, Pokrovsk became the republic's capital (Römhild 1998: 113).[43] According to Hyman (1996: 464), the republic had a 'flourishing cultural life': twenty-one German language newspapers were published, a German theatre was founded, and Germans were to a certain extent even permitted religious freedom. However, Römhild (1998: 112–15) remarks that the Volga Republic did not possess a university and, furthermore, because ninety-one per cent of Volga Germans were peasants, a politically active elite was almost non-existent.

Aside from the Volga Republic, many more German areas existed at lower administrative levels. As of 1933, a total of 550 German village soviets and sixteen German national districts were established, eight of them in Ukraine, six in the RSFSR, one in Georgia, and one in Azerbaijan. All German nationality-based areas were permitted to implement German as the official language (Römhild 1998: 113).

National areas were comparatively numerous in Ukraine.[44] In 1924, the first two German districts, Prishib and Molochansk, were formed; by 1927 there existed seven national German districts and 237 German national village soviets in Ukraine (which had a total of 872 national village soviets) (Martin 2001: 40). The reason for the numerous national areas is seen by Martin (ibid.: 35) as a result of the influential positions held by many Poles, Germans, Bulgarians and Greeks.[45] However, the fact that many of them were better off in terms of wealth and education than most Russians and Ukrainians, as well as the fact that most of them were more religious, also made them subject to suspicion. According to Martin (ibid.: 44), the formation of the numerous national areas involved ethnic conflicts and, furthermore, 'the combination of ethnicity, control of territory, and land ownership led to a politicization of ethnicity'.

The delineation of Central Asia in 1924 is often seen as a divide-and-rule policy. However, Hirsch (2005: 160–64) asserts that, in Central Asia in particular, local elites were involved in the process of delineation, and that the Soviet Union's leaders did not intend to oppress its 'backward peoples' but, on the contrary, aimed at 'developing' all of its areas and citizens.

The nationality policies decreed in 1923 focused primarily on promoting national languages and elites and later on were called *korenizatsiya* (indigenization). The decree aimed at making Soviet policies more '"native" (*rodnaia*), "intimate" (*blizkaia*), "popular" (*narodnaia*), and "comprehensible" (*poniatnaia*)' (Martin 2001: 12). In Kazakhstan its implementation is seen by Dave (2007: 73f) as a means 'to appease indigenous claims' and 'a tool to entrench Soviet rule in non-Soviet territories'. *Korenizatsiya* in principle stipulated that all appointed Soviets spoke Kazakh, which was unfeasible in Kazakhstan since there were too few educated Kazakhs. In the first four decades only Europeans took positions in the upper echelons of leadership; only at the lower levels were some Kazakhs appointed. Initially Russian chauvinism was held to be responsible for the failure of *korenizatsiya* in Kazakhstan. However, from the 1930s Kazakh nationalism was seen as circumventing Soviet policies, which argument was also used to legitimize the murder of Kazakh *intelligentsiya* (cf. ibid.: 72–77).

Collectivization

In 1928, Stalin introduced the first Five-Year Plan, and several months later the Soviet Union embarked on a violent campaign to achieve efficient economic and social transformation, a 'revolution from above'. The elimination of all backwardness was hoped to be gained by rapid industrialization and the thoroughgoing implementation of collectivization. The quickest possible building of socialism was, furthermore, supplemented by the intensified search for 'class enemies' (Hirsch 2005: 138).

Collectivization had disastrous consequences for the Kazakhs:[46] over 1.5 million died of starvation during this period and their livestock holdings decreased by nearly eighty per cent in the 1930s.[47] Olcott asserts (1981: 138) that 'the collectivization drive brought an end to pastoral nomadism in the steppe, but oftentimes without an adequate substitute'. At the beginning of 1930, when the collectivization decree was first issued, there was an immediate and huge outflow of Kazakhs to Chinese Turkestan, Uzbekistan, Karakalpakstan and Turkmenistan (ibid.: 126–28).[48] Furthermore, many Kazakhs were killed or arrested for resisting collectivization. But the huge loss of life was mainly due to famine; the slaughtering of livestock, which was done in order to circumvent the livestock's forceful collectivization or to save them from starvation, drastically reduced the number of sheep and beef cattle (ibid.: 136–38).[49] Moreover, Soviet authorities did not anticipate the encountered difficulties and failed to provide the settled Kazakhs adequately with resources. There was not enough arable land and seed available, and Kazakhs were not provided with sufficient assistance to implement the new technologies (ibid.: 137). Therefore, 'by the end of 1932 Kazakh economy was practically at a standstill' (ibid.: 134; cf. Hirsch 2005: 247f).

Collectivization was, in theory, 'not supposed to have an ethnic dimension, but in practice it quickly developed one' (Martin 1998: 837). According to Martin (ibid.),

> NEP [New Economic Policy] 'losers' took revenge. In Kazakhstan, Russians revenged themselves on the suddenly vulnerable Kazakh nomads. Likewise, in Ukraine, popular opinion viewed all Germans [as] kulaks. ... Such popular attitudes had likewise surfaced during the civil war and were linked to the Germans' privileged prerevolutionary status.

In particular in Ukraine, Germans were disproportionally negatively affected by collectivization measures, which Römhild (1998: 115) contends was largely due to their comparatively prosperous circumstances.

Ironically, at the same time the 'Great Transformation of 1928–32' can be seen as 'the most extravagant celebration of ethnic diversity that any state had ever financed' (Slezkine 1994: 414). The campaign for 'cultural revolution' in

Central Asia and throughout the Soviet Union in 1931 was launched with the standardization of national languages, literatures and histories as its primary objective. To that end, it was considered necessary to eliminate those elements that were assumed to derive from pre-Soviet customs in order to speed up the consolidation of tribes and clans into nationalities (cf. Hirsch 2005: 261–63). Moreover, Russian chauvinism was said to have been eliminated by the mid-1930s, with Soviet authorities proclaiming that all 'fraternal people' were equitably experiencing development (cf. ibid.: 267f).

Facing the Menace of the German Reich: The Passport System and Deportations

The Soviet passport system of the late 1930s was in part a response to major geopolitical threats by the German Reich, with its primordial concept of 'Germanness' and its proclamation to intervene in the affairs of all ethnic Germans (cf. Hirsch 2005: 268). In 1938, Hitler claimed Austria and Czechoslovakia's Sudetenland on the grounds that the territory was mainly inhabited by ethnic Germans (ibid.: 274). In this context, the allegiance of all 'diaspora nationalities' was questioned, and as Hirsch states (ibid.: 291f), they were set apart as different from the Soviet people:

> By 1938, the distinction between 'Soviet' and 'foreign' nations had also become part and parcel of an official narrative about the 'friendship of peoples'. … Significantly, this friendship did not include 'foreign' nationalities; those mentioned – the Poles, Germans, Swedes, Lithuanians, and Japanese – were presented in the worst possible light, as former conquerors.

The passport system aimed to determine someone's 'true nationality'.[50] By a decree of April 1938, each Soviet citizen's nationality had to be in accordance with that of their parents (Hirsch 2005: 268f).[51] In cases where the parents belonged to two different nationalities, both had to be documented if one of them belonged to a 'diaspora nationality' (those nationalities with homelands outside of the Soviet Union). Furthermore, everyone had to prove their nationality with a birth certificate, but the People's Commissariat of Internal Affairs (NKVD), which enforced the passport system, was also interested in other personal documents that might help in determining someone's 'true nationality' (ibid.: 293f).

By 1937, the NKVD had begun deporting diaspora nationalities from the borderlands (Hirsch 2005: 274f).[52] Furthermore, diaspora nationalities lost their native-language institutions, land and possessions, and individuals were deported or arrested if the NKVD accused them of attempting to conceal their true identity (ibid.: 297). The German Reich's invasion of the USSR drastically raised the number of deportations: about 1.2 million Soviet Germans were immediately deported to Siberia and Central Asia (Martin 1998: 820). The Soviets first resettled all Germans from the southern regions; however, because of the rapid invasion of the German Wehrmacht, only those Germans living east of the Dnyepr River could be resettled in Central Asia.[53] Moreover, by decree on 28 August 1941 the Volga Republic was dissolved, and all Germans were deported to Central Asia or Siberia.[54]

The areas in Siberia and Central Asia receiving the deportees were not prepared in advance by Soviet officials with regard to food supply or housing to accommodate such a huge number of people. The deported people were therefore dependent on the help of the local population. Beginning in the autumn of 1941, men and women with no small children (about one hundred and twenty thousand) were recruited for the *trudarmya* (labour army). Most were deployed in mining, road construction and heavy industry, and usually housed in separate camps that resembled the conditions of gulag camps. The *trudarmya* was gradually dissolved after the Second World War. However, migration to former homelands in Ukraine or the previous Volga Republic was forbidden; by way of enforcement the *komandatura* demanded registration (at first weekly, and eventually monthly) with the local administration, and this practice was not abolished until 1956 (Brake 1998: 66–68; Eisfeld 1999; Römhild 1998: 118f).

With far-reaching consequences in terms of Kazakh history, the Kazakh territory 'served as a dumping ground for groups perceived as "dangerous" by the Moscow government' (Otarbaeva 1998: 428). In 1943–44, the entire Crimean Tatar, Kalmyk, Chechen, Ingush, Balkar, Karachai and Mesketian Turk populations were deported to Central Asia (Martin 1998: 820). The number of Germans increased from 92,571 in 1939 to 659,751 in 1959 (Diener 2006: 202).[55] The deported Germans were confined to special settlements dispersed throughout the Kazakh SSR. The settlements contained only small numbers of Germans, and most of them were located in isolation from regional centres. Furthermore, the areas were sparsely populated and, due to the harsh climate and poor soil, often unfavourable for agriculture (Diener 2004: 63).

The Kazakh SSR after 1945

As immigration continued, the Kazakh SSR became even more 'international' in the 1950s and 1960s. In 1954, Khrushchev launched the 'Virgin Lands Programme', which aimed at cultivating huge territories in the north and triggered an immigration of over one million settlers, mostly Russian and Ukrainian (cf. Svanberg 1996: 320).[56] This huge inflow of European settlers was celebrated by Soviet authorities, who proclaimed it 'internationalism'. As a result of destructive collectivization in the 1930s and massive – forced and voluntary – immigration in the 1940s and 1950s, the proportion of Kazakhs in the Kazakh SSR decreased to only about thirty per cent of the total population in 1959 (cf. Dave 2007: 59).[57]

Kazakhs were confronted by new urban areas that were largely Russophone, and even Almaty in the south was considered a 'Russian town'. Nonetheless, many Kazakhs were attracted by the better living conditions in the newly built towns; in exchange, they had to accept the Russian 'rules of the game' and learn the Russian language (cf. Dave 2007: 60f).[58] A good command of Russian became essential in order for a career, and by the mid-1950s, Russian had become a mandatory subject in the entrance examination for universities (ibid.: 65).

On the other hand, Dave (2007: 78) states that the policies of *korenizatsiya* finally had an effect by the 1950s in that 'the twin idea that the republic must bear an ethnic face and the titular language be accorded priority had already acquired a popular resonance'. Nationality categories became crucial for access to higher education, in which the introduced quotas for all institutes of higher education privileged Kazakhs (ibid.: 79–82). In this context, a 'silent indigenization' in Kazakhstan is also seen as the result of the long incumbency of Kunaev (1964–86) (ibid.: 83). According to Hirsch (2005: 318), nationality categories gained in importance and, furthermore, 'the division between socialist and outsider nations – and the idea that only the former were entitled to land and resources – became taken for granted'.

There are two divergent aspects regarding the ethnic awareness of Germans in the Soviet Union after 1945. On the one hand, discrimination and forced assimilation reduced being German to the German language and folkloristic elements,[59] only practised in the sphere of the family. Although, by a decree of Khrushchev in 1964, Germans were cleared of the charge of collaboration, the German issue remained invisible in public discourse; as Brown (2005: 627) puts it: 'The German minority maintained a very low profile'. On the other hand, the shared memory of traumatic experiences during and after the war is said to have created a sense of belonging, which evoked and supported a collective (Soviet) German memory for the first time (cf. Römhild 1998: 124–26).

The Soviet Union after 1945 is associated with its self-created labels of 'internationalism' and 'friendship of the peoples',[60] which were not seriously challenged until the uprising in Almaty, fomented by the replacement of Kunaev by Kolbin in 1986. After the announcement of Kolbin's appointment, several thousand demonstrated in Almaty on 17–18 December 1986. The demonstrations became violent after the police attacked the demonstrators. Thousands of demonstrators were arrested and several died (Crowe 1998: 407f). These events are interpreted by Graham Smith (1996: 14f) as 'ethnic unrest on a scale previously unknown to Soviet society' and might be seen as 'an indication of the depth of anti-Russian sentiments' (Chinn and Kaiser 1996: 196). Dave (2007: 84–88), however, holds a different view since – according to her – the uprising after Kunaev's replacement by the Russian Kolbin was not triggered by anti-Russian sentiments. Furthermore, Gorbachev initially intended to replace Kunaev, who primarily had to resign because he was an ally of Brezhnev, with a Kazakh politician who ideally – unlike Kunaev – should not belong to the *Uli Zhuz* (Big Horde). However, since no suitable candidate was available, Gorbachev finally opted for the presumably neutral outsider Kolbin.

Gorbachev's response to the Almaty uprising consisted of 'greater internationalist education' (G. Smith 1996: 15), and in principle, his policies were a follow-up of Stalin's notion of national self-determination. However, this time the First Secretary was not able to circumvent the Union's dissolution: in 1989, the Lithuanian Parliament was the first to declare its independence from Moscow (cf. ibid.: 14–17), and in December 1991, the Kazakh Parliament was the last.[61] The Union dissolved corresponding to the (by then) well-established territorialized nationality categories that arose as the most natural and convenient form of organizing nationhood.

In Kazakhstan, there was no intense aspiration to independence in 1991. But shortly after the Soviet Union's disappearance, many of its long-term observers predicted ethnic unrest and the rise of nationalism in all of the independent states that were to follow. With regard to most of the countries, and in particular Kazakhstan, both have largely failed to occur. These inaccurate predictions had their roots in the misassessment by most sovietologists of the role of ethnicity during Soviet times.

Research on the Soviet Union was largely forced to rely on the interpretation of materials – through modelling and analytical abstraction – that were available outside of the USSR, since field research within the country basically could not be conducted. Therefore, it was simply supposed (e.g., Beissinger 1992; Carrère d'Encausse 1995; Naumkin 1994) that the creation of national republics and the policies of *korenizatsiya* had generated strong national identities. Jones Luong (2004a: 6f) further explains the misinterpretations by sovietologists in that many of them still conceived of society as evolving within the paradigm of totalitarianism (though most actually intended to reject it) and, thus, assumed the state's omnipresence and its ultimate control over its subjects. Therefore, the Union's end is seen as a result of a strongly implemented nationality policy, which inspired nationalism and ultimately was one of the fundamental causes of the Soviet Union's dissolution.

Some scholars on Central Asia (e.g., Allworth 1989; Fierman 1991) assert exactly the opposite. They act on the assumption that Central Asian pre-Soviet identities, beliefs and practices were significantly more resistant to Soviet rule than pre-Soviet beliefs and practices elsewhere in the Union. In this interpretation the Central Asian Republics are seen as colonies rather than integral parts of the state, and therefore scholars see a clear boundary 'between the Soviet "state" and Central Asian "society"' (Jones Luong 2004a: 10). This line of reasoning led to the conclusion that the Central Asian states in particular were fundamentally unprepared for independence (e.g., Olcott 1997) and that after the Union's dissolution, tribal, religious and other 'traditional' long-hidden identities would resurface (e.g., Roy 2000).

Kazakhstan: The Formation of a Nation State and the Role of Nationality

The analysis of the nation states and societies that arose after the collapse of the Soviet Union has often been framed in terms of transition and transformation. Such a 'transitology approach' has become criticized for its teleological presupposition (e.g., Dave 2007: 27; see also Beyer 2006) and – with respect to the related notion of postsocialism – because there are time limits for the usefulness of concepts. Dave herself avoids firm teleological interpretations, but she still overestimates historical trajectories because she interprets present-day Kazakhstani society as largely determined by its past, speaking of 'the enduring effects of the Soviet cognitive frame, institutional framework and ideological categories to navigate in the post-Soviet world' (Dave 2007: 28). In the case of Kazakhstan, those 'enduring effects' of the Soviet past may seem overly obvious, considering that the nation is still headed by the person who came to power on the eve of the Soviet Union's dissolution in 1989.

Nursultan Nazarbayev, Kazakhstan's only president as of this writing, was the Chairman of the Supreme Soviet of the republic under Kunaev. Nazarbayev distanced himself from Kuneav during the 1986 incidents, although he publicly condemned the protests (Dave 2007: 89).[62] In September 1989, he became chairman of the Supreme Soviet.[63] Though there might initially have been some hope for democratic reforms in the nation state's early phase, the first constitution, passed in January 1993, referred to Kazakhstan as a 'presidential republic' (Cummings 2005: 24), whereupon Nazarbayev 'began in early 1993 to create top-down political parties' (ibid.).

Most scholars on Kazakhstan are concerned with state and nation-building processes (e.g., Aydingün 2008; Cummings 2005; Dave 2007; Diener 2004; Holm-Hansen 1999; Surucu 2002). As a result, the formation of political institutions and identities is mostly explained in light of the country's Soviet past. Surucu (2002: 385) states that 'post-Soviet nation building in Kazakhstan is a textbook example of how the past fragments the post-colonial collective imagining'. All kinds of movements, whether oppositional or ethnic, are often ultimately explained by the existence of an omnipresent state, which itself has been deeply shaped by the all-powerful state that preceded it.

In this spirit, Nazarbayev and his regime are often depicted as exceptionally powerful. Dave (2007: 141), for instance, highlights that the country is a 'strong state' and that 'it is common knowledge that all the key sectors of the government (national security, taxation, media) and the economy are under the personal control of Nazarbayev and his "extended family" (*bol'chaia sem'ia*) of family, friends and clients'. Dave (ibid.: 142) speaks of a 'strong patrimonial presidency' and underlines its effects by mentioning that Nazarbayev's party 'Otan' had around one million members in 2006. Furthermore, it is often emphasized that Kazakhstan – like the Soviet Union – is a highly centralized state that does not permit any kind of federalism; indeed, there are no elections at the oblast level, nor are citizens allowed to elect their own *akim* (Kazakh for mayor) (cf. ibid.: 120). However, Jones Luong (2004b: 183) criticizes this 'view from above that relies on formal state institutions and overlooks the informal bargaining and tacit agreements that take place between central and regional leaders'. Certainly, Kazakhstan must be referred to as a *de jure* centralized state, which, however, does not mean that this is *de facto* always the case.

'Kazakhization'

Kazakh nationalism and the gradual shift from Russian to Kazakh cultural and language hegemony – mostly referred to as 'Kazakhization' – is another topic of discussion among scholars. Debates often centre on the firmly established dichotomy between national and civic concepts of the state, by aiming to position the Kazakh state as a whole or its individual actors within this framework (e.g., Diener 2004; Holm-Hansen 1999; Surucu 2002). In the case of Kazakhstan those oppositional poles are mostly labelled 'nationalists' vs. 'cosmopolitans' or 'internationalists'. Surucu (2002: 394), for instance, explains the controversial positions as follows:

> While cosmopolitans project an inherent dichotomy between modernity and Kazakh traditions, nationalists suggest a path within, a model that 'won't repeat the sins that the colonial power had committed'. They articulate an alternative discourse to accommodate modernity within the context of their own historical and cultural experience. According to nationalists, Kazakh historical legacy does not entail an authoritarian closure as cosmopolitans argue; in contrast, it provides the ingredients of pluralism, tolerance, diversity, and progress.

According to Surucu (ibid.: 396), the cosmopolitans' project is likely to fail because they do not have the ability to transgress the Soviet categories; they 'appear to be very restricted in their efforts to develop an alternative project based on a shared collective memory and the recognition of diversity. In a sense, they are cursed by the failure of the "Soviet man"'.

Most authors, however, take a different approach to the nationalists-internationalists dichotomy. They (e.g., Holm-Hansen 1999) argue that the state can only peacefully continue to exist by adopting a 'supra-ethnic' or 'civic nationalism' model (Diener 2004: 140). Kazakhstan, however, is criticized for its lack of a 'supra-ethnic' model and for its disguised nationalism. By 'disguised nationalism' Holm-Hansen (1999) and Diener (2004) have in mind that all nationalities – and not only Kazakhs – are encouraged to 'rediscover' their ethnic belonging. Nonetheless, such policies are held responsible for eventually circumventing the integration of all people residing in the country's territory and for creating 'more boundaries' (Diener 2004: 142).

The establishment of minority institutions is mostly interpreted as a means of concealing the subtle process of 'Kazakhization' (e.g., Cummings 2006; Diener 2004; Oka 2006). There are two minority institutions in present-day Kazakhstan. The Assembly of the People of Kazakhstan was established in 1995, with the official aim to 'strengthen public stability and interethnic accord' (Oka 2006: 367). As the president's consultative body it unites pro-regime ethnic movements, consisting of over three hundred representatives of various ethnic groups, and it has branches at the oblast level (Dave 2007: 131). Furthermore, many nationalities maintain their 'national-cultural centre', which nominates some of the delegates to the assembly while the president nominates others (ibid.). For Cummings (2006: 187) both assembly and national-cultural centres are 'largely symbolic outfits' that lack any legislative power or political influence.[64]

The national-cultural centres of the German minority are called *Wiedergeburten* (Rebirth). In 2007, there were sixteen local Rebirth organizations under the umbrella of the association of Germans in Kazakhstan, headed by Alexander Dederer. The organization was initially founded by Russian German political activists who were demanding the reinstallation of an autonomous district in the Volga area in 1989. But against the background of strong opposition from Russian settlers in that region, they soon relinquished their claim (cf. Römhild 1998: 128–30). The role of the German Rebirth organization in Taldykorgan will be explored in Chapters 7 and 8.

'Kazakhization' is most often referred to as a political tool, with the objective of weakening Russians. Along these lines, the reconstruction of oblast boundaries in the north during 1994–97 is cited, wherein 'all Russian-dominated regions were merged with the neighbouring Kazakh-dominated regions' (Dave 2007: 122). Also the capital's shift to Akmola (now Astana) in 1998 is seen as a measure taken to achieve 'a greater vigilance over the Russian-dominated regions, and to secure the loyalty of the Russified Kazakhs in these territories' (ibid.: 123). In particular, minority policies are interpreted as a disguised form of 'Kazakhization' because they are assumed to aim at isolating the Russophone community, which is currently labelled under the category 'Russian'.[65] By protecting small ethnic groups, Nazarbayev's regime has sought to 'activate "anticolonial" and anti-Russification sentiments among Slavs and other Russified groups' (ibid.: 133). Dave (ibid.) offers the example of Ukrainians who now publicly stress their common fate with the Kazakhs under the Soviet, i.e. Russian, rulers. Moreover, the offspring of interethnic marriages are encouraged to change their passport designation from 'Russian' to their 'real' ethnic identity.

Furthermore, the process of 'Kazakhization' is generally used to describe the replacement of anything Russian by anything Kazakh, based on the fact that 'numerous positions in all spheres of administration and public life'

(Dave 2007: 151) have been occupied by Kazakhs. In addition, changing city and street names, erecting new statues and rediscovering (local) histories have a direct effect on the visible image of the nation: 'Individual locales began to identify and glorify *ru* and *zhuz*-based heroes, to rename streets, schools and former state farms in their own honour, and to emphasise the role of particular lineage segments in the Kazakh history' (Schatz 2000: 500; cf. also Aydingün 2008). At least in public, however, it is not so much about stressing particular lineages as creating a fine balance, taking one hero from each (comment by an anonymous reviewer).

Language Policies

Another hotly debated topic concerning the gradual 'Kazakhization' is the designation of the Kazakh language as the official language of the country. The shift to the Kazakh language appears, first of all, to be logical since 'throughout history, more powerful social groups have sought to impose their language on the less powerful by requiring linguistic accommodation as a condition of economic and political opportunities and advantages' (Patten 2001: 696). Language policies and the actual significance and use of Kazakh and Russian garner the most attention in the works of those who are concerned with the building of a Kazakh nation as well as in virtually all studies dealing with interethnic relations in Kazakhstan (e.g., Dave 2004, 2007; Davis and Sabol 1998; Fierman 1998; Peyrouse 2007; Sarsembayev 1999; Schatz 2000, 2004). Though language policies are often seen as 'balanced', Dave (2007: 104) asserts a connection between Kazakh language, territory and culture which implies for her that Kazakhs perceive their language as 'a vital cultural resource exclusively possessed by … [them] and unavailable to Russian-speakers'. In her view, non-Kazakhs (who are logically non-Kazakh speakers) are categorically, by birth, excluded from the Kazakh nation. Furthermore, the preservation of the Kazakh language is, then, connected to the question of survival versus extinction of the Kazakh nation in general, and thus must be given priority. The concern about the Kazakh language was not without merit, since its prevalence was weak and speaking it was often associated with 'backwardness'. According to the 1989 census, only 0.9 per cent of Russians spoke Kazakh, whereas 62.8 per cent of Kazakhs indicated they were fluent in Russian (Khazanov 1995: 255).

Kazakhstan's laws on language(s) have been discussed in detail, both in academic writing and in public discourse within the country. The law passed in 1989 on languages laid the foundation for further legislation. Here, for the first time, union and autonomous republics were permitted to establish 'their language' as the (single) 'local official language' (Fierman 1998: 176, 180), whereupon, within the Kazakh SSR, Russian was accorded the status of a 'language of interethnic communication' (*yazyk mezhnatsionalnogo obsheniya*). The reversal in status of the two languages triggered feelings of discrimination among some and prompted the first wave of emigration of non-Kazakh speakers (Davis and

Sabol 1998: 474). Since then, Kazakh has been approved by all subsequent laws on language as Kazakhstan's sole state language.[66] The official status of Russian as a 'language of interethnic communication', however, leaves room for interpretation. Both the 1995 constitution and the 1997 language law state that 'in state organizations and organs of local administration the Russian language is officially used on par with Kazakh' (Art. 7 of the constitution; cited in Fierman 1998: 179). Hence, this 'ill-defined distinction between "state" and "official" language' (Schatz 2000: 494) can be used for different juridical interpretations. This indicates that the initially envisaged rapid switch to Kazakh was unrealistic, because few people had a good command of Kazakh.[67]

Despite the less-than-sweeping results of Kazakhstan's language legislation, its overriding intention – to strengthen Kazakh while gradually replacing Russian – is clearly recognized by people in Kazakhstan. For instance, Kazakh primary and secondary education as well as university education has been promoted nationwide, and the 1997 law on languages also stipulated that at least fifty per cent of all television and broadcasting should be in Kazakh (Dave 2007: 102; Schatz 2000: 494). While Kazakhs are generally assumed to appreciate the course of the state's language policies, viewing it as 'a symbolic affirmation of their sovereignty and of their identity as a nation' (Dave 2007: 104),[68] non-Kazakhs, on the other hand, are assumed by Dave (ibid.: 103) to regard 'Kazakhs as the new proprietors of the state' in which they see 'no future' for themselves. The effects of language policies on people's identities and on the process of identification will be explored in Chapters 3 and 4.

Kazakhstani Identity

The concept of nationality is generally seen as an unchallenged continuation from Soviet times.[69] Dave (2007: 130), for instance, contends that 'consistent with the Soviet socialist formulation, nationality is imagined as "cultural", that is, a non-political community. Within this framework, the state allows, in fact encourages, official national-cultural centres to engage in "cultural" and "ethnographic" activities'. Thus, 'culture is constructed in a folkloristic sense, with fixed meaning and insignias, devoid of a subjective identity dimension'. Therefore, also 'the concept of the "people of Kazakhstan" enshrined in the constitution is modelled on its ideological precursor, the "Soviet people"' (ibid.: 135).

Kazakhstan has been the most 'international' of all the former Soviet Republics and, according to official statistics, more than a hundred different ethnic groups reside in present-day Kazakhstan.[70] Furthermore, Nazarbayev repeatedly states that all peoples living within the territory of Kazakhstan are Kazakhstani citizens and equal under the law (cf. Diener 2004: 22). The president is often characterized as having 'successfully recast himself as a promoter of economic reforms, prosperity, and ethnic harmony, along with Kazakh national and cultural regeneration' (Dave 2007: 4).[71]

One of the methods employed by Nazarbayev to establish an all-encompassing national identity is making use of the concept of 'Eurasia'. However, for Schatz (2000: 492) the notion of 'Eurasian' is no more than an updating of the old Soviet notion of 'international', and therefore, tainted with the same brush:

> But, just as Soviet era internationalism ultimately had a Russian face (holding a privileged position for ethnic Russians in the evolutionary march toward the 'bright future'), post-Soviet Kazakhstani state ideology had a Kazakh face, singling out Kazakhs for linguistic, demographic, political and cultural redress.

In this context, it is often mentioned that the country's name 'Kazakhstan' defines the state in ethnic terms, as the land of the Kazakhs (cf. Diener 2004: 21). Furthermore, the fact that Kazakhs have only recently come to form the majority of their country's population,[72] and that these demographic figures attained great importance in public discourses, causes Holm-Hansen (1999: 162f) to note that this reveals an 'underlying pattern of exclusion' and the assumption of 'fixed ethnic identities'.

Thus, a Kazakhstani identity is widely questioned as an appealing mode for non-Kazakhs (e.g., Cummings 2006: 191). It is stated that the poorly developed civic concept of nationhood is not able to incorporate non-Kazakhs because of the lack of a true institutional guarantee of pluralism by the state (cf. Holm-Hansen 1999: 162). Dave (2007: 135) adds that 'a distinction between "Kazakh" and "other" people of Kazakhstan remains deeply embedded in semi-official, academic, journalistic and popular references', and Holm-Hansen (1999: 162) concludes that 'there is a widespread feeling among nontitulars in Kazakhstan that they are discriminated against'. Chapters 2 and 4 scrutinize these assumptions about Kazakhstani identity by assessing individual variation and the complex phenomenon of people's attachment to a Kazakhstan homeland. Chapter 6 explores the effects of transnational connections and views about Germany on the construction of Kazakhstani-German identities.

Kazakhstani Germans

Though ethnic unrest largely failed to take root after the collapse of the Soviet Union, some Russian political activists strove for more autonomy, particularly in Kazakhstan's northern and eastern oblasts at the beginning of the 1990s. The above-mentioned redrawing of oblast boundaries, as well as the replacement of the previously Russian oblast leadership by loyal Kazakhs, has, however, succeeded in circumventing any efforts to gain more autonomy for Russian districts (cf. Dave 2007: 126).[73] Also German political activists strove for the establishment of German *rayons* (districts) in northern Kazakhstan; this effort was equally impeded (Diener 2006: 203f). Nonetheless, the question remains as to why non-Kazakhs did not push their claims further.

The lack of ethnic turmoil is most often explained by the fact that disenchanted non-Kazakhs opted for emigration instead of fighting for additional minority rights within the country (e.g., Masanov 1999; cf. Peyrouse 2007: 492–94). Between 1989 and 1999 alone, about 1.5 million people left the country (Peyrouse 2007: 492). This huge outflow had the largest effect on Kazakhstan's Germans, more than eighty per cent of whom emigrated.

For Dave (2007: 139) the vast number of emigrants indicates that those who left had felt discriminated against as non-Kazakhs. Others (e.g., Davis and Sabol 1998; Yessenova 1996) argue that the decision of many to leave Kazakhstan was not primarily due to feelings of ethnically based exclusion but to the disastrous economic conditions during the 1990s. Furthermore, it is mentioned that feelings of insecurity after the Soviet Union's collapse, in combination with the creation of a new and unfamiliar nation state, contributed to the huge migration (cf. Brown 2005: 628; cf. Diener 2004: 33f, 89).

Specifically concerning Kazakhstani Germans other aspects have to be taken into consideration: Germany's constitutional guarantee of citizenship and the visions of homeland among Kazakhstani Germans.[74] Germany's ethnically delineated immigration policies, as well as benefits for immigrants from the former USSR during the late 1980s and early 1990s, were certainly the prerequisites for massive immigration to Germany. Furthermore, the life stories of Kazakhstani Germans suggest that some of them had already dreamed for a long time of returning to the land of their ancestors, which also helped account for the exodus of Kazakhstani Germans in the early 1990s, once the opportunity for immigration to their historical homeland was given (Ingenhorst 1997; Pfister-Heckmann 1998; Römhild 1998). However, this immigration eventually came to a near-standstill due to subsequent changes in Germany's immigration policies.[75]

Those Kazakhstani Germans who remained have been depicted as lacking ethnic awareness but are, on the other hand, deeply influenced by the various relations to their 'kin-state'. Diener (2004: 107f), relying on the concept of 'territorialization', describes Kazakhstani Germans as 'de-territorialized' with regard to their local settlements, which he views in connection with the 're-territorialization of Germans toward their kin-state' (ibid.: 138). Diener considers this as critical because the Germans' transnational interconnectedness impedes them from becoming 'members of the Kazakhstani civic nation' (ibid.: 135). Aid from Germany, as well as personal connections to relatives and friends in Germany, have resulted in 'many Germans, for their part, resist[ing] in varying degree, the reality of Kazakhstan's independence and the need to find their place within it' (ibid.: 138).[76]

Continued connections to relatives in Germany are also relevant from an economic perspective. Brown (2005: 632), for instance, underlines the fact that because so many Germans moved to Germany, it allowed others to stay in Kazakhstan. Remittances from Germany have played a crucial role: 'The network of family and associates is still where people invest their resources. In that sense, a set of networks that spans the distance from Almaty to Ulm is something that bears examination'.

Moore (2000) analyses the impact of Germany's repatriation policies on construction, mobilization and the strategic employment of ethnic identity. In particular he focuses on German language tests conducted by officials of Germany's Federal Administration in Kazakhstan. The procedure is a threefold process encompassing German language proficiency, evidencing German descent through official documents, and the ability to distinguish oneself from 'others' through particular folk customs (ibid.: 172f). Moore argues that Germany's immigration policies presuppose the existence of measurable fixed ethnic identities, in particular along linguistic lines: '"Russian", "Russian-German" and "German" identities are assumed to be immutable natural essences' (ibid.: 174). Therefore, these tests require the construction and preservation of an ethnic identity assumed and defined by Germany in essentialist terms.

Most of the above-mentioned studies and analyses, which are primarily concerned with the Kazakh nation-building process, the position of the state's minorities, and minority policies, also touch on the notion of identity. By examining state institutions and state policies, either directly or tangentially, they investigate the 'politics of identity'. All too often, however, the effectiveness of policies is simply presumed, with the result that their objectives (which, of course, do not have to be consistent) are implicitly assumed to be lived by every person (cf. Brubaker 2004: 68). This holds true for the great attention that German state policies are given in the analysis of the identity of Kazakhstani Germans, as well as when debating 'Kazakhization' and its effects on Russian and Kazakh identities.

In the following chapters, the themes of this chapter will be explored through ethnographic research. I will seek to show how people in diverse circumstances cope with large-scale changes in their everyday lives; whether and how they align their feelings towards belonging, identification and social relations; and the different ways in which they interact with state policies and politicians.

Notes

1. Most studies on memory in social anthropology and history refer to the notion of 'collective memory', coined by Halbwachs in 1925. The shared knowledge of a particular group about its past is seen as crucial in establishing a sense of groupness. Memory might therefore be seen as something that exists beyond the individual, whose memory only develops through social interactions. One critique of Halbwachs' memory concept is that it leaves

little room for counter-memories, instead highlighting the hegemonic power of memory (cf. Niethammer and Trapp 1985: 16; Pine et al. 2004: 10f).
2. By a decree in 1964 (under Khrushchev), Soviet Germans were officially rehabilitated and the general accusation of collaboration with Nazi Germany was repudiated.
3. Römhild (1998: 126) raises the question of whether the experience of deportation and exclusion might have fostered a 'collective trauma', which for the first time might have created an ethnic consciousness as Soviet Germans. Before 1941, Russian Germans did not have much in common since they were very diverse with regard to language (speaking various German dialects), religion and regional settlements, thus first traumatic experiences due to deportation and persecution could level those differing experiences and produce an awareness of being an ethnic *Schicksalsgemeinschaft* (community sharing a common destiny) (ibid.: 161).
4. Many asked me directly before the interview if they could start with their parents' life story, which of course I agreed to.
5. All names are anonymized. In the text I use only first names though, of course, people have surnames and fathers' names as well. But I was on first-name terms with most of the people cited, and I wish to impart this degree of intimacy to the reader.
6. I use the term 'memory of deportation' in a broad sense, subsuming also the experiences of the *trudarmya* (labour army) and *komandatura*.
7. Römhild (1998: 226f) comes to the same conclusion: the young Russian Germans she interviewed spoke with a distinct emotional distance about the deportation of their ancestors. In this respect the Russian-German memory of deportation supports Humphrey et al. (2003: 17), who claim that 'in the Soviet era people did not engage openly in the search for their roots and certain stories were concealed from the younger generations, just to make their life smoother and less traumatic. People changed their family names so as not to be identified as Jews or Germans or Finns'. See also Strutz (2008: 91f) on the memories of Austrian Jewish refugees in the United States, who similarly did not focus on relating their experiences of suffering to second and third generations.
8. 'Oppositional memories' are often seen as a 'potential source of power' and a 'tool of opposition'. They might foster identity claims and identity formation (Pine et al. 2004: 3f).
9. Olga holds a high-ranking position.
10. It is stressed that they were not guilty of anything because they were born after the Second World War. This leaves open whether those Russian Germans born before the war might be, in a sense, guilty.
11. In 1979, only 4.3 per cent of the Germans in the Kazakh SSR had university degrees versus 11.7 per cent of the population of the republic as a whole. In 1989, only 5.7 per cent of Germans had university degrees (Pohl 2008: 412).
12. Bourdieu developed the concept of 'habitus' in his *Outline of a Theory of Practice* (1977).
13. One also has to keep in mind that this question is often asked in a similar way at the German embassies in the context of immigration approval in order to 'prove' someone's genuine 'Germanness'. The source of Oleg's anger could also probably be traced to the fact that his application for immigration had been rejected.
14. Chikadze and Voronkov (2003) describe a similar shift of ethnic identity and memory for Jews in St Petersburg. Those who grew up in times of severe discrimination in the 1930s and 1940s tried to rid themselves of their ethnic belonging: 'All these strategies led to the deliberate destruction of social (ethnic) memory, and to the ousting of references to Jewish ethnicity not only from public but also from private life' (ibid.: 250). However,

particularly since the 1980s 'ethnic pride' has developed and the younger generations now highlight the importance of their grandmothers who spoke Yiddish and from whom they learned about Jewish culture. Nowadays, belonging to the Jewish community permits someone to immigrate to Israel or to take part in a Jewish network in Russia, which is also related to foreign support. They conclude by stating: 'First Jews converted to Russians, then Russians converted to Jews' (ibid.: 259).

15. In 'Kurs russkoi istorii' (reprint 1948: 20–21).
16. This line of forts included the towns of Omsk (established in 1716), Semipalatinsk (1718), Pavlodar (1720), Ilek (1731), Orsk (1735), Orenburg (1743) and Petropavlovsk (1752) (Sabol 2003: 27).
17. However, those territories were inhabited, mostly by Chuvashes and Mordvins, with whom the new German settlers often came into conflict (Römhild 1998: 41).
18. Part of Catherine's civilizing project was the sending of Tatar mullahs from Kazan into the Kazakh steppe (cf. Sabol 2003: 34).
19. The Resettlement Administration, established in 1896 to deal with the allocation of land and to define the permitted uses of such land, was often ignored. Furthermore, Kazakh households were allocated only fifteen *desiatyn*, whereas Russian households received between ten and eleven *desiatyn* per person. This also resulted in many Kazakhs being essentially forced to settle, since the allotted land was far too little to support a nomadic mode of existence (Sabol 2003: 44f).
20. The reform decreed that nineteen million hectares of land were set aside for farming in the Kazakh steppe (Svanberg 1996: 320).
21. Chinn and Kaiser (1996: 188) further argue that each wave of immigration subsequently intensified the development of a Kazakh national consciousness, which they view as both anti-Tsarist and anti-Russian.
22. For a detailed discussion of the Kazakh intelligentsia see Sabol (2003).
23. Due to the eastern expansion of the *Deutsche Orden*, many Germans settled in Estonia and Latvia. They were able to maintain their leading positions under the Russian regime from the beginning of the eighteenth century (Römhild 1998: 51).
24. The manifest attracted German settlers by guaranteeing the following privileges: freedom of religion, tax exemption, exemption from military service, and local self-administration (Hilkes 1996: 152).
25. It is unlikely that the German Catherine the Great was especially interested in German settlers, which is often asserted by Russian Germans. Rather, the devastated areas and weakened authorities in Hessen, in particular after the Seven Years' War (1756–63), combined to encourage subjects to emigrate while removing any possible obstacles to emigration. The manifest was also intended to be published in other European states, which, however, were able to restrict its distribution or prevent the emigration of their citizens (Römhild 1998: 42f).
26. Immigration since 1804 involved mostly southern Germans, but some migrated from Prussia, Saxony and Thuringia; furthermore, this immigration wave included many Mennonites who had escaped military service in Prussia (Ingenhorst 1997: 24; Römhild 1998: 51–53, 65).
27. Another reason for the more successful Black Sea Coast settlements was the different legal succession. While Volga Germans practised a kind of *mir* system, which led to smaller allotments with each new generation, settlers of the Black Sea Coast passed on the land to only one son. Furthermore, Black Sea settlers were allowed to acquire new territories, which was denied to Volga settlers (Römhild 1998: 66f).

28. Only through the establishment of local self-governing bodies (*semstvo*) in 1864 was contact increased between Russians and Germans (Römhild 1998: 68).
29. In the beginning of the nineteenth century, there were seventy-two Protestant villages (among them a few Calvinist villages) and thirty-two Catholic villages along the Volga (Römhild 1998: 60).
30. The abolition of exemption from military service caused the eastward migration of many Mennonites, in particular to Kazakhstan and Siberia. Furthermore, poor harvests in the years from 1890 to 1992 forced many Volga settlers to move eastwards (Ingenhorst 1997: 29–31).
31. Though recruitment of settlers officially ended in 1819, many Germans immigrated afterwards, mainly to Wolhynien and Ukraine, on their own initiative and without the lure of the previous privileges. In the beginning of the twentieth century, two hundred thousand German settlers alone immigrated to previously Polish territories. In 1897, the total number of Germans in the Russian Empire is stated to be 1,790,400, or 1.43 per cent of the total population. By 1914, almost 2.5 million Germans lived in Russia; their number dropped to 1,619,655, as officially stated for the year 1959 (Hyman 1996: 463; Römhild 1998: 52, 72–74).
32. The article 'Marxism and the National Question' (originally published as 'The Nationality Question and Social Democracy') was probably at least partly written by Stalin himself and was directed at Austrian Social Democrats who assumed nations to be stable entities and who favoured the principle of extraterritorial autonomy. Stalin contended that nations had only developed during the period of rising capitalism (cf. Hirsch 2005: 26–28; cf. Weitz 2002: 21).
33. I use the English term 'nationality' here to encompass the three Russian terms *natsiya*, *nationalnost* and *norodnost*. However, the English term 'nation' only refers to the Russian *natsiya*.
34. Belinskii was, like Nadezhdin, influenced by German Romanticism, but in contrast to Nadezhin, he favoured the 'advanced category' of *nationalnost*. On the interaction of Russian and German scientists during the nineteenth century see also Abashin (2008) and Weitz (2002). Weitz (ibid.: 19) highlights that the subsequent 'ambivalences of Soviet nationality policies' were not exceptional but reflect the 'general Western discourse on race and nation'.
35. The merging of nationalities was increasingly postponed in official discourse. Stalin had intended this process to be completed by the 1930s, Khrushchev by the 1980s, and Brezhnev – quite vaguely – stated that the Soviet Union would remain in the transition phase for a long time (Hirsch 2005: 319f). On the ascribed role of interethnic marriages in the process of nationality merging see Edgar (2007).
36. Certainly, the category 'Russian' had a prominent position in Soviet culture, but Slezkine (1994: 435, 443) and Hirsch (2005: 317) stress that at no time was Soviet culture equated with Russian culture. There was never such a thing as a 'Soviet nation'. However, from the late 1930s onwards, Russian became an obligatory second language in all non-Russian schools and primarily Russians occupied important positions in the party and the state, and therefore 'Russians were increasingly identified with the Soviet Union as a whole' (Slezkine 1994: 443).
37. Lenin's 1914 article 'On the Right of Nations to Self-Determination' articulated how national self-determination facilitates socialism at certain stages of historical development. Furthermore, he asserted that the guarantee of equal rights would deter the threat of secession (cf. Hirsch 2005: 28f).

38. At the Eighth Party Congress, a dispute arose between the advocates of the nationality policies, namely Stalin and Lenin, and the so-called internationalists – Georgii Piatkov and Nikolai Bukharin among others (cf. Martin 2001: 2f).
39. Hirsch (2005: 103), however, rejects the concept of 'affirmative action empire' because it was not aimed at developing minorities at the expense of the majority. Instead, all nationalities were to develop; therefore, she speaks of a 'state-sponsored evolutionism'.
40. These ten were the following: Soviet Union, Federal Republic (RSFSR, ZSFSR), Union Republic (e.g., Ukraine, Kazakhstan), autonomous republic (e.g., Tatarstan, Volga Republic), autonomous oblast (e.g., Komi, Chechen), autonomous okrug (e.g., Komi, Perm), national district (e.g., Polish, Finnish.), national village soviet (e.g., Roma, Assyrian), national *kolkhoz* (all nationalities) and personal nationality (Martin 2001: 47f).
41. The republic was based on the German *Arbeiterkommune*, which was established in 1918 (Römhild 1998: 113).
42. That Lenin's mother, Maria Alexandrovna Ulyanova, was a Volga German and that Lenin grew up in the Volga region is cited by Hyman (1996: 463f) as one reason for the quick establishment of the Volga Republic in 1924. Römhild (1998: 113f) sees the establishment of a German republic in particular with regard to foreign affairs. The Soviets had hopes that – after uprisings in 1923/24 – a revolution might be imminent in Germany, too. Against this background the German republic was meant to demonstrate positively a German nationhood within the framework of socialism.
43. Pokrovsk's German name was Kosakenstadt; the city was renamed Engels in 1931.
44. Martin (2001: 38) states: 'There was striking emphasis on maximum ethnic segregation'. Already by 1927, 67.8 per cent of Germans lived in their own national areas (ibid.).
45. Another reason was that Stalin did not want the Ukrainians to become too powerful; the many non-Ukrainian national territories within Ukraine served to weaken the Ukrainian position within their own republic (Martin 2001).
46. On the eve of collectivization, over ninety-seven per cent of Kazakhs were employed in the rural sector: 38.5 per cent engaged in livestock breeding, another 33.2 per cent combined agriculture and livestock breeding, and 24.5 per cent engaged only in agriculture (according to the 1926 census data) (Olcott 1981: 124).
47. The 1926 census reported 3,968,300 Kazakhs in Kazakhstan; the number had declined to 2,182,000 by the time of the long-unpublished 1937 census (Svanberg 1996: 320).
48. Olcott (1981: 128) writes: '15–20 per cent of the Kazakh population left the Republic during 1930–31'.
49. Olcott (1981: 137f) states that 'archival sources record widespread slaughter of animals from March 1930 until mid-1932. In many areas up to 50 per cent of the herd was destroyed during the first few weeks of the collectivization drive. One Soviet source records a loss of 2.3 million beef cattle and 10 million sheep during 1930 alone. … The loss of animals was proportionally far greater in Kazakhstan than in the USSR as a whole'.
50. As early as 1932, each person's nationality became fixed in his or her passport. The census, however, was preceded by a complicated debate. One of the most disputed issues revolved around whether to define nationality according to an individual's self-determination, or along certain objective criteria. This unsolved scientific question also allowed for different interpretations of the nationality concept in the use of two important political tools: the census and the passport system. See Abashin (2008), Hirsch (2005) and van Meurs (2001) regarding the relationship between social science (in particular, ethnography) and political rulers in the first decades of the Soviet Union.

All authors highlight the belief of politicians in scientific rules and the influence of ethnographers on political decisions, since scientific knowledge was intended to aid in the implementation of socialism which, later on, was supplemented by 'internationalism' and the 'friendship of peoples'.

51. The decree only concerned inhabitants of the so-called 'regime zones'. The passport system subdivided the Soviet Union into three distinct zones. The 'regime zones' were characterized as regions of geopolitical or economic significance, in which all people above the age of sixteen received a passport (indicating someone's occupation and nationality). This category comprised most areas inhabited by Germans. The other two zone categories were 'nonregime zones', which basically referred to rural districts not located in border zones, and 'extra-administrative zones' (e.g., gulags) (cf. Hirsch 2005: 268f).

52. Martin (1998: 848) states that deportation began much earlier. In 1935 about 41,650 persons were deported from the border area of Kiev and Vinnitsya oblast to eastern Ukraine and 'although Germans and Poles made up only a few per cent of the local population, they represented 57.3 per cent of the deportees'. Moreover, 'in January 1936 ... the order was given for a massive new deportation of 15,000 German and Polish households, now to Kazakhstan rather than eastern Ukraine. ... The deportations of 1935–36 included approximately half the German and Polish population of the Ukraine border regions' (ibid.: 849). Between 1937 and 1939 Ukraine's German population declined further by about forty thousand persons (ibid.: 853, n. 246).

53. Germans living in the areas occupied by the German Wehrmacht of Ukraine were chaotically resettled by the latter after the battle in Stalingrad in 1942/43 to western areas of Poland and Germany. Most were directed to the Warthegau for the purposes of *Germanisierung*; as early as 1940, Baltic Germans had been settled there. After 1945, they were deported mostly to Siberia by the Soviet army. This also affected those Soviet Germans who lived in the *Altreich* (by the Yalta agreement of 11 February 1945). About half of them (roughly 150,000 persons) successfully hid and avoided deportation to Siberia (cf. Brake 1998: 66, 184f; Lemberg 2008: 365; cf. Riek 2000: 4; Römhild 1998: 122–24). On the attitudes of Germans living in Ukraine about Nazi Germany see Brake (1998: 166–94).

54. Most Volga Germans were deported to the Kazakh SSR (Diener 2004: 63; cf. Svanberg 1996: 325).

55. In 1897, 7,049 Germans lived on the territory of current-day Kazakhstan. After the Russian Revolution and large-scale transfers of people, their number increased to 51,097 in 1926 (Diener 2006: 202).

56. The programme comprised fifty million hectares in Kazakhstan, the northern Caucasus, western Siberia and the right bank of the Volga. In Kazakhstan, by 1960, about nineteen million hectares were devoted to the programme. All in all, the programme did not achieve its aim and, in Kazakhstan, imperiled livestock production (Crowe 1998: 404f).

57. Kazakhstan's German population was estimated at 7.1 per cent of the total population in 1959 (Crowe 1998: 406).

58. On ethnic segregation in housing see Gentile and Tammaru (2006).

59. Because of Russification, however, German language proficiency in general became weaker during this time. The census of 1959 indicates that fifty-nine per cent of Germans possessed an exclusive knowledge of Russian, but Kazakhstani Germans could 'retain greater cultural distinctiveness than those living in Russia' (Diener 2006: 203).

60. For an elaboration on the implementation of *druzhba narodov* (friendship of the peoples) during Soviet times see also Sahadeo (2007), who argues, using the example of Soviet

Asian migrants in Moscow and Leningrad, that nationalist and racist ideas challenged *druzhba narodov*.
61. On 8 December 1991, the Soviet Union was dissolved and a Commonwealth of Independent States (CIS) was founded, but Kazakhstan did not declare its independence until 16 December 1991 (Cummings 2005: 16).
62. Nazarbayev's regime avoided coding the 1986 events in ethnic terms; they were referred to as the '1986 incidents' (Dave 2007: 89). There is, however, a street in central Almaty named *Zheltoksan* (December) to commemorate the events of 1986 (comment by an anonymous reviewer).
63. Nazarbayev converted this chairmanship to a presidency, which was confirmed by parliamentary elections in March 1990 (Cummings 2005: 22).
64. There are, however, also specific policies that arise from the assembly, such as quotas for students belonging to national minorities (Holm-Hansen 1999: 213f).
65. The Russian category is assumed to encompass most non-Kazakhs in present-day Kazakhstan, which is reflected in the saying: 'My mother's a Tatar, my father Greek and I am a Russian' (Dave 2007: 127). I will explore the Russian category in Chapters 3 and 4.
66. In Kazakhstan's first constitution in 1993, as well as in its second passed in 1995, and in a law on languages, which was passed in 1997, the status of Kazakh as the sole state language was confirmed (Fierman 1998: 176–78).
67. Also in the Language Law of 1997, 'the requirement that state officials learn Kazakh within a 10-year period was dropped' (Fierman 1998: 494).
68. However, it is worth noting that, as of this writing, not all Kazakhs speak Kazakh fluently; hence they face the same difficulties due to the weakened status of their mother tongue Russian as any other non-Kazakh speaker. Dave (2007: 111) makes the point that Kazakh is primarily 'an instrument of nationalization' and that businesses operate almost entirely in Russian.
69. The term 'minority' (*menchenstvo*) is not used in official statements for it 'implies Western-style policies and minority rights' (Dave 2007: 131). On the other hand, nationality (*natsionalnost*) involves the idea of the 'equality of all ethnic groups' (ibid.).
70. In 1991 all permanent residents in the territory of Kazakhstan became eligible for citizenship; dual citizenship is only allowed for Kazakhs living outside of Kazakhstan (cf. Holm-Hansen 1999: 175f).
71. With respect to economic reforms, Nazarbayev's statements are supported by the fact that the country has the highest per capita GDP in Central Asia (with a GDP growth of about 8 to 10 per cent since 1999) which is, however, almost entirely fuelled by oil exports (Dave 2007: 4). Furthermore, the country possesses substantial gold deposits, and rich unmined veins of copper, chrome and aluminium, and, therefore, appears to be 'a state of enormous potential natural wealth' (Olcott 2002: 10).
72. Only as of the 1999 census did Kazakhs outnumber non-Kazakhs (see, e.g., Cummings 2006: 178).
73. On the movements of Russian political activists such as Slaviya, Lad-ROSD (Respublikanskoe Obshchenstvennoe Slavyanskoe Dvizhenie) and Edinstvo see Peyrouse (2007). None of them still exist, 'the political activity of the Russian minority [having] collapsed at the end of the 1990s' (ibid.: 489).
74. Germany's juridical construction of citizenship is referred to as the principle of *jus sanguinis* (e.g., Brubaker 1992). Römhild (1998: 130f) adds that this principle was not valid in every context and that the construction of *Volksdeutsche* and the opportunity of

incorporation into the German state was in particular used to stress the inhuman character of the Soviet Union during the Cold War.
75. In order to reduce the scale of immigration from the former Soviet Union, the German law has been changed several times. From 1990 onwards, immigrants had to fill out the immigration application form within Kazakhstan. A quota of two hundred thousand immigrants per year was introduced in 1992. From 1996 onwards, a German language exam further reduced the number of immigrants and applicants. Between 1996 and 1998, about half of the applicants did not pass the language exam (Info-Dienst Deutsche Aussiedler 2001: Heft Nr. 110; cf. Ingenhorst 1997: 102–04; cf. Riek 2000: 136–39).
76. Diener (2004), however, contradicts his own analysis for he also describes those who stayed as the 'most highly adapted to Kazakhstani society' (ibid.: 116). Furthermore, he states that the 'out-migration of Germans appears to have drained the community of its most nationalistic members, leaving those with lower levels of ethnic awareness or at least lower levels of assertiveness to determine the fate of their community within Kazakhstan' (ibid.: 111). This does not support his 'territorialization analysis', which suggests that those who stayed continue to feel strongly connected to their kin-state Germany by holding on to an ethnically defined vision of a homeland.

Chapter 2
The Enmeshment of Identities and Life Stories

At the outset of my fieldwork, I asked people directly what it meant to them to be German (of course, only in cases where they had identified themselves beforehand as German). Often, their response was an elaboration of their life story, usually incorporating themes of deportation and discrimination – if not based on their own experiences then on the experiences of their ancestors. Equally often, they concluded by emphasizing that Germans in present-day Kazakhstan are highly esteemed. I soon realized that while telling the story of one's life is a fairly common and well-established means of communicating to others who one is and how one got to be that way, in this particular research people felt it was important to legitimize their ethnic belonging by focusing on what they perceived to be evidence of their German identity. In light of such responses I changed my approach, simply asking people to tell me their life stories, rather than putting to them the more limited question of what it meant to be German. As a result of this altered method, I heard about such varied subjects as careers, migratory movements and medical conditions, in addition to the central theme of ethnic belonging.

This chapter concerns diverse Kazakhstani-German life stories as they were related to me in an interview setting.[1] It will be argued that these stories account for divergent interpretations of German identity. Life stories are particularly helpful in assessing different degrees of emotional attachment to ethnic belonging, which I regard as a key element in defining the parameters of one's identity claims. When, how and why Kazakhstani Germans identify themselves as German is, thus, shaped by the meaning they personally attach to a German identity. This chapter provides four life stories that represent four distinct types of German identity. Each is organized according to two major criteria: the relationship towards Kazakhs and Russians and the relevance of ethnic belonging. It will be shown that only some Kazakhstani Germans define themselves primarily in ethnic terms, whereas others construct their personal identity by referring to a superordinate system, i.e., either the Kazakh state or the former Soviet Union. Thus, the chapter presents multiple interpretations and meanings of German identity. Chapter 3 will further explore these findings by explicating what Kazakhstani Germans hold in common about a German identity. Before discussing the four life stories, however, it is helpful to reflect on what life stories can tell us; that is, what they can reveal about 'real lives'.

The Truth of Life Stories

One may associate the investigation of life stories with the postmodern shift that has affected the analysis of narratives. No longer is the primary aim of such analysis to bring to light the 'real life' behind a story, while viewing 'story-telling as a fabrication' and an 'act of speech' (Plummer 2001: 402). The interpretation of the text as such and its internal structure, key patterns and key phrases are therefore seen as the main tasks in the analysis of life stories (cf. Chanfrault-Duchet 1991: 77–82).

Moreover, the context in which stories are fabricated and in particular the relationship between interviewer and interviewee are regarded as fundamentally influencing the process of constructing the story of someone's life. In a more general sense, Linde (1993) points out that we build and rebuild our life stories by telling them to others at different times over the course of our life. The ways in which these stories are received leads us to a better understanding of what kinds of stories and which ways of telling them are socially accepted. On the basis of this negotiation process we constantly reformulate what we tell others about ourselves. According to Linde (ibid.: 3) life stories are told for the following purposes:

> Life stories express our sense of self: who we are and how we got that way. They are also very important means by which we communicate this sense of self and negotiate it with others. Further, we use these stories to claim or negotiate group membership and to demonstrate that we are in fact worthy members of those groups, understanding and properly following their moral standards.

Earlier, in the 1970s, a rather different approach to biography research developed, which aimed to add to the official history the too long 'forgotten lives' of ordinary people (Niethammer and Trapp 1985). It was asserted that only by taking into account the perspectives and way of life presented in such biographies could the (oral) historian be capable of writing a more complete and accurate history.[2]

A similar discussion surrounds the substantial body of research on 'victims' and 'suppressed people'.[3] A central question is: how do people resist suppressive historiography, or put another way, how do they preserve those memories that run counter to such a historiography (cf. Passerini 1992; Sherbakova 1992a,

1992b)? Those predominantly orally stories are analysed as to their capacity to dispute hegemonic discourses. Furthermore, such oppositional memories might be re-evaluated if a political system changes and may even serve the function of encouraging identity claims. Sherbakova (1992b: 190), for instance, indicates that in the former USSR oral accounts of victims were taken in the period of *glasnost* to be the 'historical truth about decades of totalitarianism'.

Most research on biographies in the former Soviet Union is therefore focused on providing a 'realist perspective', primarily concerned with giving a voice to those who had not been previously considered in the writing of their history.[4] People's narratives have come to be regarded as a window onto the 'real world': 'Thus any biography, if a researcher manages to discard the mask of biographical illusion, becomes a personalized piece of evidence of the socio-cultural world of an individual of a certain type – and not just of his or her life-world' (Golofast 2003: 58).

Questions, however, remain: What kind of account do life stories provide? What is their value? What do they tell us? Certainly, they do not simply mirror what someone has experienced, and they cannot be wholly accepted as constituting an uncontested piece of history. Even after accounting for all possible levels of reflexivity (cf. Davies 1999), one may contest their 'truth'. The least contentious approach treats the life stories purely as narrative statements, which still allows for addressing a set of relevant questions, such as how people arrange the things they tell, how they create coherence, which stylistic devices they use and what they stress (cf. Cortazzi 2001). But a crucial consideration – assessing what people tell you and what they do not – can only be resolved against the background of some degree of historical truth, however difficult it might be to uncover. One of the main interests of this study is to present contrasting views of Russian-German history, not solely for the purpose of adding to the historical record but also as a means of studying how identities are formed during a person's life. Drawing upon insights from cognitive anthropology and relying on the idea proposed by Linde that life stories are created throughout one's life and with them one's identity(ies), it is ultimately impossible to decode this process of identity (and generally schemata) formation since identities are created through the dialectical process of self-identification and categorization (Jenkins 1996). However, since they are built and rebuilt through engagement with the social environment, the life stories entail a truth and are furthermore unlikely to be predominantly fictionalized. Therefore, life story narrations – as one crucial means of communicating one's identity – are not arbitrarily altered for they are presumably deeply felt.

Four Life Stories, Four Identity Types

Identities are continually rebuilt and adapted to new circumstances, but I argue that the range of possible identities that someone has or is able to assume is limited. This is first of all constrained by the categorization of others, which will be investigated in the next chapter. But furthermore, personal experiences – which encompass all earlier categorizations – deeply affect one's identity and do not allow for purely opportunistic identity alteration. Kazakhstani Germans grew up in very different social environments, and thus their identities differ substantially.

In order to depict the different identity types, I will provide the example of one life story for each identity type. All in all, I conducted over sixty life story interviews which,[5] however, cannot be assigned in equal shares to the four identity types; nonetheless, I am able to set forth with confidence the characteristics of the bearers of these identity types. The four life stories were also chosen because these four interviewees were among the people to whom I had the most access, which allowed me to get a more comprehensive picture of their attitudes and practices. The fact that we had known each other before the interview, furthermore, helped them to trust me, which can be particularly important with regard to research in countries of the former Soviet Union. It is often pointed out that people during Soviet times clearly differentiated between private and public biographies. The former (in particular during official interviews) were adapted as much as possible to public demands in order to avoid the various repercussions that often resulted from disapproved traits or behaviour. Therefore, the trust of an interviewee is crucial in order to be able to obtain the more private version of his or her biography (Humphrey et al. 2003: 17–19; Chikadze and Voronkov 2003: 244f).

It is often mentioned (e.g., Brake 1998) that Russian Germans tend to tell their life stories very openly to everyone. I would, however, argue that these stories are mostly the official versions of their lives. In present-day Kazakhstan this can lead to an overestimation of 'Germanness' since many Kazakhstani Germans, at first, tend to stress a German identity, at least when being interviewed by a German ethnographer or historian. One can easily elicit descriptions of deportation and German celebrations, but these are often only at the surface of Kazakhstani-German identities.

Soviet Identity

The first type of German identity is represented by Valentina.[6] She was born in the Volga Republic in 1937. Together with her family, she was deported to Siberia in 1941. Although she only started school at age ten, she managed to pursue a limited career as an economist. In the 1960s she followed her (German) husband, who had to move to a small town near Taldykorgan for occupational reasons. She divorced her husband, with whom she had two children, in the 1970s. After the dissolution of the Soviet Union she was forced to retire at age 54 because the factory where she had been working closed. She moved to Taldykorgan because the living situation in terms of water supply and heating was (and still is) better in the bigger towns. Today Valentina has an apartment of her own; both her son and her daughter live with their families in Taldykorgan.

Valentina began her life story by describing several everyday incidents of her early childhood in her hometown in the Volga Republic. She then recounted the day of her deportation in great detail: how her parents had slaughtered all of their livestock, and how she – although only four years old – had to shoulder a heavy burden to the train because one was only allowed to take what one could carry. She recalled that she and her three brothers were excited to go on a journey, and she did not relate any instances of cruelty or fear. She did talk of the long journey to Siberia and, for instance, how they thought they had lost their father because he had expected the train to stop for longer than it actually did when he disembarked to shave. Only at the next stop, some days later, did they discover that their father had been able to cut his shaving short and jump on the last car of the departing train at the previous stop.

This tone of adventure and excitement contrasted sharply with Valentina's description of the disastrous circumstances in the Siberian village. There was a massive crowd of people at the train station in Siberia, and her father was taken away without any information being provided to the family about where he was going or for how long. Her mother was allowed to stay with the four children, but since she had to work all day, Valentina and her brothers were sent to a kindergarten. She characterized the governess of this kindergarten as very cruel and unjust and she recalled many incidents of humiliation, such as the following:

> One day, we were playing in the streets and in the street stood a basin filled with water; well, the water was still hot, and in this basin were nappies. And suddenly these educators, I was just passing by, they said to me: 'Go, wash the nappies!' At that time I was maybe five years old. 'Go, wash the nappies, you fascist …' I do not want to talk so rudely. [She does not want to utter the swear word.] This was a command. Then, I bent down and washed these dirty nappies with my child hands. All the educators jeered and laughed at me, and I felt as if I were mentally deficient. Something had happened to me, so I could neither cry nor say anything. I became somehow mentally deficient. I stood there and bent down. It was already lunchtime when all the children were eating, and afterwards there was a break. Nobody had come for me, not for the lunch, not for anything. I just stood there at the basin like an idiot. Then, finally, in the evening when my mother came to pick me up, it spilled out of me – a flood of tears. As if I came to myself. My mother took me, embraced me. I told her what had happened. And then she took us out of that kindergarten so nobody could ridicule us anymore. And after that, we were at home, we were alone.[7]

Valentina described in significant detail several other incidents of humiliation and assault, and she unquestionably perceived such treatment of her and her family as entirely unjust. Nevertheless, she avoided accusing all Russians of being cruel. She made no sweeping statement of blame against either the Soviets or against Russians in general for her and her family's hard life. Rather, she blamed the war for their hunger and poverty more often than she blamed their German identity. In fact, Valentina often brought up situations in which Russians had helped them:

> And something else I remember, it was still during the war, when, one day, children were sent to our *kolkhoz*, from the Leningrad blockade. And together with them an educator was sent. Her name was Vera. She was very beautiful, she had curly hair, and she was very intelligent. And, yes, when they sent these children, at that time, we were living in a kind of burrow and we were, somehow, regarded as the people's enemy. But those children were Russian children and they were as thin as we were; however, it's true, they were older than we were. … Yes, the locals, they had gardens in which they could cultivate something. Well, I remember, on the roof of the house of one of the collective farmers lay a gourd, a frozen one. And those children reached the gourd and rolled it down, smashed it, and ate it. Sometimes they even gave us some small pieces of it. And this woman began to talk with the *kolkhoz* women and told them that we Germans are not the people's enemy, that we are also unfortunate people, and maybe even more because – they took the husbands of the local women but they still had their houses, their gardens – but we were completely desolate. And then, they started behaving a bit better towards us. Because earlier it could even happen that they didn't give us salt. There were days we had not a single crumb. Not that something in particular was missing; we did not even have a single crumb of salt. That's why we all had scurvy, we lost our teeth. That's it.

Many of Valentina's accounts ended by pointing out that their situation improved remarkably after the end of the Second World War – in terms of both the general food shortage and discrimination against Germans. Furthermore, she even mentioned that her mother was rewarded for her hard work:

> Well, [the war] ended and, well, they looked at us in a better way, that we're not the people's enemy, that our women are very honest, kind, that they had worked very well. My mother was given even some kind of decoration. Well, I cannot say now what kind of decoration. But finally – when we were already living in Barnaul [a city in Western Siberia] – it was written in the newspaper. But she didn't get anything in her hands.

> We were just told that our mother received a decoration, but it was not handed to her.

It seemed important to Valentina that Germans were also respected, and that some of them even received a medal. She also emphasized that her parents spoke Russian as well as German, and that they had always been on good terms with Russians.

Until the deportation in 1941, Valentina's father had worked as a railway employee and a policeman. Finally, after 1945, her father was allowed to leave his labour camp and visit his family. They were still living in little more than a shack, where Valentina was on the verge of starvation. Her situation had become so serious that her parents agreed to have her father take her because there was no food shortage at the labour camp. Valentina recounted how her father had taken her with him to Barnaul without a train ticket:

> He brought me to the station, but he had no ticket. However, my father had worked as a railwayman until the war. He went to one of the train cars and asked there, went to the next, to the third, he asked all the staff. This was in the Altay Krai, in the city of Rubtsovsk, there at the train station. His tears were flowing, and then, in the end, he went to the engine driver. He [Valentina's father] was a tall, handsome man, I remember his words, 'Guys, if you won't help me, here, with my child – you see, I'm carrying the living dead, I'll just have to throw her in front of your train'. He was saying: 'I myself worked as a railwayman until the war, but now – fate wanted it this way – I have become the people's enemy. We were all resettled, that's it. My family lives here and I live there. And I only have one week off, and when I won't be there again in time, they will arrest me again and my family remains hungry again and will perish'. Those men agreed to take him, and found a place for me, in a frozen corner. In that way we were travelling. … And when we arrived in Barnaul, the soldiers [there were only soldiers in the train] took me out of the train, and they all gave me something to eat. They all had their families at home, and most were in the same miserable situation. And this is how my father brought me to Barnaul, [where] he lived in a residential accommodation for men.[8] Only Germans were living there, and they all felt pity for me. They all started crying because of me – because one had four, the next, five children. They all had their families. And they were happy to see me, but they were crying that they too, somewhere, had their children.

Again, while the circumstances of the German situation were marked by isolation and deprivation, Valentina nonetheless brought up instances where she and her family had been helped by the Russians. Moreover, she stressed that the situation of the Russian soldiers was no better than hers. The topic of Russians coming to the aid of her family took on the character of a recurrent theme in Valentina's narrative.

Because she was malnourished, and there was no money for pencil and paper, Valentina only started school at the age of ten in 1947. Like her parents, she spoke both Russian and German as her mother tongue and she was encouraged by her teacher to study German and to work as a translator:[9]

> My German language teacher asked me – I learned very well but was dressed very badly – well, he asked me: 'You should enrol at a university for foreign languages'. However, at that time we were afraid of speaking [German]. Well, it was forbidden in the families, that's it. And at that time, I was already in the ninth grade, and though I learned better than anyone else, I had to ask for leave and had to go to the *komandatura* in order to register. I usually was the oldest in class because I started school late and all the others were younger … Once, during a lesson, this was still in the sixth grade, I asked for leave, and my friend, she was four years younger than me. She raised her hand – we were learning at that time about the constitution of the Soviet Union – and asked our teacher: 'Why do you say that all are equal? And why do they not call me to the *militsiya* [civilian police in the Soviet Union] but they call Valentina?' Our teacher was standing there, she blushed, and she didn't know what to say. 'We learned it this way, but it turned out that we're not all equal. You children don't go to the *militsiya* but Valentina, although she's the best in our class, she must go to the *militsiya* in order to register'.

In the above excerpt, it is clear that being forbidden to speak German and regularly forced to register at the police station is secondary to the memory of her classmate speaking up for her. Another recurrent theme is the good relationships that she and her family enjoyed with both German and Russian neighbours. She described how her mother got along with their Russian neighbours:

> Well, though she was such an unschooled woman – she never left the house – she was very warm-hearted. She had only finished one and a half years at a German parish school. Well, I don't know why our neighbours – young women – always asked her for advice. She always helped them, she always calmed them down. Some of the Russian men drank a lot, they struggled. She went to our neighbours, called the name of that person who was drunk, who quarrelled, and that's it. You see, she just said, 'Vanya, what are you doing?' That way she brought peace to those families. … So many people came to her funeral because in such a

way she was able to be on good terms with them. They always held her and my father in high esteem. They [her mother and her father] were so funny, so humorous. You see, one of their friend's brother played in an orchestra at his factory. And the whole orchestra came to us and played for us for free [at her mother's funeral]. This is always very expensive. But for my mother they were playing so well; the cemetery in Barnaul was in a forest and they even organized a gravestone for free. This is how people were always helping us. And they even collected money so that we could have lunch, and we were so grateful to those people who helped us so much.

In the late 1940s, her father was released from the *trudarmya* and her family received a small flat. Valentina describes her life in the flat as mostly a happy time:

Well, when they gave us this one-room apartment – it was already well equipped. There was a toilet. We were living on the third floor. From time to time my grandmother came to us. Then, after some years my brothers began [to marry]. It even happened that eleven people were living in this one-room apartment. There was all in all only one bed; the others had to sleep on the ground. But instead, it was very funny. I had such a fun-loving family. We were always singing. There was always laughter in our house, there was always humour. We laughed at our poverty; we were no longer mourning because our parents were with us.

Remarkably, Valentina's narratives do not touch on any kind of particular German traditions, for instance, how they celebrated Christmas. She mentioned several times that her parents spoke German at home, but this was always said as an aside without additional comment. On the contrary, she emphasized the fact that her parents spoke – unlike the other Germans of her parents' generation – fluent Russian. Valentina also explicitly said that she loves the Russian language.

Valentina characterized herself as a hard-working person who had been forced to take on responsibility from her early childhood. Besides going to school and running her family's household, she worked in a neighbour's household to earn extra money for her family. She finished school and her further education successfully, and she was very proud of always having been one of the best pupils and workers. She married a German who, like her, was able to have a career, failing to mention that this was not necessarily a matter of course for Germans:[10]

My husband was a German. He had also graduated from an institute. He was an agronomist, and he had a high-ranking position. But – this is our Russian habit – he started drinking vodka. He was a good specialist,

> everything, but once somebody drinks vodka, there will no longer be any peace in the family. He started to misbehave at home. And one day when my second child was one and a half years old, he came and he was so drunk and he started to quarrel and that was it … What more to say …

She wanted to live apart from her often drunken husband but did not know with whom to stay. Once more, it was her Russian colleagues who helped her out of her predicament:

> I worked in the planning section. Only men worked there. They all took part in the war – Russians. Well, very remarkable, good natured people. One of these men, our chief, was even in a concentration camp. Two others fought.[11] They always felt pity for me. I was like a daughter to them. All the more because I worked well – that's the most important thing. There were also other sections, and in the administration, women were working and one of those women took me in. She said: 'This is the most important thing for you now; you'll live together with me as long as you're not divorced or they give something [a flat] to you'. She accommodated me, so that I didn't have to sleep in the streets.

All in all, Valentina described her life as successful with regard to her career during Soviet times, and she presented her relations with Russians in a positive light. This is also why she regarded the Soviet Union as a good state, which enabled her to make a living and to live in harmony with others. The time following the collapse of the Soviet Union, on the other hand, is perceived by Valentina as 'another war'. The loss of 'all civilization' and concomitant feelings of uneasiness with the now-ruling Kazakhs still saddens her. However, she never considered migrating to Germany:

> Certainly, it's easier for me. Nevertheless, I have my daughter who is very successful. If she hadn't married her husband, maybe I would have thought about it. Maybe I would have asked Germany. Well, you see, I do not have anybody there. My father grew up as an orphan and all my mother's relatives have already died.

Both her son and daughter run successful businesses. Her son started by importing cars from Germany to Kazakhstan and Russia in the early 1990s, and now runs his own garage. Her daughter, together with her husband, cultivates a large plantation.

Valentina, through her life story, strove to give a balanced account of German life in the Soviet Union. With reference to Linde (1993), who analyses different kinds of coherence systems in life stories, one may conclude that Valentina's life story demonstrates the correct degree of causality. Linde points out that middle-class U.S. speakers strive for a proper balance between fate and determinism with regard to causality in order to be able to stress a person's individual achievement (ibid.: 129). I would say that Valentina does exactly the same: she does not describe herself as being defined by the fact that she is German (or something else), and she highlights that she was able to 'get that far' due to her own talent and education. On the other hand, she does explain why she, for instance, could only finish school at age twenty-one (because she is German). Valentina presents herself as an independent person who is above all grateful that her good education allowed her to take charge of her life. Moreover, she never mentioned that it was necessary to hide her ethnic affiliation. In fact, the opposite was true, since several teachers encouraged her to study the German language in order to work as a German translator.[12]

Valentina does not conceal that she was subjected to humiliation and discrimination, but this is certainly not at the centre of her life story; nor is it an accusation, for she blames no one for any wrongdoing. From time to time the fate of the Germans seems to be somewhat determined by external forces, but the close social environment is predominantly depicted as accommodating and hospitable and she often explicitly mentioned that the Russians were the ones who helped her and her family.

Altogether Valentina regarded the USSR as a just system, and she continues to believe in its values. She deeply regrets the Soviet Union's dissolution and defines her personality by the fact that she was a successful member of that system. Ethnic belonging does not appear to have the status of a primary identity for her. The fact that her parents were solid Soviet citizens may be of major importance in this context. Deportation, *trudarmya* and *komandatura*, as specific punishments reserved only for Germans, are put into perspective since Valentina often mentioned that other nationalities had to suffer in much the same way during the Second World War.

After the taped interview, Valentina told me that, although she had started the interview by saying that she is German, she actually does not know who she is – German or Russian. She is certainly not proud of being German for she seems to have internalized the Soviet conception of the 'evil Germans'. It is easy to believe that she would like to be Russian, but since this is simply not possible, she avoids this predicament by perceiving herself as a citizen of the Soviet Union. I would even argue that, from time to time (unconsciously or consciously), she downplayed the difficulties she had had to face as a German so as to preserve her vision of a Soviet system – that is to say, the system of her homeland.[13]

Valentina's life story does not stand alone, but is one example of many Germans of her generation and especially of those who grew up in Russia and were quite successful in Soviet times. They do not feel at home in Kazakhstan and mostly view the perceived ethnicization policies of Nazarbayev with a critical eye.

The Germans contend that ethnic belonging was not very important in the Soviet Union, which they likewise appreciated since – according to them – this was the prerequisite for well-being and peace during the Soviet era.

Kazakhstani Identity

The example of Edik illustrates the second type of German identity. Edik was born in Taldykorgan in 1970 and has spent his entire life there. He is married to a (Russian) woman with whom he has two teenage daughters. In the late 1990s he started a fairly prosperous business. Edik decided against migrating to Germany in 1998 with his parents and his own family when they received permission to immigrate.[14]

Edik started his life story by talking about his parents, depicting how they had had to suffer because of their ethnic belonging:

> Well, of course, my parents were more affected than I was because they lived during the years of repression, and they were oppressed together with their parents. That means that their childhood was impaired in this respect. During our childhood, we were all called fascists. Patriotic films, documentary films and the education of our people – it was our people's [the Soviet people's] comprehension that Germans are fascist. That's also why at school there were lots of brawls; many things happened. My generation was less affected but more harm was done to my parents because they lived in the post-war time. Both my grandfather from my father's side and my grandfather from my mother's side were oppressed. They had to work during the war and after the war. They were in labour camps. They worked at Belomor-Kanal, where, according to what my grandmother told me,[15] they were involved in land reclamation. For them it was considered a privilege that they were sent there. But in actual fact they did not go there – one may say – voluntarily. They were persecuted, well, and as a result of this persecution, that means that they could not give the necessary education to their children. Because once you're on the list of the NKVD,[16] that means that my father could not go to university. He could not receive the necessary education. Cases of persons with higher education in that generation are rare exceptions. Already for our generation that was easier. Now they look at us differently. Already they talk like: 'Uh, a German!' That means orderliness; that means all the rest. This changed in the 1990s after perestroika. This was highly noticeable – *glasnost*, democracy and everything else. Well, after all, people understood that culture remains culture, and since then one may find advertisements: 'House of German construction for sale'. It is considered a privilege to buy a car or a house from a German. That's why there's something you can be proud of.

As explained in the discussion on memory in the previous chapter, it is quite typical for the younger generations to start their life stories by saying that their parents or grandparents were discriminated against as Germans. According to Linde (1993: 87), they do so by reporting a 'chronicle', which typically begins with the incident of deportation of their parents or grandparents, often followed by a broad overview of their own life up to the present time. After such an introductory chronicle many return to their childhood by narrating particular incidents.

With much emotion and at length, Edik described his professional career after his introductory remarks about his German roots. He proudly illustrated how he has always been flexible and that he has held very different kinds of jobs because he has never been 'caught napping':

> Already in 1988 after I had graduated from the institute, I became unemployed. I could not find a job in my profession because the factory trained its own specialists. At that time, I understood that it's not advisable to have hopes in the state or in anyone, but that you should believe in your own strength, in what your gifts are. And when – as we say – 'you do have a head on your shoulders', you'll only move forward and forward.

Edik sees himself first as a businessman who acts autonomously, but he also feels part of a community, that is, a citizen of the Kazakh state:

> That's why, as a businessman, I also worry about things. ... When the state raises the prices, we are also forced to raise the prices of our products, for our work. And, as a result, the people suffer from that. I dislike that because we live here. I consider someone a good person if he worries about himself and about his state. When we live here I worry about this and about everything. How could it be different? These are no empty words that I am such a person. This is really true, we talk about this every day, and we discuss this in our family and with our friends. All in all, of course, I dislike, for instance, that the degradation of the underclass and middle class proceeds here in Kazakhstan very considerably.

Edik explicitly emphasized that Kazakhstan is his homeland and that he is not going to leave his home:

> I was born here in Taldykorgan. Here I got my education. I went to the institute in Taldykorgan. When this 'bang' started, everybody thought about leaving this place; I also wavered. My friends went to Russia to have a look at places there. I also wanted to leave, and I went with them

to have a look there. I cruised around, looked about, and I drew a conclusion: Where you were not born and where you didn't grow up will never be your hometown. That one should live where one was born, where one's homeland is. To give you an example: I have a great many friends who went to Germany or Russia, and among them there are some, even of my age, who didn't become old, they became ill because of the change of the climate, and some of them even died. … That's why one should live where one was born. Even if we consider Germany our historic homeland, I was born here, and if no war or other things happen, I'm not going to leave this place. At least for today, I think.

Edik turned again to his professional life by providing details on how he started up his business; after more than an hour, I felt the need to steer our conversation back to his childhood. He began by explaining his language situation:

Our parents, our grandfathers and grandmothers spoke an old German dialect, and even when my relatives, who knew German very well, went to Germany they had to face the problem of relearning the language: many new words, a different pronunciation. Well, there was a period of time in our family when we spoke mainly German. When I was young and my grandparents were still alive – at home they talked only in German – and when I went to kindergarten, they were laughing at me because my Russian was so bad. I spoke it strangely and poorly. Well, it's just very difficult when there are three languages in the family.[17] When I went to school, everything was in Russian and this language became more ordinary in my family, and my parents spoke Russian. Therefore, Russian is more native to us. To my mind that language in which you're just reasoning is your native language. We think in Russian. That's why I hold that this is our mother tongue. Well, I know some words, I can say some sentences in German, but it's just for laughing a bit and that's it.

Many Germans – even of Edik's age – who were raised by their German-speaking grandparents mention that other children laughed at them because they could not properly speak Russian when starting kindergarten or school (cf. Stoll 2007: 176). However, Edik's Russian was weak for another reason, since he partly grew up in a Kazakh-speaking family:

We lived in a one-room flat. In Soviet times, it was very difficult to get a place in kindergarten. Only those who had *blat*,[18] who had some kind of connections, could get a place. Well, my parents were very ordinary workers, my mother worked in a shoe factory, and my father also worked in a factory. And there was no place for me in kindergarten, there was a queue, like for cars, like for flats, like for everything. And it often happened that they couldn't leave me with my grandparents, and they left me instead with our neighbours. And our neighbours were Kazakhs. And one may say that my entire childhood took place in a Kazakh family. Also my brother was raised like this. Even when we moved out of this flat – Kazakhs have this tradition of the youngest child, they always give the child to their parents – and our neighbours asked: 'Please leave us Edik, we have raised him'. But my mother [said]: 'Well, how can I give him to you? He is after all my son'. The relationship was close in this way. These people were so close. They're still alive. God grant them well-being and everything else.

Edik said that his Kazakh is nowadays no better than his German, but he reiterated that he is eager to speak Kazakh whenever he is able to express something in that language. He added that Kazakhs are grateful if one simply tries to speak Kazakh, even if only to ask, 'How are you?' Edik also encourages his daughters to learn Kazakh properly:

We live in Kazakhstan and it is necessary to learn Kazakh. ... My children learn it. I force them because I say: 'You intend to live in Kazakhstan, you're the future of Kazakhstan, and you must know it'. Likewise, if we lived in Turkey we would speak Turkish. If we had immigrated to Germany we would have learned German. But you have to know Kazakh.

The ethnicity of his daughters' prospective husbands does not bother Edik, and he generally held that someone's nationality does not interest him very much:

All in all, nationality does not play a role for me because I myself live in an interethnic marriage since my wife is Russian. ... If [my daughter] falls in love and if she chooses a worthy husband, I will agree. The most important thing is that she herself wants it. We live up to date, and we won't take *kalym* [Kazakh for bride price]. Certainly, it is desirable that it would be a decent family, that they are not drunkards. And although I'm an entrepreneur, I do not want her to marry someone whose parents are also dealing with some kind of business or something else. This is not important to me. Let them be ordinary people, working somewhere, doing something.

Towards the end of the interview, I asked Edik directly whether he perceives himself as German. He answered as follows:

I'm, it turns out somehow also a German. But at the same time it's difficult for me to say who I am. I'm both a Kazakh and a Russian, and a

German. Here others have to judge. You see, in our case – if there was only one state, for example, if we lived in Germany, spoke German, lived in line with German habits, celebrated German celebrations, I would certainly say that I'm a German. But considering we live in a multiethnic country, we have here Kazakhs, Kyrgyz, Uzbeks, Tajiks live here, Tatars live here, and Russians live here and Koreans, and among all those people I have friends. That's why we have – in case someone has died, it's somebody's birthday, whatever kind of celebration – and we meet, celebrate, and we're invited, and for me it's difficult to say that I'm German. Yes, as for the passport, I say that I'm German, but in life, I don't know …
RS: *And who are you in life?*
In life, I'm just a man. And others have to decide what kind of man I am, a bad one or a good one. I see it this way.

Edik repeatedly asserted that one cannot say that people of one nationality are generally better than those belonging to another. In order to strengthen his argument, he gives the example of his own employees. He mentions that many Russians categorically do not employ Kazakhs. He, however, does not consider nationality to be a decisive criterion – he employs whoever is willing to work well for him.[19] Furthermore, Edik alludes to his interethnic marriage:

Among each nationality, there are good and bad people. Therefore, to beat my chest and say that I'm a German, I cannot do this. In our family, even my conscience does not allow me to do this. Well, my wife is Russian, and we've already lived together for seventeen years and, at the same time, I cannot say, 'You're Russian and I'm German'. We live together and follow both their and our rites. Well, of course, there are also disputes, sometimes we quarrel over something, or we agree, but this rather concerns our personal matters. Germans are, after all, a spirited people, you yourself know [we are both laughing].

Edik's wife joined us towards the end of the interview. While Edik was explaining that he and his wife quarrel from time to time because of different attitudes, partly caused by their different ethnicities, she chimed in:

Well, I don't regard him as a German. Their habits do not in any respect differ from ours. I haven't recognized any differences in his family, or that his family differs in some way from mine.

Edik tried several times to enumerate certain differences – such as how Christmas is celebrated – but each time his wife countered his argument, for instance, in the case of Christmas, by saying that they do not celebrate the holiday anyway. Edik finally resolved the situation by respectfully silencing his wife and lecturing on the history of Russian Germans, starting with Catherine the Great. It turned out that he was well grounded in 'his history'; he gave detailed descriptions of the lives of his great-grandparents and grandparents in order to distinguish himself from Russians.[20]

Edik does not perceive himself first as a German but simply as a human. He loves his hometown and, to a certain extent, Kazakhstan in general. It is very important for Edik to establish good relationships with persons belonging to all of the various ethnic groups. He perceives Kazakhstan as a multiethnic country, a characteristic that he openly appreciates. Moreover, he even welcomes the highly criticized Kazakh language policies as a way to ensure a Kazakh cultural revival. The fact that he partly grew up in a Kazakh family might explain his attitude. Last but not least, it is the collapse of the Soviet Union and the formation of the Kazakh state that were the prerequisites for his economic success.

Though Edik's German identity does not seem to be particularly important to him, it is not negligible either. The brief quarrel with his wife clearly shows that he is not entirely indifferent towards his German roots. Moreover, even the fact that he stressed several times that he lives in an 'interethnic' marriage demonstrates that he makes a distinction between Russians and Germans.

Edik's life story reads like a call for interethnic harmony, and it shares much of Nazarbayev's proclaimed worldview, namely that interethnic harmony is the prerequisite for economic well-being. Therefore, I call this type of ethnic identity 'Kazakhstani identity' – but the homeland Kazakhstan is a multinational one that provides a place for all ethnic groups.

Edik's example is typical of younger Germans who grew up in an environment that was neither exclusively German nor Russian and who perceive themselves as successful. Their ethnic identity is especially marked by the fact that they are flexible. Edik can behave very much 'like a German', when stressing his work ethic, his parents' hard times and how he managed to get out of a difficult situation. But he is also very Russian, such as when he stresses that Russian is the language closest to him. Finally, he can also highlight his Kazakh connection by talking about his 'Kazakh quasi parents'. While running his business, all these identities help him to create trusting relationships that surely benefit him substantially.

This flexibility is one of the main differences between the first two types of ethnic identity and the last two. Both Valentina and Edik hold that ethnic belonging should not be relevant, that it is in principle not important whether someone is Korean, Russian or German. I would argue that this devaluation of ethnicity also allows them to play with their ethnic identity. The fact that they both chose to describe, and emphasize, an interethnic and helping environment in their early socialization and throughout their life may reveal an awareness gained over time that cultivating flexibility with regard to ethnic belonging can prove to be personally advantageous.

Russian-German Identity

The other two types of German identity discussed in this chapter are characterized above all by the fact that ethnic identity is perceived as crucial. Rosa represents the first of these two types, where being German is perceived as a subtype of being Russian.

Rosa was born in a village close to Taldykorgan in 1961. She has worked many different kinds of jobs, ranging from the retail sector to a job as a film projectionist during Soviet times to merchandizing after 1991. In the 1980s, she moved to the city of Taldykorgan. She had a long-term (Russian) boyfriend who died about ten years ago. She has no children. Rosa commenced her life story by describing her childhood as a happy time:

> Well, we had a happy childhood. We grew up in a village, our family was big. And since childhood, somehow, this [discrimination against Germans] wasn't there. One says that for many it was forbidden to speak German. I say, thank God, this didn't affect us. Me personally, somehow, no one insulted us as fascists, our parents – yes – but there wasn't anything like that in our case – because we were living in a huge German settlement. ... There was all in all only one Kazakh and one Korean family. That's it. All the others were Germans and Russians.

Rosa added that she has always been proud of her German identity:

> I had a good childhood. I cannot say otherwise. Somehow we were not treated badly. I always say to everybody – in case somebody says, 'Yes, we were always afraid of saying that we are Germans'. And I always say, 'Thank goodness that this didn't concern me'. I have always been proud of being a German.

Though Rosa recalled her childhood as harmonious, she nevertheless linked her description of that time to the wider discourse of German discrimination and name-calling. She highlighted on several occasions that she grew up in a predominantly German environment, which is why she was not affected by the general difficulties faced by Germans. Not only were there mostly Germans living in her home village, but she identified her own family as being very German, namely by respecting German traditions and customs. Rosa depicted, for instance, in detail how they celebrated Christmas:

> My mother dealt with sugar beets; she worked in the fields, harvesting sugar beets. But our father was very intelligent, he had a very intelligent family – they were teachers and doctors. He somehow imparted more of German culture to us. He was musically educated. And thanks to

our father – he invested a lot in us. German celebrations, we celebrated them all. Christmas was for us a grand celebration. We came back from school – on the twenty-fourth of December, we were running back home because we knew that our parents – well, we weren't very well-off – a big family with many children. Our parents certainly cared to work hard for everything, to do everything for us. We had a big house and a big garden – we cultivated everything ourselves. And in the evening, we came back home and knew already that our parents had put presents under the tree. Well, what kind of presents, there were sweets and nuts. Usually we didn't eat apples and nuts. This was maybe the case in town, but in the village we couldn't afford this. But for Christmas we always had nuts, apples and sweets. We were so happy about this celebration. Well, we celebrated Christmas in the German way, in our family. For example, in case some teenagers went to the disco or in case there was some kind of festivity at school, my mother was always asking us not to amuse ourselves too much that evening – on this evening before Christmas – in order not to offend anybody. Well, this is how it was. This is something you treasure.

Rosa also stressed the importance of the German language:

Well, somehow it was in our family simply that way – our father always spoke German and our mother, too. They always spoke German with one another. We listened to all of that; however, to be honest, we didn't answer in German because we were uncomfortable with it. In some way, it wasn't very acceptable to speak German. But the spirit in our home was German. Everything was German – like our parents. And they prepared German dishes and everything, which was pleasant.

Rosa elsewhere emphasized that she loves listening to German. Nevertheless, she said that she always felt uncomfortable speaking it. Although she remarked on her happy childhood several times, the wider context of discrimination left a mark on her life story. Furthermore, Rosa – like all the others – described the fate of her parents within the framework of Russian-German history:

Well, for example, my parents, my mother was born in Ukraine. How beautiful it was! And such places there were before the war. It was afterwards, when everything was already destroyed. ... Such nature! What a rich district – Ukraine! They were also resettled, from Ukraine to this place. And here, what they experienced! My father was in the *trudarmya*. He worked in a mine shaft. They went through all of this. How hard it was.

Rosa then explained the importance of her German identity:

> It means everything that I'm German. I think so. I have it in the blood. I'm a German and not anyone else. Like many others say: 'No, I don't feel myself [German]'. But I'm really a German. And my heart is aching for all the Germans, not because I'm a nationalist. No. I have many Kazakh friends … Towards this [interethnic relationships] I behave normally. Towards everybody. In my soul, I'm German, a genuine one.

Throughout the interview, Rosa stressed that being German is a crucial part of her personality. She characterized her German identity as something deeply felt that she could not change even if she wanted to.

In talking of her professional career, Rosa stressed that the collapse of the Soviet Union brought about more problems than advantages. Furthermore, she became uncomfortable when she began dealing in goods from China and Turkey. But in the end, although she explained the details of her business to me at length, she had not touched on one of the primary concerns of the 1990s – the difficult decision of emigration. Only after I directly asked her why she did not emigrate to Germany did she talk about this painful time:

> Well, I try not to shout it from the rooftops because at first I felt very miserable. At that time I had a very critical moment. I emigrated together with my family. I did not want to emigrate! My entire family emigrated. This was in 1991. Well, they of course organized everything for me, registered me there. I had to go. But I left my boyfriend behind here. Well, of course, probably because of him I didn't want to. It was very hard for me to part company with him. Whenever I remember this, I feel bad. Well, I will tell you a bit. I left him behind here, and we emigrated. You yourself understand how difficult it is when people from here resettle. The mentality is completely different, irrespective of the fact that I didn't have big problems with the language. I understand what people say, and I get my ideas across. There weren't big problems with this, but I had a terrible nostalgia. I was constantly crying, I wanted to go back home. At that time my mother became sick. There, we were living at somebody's place. Everything was alien. We lived in a cellar there.

Her younger brother suggested that Rosa visit Taldykorgan again for a couple of weeks. Only then, he argued, she would finally realize that living circumstances were rapidly worsening after the collapse of the Soviet Union, and that living in Germany would be much more desirable for her:

> This is how we did it. We didn't talk to anybody, nothing. He also brought my things and he bought the ticket. … I arrived here and

> I stayed! My boyfriend was here, my beloved spirit. And the job that I had before, they gave it back to me. And also the flat I had was given back to me. Which means I stayed. This was a terrible moment in my life. Now I suffered from being alone here. How would I go on living? I blew myself up into little bits. I didn't know what to do. That was horrifying. Well, at this time, I started believing in God. I understood that there has to be something. I agonized. I don't know for how long, two to three months. I had no rest. I couldn't sleep normally at night. My mother and my father were far away. In all of my life, I hadn't been separated from anybody. And here I stayed alone. My boyfriend told me all the time that we would be together and to calm down. 'Everything will be fine'. This is understandable. However, relatives remain relatives. And then, I don't know what jogged me, I anyhow decided that I should live there [in Germany]. This would be more correct. And once more I tempted fate. … And I came back here to Taldykorgan again. Can you imagine? This was so dreadful. Now I remember all this, and I don't know. That's it.

Although Rosa twice tried to emigrate to Germany, she simply couldn't bear living away from what she considered home – Taldykorgan. Also, after her boyfriend's death, she could not imagine herself in an alien country. But the fact that she is the only one from her family who chose to remain in Kazakhstan distresses her:

> All my relatives are far away and I'm here alone. Well, what to do now? And since then they have been asking me, 'You do not want to come here [to Germany]?' But I don't want to. That's it, I'm such an abnormal person. I think here's my house, here's everything. … Well, this is how it happened. My father was always writing me: 'You chose the most negative. You always choose the negative', he said to me. 'Conversely, you should strive for the good, but you go towards the bad'. He had always been dreaming of going to Germany. He also went through a lot. They wanted to go to Germany, where they are among their own kind. But when they arrived there, maybe it was not completely one's own kind. Also there, they are foreign. There, they are Russians.

With regard to the dissolution of the Soviet Union, Rosa focused on her sense of loss. She lost her beloved job as a film projectionist, and more importantly she lost her family. This latter loss especially may have an impact on how she now perceives her childhood, a time when she recalls the entire family living happily together. The additional reality that almost all of her German classmates and neighbours have also emigrated to Germany has reinforced her feelings that the entire 'German world' of her childhood has vanished. Thus, for Rosa, feelings of loss are deeply enmeshed in her German identity, which, for precisely this reason, validates the intensity with which she views that identity.

Although Rosa regrets the end of the Soviet era, this (in contrast to Valentina's opinion) is not to be understood as a general critique towards the Kazakh state. For the most part, she agrees with the state's policies, and she in particular admires the 'typical Kazakh characteristics':

> In Kazakhstan, for example, there are a lot of good things that the Kazakhs have. For instance, how they honour aged people. How they esteem them, with such respect. Well, this means a lot. How hospitable they are. This you cannot deny them. You see, many Germans, who came here to Kazakhstan [after deportation] are very grateful. Those who were hungry and who were freezing, Kazakhs put them up. Many children were provided with food. They shared the last things they had. This you cannot deny.

Moreover, Rosa casted current German-Kazakh relations in a positive light and presented the 'German qualities' as reasons for the good relations between Germans and Kazakhs:

> Well, and I would like to say that Kazakhs really esteem Germans very much, I have already told you. They really esteem them. They behave well towards Germans. I haven't heard so far, not from a single Kazakh, something bad uttered against Germans. Something like this I haven't heard. So they esteem them – because Germans recommend themselves as hard-working and thorough people. Moreover, they never raise any kind of quarrel, they do not brawl, and this is how they are. They are always calm, good, and family-oriented people. They live very well among their families. Germans, in comparison to others, know that the family is holy.

However, while Rosa has several Kazakh friends, she does not attempt to act like them:

> Well, I say, I'm in my heart of hearts a German, a genuine one. Well, for me this concerns my mode of life. Well, in a way, I'm always – myself. I cannot get out of it. Well, for instance, when they sit in this traditional way – even Kazakh traditions. We live in Kazakhstan, this is all understandable. When they sit there – for a wedding ceremony or a commemoration – and everybody sits like this and holds his hands like this [she makes a circular motion with her hands while bowing]. I cannot even do this. This is not because I do not esteem them. I sit among them. Many Russians sit and hold [their hands] this way [she again demonstrates the

circular hand motion]. But I will never do that. I cannot do that. I do not want to do that. I can fold my hands together, like my parents did. Just folding one's hands together, like this [she demonstrates]. I can sit like this. I give my tribute to everyone. But what I don't have to do, I'm not going to do. This is my opinion. It's mine.

Interestingly Rosa distinguished herself from Kazakhs during the interview by generally including Germans in the Russian category, such as when she speaks of 'many Russians' above. She equated the term 'Russian' with 'European Kazakhstani', and by doing so conceptualized her German identity as in fact a subtype of a Russian identity.

Rosa's case is typical for the few who had grown up in a German village but remained in Kazakhstan. They in particular feel left behind and alienated by the loss of everything with which they were familiar.[21] The entire environment of her childhood is characterized by Rosa as German, for she speaks of her German family, her German street and her German village, and she depicts German customs and habits in detail. In this regard, the end of the Soviet Union marked the turning point in her life story. Since then the German village has vanished and, with it, those who were closest to her. She has not only lost her family but also almost all of her previous neighbours and classmates. Furthermore, she views the fact that she was not able to manage living in a foreign country as a personal failure, and in this way appears to concede that she did not truly choose Kazakhstan, but rather returned because she could not overcome her negative feelings about her life in Germany. That being said, she copes with her situation by viewing Kazakhstan as a prosperous country, inhabited by congenial fellow citizens.

The reasons for staying are diverse but often rooted in deeply personal conflicts within the family.[22] The families usually put a lot of pressure on them to migrate at last to their 'historic homeland', but many instead have decided to sever all ties with their relatives in Germany.[23] Even in such cases, an ethnic identity is perceived as very important since being German has affected their lives so deeply. The fact that they grew up in a 'German world' that has disappeared has conversely served to validate the necessity of holding on internally to that 'lost' world. Hence, it is not a hostile environment that has enhanced their ethnic identity, but the loss of everything that had connected them to that identity, and which now keeps alive in them a desire not to betray their 'German' past.

Kazakhstani-German Identity

Peter represents the fourth type of German identity. He began his life story as follows:

In 1941 our parents were banished from Mariupol, from Ukraine, here, to Kazakhstan. They ended up in Akmola, where they now are building

Astana; at that time it was Akmola.[24] Then, my father was a pitman, working in a mine shaft. They were sent to Ayagus where the atomic firing range was located and they mined some kind of mineral. Only Germans and Kazakhs were living there. That's where I was born in 1951. Then, I went to school, to a Kazakh school because in our village there was no Russian school, there were only Kazakhs and Germans. … In 1965 we moved to Urdzhar. In Urdzhar, my father told me that I should learn Russian. I only knew German and Kazakh. I didn't know Russian. We were singing only Ukrainian songs, more or less [in correct Ukrainian] at home. Well, half Ukrainian, half German. My grandmother spoke only German. Well, we were children and since my father and my mother were working, we grew up with our grandmother. And then, two years in the fifth grade, I could not speak Russian. Two years in the sixth grade, I could not speak Russian. Then, they kicked me out of school. That was it.

Peter went on to describe his first day at the Russian school:

When I came to school [for the first time], I stood up and said my surname. That's saying something, a German! 'Ugh', someone was saying, 'a living fascist'. I punched him right in his face. They sent me home. I came to my father; my father asked me: 'Why did they send you home?' 'I somehow hit someone', I said, 'but not very hard'. 'Then you should have hit him harder'. This was the answer my father gave to me. Then, the entire following month, my father accompanied me to school. The relationship with the Russians was constantly tense; however, with the Kazakhs, it was alright. Why should I tell a lie? I'm speaking about myself; this is how it was in my case. And today, there are those idiots who say: 'Well, you're a good guy, but it's bad that you're a German. It would be much better if you were a Russian'.

The incident at his new school reflects one of Peter's central themes: his poor relationship with Russians on the one hand and his good relationship with Kazakhs on the other. Peter finally learned Russian, and even went on to receive a technical education.

His life has been marked by two critical periods: he was a soldier in the Afghanistan war, and he was forced to work as a technician in Chernobyl after the catastrophic nuclear accident. He considers Russians, in particular, to be guilty for his and his family's misfortunes:

This was done especially by Russians, with guns everywhere. A gun gave them the right to kill and rape everybody everywhere. This was the history, this is kept secret but our parents [told] us and we know that although we didn't see it ourselves. I served [in the army in the Afghanistan war] and I saw how they regard it. Where it's bad, Germans are sent; where it's good, others are sent. Openly they do not talk about it, but where it's bad, they wouldn't send their own people but only the others. I went through this, I know this. And in Chernobyl, everybody [was evacuated] – their own people – and I was sent into the grave.

Peter compared his fate with the fate of his parents. In his view, Germans were constantly discriminated against in the Soviet Union; for him, there was no substantial improvement after the Second World War. Moreover, Peter is aware of the Russian Germans' history in general, and he feels very much a part of it. He describes how an acquaintance in Russia told him about the Germans who were killed:

He says: 'Son, do you see these accumulated stones? These are no stones; these are the skulls of our Germans'. 'Here', he says, 'from top to bottom are only German corpses'. 'Nobody has interred them'. That was something. Communists didn't talk about that. How many Germans did they destroy here? How many were we? … I don't know, maybe in Germany, those statistics are available, how many they were until the revolution, and how many remained after the war, and how many now in the Union [referring to the territory of the former Soviet Union]. And Germans increased in number only in Kazakhstan. Thanks to Kazakhstan, we are so many.

Peter went on to emphasize that, even during the Soviet era, the situation for the Germans in the Kazakh SSR was better than in present-day Russia. Only after the dissolution of the – according to Peter – entirely inhuman Soviet Union could one truly find relief, and only those who are lazy long for the Soviet times to return:

I, for instance, do not want communism back. This is only wished by those who do not like working. But our loafers want the old times back. But those who want to work, now please start working. Learn something, think, make decisions and act. But these [loungers] do not want to do anything and [want to] receive money for that.

As mentioned earlier, Peter contrasts his negative feelings towards Russians with his positive feelings towards Kazakhs. He offered the example of a German friend who became, in the course of the Second World War, an orphan and grew up in a Kazakh family:

Arthur, for example, I know it because I was there. He grew up as an orphan in a Kazakh family. His father was Kazakh and his mother was

Kazakh but he – although the parents were Kazakhs – they let him be a German. His surname, first name, they left everything like it was. But in Russia, who would he have become? Ivanov or Petrov? They would have altered him quickly.

According to Peter, Kazakhs, in contrast to the Russians, have never tried to assimilate Germans, but they have allowed them to remain who they are. Consequently, Peter would never say that he himself is Kazakh, but he makes a point of stressing his good relations with this other ethnic group of which he never tried – and was never forced – to become a member. He identified German as his mother tongue, but was simultaneously proud of being able to speak Kazakh like a native speaker. Peter became particular angry when talking about the refusal of Russians to learn Kazakh:

> If you want to work in the administration, know the state language. Please. 'We're discriminated against because of our nationality'. This is what they themselves want [to believe]. 'These *kalbity* [a vulgar term for Kazakhs], these *kalbity*'. I say to them: 'The time of *kalbity* is finished, now they're Kazakhs'. That's it. They fume at this. Especially the Russians, you see. A German doesn't say *kalbit*, only Russians say *kalbit*, and only Russians say 'fascist'. This is the reason they fume, you see. In Russia, they're now not welcomed. But here, they have to learn the language, but they don't want to learn it. This is the reason. You see, they don't want to, but my granddaughter will speak it, let her learn it. But all the Kazakhs do speak both Russian and Kazakh. And they're not uncomfortable with it. But why are Russians uncomfortable with speaking Kazakh? Well, this means they perceived themselves as gods, or how did they say it, a 'great race', 'great people'.[25]

Although Peter's granddaughter attends a Kazakh kindergarten in Taldykorgan and he speaks mostly Kazakh with her, he also believes it is important to pass on something German. Peter describes how he calls on his daughter (the mother of the above-mentioned granddaughter) to behave like a proper German:

> I still say today: 'Daughter, keep in mind, being German implies to be proud of it and to do everything well. You have to wash well, to clean up well. You have to do everything well. Everything you have to do well because you're German'. This is how it is.

Peter, nonetheless, never seriously considered emigrating to Germany. He feels too close to the Kazakhs and, because of this, he cannot leave his homeland:

> We grew up here, we have our own mentality. You see, we've become Kazakhs. We know the language, we know that we're Germans, but in actual fact, we won't integrate there. For our children, who would grow up there, I agree. But we're old, well, think of it yourself. Going there, becoming melancholic and then coming back. I know that there's abundance, I know that it's fine there, and that I would live in abundance. But maybe I want to chat with Kazakhs. You see, well, we grew up here.

At the end of the interview, I asked Peter directly what it means to him to be a German:

> First of all, it's pride in my parents. My father was German, and my mother was German. So who am I? How can I change them; all the more, I had very good parents. You see, I loved them. And still love them. How will I become a Russian or a Kazakh? No way. I'm a German, I now say to everybody. They say, 'Uh, well, how?' I say, 'I agree, but in spite of everything my bones are German. Let Kazakh flesh grow upon them, but after all, in spite of everything, I'm a German. You cannot change it'. … I say to everybody, always and everywhere that I'm German. I'm proud of it. You understand?

Peter's life story is marked by his complicated relationship to Russians. Language played a crucial role: his weak knowledge of Russian throughout his childhood did not allow him to be Russian or simply a well-educated Soviet citizen. Instead, he associated with rural Kazakhs, whose language he speaks perfectly. This alone appears to be the most plausible explanation for why Peter was unable to establish a successful career during the Soviet era.

Aside from the language issue, however, Peter asserted that the fact that he was German also dictated how he was treated by the Soviet Russians. He believes that he was assigned to Chernobyl because he was German, adding that the overwhelming majority of the workers in Chernobyl belonged to one of the nationalities detested by the Russians. In general, he contends that the Soviet Russians were bent on trying to eliminate the Germans. He views discrimination against Germans as being ever present during the Second World War and continuing up to and beyond Stalin's death, and in fact until the fall of the Soviet Union. Only the collapse of the Soviet system and the pushback against the Russian rulers allowed for the free expression of any kind of ethnic belonging.

Though the example of Peter is extreme in its directness, it stands for many other Germans who grew up in a predominantly Kazakh environment and who, at least during their childhood, knew Kazakh better than Russian because they went to Kazakh schools.[26] They do not identify themselves as Russians and would consider it an insult if somebody referred to them as Russian. On the other hand, none of the Germans define themselves as Kazakh, although relations with Kazakhs are seen as quite good. In this context, a German identity has firmly taken root. Being German is perceived as the main reason for the misfortunes of life, but at the same time no other identity is available.

The life stories of Rosa and Peter strive to demonstrate that they are German and that their lives are deeply shaped by their ethnic belonging, although in very different ways. Rosa has never perceived her ethnic belonging as a disadvantage, but the collapse of the Soviet Union and Germany's immigration policies, which allowed her family to migrate to Germany, have complicated her life. Furthermore, in the context of European Kazakhstanis, she refers to herself as a Russian. On the other hand, Peter sees his life as being negatively affected by the fact that he is German, and that Russians are to blame. In light of such an apparent dichotomy, do they share the same meaning when they stress their German identity? That is, do they refer to the same concept of a German identity? For the most part, I would say yes: they would be able to relate to one another's idea of German identity without any significant misunderstanding. First, although Rosa herself did not experience it directly, she mentioned on several occasions that she was aware of other Germans being subject to discrimination by Russians, which accords with Peter's account of his background. Second, Peter realizes that his case is atypical because he learned Russian very late, whereas Rosa learned Russian from an early age, even though her parents spoke to one another in German, and she was aware that her knowledge of Russian helped her during Soviet times. On the other hand, their perceptions of other ethnic groups and their daily relations to Kazakhs and Russians differ quite substantially, which has had an impact on their position in present-day Kazakhstan and might someday also fundamentally affect their perception of ethnic belonging.

Summary

This chapter has presented four distinct types of German identity in Kazakhstan. It has become clear that there is no single criterion, such as the generation to which one belongs, to account for the diverse identities, although these identities share several overlapping features. One general distinction can be drawn between those who feel at least partly Russian and those who see themselves as closer to the Kazakhs. Another cross-cutting distinction separates those who identify themselves above all as German and those who view themselves predominantly as a member of a greater group, such as the Soviet Union or Kazakhstan. Both of these distinctions can be at least partially explained by the social environment that the individual experienced, especially during early socialization. In the first case, those Germans who grew up in a predominantly European setting are unlikely to feel particularly close to the Kazakhs today and tend to identify themselves as Russians. The second case is more related to the perception of a threat or crisis. Those who experienced severe discrimination and a predominantly hostile social environment, as well as those who might not have experienced discrimination and hostility directly but suffered in some way due to their ethnicity, tend to identify themselves first and foremost as Germans because their German identity is perceived to have affected their lives more decisively than any other identity.

The telling of life stories does not exhaust the issue of identity, and the findings presented here reveal even less about the process of identification. Nonetheless, life stories, such as the four discussed in this chapter, are helpful aids in depicting the deeply personal views of individuals, particularly concerning how their attitudes about identity have evolved over the course of their lives, as well as providing a window onto their perceptions of the effects of social environment on identity formation. Accordingly, life story narratives deliver insight into the momentousness of belonging by elucidating a person's emotional attachments; at the same time, however, their ultimate validity is restricted to the specific situation of the interviewee and affected by the circumstances of the interview situation itself, in this case with a German ethnographer. In the following chapter, therefore, I will seek to relate these individual accounts to a shared notion of a German identity and investigate how both – shared notion and emotional attachments – impact upon identifications.

Notes

1. I employed a 'grounded theory mode of interviewing' (R.L. Miller 2000: 92–95; cf. also Charmaz and Mitchell 2001); i.e., before the interview I only mentioned my research topic ('the life of Germans in Kazakhstan'), and during the interview I asked as few questions as possible, and then only general questions. Since most of the interviewees enjoyed telling their stories, this approach proved the most fruitful because it predefined the course of the narratives as little as possible. This is also why some of the life stories, at first glance, may reveal little about 'being German'. In such cases, I waited until the end of the interview to inquire specifically about the significance that being German had for them at various times in their lives. In some cases I received a second version of the interviewee's life – an 'ethnic version' – but in most cases I was told that ethnic belonging had not been particularly important to them.
2. German and French (oral) historians were influenced by the much older debates on oral history that had taken place in the United States, initially by Franz Boas, who strove to record the oral accounts of the 'last Indians'. Oral history came under pressure during the structuralist (and synchronic) turn. Those anthropologists dealing with mental structures (e.g., Lévi-Strauss) and those dealing with social structures (e.g., Radcliff-Brown) questioned the historical truth of such oral accounts by holding that they only contain information about current cosmology and current social institutions. The historian Joseph C. Miller (1980) countered that if one considers the mnemonic techniques that were used, then the historian is able to distinguish between historical truth and pure narrative clichés (cf. also Vansina 1985). This relates to the discussion about mnemonic techniques in

societies with different kinds of media and their consequences on memorizing and the formation of memory in general (cf. Assman 1995; cf. Goody 1987).
3. This method of biographical research has been used extensively with regard to the Second World War and the Holocaust (see, among others, Rosenthal 1998).
4. Widening the number of heard voices is certainly associated with the postmodernist agenda.
5. All life story interviews were taped, transcribed by me or an assistant, and translated by me. The interviews mostly took place at the interviewees' homes and were (with two exceptions) conducted in Russian. Before we began the interview, I explained only that I was interested in the story of their lives, although all of them were aware that my research focused on the German minority in Kazakhstan. Each life story interview lasted approximately one to three hours. During the interviews I adhered mainly to the 'realist approach' advocated by R.L. Miller (2000: 92–95), i.e., I avoided asking questions as much as possible. In cases where a question or a reaction was necessary to keep the conversation going, I interjected in a general way (e.g., 'How was it at school?', 'Let's go back again to your childhood.', 'How did you get to Taldykorgan?'). Only after I sensed they had concluded the telling of their life story did I ask more focused questions.
6. While all names are anonymized, I am aware of the ethical problem of 'playing with another person's life' (Plummer 2001: 403). All of the interviewees knew that I intended to publish their life stories. Several days after the interviews I asked the persons who are cited here at length whether they still felt comfortable with what they had told me. Nevertheless, I excluded passages that, in my judgement, could cause problems for them, and those which I found to be too personal.
7. Regarding the analysis of life stories, Linde (1993: 61–94) distinguishes between three distinct discourse units: the narrative, the chronicle and the explanation. The passage cited above belongs to the narrative type. I have mostly aimed at quoting distinct narrative units which start with 'abstract' or 'orientation' clauses (such as the example above: 'one day we were playing in the streets …') and which often end with phrases such as 'that's it' (as in the next narrative segment).
8. Valentina was referring to the labour camp but used the term *obshezhitie* (residential accommodation).
9. Valentina is still fluent in German, though she does not like to speak it. She harbours negative feelings towards the German language, which might be the result of experiences of discrimination as a German and the negative attitudes towards the German language in particular during her childhood.
10. The Germans of Valentina's and her husband's generation were the beneficiaries of the comparatively liberal nationality politics of Khrushchev. For a few years at the beginning of the 1960s, Germans were given the opportunity to study. German as a mother language was introduced in several schools, and in 1961, a German study programme was started at the University of Novosibirsk to produce instructors capable of teaching German. In particular those Germans who at that time spoke German as their mother tongue were encouraged to enrol (cf. Römhild 1998: 191, 205).
11. To take part in the Great Patriotic War was seen by Valentina as a privilege denied to Russian Germans. Many of them regarded this as a kind of fundamental discrimination, since it prevented them from proving that they were willing to fight against Nazi Germany. They argue that this restriction led to lifelong feelings of exclusion, since each of the many ceremonies celebrating the Great Patriotic War continued to remind them that they had not been allowed to take part in the heroic fight against fascism.

12. Römhild (1998) points out that many of her respondents (and in particular those of Valentina's generation) told her that they felt encouraged to feel like Soviet citizens and to be part of Soviet society. She describes the cases of two women for whom being German was only one aspect, and by far not the dominant one in their lives in the Soviet Union. Römhild remarks, however, that this gradually changed for those Germans born after 1950 who grew up under the more restrictive policies of Brezhnev (ibid.: 215).
13. Also Flynn (2007), in her study on Russian migrants from the other former Soviet republics to the Russian Federation, states that a number of migrants related homeland 'to the temporal and spatial territory of the USSR as a whole' (ibid.: 469).
14. As a consequence, his parents and his brother did not emigrate to Germany either. His brother currently works in Edik's business.
15. It is usually the grandmother who tells the younger generations about the past.
16. The NKVD is the People's Commissariat for Internal Affairs (*Narodnyi Komissariat Vnutrennikh Del*), which was the public and secret police organization of the Soviet Union.
17. The presence of three languages will be explained below.
18. *Blat* is difficult to translate directly into English; it is defined by Ledeneva (1998: 1) as 'the use of personal networks and informal contacts to obtain goods and services in short supply and to find a way around formal procedures'.
19. However, Edik did mention elsewhere that it is currently very difficult to find good workers because so many Russians and Germans have left the country and Kazakhs 'do not like working'.
20. Edik's strategy of claiming a German identity by referring to his ancestors is a common means of positioning oneself as German. For this purpose, life stories (or rather those of one's ancestors) are often told in everyday life.
21. Only about ten per cent of Russian Germans remained in small German settlements after deportation in 1941, and the vast majority of that ten per cent emigrated to Germany during the late 1980s and early 1990s (cf. Ingenhorst 1997: 57–61). Diener (2006: 219) states, with regard to the former 'areas of compact living', that 'those remaining often express feelings of abandonment and consider their place of ethnic refuge diluted and ephemeral'.
22. There are also those who were not allowed to immigrate to Germany. If they did not voluntarily choose to stay in Kazakhstan, and most of their close relatives now live in Germany, they are likely to feel left behind. Many had tried to pass the language exam several times, and had spent a lot of money doing so. Though they were angered by Germany's immigration policies, they nonetheless continue to identify themselves in predominantly ethnic terms. The impact of Germany's immigration policy will be discussed in detail in Chapter 8.
23. It is often stated that the decision of whether to migrate is a family decision for Russian/Kazakhstani Germans. To choose to stay in Kazakhstan, when the rest of the family has chosen to emigrate to Germany, therefore threatens to undermine the fundamental basis of Russian/Kazakhstani-German tradition, namely to act as a member of one's family (cf. also Römhild 1998: 202).
24. In 1941, the city's name was 'Akmolinsk'. It was renamed 'Tselinograd' in 1961, 'Akmola' in 1991 and 'Astana' in 1994. See Laszczkowski (2016) for a detailed account of the changing status of this city and the different identifications within it.
25. Peter's life story contains, in contrast to Valentina's, many 'explanations', such as those cited above. Linde (1993: 94) points out that the 'explanation' discourse unit begins with

a statement, which then is proven by a sequence of supporting reasons, the main purpose of which is 'to demonstrate that propositions that may appear dubious, false, problematic, or stupid do in fact have justification that should lead to their addressee's believing them'. Peter may know or feel that his statements are not widely shared and, thus, they need to be confirmed through a series of examples.

26. A prominent example of this identity type is the Kazakhstani German author Gerold Belger, who writes in German, Russian and Kazakh, and who shows that Kazakhstani-German dialects have incorporated elements that derive from the Kazakh language. Belger grew up in a Kazakh village (cf. Stoll 2007: 185).

Part II

Nationality, Power and Change

Whenever I was introduced to someone during my fieldwork, their ethnic belonging was usually among the first things I learned about them, often followed by a discussion of the stereotypes generally associated with their own and other ethnic groups and how the groups related to one another. During a taped interview a young woman explained to me:

> After all, stereotypes persist. We have, for example, for every people a set of stereotypes: Koreans like spicy dishes, Russians vodka, Germans have punctuality and cleanliness, and Kazakhs are hospitable, which is their main attribute. For them [such stereotypes should] be sown and blown. (Anna, 22 years old)

In Kazakhstan, it seems that ethnic clichés help to maintain a certain order in the social world, and are even relied upon to demonstrate how diverse ethnic groups are able to live together peaceably. Anna's statement can be understood as a late homage to the formerly held Soviet idea that each nationality has to develop its own characteristics in order to contribute to the Soviet people as a whole, or, as in the present case, the Kazakhstani people as a whole. In this view, stereotypes are considered to be beneficial and thus should be spread, or in Anna's words, 'sown and blown' among the people.

Herzfeld (2005) investigates stereotypes as essentializing strategies. He argues that 'the act of stereotyping is by definition reductive, and as such, it always marks the absence of some presumably desirable property in its object. It is therefore a discursive weapon of power' (ibid.: 202). Herzfeld advocates for analysing stereotypes in the context of social action, and he criticizes anthropology for having investigated them mainly in connection to group boundaries and hostility. Instead he believes that anthropologists should ask: 'Who uses stereotypes? Under what circumstances? How stable are the forms of stereotypes and the meanings people attribute to them?' (ibid.: 26).

Furthermore, Herzfeld (2005: 207) hints at a 'dominant discourse' that people use in order to pursue their goals. Thus, the content of stereotypes cannot be endlessly malleable; instead, there must be some stable element to them, although this conclusion was not the intent of Herzfeld's arguments. Therefore, in the following I seek to combine Herzfeld's insights into investigating stereotypes as social practice with D'Andrade's focus on the stable aspects of people's knowledge and opinions, which he analyses as mental schemas. D'Andrade (1996) argues that how we act in a given situation depends on which of our schemas are activated by that situation. Such schemas are, first of all, the result of people's individual experiences, but they have particular significance with regard to how people act if the schemas are shared and if they exhibit normative power.

Along with Schlee et al. (2009) I treat identities and other stable concepts such as schemas, categories and stereotypes as mutually dependent upon such concepts as identification and stereotyping by which action is analysed. This part of my study, therefore, approaches the issue of identities and identification from both angles: schemas and action. In this endeavour, I seek to show that only by carefully investigating people's categories can we fully understand when, why and to what end people make use of them.

Chapter 3
Assessing Nationality

This chapter deals with the dominant discourse on nationality. In this endeavour, schema theory helps me to analyse people's understanding of nationality, their attitudes towards the concept, and how their understanding and attitudes relate to their actions. The nationality schema is complex because it is composed of many interconnected aspects that, in part, contradict one another. Firstly and fundamentally, it encompasses a definition and thus defining dimensions such as language and religion; secondly, it refers to individual nationality categories such as Russians and Kazakhs, and how those relate to one another; thirdly, it comprises people's appraisal of the nationality categories. All of these aspects relate to action, though schema theory usually focuses on the analysis of a system of meaning.

In the following, I show that the nationality schema is distinguished by two features. People seek to construct nationality categories by applying a fixed set of dimensions, namely (origin) territory, religion, language and 'mentality'. These categories then form the basis for a national binarism of Kazakhs and Russians, though this contradicts the first feature. This contradiction is then examined in light of Herzfeld's contention (2005) that essentialism and binarism are conflicting strategies that deny their own existence. Subsequently, I elaborate on the Russian and Kazakh categories and how their bearers relate to the German category. But first it is helpful to provide a review of recent literature on Kazakhstani-German nationality.

Barth's (1969) plea to overcome the analysis of the 'cultural stuff' resulted in partially disregarding the role of identity dimensions such as religion, language and customs for drawing boundaries. This approach is criticized by Jenkins (1997), who argues that the cultural traits from which ethnic categories are built are not irrelevant. For instance, those features that are used to show differentiation from others might have an impact on the flexibility of group boundaries. Therefore, some ethnic attachments are likely to be more mutable than others (Finke 2014).

Research on ethnicity in Central Asia, however, should not be criticized for an overly extreme constructivist stance; in fact, the opposite is true. Studies dealing with minorities in Kazakhstan (e.g., Akiner 2005; Diener 2004) tend to engage with nationality categories as if they exist beyond time and space. Diener (2004: 4) points out the importance of nationalities by asserting: 'Simply stated, ethnicity remains the primary identity'.[1] Often, the Soviet assumption of inherited ethnic affiliations is taken for granted by, for instance, directly applying the concept of diaspora to the 'nationalities' in Kazakhstan (e.g., Akiner 2005: 23).[2] The notion of diaspora and its relevance to Kazakhstani Germans will be discussed in Chapter 6.

This simplified criterion of inheritance raises, however, a set of questions. What, for example, about the children of interethnic marriages? Furthermore, how to 'define someone's ethnicity' who is by descent German but claims a Russian identity?[3] Or, in the opposite case, what if, for example, a woman's passport says 'Russian' and most of her ancestors are Russians, but she identifies herself as a 'proper German'? Certainly, Kazakhstani Germans cannot be 'objectively' defined by inheritance, and there is no such thing as a fixed group of people being German. But studies on nationality in Kazakhstan operate almost exclusively with the numbers provided by census data for the different nationality categories.

The 'culture' of Kazakhstani Germans is the focus of another body of literature (Kazakhstani-German authors such as Seifert 2006; Wensel 1998, 2006; see also Dorlin 2005). Through the examination of German newspapers, folk music and dances, German poets and theatres, most authors aim to show the value of particular cultural traits. In this context, the German language is widely seen as a prerequisite for a distinct German culture. Dorlin (2005: 173), for instance, writing on Kazakhstani-German culture after the Second World War, asserts that there is no ethnic identity without the accompanying language:

> Language is certainly the fundamental trait which allows for characterizing and identifying an ethnic group. A distinct language allows for distinguishing one ethnic group from the other and, at the same time, serves as a special bond among its members. Consequently, it is at once an external sign and a device for internal cohesion. Promotion and defence of the ethnic language have always been perceived as a fundamental duty, as a collective need for the survival of the group.[4]

Likewise, Stricker (2000) questions a German identity without German language proficiency. In his article 'Ethnic Germans in Russia and the Former Soviet Union', he quotes Eugen Müller, editor in chief of the German newspaper *Rundschau* in Ulyanovsk, who deplores the loss of the German language among Germans of the former Soviet Union: 'What is left are assimilated Germans, who no longer maintain any kind of Germanness' (ibid.: 178).

Therefore, very often German identity is equated with German language skills. One reason might be that language proficiency is measurable and can be assessed statistically. It is mostly intended to show that Kazakhstani Germans are Russified and perhaps can no longer be regarded as (proper) Germans. Assimilation into the Russian population is also a decisive topic in Kazakhstani literature on the Germans. Sakenova (1998: 177f), for instance, regards in particular interethnic marriage with Russians as a reason for ongoing assimilation. Furthermore, she states that 'the German language is dead' and asserts that, while some Kazakhstani Germans wish to retain their German tradition, the overwhelming majority are deeply influenced by Russian culture.

All in all, studies concerned with the status of German language and culture call into question the practice of defining the German category by inheritance. However, this research, framed in a pre-Barthian manner, completely lacks the perspective of those who are assumed to be the owners of that ethnic identity and, therefore, cannot comment on whether the described cultural traits have any significance for the process of self-identification and differentiation from others. Therefore, the next sections elaborate on how people themselves define the national categories and how the categories have an impact upon their actions.

Nationality as a Unifier of Territorial Belonging, Language, Religion and 'Mentality'

People in Kazakhstan generally consider a nationality to be a distinct group of people who share certain features. In my investigation of the emic concept of nationality (*nationalnost*), I also refer to cultural domain analysis and, in particular, to two cognitive tests that I applied in combination: free lists and pile sorts (for the application of this method see Bernard 1995: 237–55; Weller and Romney 1998: 9–31). To this end, I asked forty-two people[5] to note down every nationality that lives in Taldykorgan on a separate sheet of paper.[6] Secondly, I asked them to sort the nationalities and to explain the criteria they used to do so.[7] Most often, people categorized the nationalities in between four and seven distinct groups. Further, it seemed as if the definition of 'nationality' given by Stalin in 1913 was still employed as a device for classifying people. Thus, most interviewees elaborated on a combination of the criteria defined by Stalin of 'a common language, territory, economic life, and psychological make-up manifested in a common culture' (Stalin 1913: 307, 'Marxism and the National Question', cited in Weitz 2002: 21); the most common addition to the features listed by Stalin was 'religion'.

Moreover, the general underlying assumption was that those criteria could be consistently applied – besides exceptional cases, such as the non-Turkic-speaking Tajiks or the Muslim Turkic-speaking Uighur from China. However, some interviewees said they simply did not have adequate knowledge of a particular nationality to make any claims about them. Young people below the age of thirty made their choices in the same way as older people did, although they often had only minimal knowledge of the nationalities. For instance, some of them grouped Koreans and Chinese together because they mistakenly assumed the two shared a common language and religion. Thus, young people tended to stress people's physical appearance, and sometimes openly admitted that that was the extent of what they knew about a certain people.

Though a combination of criteria was applied, a single criterion – namely (origin) territory – appeared to be prevalent. Thus, most often people constructed a Central Asian group, a Caucasus group, a European group (most often further divided into a Russian group and a more Western group comprising Germans, Poles and others), and separately Chinese and Koreans. However, the interviewees themselves usually did not explain their decisions in the context of the single criterion of territory, but instead argued that those grouped nationalities share a common 'mentality' (*mentalitet*), customs, habits, religion and language. In this vein, the nationalities from the Caucasus were most often described as 'hot-blooded', the European nationalities as more civilized and advanced, the Koreans and Chinese as hard-working, and the Central Asians as hospitable. Furthermore, people often mentioned the characteristic dishes associated with a particular nationality in order to underscore their assertions about that nationality's distinctiveness.

In the following, I approach the nationality issue from the opposite perspective. Instead of asking how people differentiate the various nationalities from one another and by which criteria they do so, I investigate the relevance of those criteria for defining one specific nationality, namely the German nationality. To this end, I enlarge upon the use of language, religion and 'mentality' as national markers. I begin, however, with common ancestry, which in the case of Kazakhstan is connected to territorial belonging since that refers to the territory from whence one's ancestors had come, usually many generations ago.

Common Ancestry

In principle, there is only a single criterion: a German is German when his father and/or mother is/are German. Kazakhstani Germans mostly say that ethnic belonging is 'in the blood' (*v krovi*). Such a definition of ethnic belonging is generally widespread and can be traced back to Soviet times. Lemon (2002) points out that although the Soviets did not have a concept of 'race', discursive practices were nonetheless often racist. For instance, in media: 'Since at least the 1960s, Soviet films and television have fleshed out a motif of detecting hidden identity "in the blood", and they played this trope of connections under the skin without naming those connections as "racial"' (Lemon 2002: 59; cf. Weitz 2002). For Herzfeld (2005: 122), Soviet racism would not come as a surprise, since he alludes to the fact that 'the central concept of blood is not uniquely Greek or even Balkan – indeed, it has a long history in Indo-European and Semitic culture as a marker of social inclusiveness'.

Common ancestry is, thus, the primary defining feature of being a German. Often, the blood criterion is so powerful that it constitutes being German in and of itself:[8]

> You see, I'm baptized according to the Russian rules. My parents mainly talked in Russian. Well, that's how it is. But, anyhow, you have your blood. (Karla, 65 years old)

Mostly, Kazakhstani Germans argue that being German is transmitted through the father's line. However, some Germans only have a German mother, and they nonetheless hold that the mother's ethnic belonging is decisive in defining the offspring's ethnicity:

> In our case all children are German. Well in Asia, for instance, one takes the nationality of one's father. Jews take the nationality of the mother and in Germany, they say, it is also the mother's. Here [in Kazakhstan], this is not customary; here one takes the father's nationality. (Lena, 48 years old)

Interestingly, Germans appear to be conceptually influenced by the unilineal descent system of the Kazakhs. Quite often, people hold that ethnic belonging is unambiguously traced from parent to child, but it seems that Kazakhstani Germans are very flexible in adopting descent concepts to their own needs, since they might refer alternately to the patrilineal Kazakh descent system or to the (assumed) matrilineal German/Jewish descent system. Although the issue of how to correctly trace ethnicity comes up often, it is rarely with the intention of blaming others for not being proper Germans because they only have a German mother or father. Kazakhstani Germans rather feel insecure about the issue, which is why I was often asked for confirmation when the 'matrilineal German descent system' was brought up by them.[9] Nevertheless, the number of German ancestors that a person has can be important:

> I think that as far as my own ancestry is concerned, probably seventy-five per cent is German. This is because my father is fifty per cent Russian and fifty per cent German and that means that my mother is one hundred per cent German. I would say that this says something; that seventy-five per cent is German. (Sasha, 50 years old)

Germans often list in detail how many German ancestors they have, and it is often discussed among them to what degree a person is German. This certainly contradicts the conceptual rigidity described above of passing ethnic belonging from parent to child. But someone who has, for example, only one German grandmother is most often considered 'less German' than someone whose ancestors are all German. Therefore, depending on the context, it might happen that 'pure Germans' try to exclude non-pure ones. Such a 'purity discourse' in the context of the German Rebirth organization will be explored in Chapter 7.[10] However, the great majority of Germans in Taldykorgan do not only have German ancestors and, in most contexts, it seems to be sufficient to have one German grandfather or grandmother in order to claim German ethnic belonging, at least in relation to Kazakhs. Having a bit of German blood running through one's veins is, moreover, sufficient for becoming a member of the youth club (*Jugendclub*) in the German Rebirth organization – usually referred to as the 'German House' – as one of its members explained:

> Those guys who regularly come to us [to the youth club in the German House], they are not pure Germans. But German blood to some degree does exist. (Sonya, 22 years old)

Language

As indicated above, the literature on the Germans of the former Soviet Union interprets German language proficiency as decisive for a German identity. Decreasing numbers of native German speakers serve as an indicator of the loss of a distinct German identity and an ever-increasing Russification. It is certainly true that the vast majority of Germans in Taldykorgan, and in Kazakhstan in general, do not speak German, but this is not widely perceived as precluding a German identity.[11]

In Taldykorgan hardly anyone below the age of sixty-five speaks German. The generation older than sixty-five has at least some passive knowledge of German since this is the language they heard during their childhood. Some of them stress how poorly their parents or grandparents spoke Russian, but in reaction to their stigmatization as Germans, they mostly stopped speaking German at home during the 1950s. Karla explains her feelings towards her mother tongue:

> I know some Uighur, I know Kazakh, and I know Russian but the point is that I don't know my mother tongue. This is painful. Anyway, I'm a bit resentful [she's crying]. Maybe my parents didn't do this correctly. Certainly, I regret – but I'm already 65 years old, what should I do? I think that I won't be able to learn my language entirely. However, when our Germans [the Germans who regularly meet in the German House] are talking, I understand a little bit. The only problem I have is that I can't say anything. For example, Ira, when she is talking, I can

understand her very well. But Adam for example I can't understand him at all. He belongs to the Germans coming from Ukraine. They have a completely different language, another dialect. My mother always tried to speak German. But my father always answered, 'Sei ruhig!' [Keep quiet!]. That's what I remember in particular. (Karla, 65 years old)

Everyone of this generation told me that they deeply regretted having forgotten their mother tongue.[12] Remarkably, no person(s) or no particular event or situation is consistently blamed. The loss of the German language is perceived rather as a personal tragedy, with perhaps some blame placed upon one's parent(s), as Karla's statement exemplifies.

Only Germans above the age of seventy-five who still speak German fluently sometimes deny a German identity to someone with insufficient German language skills (cf. Stoll 2007: 167). When the language issue came up in the *Seniorenclub* of the German House,[13] the advocates of the German language were always harshly attacked by the younger non-German-speaking participants, who emotionally defended their 'Germanness' by stating that they are not at all 'second-class Germans' and not to be blamed for the loss of their mother tongue. These disputes were often solved by resorting to the 'common blood' argument, probably because it was something upon which everyone could agree.

Only a few younger Germans intend to learn German, among them Sveta:

I love German very much. I put my heart and soul in it, you see? To be honest, I have an obsession. I have to learn and to learn it. And generally, God willing, in case it works out, I will be able to read and write it. I just need, you know, to be honest, Rita, I do need communication, something like a month living in a German family where they only speak German, maybe living for a while in Germany. (Sveta, 47 years old)

But most often younger Germans, if they learned any German at all, only learned it to pass the language exam for intended immigration to Germany. Those who changed their plans, or realized that they might not be able to pass the language exam, gave up on learning the language. However, many parents encourage or sometimes even force their children to learn German in order to improve their chances for immigration to Germany. Here a mother describes her son's failure to learn German:

My son didn't learn the language either. He doesn't know anything. I brought him to the German House for the German classes, ever since he was a little boy. Last autumn he was still going there but then he started sobbing and saying that he is not going to go there anymore. And then I thought, anyway, we will never go there, I mean to Germany. Not at any time we will go there. (Lena, 48 years old)

Thus, most often, the issue of learning or not learning German is linked to the immigration decision. For life in Taldykorgan, German language proficiency is practically irrelevant. Since few people speak German, language in principle cannot be used to distinguish oneself from others in daily life. However, most Kazakhstani Germans I met know at least a couple of German words, which some of them from time to time use to stress their ethnic belonging. In particular elderly people often feel emotionally bound to their mother tongue and deeply regret its loss. They often express their emotional attachment by using German words such as *tschüß* (bye). Therefore, the German language can provide a basis for identity claims though it is actually not spoken or understood. To what extent others accept such claims for a German identity will be discussed below.

Religion

As has been stated above, next to language, it is religion that defines nationality categories. As for Kazakhstani Germans, religious affiliation can be asserted on principle to distinguish oneself from Orthodox Russians or Muslim Kazakhs. Many Germans in Taldykorgan are either Protestants – in particular Lutherans – or Catholics.[14] The Lutheran parish is even referred to by Taldykorgan citizens as the 'German parish' and most of its members are in fact German (see also Chapter 7). Nonetheless, I would argue that religious affiliation is even less important for drawing boundaries than language. Lena's position illustrates this:

> In our place there is also an Orthodox parish, that's where we go. I let my son be baptized there. … When my son was born I wanted to have him baptized according to the German rules, there, in the German parish.
> *RS: Do you mean the Lutheran parish?*
> Yes, the Lutheran parish. I tried to find out something about it, but nobody could give me any kind of information. Then, after a while, and before he had to go to school, it was necessary for him to get baptized. Therefore, I addressed the Orthodox parish and he got baptized there. For example, I don't know where I was baptized, I was born in the north where the climate is very harsh, and it was a polar night. My father said that, when I was seven, eight months, I almost died. Then, my grandmother baptized me in a barrack, but according to what kind of religion, I don't know. And nobody knows. But it is true that I am baptized. I addressed the priest [of the Orthodox parish in Taldykorgan] and he asked me: 'Do you perceive yourself as baptized?' I said, 'Baptized', and he said, 'That's it, so you are baptized'. (Lena, 48 years old)

Lena's case is relatively typical for Taldykorgan. Many Germans do not even know whether they were baptized and they sometimes feel uncertain about their statement of belief. Furthermore, many Germans in Taldykorgan expressed their indifference towards the issue. Although most Germans do characterize themselves as religious – that is, as believing in God – only a few were raised in a religious environment. After the collapse of the Soviet Union many people searched for a religious community to suit their needs. In the process, people often changed their religious affiliation several times. This might also be the reason why religion, in contrast to language, is generally not an emotionally sensitive issue. Most people in Taldykorgan do not pay much attention to someone's religious affiliation, beyond arguing that there is only one God.[15] Therefore, Germans rarely distinguish themselves from other Christians along religious lines. The relevance of the Christian/Muslim distinction will be explicated in the next section, taking into consideration the perspectives of Russians and Kazakhs.

The Lutheran parish attracts very few people, and many, as indicated by Lena's statement, do not even know where the parish is located. Beyond the Lutheran parish, there exists a wide variety of other Protestant and Catholic parishes in Taldykorgan. Therefore, those very few Germans who are affiliated with a religious community are spread over several Protestant parishes, two Catholic ones, and several Orthodox ones, and in each of those communities they form only a small minority. Thus, neither on the grounds of a distinct belief nor of a religious community can people in Taldykorgan identify themselves as German.

Germans in present-day Kazakhstan, therefore, draw their ethnic identification primarily from neither language nor religion. Fuller (2008: 14f), in her analysis of German communities, concludes that 'a review of German enclaves in the diaspora has shown that not all of those who claim German identity use the German language'. Secondly, she hints at a connection between language use and religious communities. She remarks that 'in fact, religious group identity has been shown to be more effective for language maintenance than ethnic group identity' (ibid.). Thus, the fact that only a very few Germans in Taldykorgan belong to a religious community might have contributed to the loss of the German language.

'Mentality'

'Mentality' [*mentalitet*] is an emic concept that is very widespread in Kazakhstan. It refers to 'typical national characteristics' and is related to the emic concept of stereotypes. Herzfeld (2005: 116f) rightly criticizes those anthropologists who have dismissed such a static concept because it reminds them of the previous conceptual flaws of their discipline. But if we ignore people's view on 'mentality', we are likely to miss an important construction of sameness and difference.

As shown above, most Kazakhstani Germans view ethnic belonging as being transmitted from parent to child, and thus most of them hold that their ethnic belonging is in their genes. Many of them argue further that their German genes are responsible for a particular manner of acting that makes them different and by which they can identify themselves as German,[16] as exemplified by Olga:

> Well, Germans, that's a certain kind of more punctuality, somehow. Some kind of, well, considerateness, somehow, maybe, some kind of more planning. Russians are a bit different in that they are more unmindful than we are. Germans, anyhow, well, they have, probably on a genetic level, that there has to be orderliness. (Olga, 55 years old)

Many Germans are proud of being more reliable, hard-working and punctual. They usually support their assertions by hinting at the high quality of all German products. Along these lines, people often mention the high standards of German houses and the efficiency of the former 'German *kolkhoz*' in Taldykorgan.

Many Germans also remarked that not all Germans live in accordance with what such 'typical German characteristics' suggest. But this deviating behaviour is still primarily explained in the context of the same 'genetic framework'. Since most Germans in Taldykorgan also have Russian ancestors, it is, in the case of non-German behaviour (especially drinking and not working), often said that the Russian genes may unfortunately predominate over the German ones. Therefore, being German is also a duty, and I observed several times that somebody was questioned on whether he is a proper German just because he was late by a few minutes.[17] Lena, for instance, explains how a German ought to be:

> Well, that is some kind of obligation. A German, that means, he has to be accurate, to always come on time, never be late, he has to be reliable. And let's say, Germans should always offer a 'well-set table'. (Lena, 48 years old)

When attempting to elaborate what constitutes specific German qualities, Germans very often seek to distinguish themselves from Russians:

> The Germans who live in Kazakhstan, they're especially conscientiously, they are hard-working. This characterizes, I think so, our Germans here. And Russians – that's something completely different. (Kolya, 48 years old)

This is not to say that Germans distinguish themselves less from Kazakhs; in fact, exactly the opposite is true. Kazakhs are generally said to be even less reliable and hard-working than Russians (with the exception that they are said to drink less). But it seems that Germans feel more of a need to distinguish themselves from Russians, with whom they have much more in common.

Next to the pure genetic explanation for specific German qualities, many Germans also mention their particular education and history:

> For example, our grandmother, she was always saying, 'Remember my son, everything starts with a sewing needle. If you steal the sewing needle, that's bad. If you just take it, without asking for it, that's also bad. So even taking the sewing needle without asking is forbidden. Ask for it and then take it; if they don't give it to you, don't take it'. That's the way we were educated. Only acquiring something by means of your own work and that's it. (Peter, 56 years old)

In particular the working ethos is connected to the hardships endured during and after the Second World War. Many Germans argue that they only survived labour camps because they were able to work harder than everyone else. Others see it the other way round – it was the experience of deportation and *trudarmya* that forced them to work harder. Sofia describes the situation in the 1950s and 1960s as related to her by her mother and grandmother:

> First of all, yes, they [the Germans] are hard-working and maybe, this people, yes, anyhow, I've heard from my mother, from my grandmother, that they had, maybe, a comparatively hard life. They had to, well, live like this, yes, how to say – they could only achieve something in their lives thanks to their efforts. And they are not like the Russians. They are first of all, as I've said, maybe that's why – because many believed and they didn't drink. I didn't see such drunkards among the Germans, as among the Russians. They always strove for something. They always tried to help someone. But from the Russian side and also from the Kazakh side, the relationship was kind of – well, because of the war, obviously. They behaved towards us – we were always fascists. (Sofia, 37 years old)

As has been explored in Part I, history is a crucial feature of a German identity. The shared memory of traumatic experiences during and after the Second World War defines being German, at least for the older generations. Thus, it happened several times that someone at first declined to be interviewed, arguing that their life story was not relevant because they had not experienced deportation and *trudarmya* or were too young to remember that time period. The younger generations, however, have largely transformed their ancestors' memory of suffering into a 'success story' of people who overcame hardship through honest labour, and by doing so substantiate the above-described 'typical German characteristics'.

As has been shown in the previous section, for most Kazakhstanis, nationalities are groups of people who share a particular (origin) territory, language, religion and 'mentality'. Thus, one might conclude that the criteria for categorizing nationalities are not really appropriate for delineating the 'German' category. Moreover, it is worth noting that most nationalities in present-day Kazakhstan are very unlikely to meet half of those criteria. Consequently, many people both identify themselves and categorize others by means of a concept that in fact does not fit. Kazakhstani Germans solve this problem by claiming that certain German traits are transmitted from parent to child. This point of view seems to be shared by others, too.

The question arises as to why many Germans and, for that matter, Koreans and Poles rescue their ethnic distinctiveness at all, instead of accepting that they do not meet the demands of the nationality categories. Likewise, while people are often disappointed in themselves because they do not meet the criteria comprising their particular nationality, they refrain from challenging the concept of nationality itself. Along these lines, Poles, Koreans and Germans usually regret that they do not speak 'their mother tongue' and that they have forgotten their 'ethnic habits'. Therefore, indirectly, the 'cultural stuff' with respect to the criteria for membership has been altered, but this has still not affected the nationality concept itself. Or more to the point, the nationality concept is not challenged because it provides the framework for rescuing nationality categories. As has been stated, most ethnic stereotypes are positive,[18] which is particularly true for the smaller nationalities. Therefore, it simply makes sense to be associated with an ethnic minority.[19] But the naturalization of nationality categories through a genetic framework is also a prerequisite for a national binarism that fundamentally contradicts Kazakhstan's image of ethnic diversity and harmony.

National Dichotomies

One of my German friends, Natasha, had offered me the use of her washing machine to do my laundry. At the time Natasha was furious because of a quarrel with her neighbours. She lives in a typical Soviet-style apartment block, and for several days she had found a garbage bag left at the hallway's entrance. The first few times she carried the bag outside to the rubbish bins, but eventually she got so fed up that she began asking her neighbours if any of them had left their garbage at the entrance. They denied having done so, but she began to feel as though she were being teased. She told her neighbours that if the situation did not change, she would dump the garbage at their doors. When the situation persisted, she carried through her threat, dumping the garbage at their doors, whereupon her neighbours insulted her on the street and threatened to call the police. At the time I was there, two days had gone by and the police had yet to show up. Natasha said she was not afraid of the police because she believed she occupied the moral high ground. She went on to explain that she is the only white (*belyi*) person in the block, the rest being Kazakhs, which is to say, black (*tshyornyj*). She sighed, saying that they probably cannot be taught to change their habits because Kazakhs are Kazakhs and would remain Kazakhs even if they were living in Africa.

In the previous sections it has been shown that most people are aware of more than a dozen nationalities, which they differentiate from one another

Figure 3.1 Pile sort and free list of Anna (left) and Tanya

according to a range of criteria. This apparent complexity concerning the nationality issue, however, is often reduced by many people to two basic opposing categories: 'black' and 'white'. In order to illustrate this point, I return to the pile sorts that have been introduced earlier. After the interviewees had explained their criteria for classifying nationalities, I asked them to merge the nationality groups that they had constructed. This second merging was less about the definition of nationality and more about the hierarchical structure of nationality. Sixteen out of forty-two persons created two piles,[20] while the others created three piles or very rarely four or more piles.[21] Most often, people built a 'European group', a 'Central Asian group' and a 'Caucasus group'.

When interviewees built only two piles, they always formed a 'European' and an 'Eastern' group (Figure 3.1 provides two examples). The inner, darker, rounded-edged rectangles indicate the first grouping; the outer rectangular groups A, B and C the second grouping; the numbers in parentheses indicate the nationalities' position in the free list. Both German Anna and Russian Tanya were in their early twenties. The decisive criterion for Anna was religion, whereas Tanya categorized the nationalities according to religion and physical appearance, but both Anna and Tanya were aware that they might be mistaken in their categorizations, which, as indicated above, was characteristic of most young interviewees. One typical feature reflected in both Tanya and Anna's examples is that while one category was organized around the Kazakhs and the other around the Russians, neither of them put Kazakhs and Russians into a single group. The Russian category comprised other Christian 'European' nationalities and sometimes, as in Anna's example, also Koreans and Chinese. Those who placed Koreans and Chinese with the Christian nationalities argued that they are not Muslims, and that many Koreans belong to one of the Protestant parishes. Furthermore, some explained that Koreans get

108 *Staying at Home*

along very well with Russians and they usually have Russian first names. The Kazakh category comprises other Muslims from Central Asia and the Caucasus and sometimes, as in Tanya's example, all non-European-looking nationalities. Thus, a national binarism is inspired by religious affiliation, physical appearance and territorial belonging.

Some interviewees, however, generally refused to merge the nationalities into broader categories, and six of them (three Germans and three Kazakhs) did not create the common category 'Europeans' for Germans and Russians. One such person is Yulia; see Figure 3.2 for her pile sort. Yulia listed twenty-one nationalities, which she classified into eight groups. She then merged those groups into three broader categories, which she labelled 'Europeans' (A), 'Slavs' (B) and 'Eastern peoples' (C).[22] Though Yulia's classification is rather atypical, it illustrates the tendency of most people to provide more detail for those nationalities with which they were more personally acquainted. As a German, most of Yulia's acquaintances and friends are either German or Russian, and, thus the category 'Eastern peoples' appears to be an 'other' category in which to include the people she does not know very well. The fact that she distinguishes Germans from Russians does not imply that she has a difficult relationship with Russians;

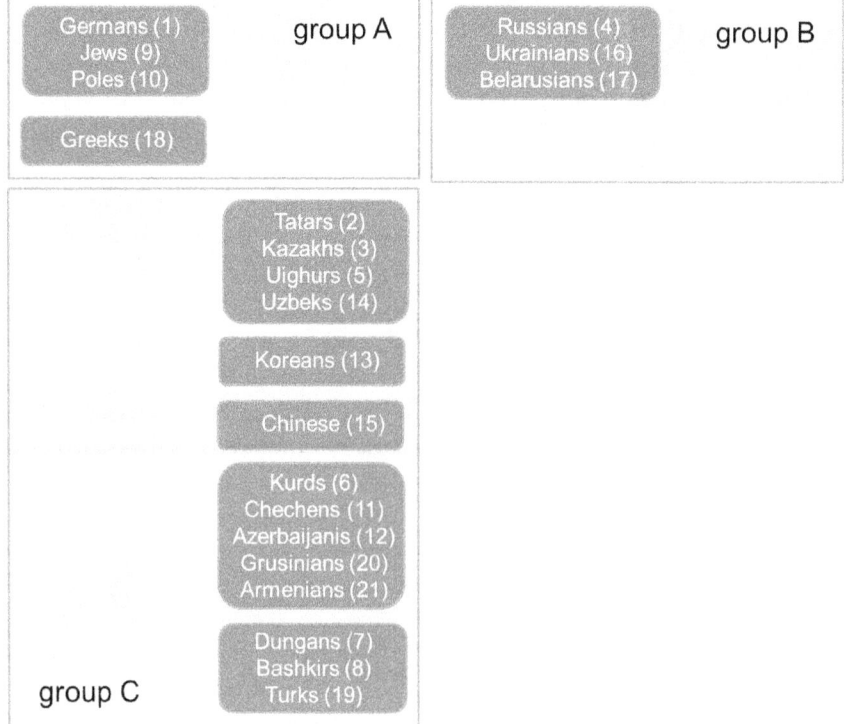

Figure 3.2 Yulia's pile sort and free list

on the contrary, very often people have complicated relations with, or hold negative stereotypes of, those persons belonging to a rather vaguely defined 'other' category. And, as has been indicated by Anna and Tanya's pile sorts, most often, people lump together the Russian and German categories. Consequently, such a 'European' category, as it is often labelled, is opposed to an 'Eastern' category, which is organized around the Kazakhs.

Most Kazakhstani Germans perceive themselves as distinct from Russians, whom they nevertheless include in the common category 'European Christians', as conceptualized in opposition to 'Muslim Central Asians and Caucasians'. The notion of 'Russian' is thus used on two levels: firstly, with regard to ethnic Russians, and secondly, as a synonym for 'European Christians'. This is also reflected by the statement of a nineteen-year-old German maid. When I asked, 'What does it mean to you that you are German?' she replied that it means, above all, individuality. Her statement supports the assertion that being German is often conceptualized as being a special type of Russian.

Some Russians and Germans label the two categories – 'European Christians' and 'Muslim Central Asians and Caucasians' – as white (*belyj*) and black (*tshyornyj*), which thus implies a racial distinction between Russians and Kazakhs, and those who are affiliated with each of them. The perception is that 'white' people are more advanced and civilized than those whom they call 'black'.[23] The German Viktor explained during his pile sort how he decided on the criteria for his 'black category':

> First of all, who do we have? [Viktor is looking at the nationality labels he had written] – Kyrgyz, Mongols and Uighur, and Kazakhs. First of all, they are all very similar to one another, as to their physical appearance. For example, I would never be able to differentiate between a Kazakh and a Kyrgyz. Mongols are also similar [to Kazakhs and Kyrgyz]. They are also dark and their mentality is the same as well. They also had yurts and horses, and they are also Muslims, and everything is basically the same. It is very difficult for me to differentiate between them. They share the same mentality, nature and culture. But the dirtiest nationality is the Kyrgyz. And the Kazakhs also got something from them. In former times, until the Russians came, they were also a bit backward. Thanks to the Russians, they could improve their situation. But the Kyrgyz remained backward. Yes, approximately, they are all the same … and these Chechens, they are also Muslims; they are also very deceitful. (Viktor, 25 years old)

Viktor's statement is more racist in tone than many of the other interviews, but in daily conversation I often encountered people referring to the 'black' and 'dirty' Kazakhs. His comments also illustrate what most interviewees intended – namely, to combine religion, physical appearance, way of life and 'mentality, nature and culture' in order to build uniform categories. Consequently, the complexity of numerous criteria, which gives binarism a scientific aspect and disguises its essentializing nature, makes racism appear meaningful. Furthermore, Herzfeld (2005: 26) indicates that 'racial stereotypes offer a particularly good illustration of how use can appear to convert transient perception into self-evidence'. Accordingly, it is not irrelevant that the Russian-Kazakh binarism and its respective stereotypes are so widespread and shared by so many people. This leads many to accept that this binarism and these stereotypes are self-evident, which is a prerequisite for racist thinking.

The relationship of the German nationality towards the Russian and Kazakh nationalities is the topic of the subsequent section. It will be shown that the Russian and Kazakh categories have very different compositions, histories and meanings in present-day Kazakhstan, which is also why Russians and Kazakhs each grasp the German category very differently.

Kazakh Primordialism vs. Russian Constructionism

First, returning to the pile sorts and the question of how Kazakhs and Russians categorized 'German', it is interesting to note that most Russians built only one group for Germans and Russians, whereas Kazakhs (to a greater extent than the Germans themselves) built a distinct group for Germans.[24] In cases where Germans were included in the Russian group, this group comprised – in addition to Poles and Baltic nationalities – Ukrainians and Belarusians (if those were mentioned). Where Germans were not part of the Russian group, they either formed a separate group of their own, or were grouped together with the Baltic nationalities, Poles and/or Jews. The criterion for building a distinct group for Germans (and the above-mentioned nationalities) was, most often, that they have distinct religious affiliations, traditions and language, and are generally more advanced because they are perceived as being 'more Western' than Russians.[25] The people asserting this argument are not saying that, for example, Latvians, Poles and Germans speak the same language (because they usually know that is not the case) but rather that their languages and religious affiliations differ from those of the Russians. Furthermore, and more implicitly, Kazakhs in particular place Russians in a different position because they were the previous rulers. It should be added that those who grouped Germans and other 'Europeans' together argued that all of them nowadays speak Russian, they are all Christians, and they look the same.[26]

The differing perception of the German category by Russian and Kazakh interviewees hints at different conceptions of the nationality schema itself. While Russians appear to focus on localized concepts of ethnic belonging, Kazakhs prefer a much broader concept of ethnic identity. Kazakh interviewees seem to have in mind 'all Poles' or 'all Germans', i.e., the nationality categories do not only comprise Poles in Taldykorgan or Kazakhstan or the former Soviet Union but also include Poles in Poland (and anywhere else they might be) – above all, because all Poles are assumed to share a common 'mentality'. Therefore, one could argue that Kazakhs tend to hold a primordial concept of ethnicity, whereas Russians tend to perceive ethnic belonging in more flexible terms. The Germans appear to position themselves between those two concepts. The next sections explore the views of Kazakhs and Russians with regard to the German category.

Kazakhs' Esteem

Many Kazakhs, as indicated above, hold a primordial view of ethnic belonging. Being Kazakh is transmitted from the father to his children; therefore, as a rule, people do not have the option to choose or change their ethnic affiliation. Although most Kazakhs acknowledge that other ethnic groups are not organized patrilineally, they tend to transfer the idea of inherited ethnic belonging to all people. Consequently, people generally do not have to 'prove' who they are in ethnic terms, and ethnic belonging can never be denied. However, one can still be a 'good' as opposed to a 'bad' Kazakh, since a certain way of being, i.e., a particular 'mentality', customs and habits, characterize 'good' – in the sense of true or pure (*taza*) – Kazakhs.

Thus, as with any other ethnic category, a German identity is perceived by Kazakhs in a primordial sense, and many of them attach certain qualities to all Germans, regardless of where they were born or raised. Furthermore, the 'typical German characteristics' as viewed by Kazakhs generally coincide with the self-description by Kazakhstani Germans. To support their view, most Kazakhs give examples of Germans they know personally, as illustrated here:

> They [Germans] are different.
> *RS: In what respect are they different?*
> Well, anyhow, their character is different. Germans are more neat, benevolent, clean and accurate. When you work together with a German you directly notice it. 'You're probably a German?' you ask, and he directly says, 'Yes, I'm German', or that there's a German grandmother or grandfather. Without fail, there's something you sense … Germans are different, for example, my acquaintances, not just acquaintances but my father's friends. I remember it from my childhood, first of all my father's friends, and my teacher – she was teaching in Lepsi – she was also a German – I also associated with. Well, in particular, those who were good people, I directly remember, those were Germans. Russians, probably, I can tell a few families that were very good families. (Aigul, 27 years old)

Aigul is not hesitant to mention several German stereotypes, and she illustrates them through her direct interactions with German colleagues and her father's friends. As exemplified by Aigul's explanation, Germans are most often characterized by the way they work. The relevance of the working ethos for the Germans' self-perception is elaborated below, and it is exactly the picture of hard-working people that is above all associated with Germans:

> Honestly said, Germans, they, how to say, when a German says, for example, at that time I'll come, or, for example, at that time will be lunch, that's it. He said it directly. Further, Germans, they're hard-working. In our place, for example, the *kolkhoz* was kept up only because of the Germans. They worked well. In many respects did they teach Kazakhs and Russian, for example, how to build a house, and orderliness. Then, they also have their own habits, which is also interesting for us … First of all, Germans are hard-working. They work well, fine fellows. I like them because they're not lazy people. (Azamat, 35 years old)

Azamat's listing of German characteristics – the orderliness of the 'German *kolkhoz*' and German houses, the punctuality of German workers – corresponds exactly with how Germans themselves comprehend the German category. Furthermore, Kazakhs value these characteristics, and Azamat's statement that Kazakhs and Russians have learned a lot from Germans is a common sentiment.

Kazakhs and Germans not only share the same notion of a German identity, but also hold a common view of the history of Kazakhstani Germans:

> Kazakhstan is such a country that regards everyone with good intention, irrespective of which people he belongs to. For example, at that time [during the Second World War] Chechens were resettled here. Kazakhstanis housed them like their relatives and now many Chechens refer to Kazakhstan as their homeland. As for the Germans, who were housed by the Kazakhs like their own – during the war and afterwards. And those Germans, who remained here, also live peacefully and in a friendly manner because at that time our grandfathers and fathers accommodated them well. They helped them to get situated, they helped them with the work, and they now live like one single family. I think there's no need for any kind of separation. And they will go on living like this. And also the Russians, again during the war, many enterprises were transferred from Ukraine or Russia to Kazakhstan, and Kazakhstan welcomed them, embraced them at that time. And also they're already inhabitants of Kazakhstan.
>
> The people live peacefully together, they associate with the Kazakhs, and mix well with other people, they know our language. For example, I have many friends, Germans, who know Kazakh. Some of them know

Kazakh even better than I do because they lived straight away in Kazakh settlements. They know German and Kazakh; some of them did not even know Russian. (Rashid, 52 years old)

Kazakhs widely acknowledge the difficulties that many Germans and others faced after they had been forcibly transplanted to Kazakhstan. In this context none of the Kazakhs with whom I talked expressed any uneasiness concerning the many foreign people arriving in their country. On the contrary, Kazakhs usually speak of this influx by highlighting that they took care of everybody, which is also borne out in the narratives of the Kazakhstani Germans (see Chapter 1). The fact that some Germans speak Kazakh is particularly appreciated and often serves to foster a kind of connectedness between Kazakhs and Germans. A close relationship is further strengthened in that many Kazakhs stress that Germans were among their best friends.

However, not all Kazakhs know Germans personally, which does not necessarily affect a Kazakh's notion of 'German':

RS: My topic is the German diaspora; therefore, I'm interested in how Germans differ from Russians in your opinion?
Uh, I don't even distinguish between them at all, they're like Russians. When somebody doesn't say that he's German, I can't even distinguish him.
RS: Do you personally know Germans?
No, I don't have such friends.
RS: Where you grew up, there were no Germans?
No, but I've heard about Germans ...
RS: And what?
That they're disciplined and accurate, though I myself haven't been to Germany, I have such a picture of them. A very high culture, that they're very punctual. Because I was told many things about them, because I've heard a lot about them, I have such a picture. Even when you just consider any kind of technical equipment, just the [German] label guarantees you – that means good products, that means, it's a high-quality thing. It already has such a meaning. (Farida, 30 years old)

As indicated above, many Kazakhs lump all Germans together, relying upon what they have heard about Germany, all of which is used to build a German stereotype. Another point arises in Farida's comments – that Germans are first of all perceived as Russians, and unless they say that they are not Russian, they will be considered Russian. Interestingly, Farida actually knows at least one German who is her neighbour, but this neighbour thus far has not seen the need to leave the Russian category and thus continues to be perceived as Russian by Farida.

In short, most Kazakhs perceive 'German' as a distinct nationality category, and above all associate the German category with a hard-working, orderly and punctual people. Thus, the Kazakh notion of a German identity resembles the self-perception of Kazakhstani Germans.

Russians' Inclusiveness

Many Kazakhstani Russians, as indicated above, view ethnic belonging in a constructivist rather than a primordial sense. In their opinion, while people in principle inherit ethnic belonging, they still must prove through their daily actions that they are truly a member of a particular ethnic group.[27] One might say that Russians adhere more strongly to the Soviet concept of a 'nation'. For this reason, with regard to people who did not have a language or territory of their own, many Kazakhstani Russians integrated them into the Russian category. This might further be seen as the eventual result of the merging of nationalities (as was intended by many Soviet rulers), which were all supposed to become Soviet in the future (see Chapter 1). However, in present-day Kazakhstan, it has had a slightly different outcome, as people are assumed to become Russian instead of Soviet.[28] But, as the dichotomy between 'black' and 'white' people in the above-shown pile sorts indicates, most Kazakhstani Russians see only those who belong to the 'white' category as Russian; those not in the 'white' category – who during Soviet times were referred to as *inorodtsy* – can never be Russian.

Against this background, the Russian perception of Germans differs in many respects from how Kazakhs perceive Germans. Most remarkably, as has been shown by the pile sorts, most Russians deny a distinct category of German in present-day Kazakhstan, an attitude illustrated here:

> *RS: And those local Germans, do they differ from Russians?*
> No! In practically no way!
> *RS: Not at all?*
> The locals, they're Russians! For example, my sister's mother-in-law, she herself is German and she's not at all different. How many Germans I know, who had moved here, it's all the same: they won't speak German at all, and they don't know that they're Germans … Only when they left [emigrated to Germany] did they come to know it. But earlier they lived here and we didn't know that they were Germans. We're all the same, all whites, and all the same. (Anatoli, 45 years old)

Above all, the fact that most Germans in Taldykorgan do not know the German language is given as the basis for the Russian assertion of the non-existence of anything specifically German in present-day Kazakhstan. Furthermore, many Russians mention that they did not know that certain of their colleagues or acquaintances were German unless one of them began preparing to leave for Germany.

The denial of difference between Germans and Russians is also expressed by Nadya:

> *RS: Do the local Germans differ from Russians?*
> No! Not at all! Only when they tell you their surname, but otherwise, no!
> *RS: Did you know that Vera [her neighbour] is German?*
> Well, how did I know that, when we first came here, I didn't know her surname. Then, I got to know it but this wasn't such a discovery for me, that, 'uh, she has a German surname', no! This I perceived, as it has to be perceived. There wasn't anything like, she has a German surname, and she is German, no! Nothing like this! Therefore, I don't remember [the details]. (Nadya, 28 years old)

As has been mentioned earlier, by denying specific German traits, Russians include Germans in the Russian category, and, most often, all 'whites' are gathered under the Russian umbrella. Further, when some Russians say that Germans are like them, this tends to suggest feelings of amity and generosity, and by discrediting any kind of German distinctiveness, such Russians also seem to promote the idea that Germans should no longer be seen as enemies or regarded as suspicious:

> For me it seems that today they're not different, those who remained here. Even when I was working in Siberia – I was sent there because of work – in the administration there was a woman, she was a German from a small place close to Leningrad. When the war started, they evacuated the factory where her brother was working. She was an old virgin, such a good woman. I came there [to Siberia] as a very young woman and she, so much, looked after me. She was even crying when we moved to Kazakhstan. We were friends.
> *RS: Does that mean that today Germans do not differ from Russians?*
> No! Virtually they're not different. We're friends and that's it. This is how it is. (Ludmilla, 60 years old)

It is exactly this often expressed combination of 'No, they are not different and we are friends' that suggests friendship between Russians and Germans has not always been a matter of course, and that if Germans were different, there might be problems. The denial of German distinctiveness on the part of many Russians stands in sharp contrast to the Kazakhs' emphasis on 'typical German characteristics', but both Kazakhs and Russians seem intent on emphasizing their good relations with their German friends, neighbours and colleagues.[29] The fact that Russians and Kazakhs argue from different angles might also be rooted in the reality that their actual relationship to Germans has been different. Kazakhstani Germans mention experiences of discrimination against them as Germans after the Second World War almost exclusively on the part of Russians, whereas Kazakhs are mostly characterized as those who helped them to survive. Negative attitudes towards Germans were only indirectly voiced by Russians, but again, this certainly has to be weighed against my presence in the discussion.[30]

However, the above-outlined delineation of the German category, as asserted by many Kazakhs and Germans, is also known to Russians, and some Russians also refer directly to 'typical German characteristics':

> RS: *Those Germans, who live here, do they differ from Russians?*
> Well, how to say, they do not differ a lot. Well, they're hard-working. Here in our *sovkhoz* many Germans were working. They were very good specialists, be they turner, metalworker, motor-mechanic, tractor driver, or combine operator. Many Germans were here, even in our street. Hard-working, good people – nobody says anything. But then, the collapse, and they left. (Nikolai, around 60 years old)

Though Nikolai mentions the positive German stereotype of hard-working people, his statement differs significantly in tone from Kazakh statements. There is no such admiration for the German characteristics; his closing remark – 'nobody says anything' in the sense of 'nobody complains about the Germans' – stands out after having mentioned only positive features. Furthermore, Nikolai only refers to the past and says that those hard-working German specialists have already left Kazakhstan. This again demonstrates how many Russians, at least when referring to Kazakhstani Germans, do not attach certain ethnic stereotypes to an ethnic group, but rather look at individual persons and how they act. In their view, Germans do not behave in a distinctly German way in present-day Taldykorgan, which is why they are not perceived as German but rather subsumed into the Russian category.

The Russian perception of a German identity is by and large well intentioned, and can be construed as an invitation for Germans also to be Russian. But this view of Kazakhstani Germans meets the concept held by the Germans themselves only halfway; many Germans surely perceive themselves as Russian, but at the same time they hold that they are also German, which makes them distinct from those who self-identify only as Russians.

Normative Entanglements

In the following, I explore the normative implications of the nationality concept by elaborating how the concept shapes action. Schlee et al. (2009: 2) points out that a 'collective identity' contains a 'normative appeal to potential respondents'. D'Andrade (1997: 96), by referring to meaning systems in general, criticizes that those are mostly understood only as representational; instead he distinguishes between four different functions:

> Meanings in general, and cultural meaning systems in particular, do at least four different things. Meanings represent the world, create cultural entities, direct one to do certain things, and evoke certain feelings. These four functions of meaning – the representational, the constructivist, the directive, and the evocative – are differently elaborated in particular cultural meaning systems but are always present to some degree in any system.

With regard to the directive function, D'Andrade (1997: 98) elaborates:

> In general, the directive functions of most cultural meaning systems are highly overdetermined: Overdetermined in the sense that social sanctions, plus pressure for conformity, plus intrinsic direct reward, plus values, are all likely to act together to give a particular meaning system its directive force.

The case of Sonya's café takes up the directive dimension of the schema 'nationality', exemplifying how a person is expected to act and in which situations ethnic belonging matters. On this basis, we can examine when people perceive it as appropriate to identify oneself and to categorize others in ethnic terms and when it is not. Fifty-seven-year-old Sonya runs a café called 'Vaterland' (German for fatherland). The café is situated in a small village close to Taldykorgan, on the main road connecting the city of Taldykorgan to Almaty. Sonya is convinced that the German name attracts many clients, explaining that the German word *Vaterland* is known to many Kazakhstanis because *Vaterland* was the answer given by many emigrating Germans when asked where they were going.

In 2000, Sonya started selling *shashlik* at a food stall that she ran with her son. At that time they had about thirty-five pigs and did not know what to do with all the meat. After two successful years they started selling, in addition to *shashlik*, two dishes, and two years later, in 2004, they opened the restaurant Vaterland in a newly built café. Their business is still expanding, and a restaurant three times the size of the original is currently under construction across the road.

Sonya says that the vast majority of her clients are Kazakh, and she is particularly proud of the fact that many prominent local politicians are regular guests and also help them with 'all kinds of bureaucratic requests'. Sonya explains that Kazakhs and Germans have always been very close and she notes that the Kazakhs' favourite dish is 'meat prepared in the German way', which is now made with lamb instead of pork in her restaurant.

Just a week before we met, Sonya had won the silver medal in an oblast-wide restaurant competition. Although she was very happy about the competition's results, she remarked that a Kazakh confidant had told her that only the votes of the two Russians on the selection committee had kept her from winning the gold medal. In general, Sonya is rather critical of Russian attributes. She describes how bad and unfriendly her Russian clients' behaviour is, and she does not like that they do not share their dishes, but instead only eat and pay for what they themselves have ordered. On the contrary, Kazakhs mostly order many different dishes for everyone at the table and end up quarrelling over who is allowed to pay for it all. Sonya points out that she feels closer to the Kazakh way of doing things and explains it by emphasizing that she basically grew up with Kazakhs.

Since her and her son's business is rapidly expanding, they recently had to hire a couple of people. Sonya herself is now mainly concerned with the business's strategic development, the creation of new dishes and arrangements, and monitoring of the construction work on the new building. Her son and his wife are responsible for all the financial issues and, furthermore, for purchasing all the necessary goods. They recently hired a Russian cook to head up the kitchen who works alongside many different nationalities, among them Kazakhs and Chechens. Sonya says that a person's nationality is irrelevant and was not at all a criterion for employment.

The case of Sonya's restaurant is particularly interesting because her behaviour reflects the nationality concept's normative power. First of all, by naming her café Vaterland, she explicitly draws on the positive image of a German identity that is widely accepted; also, referring to one's own ethnic belonging by positively highlighting its virtues is supported by the ethnic folklore proclaimed in state discourse and appreciated by most Kazakhs. D'Andrade (1997: 98) describes two motivational forces: 'There appear to be two major intrinsic motivational systems involved with cultural meaning systems: the first relatively direct personal reward; the second is reward because of attachment to a particular set of values'. As to the reference to her German identity, the two motivational forces support each other: Sonya personally profits because, firstly, her German identity attracts Kazakh clients, and secondly, it is generally appreciated when one offers 'traditional ethnic dishes'.

Moreover, Sonya's behaviour exemplifies how the nationality concept directs people to treat the Russian category and Russians personally. It is admissible to complain about Russian habits, the stereotypes of which are generally ambiguous; and since Russians are still considered to occupy a position of superiority, it allows others to criticize them. But not to hire a person because he or she is Russian contravenes the implicated norms because it contradicts the oft-stated expression, 'We don't say you're Kazakh, and you're Russian'. Thus, discriminating against individual persons because of their ethnic belonging is not accepted. This is certainly not to say that people always follow the concept's normative implications, but at least in explanations of their behaviour they usually strive to act in accordance with it.

People typically express approval for the idea of many different nationalities living peacefully together, which is often substantiated by the availability of different national cuisines and 'folk traditions'. The many positive stereotypes underline this view of national folklore. But by reaffirming the existence of national differences, national belonging also becomes a salient dimension for explaining behaviour, and, thus, also for explaining negative behaviour. In the case of the German restaurant, Sonya explains the fact that she did not win the gold medal in the restaurant competition with the ethnic belonging of two of the committee's members – that is, the Russians who do not like German restaurants. It could be that, in this case, the alliance of nationality and food as celebrated in national gastronomies gives natural meaning to someone's belonging, or as Herzfeld (2005: 28) puts it: national gastronomies 'may achieve to an even greater degree [than visual and musical iconicities] the surreptitious obviousness that the process of naturalization requires' (see also Appadurai 1988).

Summary

Mental schemas might best be understood as flexible connections of experiences, knowledge and emotions. Part of the schema 'nationality' is, thus, the knowledge about nationality that has been investigated as a cultural domain. Irrespective of someone's own national belonging, people hold a common definition of nationality: it defines groups of people who share (origin) territory, language, religion and 'mentality'.

Paradoxically, if one approaches the issue from the opposite perspective, namely by asking about the relevance of those listed features that define nationality, it becomes obvious that most of them actually have no significance: Kazakhstani Germans generally do not speak German and they do not necessarily share common religious beliefs. Consequently, the origin of one's ancestors from many generations ago is thought to impact a person's 'mentality'. This essentializing stance is also a prerequisite for a binary division between Kazakhs (and other Muslim Central Asians) and Russians (and other European Christians), which by some in the latter category are labelled 'black' and 'white'. But even without such a racially inflected terminology, it is the omnipresence of national categories, for instance in national cuisines, songs and 'mental characteristics', that turns nationality into a self-evident determinant.

The nationality schema also promotes the norm of not discriminating against people because of their national belonging and of holding in high regard Kazakhstan's national variety. Russians, however, as the previous rulers appear to some degree not to take part in this ethnic folklore. They are perhaps the easiest to criticize with regard to being less accepting of the nationality schema;

120 *Staying at Home*

it is clear, for example, that many of them question the status of the smaller European nationalities such as the German one by grouping them under the Russian umbrella. The relation of people to power and the state, and the impact of this relation on categories and the process of identification, is the topic of the next chapter.

Notes

1. Diener's study (2004) on homeland conceptions of Germans and Koreans does not reflect on the nationality categories themselves. He focuses on how they are integrated into the Kazakh state by official rhetoric and state policies.
2. However, as elaborated in Chapter 1, the definition of ethnic categories was not undisputed during Soviet times.
3. Römhild (1998: 154), for instance, states that there are a certain number of Germans who deliberately decided against an ethnic articulation of their ethnic background which has, according to her, not been sufficiently studied. Moreover, she found that ethnicity with respect to a fixation on origin does not play a dominant role according to most of the Germans she interviewed.
4. The translation is provided by the author; the original text in French is as follows: *La langue est certainement le trait fondamental permettant de caractériser et d'identifier une ethnie. Une langue propre permet à la fois de distinguer l'ethnie des autres et de servir de lien particulier entre ses membres. C'est donc à la fois un indice externe et un élément de cohésion interne. La promotion et la défense de la langue ethnique ont toujours été ressenties comme un devoir fondamental, une nécessité collective pour la survie du groupe.*
5. Nationality – Russian: 13; Kazakh: 13; German: 16. Gender – female: 27; male: 15. Age – below 30: 9; between 30 and 50: 20; above 50: 13.
6. In general, the interviewees had no difficulty in mentioning several nationalities and most of them took readily to the task. On average, people mentioned sixteen nationalities; a typical list included Kazakhs, Russians, Ukrainians, Germans, Koreans and Chinese, as well as other nationalities from Central Asia (most often Uzbeks, Uighurs, Kyrgyz), the Caucasus (most often Chechens, Azerbaijanis, Georgians), and the Baltics. There was little variation as to age and ethnic affiliation: both young and middle-aged persons mentioned on average fifteen nationalities, while persons above the age of fifty mentioned seventeen. Russians mentioned on average thirteen nationalities; both Kazakhs and Germans seventeen. The shortest list comprised nine nationalities, the longest thirty-five. Which nationalities people mentioned and in which order they were listed seemed to be influenced by whom people actually knew and by the respective positions of those nationalities in Kazakhstan generally and Taldykorgan more specifically. Most people told me that they knew a person from each of the nationalities mentioned by them, and quite often had a good friend or neighbour from one of the less numerous nationalities, e.g., Azerbaijani or Belarusian, appearing at the top of their list. However, for the most part, the lists reflect the nationalities' quantity and significance in the city of Taldykorgan – for instance, whether a nationality is represented by an active nationality centre or not.

  Furthermore, it is relevant to which nationality the interviewee belongs. Russians, in contrast to Germans and Kazakhs, list, on average, Russians before Kazakhs. (On average, the interviewees listed Kazakhs first, Russians second; Germans were placed fifth). Furthermore, Germans placed 'Germans' fourth, Russians placed them fifth, and

Kazakhs placed them sixth. Moreover, Kazakhs mention, on average, more Central Asian nationalities, whereas Russians and Germans mention more European nationalities such as Poles and Greeks and those from the Baltics.
7. It was up to them how many piles they built. I noted down the visual result and taped the interviews.
8. In this section, all quotes are from persons who self-identify as German. The perspectives of Kazakhs and Russians will be explored later.
9. I deflected such questions by explaining that I would be happy to answer any interviewee questions once the interview was concluded.
10. The expression 'pure blood' (*chistokrovnyj*) typically refers to a person who has only German ancestors.
11. German language proficiency is above all linked to generation: only 6.6 per cent of those born after 1955 indicated in a survey conducted in the former Soviet Union in 1990 that they spoke German fluently, as compared to sixty per cent of those who were born before 1930 (Stoll 2007: 175).
12. I am aware of the fact that this might be said in order to please the German ethnographer. But since discussing the loss of the mother tongue was often a very emotional moment in an interview, it is hard to imagine that this was simply a performance for my sake.
13. This is a weekly meeting of around twenty-five elderly Germans organized by the German House in Taldykorgan.
14. However, not only Germans are Protestants or Catholics in Taldykorgan. Most of the Catholic parish's members are in fact Polish, and all Protestant parishes, except for the Lutheran parish, have more Russian and Korean than German members.
15. Certainly, this does not hold true for the parishes' 'real members'. But they form a very small minority in relation to the town's population.
16. This concept of a German identity resembles that of Germans in Blumenau (Brazil) investigated by Frotscher Kramer (2008), who concludes: 'Over time … it was no longer the language but other criteria that were used to build a German Brazilian identity: the German ancestry above all and a "German concept of life", including being hard working' (ibid.: 427).
17. This happened, for instance, when people came too late to a birthday party.
18. Which is not to deny that many Germans and Russians utter negative Kazakh stereotypes; rather, here I refer to the folkloristic ethnic categories also used in state discourse, in which each of the stereotypes is associated with a certain set of positive attributes.
19. Peyrouse (2007: 483) asserts that Kazakh state policy has divided its minorities into several categories: 'The most favoured ones, symbolically, were the nationalities without a titular state (for example Dungans, Kurds and Uigurs) and the supposedly socially weak nationalities (such as Chechens and Buriats). A second group consisted of several socially well-integrated national minorities, well supported by their states of origin, such as Germans and Koreans, and to a lesser extent, Ukrainians, Poles, and Greeks. Russians alone comprised a third group, marginalized since they neither were deemed to be a national minority given their numbers, nor were they part of what is defined as the Kazakh "titular nation"'. One may question whether members of all ethnic minorities agree with Peyrouse's classification, but apparently Russians are *symbolically* less favoured by the Kazakh state than the smaller ethnic groups.
20. There is almost no variation as to age and ethnic background with regard to those who built two piles: six out of sixteen were above age 50, six between ages 30 and 50, four below age 30; four were Kazakh, five Russian, and seven German.

21. The number of piles – that is, the extent to which nationalities were merged – appeared to depend, firstly, on an interviewee's knowledge and, secondly, on their attitudes towards ethnicity. The more people know about ethnic groups the more they tend to consider the various specifications of each, which in turn tends to be reflected more significantly in nationality categories.
22. Yulia initially labelled the 'Eastern peoples' the 'Muslim group'; however, when she realized that her 'Muslim group' contained many non-Muslims, she renamed it the 'Eastern peoples'.
23. As to the categorization of nationalities themselves, there is little variation among Kazakhs, Russians and Germans. Kazakhs also most often construct two nationality categories according to religious affiliation, i.e., a Muslim group and a non-Muslim group (the latter mostly including Koreans and Chinese). Thus, although the focus differs – Russians and Germans build a Christian or European category, placing those who remain into an 'other' category, whereas Kazakhs build a Muslim category and create an 'other' category for all non-Muslims – the overall outcome is nonetheless similar.
24. Nine out of twelve Russians grouped Germans and Russians together, whereas only two out of thirteen Kazakhs and seven out of sixteen Germans did so.
25. Only one elderly Russian argued that Germans could not be in the Russian category because 'they, after all, fought against one another'.
26. Kuzio (2005: 232) underlines the relevance of language for Russians in Ukraine; he remarks that those Russians 'resist being labelled as an ethnic group and national minority'. Instead they prefer to be seen 'as part of a Russian ethno-linguistic community'.
27. Flynn (2007), in her analysis of Russian migrants' 'home/lands' constructions, states that ethnic belonging and an attachment to a 'native homeland' are not crucial for Russian migrants from former Soviet republics to the Russian Federation. Furthermore, 'official Russian state discourse and policy have not constructed the territory of the Russian Federation as a welcoming homeland. The focus on ethnic Russian and Russian-speaking populations in the policies of forced migration, diasporisation and repatriation has, to an extent, avoided an over-ethnicisation of mainstream migration debate, and reflects the historic attachment of both ethnic Russian and Russian-speaking populations to the Russian "state" (whether Tsarist or Soviet) through territory, rather than blood' (ibid.: 466f). The fact that the Russian state ultimately excludes Kazakhstani Russians from the Russian category because citizenship is not defined on the basis of common descent might also have its effects on how people in Kazakhstan view ethnic belonging.
28. See Chapter 1 for a discussion of the significance of Russian ethnic belonging in the endeavour to build a Soviet people within the USSR.
29. Of course, one has to keep in mind that all interviews were conducted by a German ethnographer.
30. Not during taped interviews but in informal discussions, it was sometimes mentioned that Germans are overly fussy, that they lack a sense of humour, or that they are boring. Surely, these negative stereotypes can be directly related to the very same positive stereotypes of Germans held by many Kazakhs, and they have nothing in common with the features of an 'enemy nation' (see Chapter 1 regarding the official Soviet characterization of an 'enemy nation').

Chapter 4

Everyday Nationality in the Kazakh Nation State

Accurately identifying and categorizing a subject group often presents the ethnographer with a difficult challenge, demanding that he or she spend many hours among the people under study and conscientiously record numerous incidents that may seem of little importance at the time, and which frequently prove to be of little significance upon reflection. Thankfully there are also encounters like the following, which began routinely but developed into something revealing and worthy of note. In Taldykorgan I had gone out with two German-Kazakhstani women whom I had known for several months. In the overcrowded café there were only three 'acceptable' places left at a single table – by 'acceptable', my companions meant a table where they could sit with other 'Russians'. We were soon introducing ourselves to the two Russian men at the table, and a conversation ensued about this particular café and cafés in general. Besides complaints about the unavailability of particular drinks and the 'always sleepy service', the main objection was that there were too many Kazakhs and too few Russians. I followed the conversation without comment, as the others continued to compare cafés and clubs in terms of their suitability for Russians.[1] Then they moved beyond cafés and clubs, discussing the situation of Russians in Taldykorgan and eventually weighing the possibility of migrating to Russia.

When the topic shifted to who worked where and at what, one of my German friends mentioned that she from time to time worked at the German House. This led one of the Russian men to ask her if she herself was German. When she replied 'yes', he and his friend laughed and happily replied that they were also German. Afterwards, the conversation took a pronounced turn. Not simply because they now replaced 'Russian' with 'German' and talked of migration to Germany instead of Russia; rather, I sensed a much more intimate atmosphere at the table, and they began asking each other about persons they might know and finally decided to meet again the following week (field notes 23/02/2007).

What transpired at the café points to a common phenomenon among Kazakhstani Germans: although they typically do not attempt to hide that they are German, they often do not make a point of mentioning it either, because it is not necessarily perceived as being important in daily interactions. All four Kazakhstani Germans at the café seemed perfectly comfortable identifying themselves as Russian, and comfortable with one another as Russians, but only after they realized that they also were all Germans, and began talking of similar experiences with relatives in Germany and their own decisions not to emigrate to Germany, did a distinct feeling of relatedness emerge that had not existed beforehand. However, no discussion developed about the general situation of Germans in Taldykorgan or Kazakhstan, as had developed earlier with regard to the situation of Kazakhstani Russians.

This chapter investigates how people relate nationality to their lives in the Kazakh nation state. My interest here with regard to the state is its role in the daily lives of its citizens, as perceived by the citizens themselves, and how state policies and discourses impact on the nationality schema, which has been explored in the previous chapter. To this end, the effects of language policies and the demographic change due to the out-migration of the Russian-speaking population and the in-migration of ethnic Kazakhs from Mongolia, China and Uzbekistan are explored. It is demonstrated that non-Kazakhs usually express their feelings of exclusion by referring to their Russian identity, even though 'at home' or among friends, and in particular Kazakh friends, they identify as German. Consequently, a German identity is perceived as a private matter, even if a person might profit from it by running a business that is intentionally promoted as German. This ambiguous position – between celebrating one's German ethnicity (and profiting from it) and downplaying it – is perfectly mirrored in state discourse on the 'friendship of peoples' (*druzhba narodov*).

It is further explored to what extent people refer to a Kazakhstani identity. Diener (2006: 201) states that 'they [the majority of peoples of the state] continue to regard their ethnic identity as primary, with the abstract notion of "Kazakhstani" citizenship taking a subsidiary position'. For Kazakhstani Germans (to whom Diener is also referring) the case is more complicated. Feelings of exclusion from the Kazakh nation have triggered a largely non-ethnic reference to a 'Russian' identity among Kazakhstani Germans, while simultaneously an ethnic German identity has been strengthened that nonetheless remains largely in line with, or part of, a Kazakhstani-German identity.[2]

'The Friendship of Peoples – Is Our Wealth!'

The state discourse over the last several decades celebrating the concept of interethnic harmony continues to have a pervasive effect on Kazakhstani society, and it remains a constant in many official Kazakhstani statements on the matter of

Figure 4.1 When people enter Taldykorgan they read: 'The friendship of peoples – is our wealth!' (photo: R. Sanders, 2007)

interethnic relations. Very often, people explicitly mention that Nazarbayev himself deserves the lion's share of the credit that all nationalities live together peacefully. His policies are widely perceived as guaranteeing interethnic harmony,[3] as explained by Farida:

> *RS: How do the different nationalities live together in your opinion?*
> This is generally good, very good. For example, when I watch TV, there's this going on, at another place something else has happened, there's some kind of clash. We don't have anything like that. On the contrary, there's such a mutual understanding; we do not even say 'You're Kazakh, you're Russian, you're Chechen'. In our town Taldykorgan, so many different peoples live here: we have many Chechens, here are many Uighurs, Moldovans, and there wasn't anything like this before. Even as far as I'm concerned – my circle of friends – there are Russians, and Chechens and Uighurs. I've never made any kind of distinction between them. This is the work of Nazarbayev. I like his policies, this is well done, not like in other countries.
> *RS: Why is it so? That so many different nationalities live together in such a friendly manner?*
> It's the politics, you see, how Nazarbayev unites all. He doesn't force anybody by saying this is the land of the Kazakhs; you all have to be like them. He doesn't put any extraordinary pressure on anyone by saying this is the land of the Kazakhs, you all have to speak Kazakh, other [languages] don't exist and if you don't like this, you can leave the country. He doesn't have such policies. On the contrary, he says that he has united everyone, that he has given a chance to everybody. If you are Uighur, there's an Uighur school, there you have the opportunity to

learn your language. He doesn't prohibit anything from anyone. You see, and therefore, I think we have peace and harmony. If there was a law, a prohibition, or another kind of force, then, of course, it would be a different relationship, and there would be other opinions, and of course then there would be all kinds of skirmishes. He [Nazarbayev] gave full freedom to everybody. If you feel like it, you can speak Russian, or if you want to, you can talk in your own language. (Farida, 30 years old)

Moreover, Kazakhs often illustrate the success of interethnic harmony by pointing to the actions of Kazakhs themselves. As indicated in the previous chapter, Kazakhs characterize themselves as hospitable and tolerant. In this regard, many of them proudly mention that Kazakhs are usually bilingual, and the status of Russian as the language of interethnic communication is widely accepted, as exemplified by Rashid, who is fluent in both Russian and Kazakh:

The Russian language still unites all nations. Every nation knows its own language, and that will continue, but the language of interethnic communication is still Russian. I think the Russian language will continue to develop, it won't cause trouble, neither among Kazakhs, nor Russians, nor Germans, nor other nationalities. On the contrary, it brings us closer to each other. Through the Russian language we communicate with each other, and its future existence contradicts neither our constitution nor our communication. In our constitution it is written that our second language is Russian; it is the language of interethnic communication. And I think that still in fifteen, still in a hundred years, it will exist in Kazakhstan. (Rashid, 52 years old)

Not only Kazakhs appreciate Nazarbayev's minority policies. The establishment of minority centres, which offer language courses in the 'mother tongue' of the minority's members (and to which Farida refers above), are often mentioned in a positive light, and many Kazakhstanis are proud that they belong to a state that actively addresses minority issues. Furthermore, most non-Kazakhs support the Kazakhs' view of themselves as hospitable and tolerant (cf. Sanders 2013b: 85–87). However, Russians tend to interpret Kazakhstan's ethnic stability as a continuation of Soviet ethnic policies rather than a specific accomplishment of the Kazakh state, and moreover emphasize that interethnic harmony is in large part due to the relative economic prosperity, as Maxim asserts:

RS: Why do the different nationalities live together so peacefully?[4]
Kazakhstan is currently developing rapidly and everybody is busy with his own business. Everybody tries to grab something, you see? Some are busy with renovation, others with construction. We don't have such

testiness that occurs when something is missing. ... Now we are all in a state of development, you see? But when there was nothing at a certain period, when there was this transition phase in the 1990s – at that time a lot of problems came up, you see? Taking away, plundering – in principle the population lived on the basis of deceiving. But now there's simply the opportunity, now you just have to think with your head. If you want to think, here you are! And there are building sites where you don't have to think. (Maxim, 30 years old)

According to Maxim, a Russian, the rapidly growing economy offers opportunities to whomever is willing to take advantage of them, and this is one of the primary reasons for the current interethnic peace, and, in particular, it explains why those non-Kazakhs who profit from Kazakhstan's economic development come to regard the nation as their homeland, as will be shown in the last part of this chapter.

Interestingly, however, despite the extensive rhetorical celebration of national diversity, virtually no one, when asked directly, asserts that her or his German identity is relevant 'in public'. The incident in the café described above exemplifies that ethnic belonging is perceived as a personal matter by many Kazakhstani Germans, and they do not feel it necessary to make a point of it in social situations with others. In fact many Kazakhstani Germans affirm that ethnic belonging is, in the public sphere, not an issue at all, an attitude illustrated by Eleonora:

RS: What does it mean to you that you're German, in general, in your life?
In life?
RS: Yes.
Well, you know, in principle, I have observed something peculiar. The people who come to the German House, they, firstly, all perceive themselves to be German. Because they're all attached to the German culture, right? But in addition to this, Kazakhstan is a country that fosters tolerant relationships towards other diasporas. Therefore, in principle, for instance, here in Kazakhstan, in our Taldykorgan, in the sphere where I operate, where I communicate, there's nothing like: You're German – in a concrete sense – you're Russian, you're Kazakh and so on. I'm not going to talk to you and so on. Here, in a way, everything is blurred and dynamic. Therefore, in principle, there's not a distinction between a German, a Russian, a Kazakh and so on. And, in principle, it doesn't make a difference to anybody who you are, right? For that matter, it is solely your personal attitude and understanding. Well, for example, I feel like a German, I position myself as a German, everybody perceives me as a German. However, in principle, this doesn't play a role, not

for acquaintances, not for work and so on. This is how it is. (Eleonora, 23 years old)

On the one hand, Eleonora contends that being German is a personal matter and is not relevant in her relationships with others or in her life in Kazakhstan in general. On the other hand, she stresses that she feels like a German and that everyone perceives her as German. This discrepancy between personal and public attitudes generally underlies many statements about the significance of a German nationality.

There is also widespread disagreement on the question of whether ethnic belonging is becoming increasingly important in present-day Kazakhstan, and often the same person utters contradictory opinions on the subject. At first, it is often stated by Kazakhstani Germans that ethnicity has become less important, and that it is likely to continue to decline in relevance:

> The nationality question even today, maybe, is set up artificially, anyhow. But I think that in ten years people will have understood that the basic thing is not nationality but mutual respect. Actually, here in Kazakhstan, it's difficult to distinguish people according to nationality features. Well, when it comes to habits, to the cuisine, here we have so many different nationalities, and all have been mixing so that it is difficult for us to say: whose cuisine, whose ceremony and so on. This is already so mixed that it has lost its purity. There's nothing pure German, nothing pure Kazakh. In any case, some other elements exist because we have been living close to each other, together with many different nationalities. Therefore, I think that our republic has a good future. (Olga, 55 years old)

Many Kazakhstani Germans appreciate that the significance of their ethnic belonging is decreasing, which furthermore is often seen as the most important prerequisite for Kazakhstan's future success. To explain this decline in importance of a person's ethnic belonging, Olga points to the difficulty in determining a person's nationality, since ethnic boundaries have become blurred due to interethnic mixing. While this at first may seem a contradiction in terms, in that 'ethnic traits' still exist according to Olga, they are also available across ethnic groups; for example, Kazakhs now cook *borshch*, though they continue to regard it as a Russian dish. Thus, the ethnic stereotype remains, even when a different ethnic group incorporates it into their own way of life.

The ambiguous nature of the concept of nationality is clearly seen in the contradiction between, on the one hand, the envisioned merging of nationalities and, on the other, the celebration of each nationality's distinct traditions and the state's 'international' image, which has been enshrined for decades in Soviet and Kazakhstani state rhetoric and policies (see Chapter 1). The concept of 'internationalism' and its positive connotations are often emphasized:

RS: How do the different nationalities live together?
We have here many different nationalities. As far as I know, I mean, for me it seems – peacefully, because here, for example, in our town [Taldykorgan], not a big town, there are many different diasporas, peoples. Even our family itself is international, the daughter-in-law in our family is Korean, and therefore – we don't make any particular distinctions between Russians and Kazakhs. In organizations, for example, Russians, Kazakhs, Germans and Koreans, all work together and there are no distinctions. For me it seems – I don't know – maybe the Kazakhs themselves on their own couldn't become a civilized people. When there's a collective composed of only Kazakhs, this is not very good. On the contrary, there has to be some kind of mixture. (Aigul, 27 years old)

Aigul states that ethnic belonging does not have any importance with respect to relationships at her workplace. However, at the same time, she does not want to work only with Kazakhs, and she appreciates the benefits that 'internationalism' brings to her office. Therefore, distinct nationalities exist in her opinion, but are at the same time irrelevant or – perhaps more precisely – should be irrelevant.

On the other hand, many non-Kazakhs state that ethnic belonging is now much more important than it has ever been, as Sofia illustrates:

Well, here in Kazakhstan, there's no strong distinction between Russians and Germans. We have the same face. All that's left are the Kazakhs, and well, it's like all the others under one umbrella – the Russians. … I won't make any career here, and also not my child – zero per cent. I look at the children [Sofia works as a teacher]. By and large everybody tries to send his children somewhere. To get a good education here, that's very expensive. Generally, Kazakhs get a stipend. I don't know how they achieve it. I don't know. Nobody tells us. … Briefly, there's a kind of barrier, in spite of everything. Even – we work for how many years – I have now worked for fifteen years at a school. Somehow, earlier, on the contrary, this nationality question wasn't raised; it wasn't even mentioned at all. But now, in particular in connection with the change-over to the Kazakh language – this state language – they behave so – even at my school, we work together for fifteen years but some of them – I don't recognize them. They perceive themselves as bosses. They're the country's boss and we – because we're Russians or Germans, this is not important, well, light-skinned, and we're just – not bosses. I don't perceive myself as a boss. In every respect I feel that I'm just a foreign person here. This attitude, I don't know, somehow subconsciously or how – but you can feel it that I'm foreign here. This is, I don't know – therefore I also think that I have to do something in any case, even if we have to emigrate to Russia. (Sofia, 37 years old)

Sofia, a German, states that in present-day Kazakhstan it is no longer important whether you are German or Russian, but it is important whether or not you are Kazakh. She expresses feelings of exclusion from the Kazakh state and clearly feels discriminated against. Sofia's assertion is in line with what has been said before: while being German is a personal matter and is declining in public relevance, being Russian is becoming increasingly relevant publicly, in that it is perceived as negatively influencing a person's future prospects in Kazakhstan. Therefore, as elaborated in the previous chapter, it is not only that a Russian identity is widely conceptualized as encompassing a German identity, but the Russian category has, furthermore, partially left the folkloristic sphere of the nationality categories. Being Russian – which basically means being non-Kazakh – is becoming more of a political category, while being German is still thought of within the framework of nationality constructed by the Soviets and adopted by Nazarbayev.

Losing Language Hegemony

Many Kazakhstani Russians are afraid of losing their previous position of superiority, both in terms of economic well-being and language hegemony. One might then ask why such a Kazakhstani Russian would not at least make a concerted effort to learn Kazakh in order to escape their perceived disadvantage as a non-Kazakh speaker. Though most Kazakhstani Russians see the need to learn Kazakh, many of them perceive learning Kazakh as too difficult, if not impossible (cf. also Aydingün 2008: 150–54). Furthermore, many Russians complain that Kazakh language lessons at school are typically of poor quality because former Russian-language teachers are often the ones teaching Kazakh. Moreover, they say that language training rarely touches upon everyday conversations, focusing instead on memorizing poems and studying other literary genres.

In the previous chapter, the Kazakh nationality was explored, and it was suggested that there is a belief among people that for a non-Kazakh to become Kazakh is categorically impossible. It may be that the reluctance to learn Kazakh is due to a widespread impression among Russians – despite the sense of a fading language hegemony – that disadvantages in the end do not stem from a lack of linguistic knowledge but rather from not belonging to the titular nationality. This is often exemplified by their assertion that a good command of Kazakh is established as a prerequisite for employment in the public sector, however, Kazakh policemen do not always speak Kazakh well, and therefore have to attend special language courses. Thus, they believe that the truly decisive factor is ethnic belonging, not language skills, in particular with regard to public sector employment. To further bolster their argument, some Russians contend that Kazakhs, especially those in the public sector, do not even want Russians to learn 'their language', which in turn provides Kazakhs with a strong reason for excluding them from the public sector.

Another complaint along similar lines is that many Russians working in the public sector have been replaced by Kazakhs.⁵ For example, Russians in Taldykorgan assert that in little more than a decade all of the school directors in Taldykorgan except for two have been replaced, and in every instance a Russian has been replaced by a Kazakh. In addition, those Russians working in the private sector often complain about being at a disadvantage, and again it is the Kazakh language that is seen as a major obstacle. For instance, since 2006, accountancy must be carried out in Kazakh, which not surprisingly, considering the technical nature of the work, often results in employing a Kazakh-speaking person.

Many Kazakhs do not share the Russians' view that the increasing importance of Kazakh may eventually threaten the interethnic peace. While most of them acknowledge that it is difficult to acquire language skills above a certain age, they expect Russian children to attend a Kazakh-speaking kindergarten. Furthermore, some Kazakhs turn the tables here, accusing those Russians who emigrated as being more 'nationalistic' since they preferred to live among their own kind instead of living together with the Kazakhs, and some Kazakhs even feel somewhat abandoned. The following general statement by Nurgul exemplifies this feeling:

RS: How do the different nationalities live together?
They lived well, in a friendly manner.
RS: And today?
Now, since the Soviet Union is dissolved, they all … The Turks have their own homeland; they also want to go there. Well, everybody is talking about their children's future. Earlier, they didn't think about that. We all lived together, and now? And now, you see, they have been separating. Now every mother thinks about her child's future. 'It's still fine [generally in Kazakhstan] but only God knows what will be in twenty years [they say]'. And the child shouldn't stay behind. Therefore, everybody strives for taking the children to their homeland, to their own kind. (Nurgul, approximately 55 years old)

Nurgul does not have much sympathy for those mothers who prefer to raise their children in their 'historic homeland', and she even wonders what the Kazakhs have done to them to make them think the future of their children in Kazakhstan will be compromised in some way. Therefore, to Nurgul, the process of out-migration itself triggers feelings of ethnic belonging and highlights the differences among Kazakhstanis. This view on interethnic relations is not shared by Russians, however, who see language policies as the major obstacle to their future success in Kazakhstan. I was told many times that Russians had emigrated to Russia, Israel or Germany because they did not know Kazakh well enough. Furthermore, many Russians strive to send their children to universities in Russia, and if their children are able to gain employment in Russia, they also begin to consider emigration.

Many Russian-only speakers feel particularly alienated by Kazakhs from the countryside, whose command of Russian is generally weak. The continuing flow of rural populations into the town is often viewed critically by 'native inhabitants', who refer to the newcomers as 'uncivilized', 'primitive' and 'badly educated'. Interestingly though, while rural Russians and Germans have also migrated to Taldykorgan, such negative attributes are only associated with rural Kazakhs rather than rural migrants in general. One important consideration with regard to this process of 'ruralization' (*ruralizatsiya*) – as it is sometimes termed – is the Kazakh language as spoken by rural migrants (cf. Sanders 2013a). Emilia explains the importance of ethnic categories in this context:

> Kazakh or Russian, I don't pay attention who speaks in which language, for me it's all fine, I grew up like this. The only thing is – those Kazakhs who came from the village, they behave primitively in town, and they can speak pure Kazakh. But as for the locals [meaning those born in Taldykorgan] I don't look at the nationality, I look at a person's character. For example, my best friends are Korean and Kazakh, and my mother's best friends are also Kazakh and Korean, and a lot of Russians. I don't look at a person's nationality but at his character. There are bad Kazakhs, Russians and also Germans. (Emilia, 22 years old)

In other words, for Emilia it is not ethnic belonging that is important, but whether you come from the town or a village. When she says that those from the villages are Kazakhs who speak 'pure Kazakh', she is implying that such rural Kazakhs usually speak Russian badly if at all, which explains why contact between rural Kazakhs and Russian-only speakers is very limited. Generally, rural migrants are often described as being 'too Kazakh', and for the most part Soviet 'backward' and 'uncivilized' stereotypes are applied primarily to *rural* Kazakhs in present-day Kazakhstan, since a broader picture of Kazakhs that includes *non-rural* Kazakhs has been disseminated widely in state discourse.

Rural-urban migration has become a major issue in mass media and scholarly analysis in Kazakhstan, with hundreds of thousands of villagers having migrated to urban areas since the early 1990s. Yessenova (2005: 662), in her analysis of 'urban discourses', states that former villagers are depicted 'as an obstacle in the society's transition from the Soviet state to a more advanced collective state of being. The fashion in which these images are structured resonates with the colonial rhetoric of the Soviet regime, defining Kazakh society as archaic, inferior, and, therefore, incapable of modern nationhood and self-governance'. Thus, Emilia's statement about the 'primitive rural Kazakhs' is largely a reflection of their representation in mass media 'in which they are discursively set apart as unwanted elements in urban society' (ibid.: 666).

The negative image of rural Kazakhs can also be viewed as a response by the older elites who feel threatened by the influx. The distinction between 'black' and 'white', with its racist overtones, along with the similarly prejudicial connotation when differentiating between rural and urban, can be traced back to Soviet state discourses about the 'backward' and 'uncivilized', and many people still fall back on the old vocabulary, but more as a result of rapidly changing circumstances than the availability of stereotypes. That is to say, the use of negative stereotypes seems to be motivated by something that affects people directly (cf. Herzfeld 2005); above all, in this case, Russian-only speakers who are afraid of losing their jobs to Kazakh speakers, and who are therefore more inclined to speak of the 'lazy Kazakhs who would not even be able to do their job'. Those Kazakhstani Russians and Germans who are well-off, and less threatened by the influx of rural Kazakhs, express negative attitudes about Kazakhstan and its titular population to a lesser extent.

Identification: Strategies and Emotions

Since ethnicity is based on cultural grounds – it is the 'cultural stuff' (Barth 1969; see also the introduction to this volume for a discussion of his notion of the 'cultural stuff') that is decisive – the means by which Kazakhstani Germans distinguish themselves from others is important. Kazakhstani Germans appear to intend to be on good terms with both Russians and Kazakhs, largely through how they position themselves among each group. In the company of Russians, Germans position themselves as Russians. This is the case both in daily encounters, such as during a bus ride or at the marketplace, and for long-term relationships such as friendships and even marriage, as has been shown in Edik's story in Chapter 2. Firstly, because Russians do not accept German self-identification without a demonstration of substantial boundary markers, particularly German language skills, and comparatively few Kazakhstani Germans speak German. Secondly, and perhaps more importantly, if Germans wish to distinguish themselves from Russians, they must do so by drawing on German memories, but considering the complicated historical relationship between Germans and Russians – especially the German memories derived from experiences of intense hardship during and after the Second World War – this would not be seen as helpful to present-day relations.

At the same time, German memories are in fact helpful in supporting good relations with Kazakhs, with both groups seeing the other in a positive light with regard to the past, which is one reason why Germans tend to identify themselves as Germans in their dealings with Kazakhs. Therefore, towards Kazakhs, but not Russians, Germans have the appropriate 'cultural stuff' at their disposal in order to achieve good relationships through self-identification as Germans. This holds true mainly in close and long-term relationships, such as at the workplace or among neighbours. In more superficial day-to-day interactions, most Germans do not make a point of letting it be known that they are non-Russian.

Kazakhstan's changing demographic is thus likely to have an impact on the significance of a German identity in Kazakhstan. Since the proportion of Kazakhs in most fields is rising, whereas the number of Russians is generally declining, Kazakhstani Germans might increasingly opt for a German identity instead of a Russian one. Furthermore, since the number of Germans has dramatically decreased, largely due to migration, it seems that the boundaries of the German category have loosened in order to allow as many as possible to be included in it. This makes sense for two reasons: (1) most present-day Kazakhstani Germans only meet a very broad definition of 'German', since they do not speak German or belong to a 'German parish' and (2) the general status of a German identity in Kazakhstan can only be maintained if there is a comparatively significant number of Germans. Consequently, the 'cultural stuff' has become transformed somewhat against a background of decreasing numbers of Germans and German speakers.

While the following excerpts help to demonstrate how this general pattern of identification is at work in people's daily lives, they also serve to remind us that individual life stories often complicate attempts to make overly general assertions:

> It was Anna's birthday party when she and her German boyfriend, her father, her Ukrainian neighbour and I were sitting together around the kitchen table. The conversation touched on the topic of the growing importance of knowing Kazakh when Anna, who works as a journalist for a local newspaper, complained that she had been asked by her employer to attend a Kazakh language course since most of the events she had to report on require a good command of Kazakh. She expressed her discontent about the language shift in many public events, and uttered that, though she was only twenty-seven years old, she was by far too old to learn a new language. Moreover, Anna told us that a friend of hers did not get a job because he was not fluent in Kazakh. Her boyfriend and her neighbour nodded. Anna went on to mention an incident she had recently experienced during a bus ride. A pregnant Russian woman was not offered the seat she had asked for; instead, the seated Kazakh man replied that she should go to Russia. The Ukrainian neighbour was filled with indignation and said that the Kazakhs would not have achieved anything without them.[6]
>
> Just a few minutes later, Anna's colleague, a Kazakh, joined our discussion at the kitchen table. Anna introduced him to all of us by also mentioning our nationalities, German and Ukrainian. She concluded by remarking that since there were no Russians among us we should all feel free to put them down, whereupon everybody laughed. (Field notes 06/09/2007)

As to the process of identification, the incident demonstrates that many Kazakhstani Germans identify themselves, depending on the context and the interlocutor, as being either Russian or German. While discussing the disadvantages of not knowing Kazakh and discrimination against Russians, Anna identifies with the pregnant Russian woman (who, of course, might be German, too). But towards her Kazakh colleague, she appears to be proud of having only non-Russian friends and clearly makes a point of being German. Thus, though many Germans feel concerned by the disadvantages all 'Russians' have to face in present-day Kazakhstan, they try to engender a relatedness to Kazakhs by stressing that they are not Russian, but German.

Individual experiences, however, can differ from this general pattern, in that not all Germans identify themselves as Germans towards Kazakhs. Peter and Valentina's life stories were explored in Chapter 2. It was shown that Peter tells his life story in order to explain his Kazakhstani-German identity, while Valentina makes plausible her Soviet identity when telling about her experiences. Two incidents will illustrate how they identify themselves in their daily lives:

> I accompanied Peter and two of his friends (a German and a Ukrainian) on a one-week trip to Usharal, where they had to do some business. Apart from this, Peter wanted to introduce me to other Germans whom he knows and who live in different villages on the way to Usharal and in the town itself. Several times we lost our way and had to ask for directions, which was always done by Peter because he was the only one of us who speaks Kazakh fluently. The point is not that the persons addressed would not be able to speak Russian, but Peter's 'Kazakh approach' opened all possible doors to us. Once a Kazakh asked Peter how a Russian happened to speak Kazakh better than he does, whereupon Peter emphatically replied that he is not a Russian but a German, which was, according to Peter's interpretation, regarded as a reasonable explanation for his fluency in Kazakh. (Field notes 17/05/2007)

> Some months earlier, I accompanied Valentina on the way to her friend's house in a neighbouring town. Sitting in the crowded bus, a Kazakh woman started a conversation with us. A relative of hers had died and she was on the way to his funeral. To keep the conversation going and, certainly, also in order to please us, the woman finally began to compare Kazakh and Russian funeral ceremonies in such a way as to demonstrate her detailed knowledge of Russian traditions. Valentina did not give any hint that she is non-Russian but instead added some further details about Russian habits. (Field notes 27/02/2007)

How Kazakhstani Germans identify themselves is linked to their emotional attachments and their personal notion of belonging. Valentina does not disagree when addressed as a Russian in day-to-day life, but Peter, who perceives his life as fundamentally threatened by Russians, does not accept being included in the Russian category because feelings of having experienced humiliation circumvent a Russian identification. Interestingly, he identifies himself as German by speaking Kazakh, and not by speaking German or demonstrating any other German boundary marker. His explanation is not unusual: Kazakhstani Germans learned Kazakh because, after deportation to Kazakhstan, they grew up in Kazakh villages, and it is thus their knowledge of Kazakh that distinguishes them from Russians. Decisive here is both an awareness of Kazakhstani-German history and the practical relevance of knowing the state language that allows Peter to avoid being pushed into the Russian category.

Rosa's life story, also presented in Chapter 2, was told by her to emphasize a German identity that she perceives as being part of a Russian identity. Her following statements stress this double identity, since she does not feel in a position to choose whether to identify as Russian or German, most often perceiving herself as both Russian and German:

> Rosa began to talk about Kazakhs, Russians and Germans in Kazakhstan while we were preparing food in her kitchen. She told me that Russians humiliated Kazakhs in the past, that they perceived them to be stupid and even inferior people. Therefore, many Kazakhs strove to speak Russian in the streets. Nowadays, however, Rosa senses that Kazakhs have gained self-confidence, which is also why they speak Kazakh more often. Rosa said that she could understand this well enough, although it was bad for her since she does not understand Kazakh. Furthermore, she gave the example of her Kazakh friends with whom she meets regularly. They speak Kazakh most of the time, and only her very close friend understands her situation and translates for her into Russian. Rosa mentions that one of her Kazakh acquaintances even hates Russians, and Rosa imitates for me the disdain with which that Kazakh woman vocalizes the term 'Russian'. Rosa says that she feels concerned by the invidious comments directed at Russians, even though she is German and she herself has had difficulties with Russians. She adds that it was the Russians who humiliated the Germans and called them fascists, and she explains that many Germans still harbour such feelings of humiliation within them. (Field notes 20/08/2007)

In matters of identity, Rosa believes people are not free to choose who they are. While it might seem rational for her to opt for a German identity, her feelings of exclusion in the company of her Kazakh-speaking acquaintances reinforces her identity as a Russian. This again indicates how language has become essential in daily life in present-day Kazakhstan – the increasing prevalence of the

Kazakh language also unites those who do not speak it, and those who speak only Russian, whether ethnically Russian or not, invariably become more connected to a Russian identity.

These incidents have depicted three modes of identification. Anna identifies as Russian when she discusses her feelings of exclusion from the Kazakh state, and as German when among Kazakhs in order to invoke a sense of relatedness. The examples of Valentina and Peter have demonstrated that some individuals are not flexible with respect to their ethnic identifications: Valentina always identifies as Russian, Peter always as German. The third case of Rosa represents those who find themselves, in certain situations, feeling both Russian and German. Thus, emotions and social strategies both impact on identification. Emotionally, there are deeply felt ethnic attachments, and possibly the fear of not having the 'right' ethnicity in the eyes of the Kazakh state. Strategically, there is the desire to position oneself favourably in daily life, whether at the workplace, in one's neighbourhood, or out in social settings.

As exemplified by Anna's case, some Kazakhstani Germans tend to stress a German identity towards Kazakhs, and sometimes even by explicitly excluding Russians. Feelings of closeness between Kazakhs and Germans also impact on how people relate to the Kazakh nation state. Despite complaints about language policies, many Germans regard Kazakhstan as their homeland, which is, furthermore, generally characterized as ethnically peaceful. Thus, in part, Kazakhstan is perceived as an inclusive state. By analysing state symbols and national identity, Aydingün (2008: 155) concludes that 'a new hybrid identity may emerge out of an inclusive ethnic nationalism and civic territorial nationalism. The existing state symbols and the pragmatic implementation of the language policy seem to support this hybrid model'. However, the case of Kazakhstani Germans also points to an ambivalence experienced by many people towards the Kazakh state, which is often perceived as both exclusive and inclusive. The following section deals with the latter aspect and investigates Kazakhstan's potential as a homeland.

Kazakhstan as a Homeland

A common expression among Kazakhstani Germans is: 'I am a German but my homeland is Kazakhstan' (*Ya nemka/nemets no rodina u menya Kazakhstan*). However, the notion of *kazakhstantsi* (Kazakhstanis) is rarely mentioned in day-to-day conversation. People usually refer to themselves and others by relying on nationality terms, and if they wish to distinguish, for instance, between Germans in Kazakhstan and Germans in Germany, people would call the former *mestnie nemtsi* (lit. 'local Germans', i.e., Kazakhstani Germans), or when non-Germans are speaking, sometimes *nashi nemtsi* (lit. 'our Germans').

Linguistically, *rodina* (homeland) is the 'place of birth': '*rod* (kin) is the stem of the verb *roditsia/rodit'*, to be born/give birth' (Flynn 2007: 468). Flynn, in her 2007 study on Russian migrants, found that *rodina* was frequently applied by migrants to the former Soviet Union when 'the connection between place of birth, kin and land was explicit' (ibid.). Thus, if Kazakhstani Germans explicitly refer to Kazakhstan (and not to the Soviet Union or a particular region or town) as their homeland, they also express feelings of belonging to the Kazakh nation, which includes a particular bond to all who were born in Kazakhstan. Therefore, the fact that the notion *kazakhstantsi* is uncommon does not necessarily mean that a civic concept of nationhood does not exist (cf. Sanders 2013b: 82).

Generally, home might be defined as a distinct and meaningful place, which is impacted by (multiple) temporalities, and to which one seeks to belong (cf. Easthope 2004: 135f). Though such a place in most cases exists as a location on a map, such feelings of belonging might transgress materiality to the extent that the phenomenon of home is one of (pure) imagination and fantasy (Morley 2000). Furthermore, for some people, home is associated exactly with loss and/or exclusion – their insistence on the existence of a home, where they can feel secure and with which they most closely identify, makes the absence of such a place especially bitter. This has led some researchers to reject the entire concept of home in the face of increasing mobility (cf. Sanders 2015: 294–97). Morley and Robins (1990: 20), for instance, state in regard to the German notion of *Heimat* (home/homeland): 'There can be no recovery of an authentic cultural homeland. In a world that is increasingly characterized by exile, migration and Diaspora, with all the consequences of unsettling and hybridization, there can be no place for such an absolution of the pure and authentic, in this world, there is no longer any place like *Heimat*'.

While I seek to show that though it is certainly correct to abandon the category of *Heimat* as an analytical tool and to no longer rely upon the concept of 'proper homelands', Kazakhstani people often strive to reside within, and to belong to, their 'real place'. It is through the notion of *Heimat* and/or *rodina* that they express their feelings of belonging and, not least of all, 'who they are'. Furthermore, places are pivotal for people to organize and recall their experiences, which, in turn, provide these places with meaning (cf. Casey 2000). But home is always, like any other place, a person's project and production, which changes throughout one's life and according to the ongoing experience of knowing places (cf. Gupta and Ferguson 1992; Malkki 1992; Massey 1995).

In the following excerpt, Igor exemplifies how people construct a Kazakhstani homeland and how they see their role in it:

> It was the first warm spring weekend when Igor, the son-in-law of my German host family, invited me to his farm, up in the mountains. On this occasion he also invited some of his friends and workers. There were about ten of us sitting outside around a table crowded with all sorts of dishes and drinks when Igor began to give the first toast. He described

at length the country's beauty, its vastness and its freedom. He compared Kazakhstan to Germany, Russia and China, where he could not imagine himself living, and he concluded by saying that he was a patriot of Kazakhstan. All the others, Germans and Russians, affirmed his words, referring to themselves as Kazakhstan's patriots, mostly by specifying all the negatives of a life in Russia or Germany and by highlighting Kazakhstan's nature, the free space and the tolerance of its people. When Igor and I were alone for some minutes he informed me about his future business plans. He intended to cultivate apples and pears in addition to raspberries and strawberries. He explained how he irrigates his fields, and he mentioned that it would work out well for him because Kazakhs were incapable of such endeavours. They were unwilling to wait for several years to harvest the first fruits, and were not even able to plan ahead for such long periods. But the Kazakhs living in the farm's neighbouring villages would admire his ability to do so, and would be grateful that some of them could work for him. (Field notes 28/02/2007)

In addition to his poor regard for the patience of the Kazakh people, Igor is also not contented with Kazakhstan's language policies, as neither he nor his wife nor his children speak Kazakh, but nonetheless he is convinced that nowhere else in the world could he realize his future plans better than in Kazakhstan. Thus, not knowing Kazakh (and also not intending to learn it)[7] and perceiving Kazakhstan as one's homeland are not necessarily contradictory. Rather, it seems to be decisive that Igor feels needed and that he has occupied an economic niche where he does not have to compete with Kazakhs. In this vein, the existence of distinct ethnic groups might be seen as an instrument of integrating people into society (Schlee 2001: 20).

Kazakhstani Germans often express feelings of home by referring to the beauty and vastness of Kazakhstan (Sanders 2015: 307). This static view of home might be seen in response to rapidly changing social, economic and political environments, which are also the result of massive emigration. Thus, for Kazakhstani Germans, change and mobility are contrasted with a static concept of territorial belonging and make the concept of homeland particularly attractive. However, interestingly, as has been elaborated in the previous chapter, the *origin* territory is actually most decisive when nationality categories have to be defined. Thus, the statement 'I am a German but my homeland is Kazakhstan' is rather contradictory, since the defining country Germany is replaced by Kazakhstan. How this relates to a diasporic identity and to Germany as a 'historic homeland' will be investigated in the next part of this study. It shall be emphasized that a German identity is not on equal terms with being a Kazakhstani (or, from another angle, that Germany is not on equal terms with Kazakhstan as a homeland); rather, a German identity is a prerequisite for a Kazakhstani identity, which is exactly the aim of Nazarbayev's nationality policies. This aim – to strengthen an ethnic identity with the ultimate goal of achieving a supra-ethnic identity – takes up the Soviet concept of nationalities (cf. Hirsch 2005). For Germans in Kazakhstan, it is this view of ethnicity that allows them to project their future hopes onto the land of the Kazakhs and to regard it as their homeland (Sanders 2015: 306–309).

Summary

Kazakhstani Germans have ambivalent feelings towards national belonging in the Kazakh nation state. They experience the usefulness of a German identity, and the esteem in which it is often held, as well as the disadvantages of being non-Kazakh. Moreover, the many statements and incidents included in this chapter have demonstrated that Herzfeld (2005) is correct to insist that stereotypes and identities should be investigated, by means of long-term fieldwork, to see how they actually play out in people's lives. Only in this way can one discern both general patterns and individual variations, and only by pooling those patterns and variations can the ethnographer perceive the actual relevance of nationality in people's daily lives.

Statements on friendship among the various peoples of Kazakhstan generally highlight the positive aspects of different nationalities living in peaceful coexistence, which is mostly attributed to the work of the country's president. Despite these proclamations, however, an ambivalence persists. Some perceive national belonging as gaining in importance, while others perceive that it is losing significance. Some contend that nationality is only relevant in private; others contend that it is only relevant in public. Such contradictory statements point to widely diverse understandings, feelings and uses of national belonging, even though the previous chapter indicated that, on a conceptual level, people share a common view on 'nationality'. But people are different, firstly in regard to their life stories and emotional attachments, and secondly in regard to how they position themselves in, and how they feel positioned by, the Kazakh state. Moreover, each person might interpret his or her condition quite differently depending on the specific situation and conversational partner(s).

The fear of forfeiting power, jobs and money in the new state, with its new language requirements, has generally strengthened a Russian identity that embodies exclusion from the nation state of Kazakhs. But this is not necessarily the case for all non-Kazakhs. As for the German Kazakhstanis under study, some of them occupy an advantageous economic niche that is in part helped by their German identity. Consequently, many Germans identify with the country and regard it as a homeland. A Kazakhstani-German identity has thus been intensified, as has a Russian identity and both of these transformations are related to state policies, in particular to Kazakhstan's view on internationalism and its language policies.

Notes

1. I had told my German acquaintances beforehand that I did not want to be introduced as 'their friend from Germany', and since I only mentioned my name, and foreigners are extremely unusual in Taldykorgan, the Russian men presumably assumed I was also from Taldykorgan.
2. Diener (2006) argues on the basis of survey data that was published in 1997 by Masanov and on his own semi-structured interviews (with twenty-seven Germans and thirty-two Koreans) that were conducted between 2000 and 2002. German respondents indicated in the survey and interviews that 'relationships between nations have worsened' (61.1 per cent in the study by Masanov) (Diener 2006: 210); that 'an awareness of my ethnic belonging' had 'greatly' (33.3 per cent) or 'slightly' (40.7 per cent) increased (in the interviews by Diener 2006: 209); and only 13.5 per cent of Germans indicated that they perceived themselves as Kazakhstani (in the study by Masanov) (Diener 2006: 209). Firstly, one has to keep in mind that the survey by Masanov was conducted more than fifteen years ago, and secondly, those questions do not account for the categories' complexity. Thus, it remains unclear whether a German felt discriminated against because of his/her German ethnic belonging (which I doubt) or because of being, as a non-Kazakh speaker, excluded from the Kazakh nation. Diener (2006: 215) attempts to explain his results with a reference to Kazakhstani-German history: 'Germans, by contrast [to Koreans], while long regarded as good workers and quality managers in Kazakhstan, continue to struggle with their deep-seated belief that the stigma of having been a "punished people" will never fully abate'. Based on my life story interviews (see Chapter 2), this does not hold true; on the contrary, the formation of the Kazakh nation state was perceived as a deliverance from 'enemy status' and has fostered a rebuilding of their memories that today, more than ever before, allows Germans to present themselves as good workers.
3. Interestingly, the language policies often criticized by Russians are to a far lesser extent associated with Nazarbayev personally.
4. That they do so had already been mentioned to me by Maxim.
5. According to Peyrouse (2007: 486) '80% of those working in the administration and academic circles are ethnic Kazakhs'. However, '75% of state employees – who are mainly Kazakh – still used Russian as their main language of communication [in 2000]'. One has to keep in mind that Taldykorgan, as the oblast centre, has many workplaces associated with the public sector. In industrial cities, Russian language skills might still prove more decisive (cf. Fierman 2006: 113).
6. The opinion that Russians brought 'civilization' to the Kazakhs is very widespread and can be linked to nationalist discourses in Russia: 'For the moment, devoid of a "self-history", the Russians in Kazakhstan develop their historical discourse based on those of nationalist circles in Russia. It is but a vulgarized and radicalized repetition of the Soviet argumentation in favour of the benefits of a Russian presence and its "civilizing mission" to the Kazakhs' (Peyrouse 2008: 109).
7. But Igor wants his children to learn Kazakh, as he is aware of its increasing importance.

Part III
Non-Migrants' Social Ties

The issue of migration is omnipresent in Kazakhstan. It is a frequent topic of discussion, and questions on subjects such as for whom, and under what circumstances, migration is appropriate are often raised. For instance, while four elderly women and I were having tea and a tart at Vera's sixty-fifth birthday party, Ludmilla began to talk about her son, who has lived in Germany for almost eight years and still does not feel at home there. She admitted that it had always been her wish that he would marry a German wife in order to emigrate to Germany, and though her wish came true, she now realized that it was wrong to have encouraged him to leave his hometown. She had once visited him in Bonn, and there she came to understand that life in Germany is completely different from life in Kazakhstan. Her son, employed by United Parcel Service, works the night shift, is constantly tired, and, worst of all in her opinion, he and his wife have no German friends there. The women all agreed that living in a foreign place is not the best solution for everyone. Raissa, a friend of Ludmilla who also lives in Taldykorgan, then added the story of her own children: immediately after the Soviet Union's collapse, her son decided to leave for Israel, and after a couple of years emigrated from there to Germany. But since he was unable to 'find himself' in Germany, he resettled yet again, this time in San Francisco, where, according to Raissa, he finally feels at home. Raissa's daughter left in the mid-1990s for Germany and moved, some years later, to France, where she still lives. The other women added their relatives' stories, which were equally complicated and had their fill of sorrows (field notes 09/05/2007).

I was left with the impression that they had told their stories, above all, in order to share the heavy burden of loss. All of them had children living in other countries. At the same time, people tell stories about the difficulties of migration to affirm that they made the right decision to stay in Taldykorgan. One has to keep in mind that currently more than eighty per cent of Kazakhstan's Germans have emigrated. Thus, in the course of a few years, many Kazakhstani Germans not only parted company with relatives but also often with former classmates, colleagues, neighbours and friends.

Migration and Social Networks

This section explores the situation of non-migrants with regard to their social embeddedness, in the locality as well as transnationally. While conditions have prompted an out-migration to an 'historic homeland', thereby establishing a transnational social field, this field has been characterized by disruption and resentment and has ultimately widened the gap between those Germans who remained in Kazakhstan and those who emigrated to Germany, which helps to explain the strengthening of a Kazakhstani-German identity over the last two decades. In the past the analysis of migratory processes focused on the migrants themselves and their incorporation into new societies, but more recently the framework of transnationalism has helped to overcome this restricted view of mobility and, furthermore, has encouraged the investigation of social relationships. Through examining social ties by means of network analysis, I, however, also intend to modify some of the assumptions about transnationalism and diaspora.

Migration is not one of anthropology's classical concerns. For a long time a nexus between place, culture and social group informed the research agenda (cf. Schmidt-Lauber 2007: 15). But against the background of globalization theories, the categories 'local', 'regional' and 'national' have been redefined. Hannerz (2007 [1996]) sees the often naturally assumed link between territory, culture and people under challenge, but at the same time he stresses the relevance of personal everyday encounters at the local level. He argues against a mystification of the global, advocating instead for a precise analysis of the interconnectedness of people and meanings. Robertson (1998), by introducing the concept of 'glocalization', argues against the dichotomization of local and global forces. He contends that, though concepts of the 'local' have become formulated in global categories, they are not pure responses to the global. Besides, it is his intention to emphasize 'space' instead of 'time' (ibid.: 201f, 216).

The debate concerning local, national and global categories has been partly inspired by research on migration and conversely has also informed recent concepts and notions concerning migration. The concepts of both diaspora and transnationalism seek to overcome the nation state container view by shifting the focus to 'non-nation based solidarities' (Anthias 1998: 557).[1] Transnationalism is defined by Basch et al. (1997: 7) as a 'process by which immigrants forge and sustain multi-stranded social relations that link together their societies of origin and settlement'. Migrants establish transnational social networks, which also incorporate those who stayed behind into transnational social fields, 'through which ideas, practices, and resources are unequally exchanged, organized, and transformed' (Levitt and Glick Schiller 2004: 1009). Thus, the concept of transnationalism highlights the relevance of concrete webs of personal relationships (Nieswand 2007: 42).[2]

Investigating migrants' networks, of course, is not new.[3] The beginnings of migratory research and urban anthropology can be traced back to the Manchester school in the 1950s and 1960s (Mitchell 1969; cf. also Schweizer 1996). However, the methods developed for studying social networks by Mitchell and his adherents have infrequently been applied in research on migration, and even less so after anthropology's postmodern turn and the rise of concepts such as globalization, diaspora and transnationalism (cf. Boyd 1989: 654f; cf. Giordano 2003: 11).[4] The 'positivistic' approach of network studies and their mathematical outlook have obviously hindered their application by those who investigate transnational social fields.[5] But the risk then is that transnational relations are assumed rather than analysed, and that transnationalism becomes a 'catch-all concept' 'viewing transnational relations in any corner' (Pries 2008: 2; cf. Al-Ali and Koser 2002: 14). Despite all (assumed) global interconnectedness, of equal interest is '(1) Why and when do personal networks fail to emerge, and (2) under what conditions do networks weaken and/or disappear' (Boyd 1989: 655). The current study addresses both questions by additionally paying attention to the effects of (fragile) transnational relationships on the local networks of those who stayed behind.

Furthermore, the oft-cited 'age of migration' (Castles and Miller 1993) primarily refers to the labour migration that occurred after the Second World War (cf. Al-Ali and Koser 2002: 4). The fact that migration has often been associated with development and the search for labour has, firstly, promoted the concept of economic individual decision making, which has been framed in the often criticized model of 'push' and 'pull' factors and, secondly, inspired its critique in that labour migrants are now seen as being embedded in transnational social fields.[6] Other types of migration, such as in the case of Kazakhstani Germans, have taken place on other grounds and, therefore, will add new insights to the study of migration.

Chapter 5 is concerned with local ties, while Chapter 6 focuses on transnational relations. In order to systematically investigate people's relationships, these two chapters are based on the personal social networks and genealogies of Kazakhstani Germans.

Notes

1. The term 'transnationalism' has been coined in the context of U.S. research on immigrants arriving in that country after 1945, whereas the term 'diaspora' has been predominantly used by British researchers who investigate groups of expatriates, immigrants and refugees (Kennedy and Roudometof 2002: 2).
2. This might be seen, however, as only one aspect of a transnational approach, namely *empirical* transnationalism. Khagram and Levitt (2008) distinguish between five aspects:

empirical, methodological, theoretical, philosophical and public transnationalism. Furthermore, Kennedy and Roudometof (2002: 1) advocate for widening 'explorations of transnational communities beyond migrants and diasporas', in order to include, e.g., global communities that are bounded by a shared occupational ethos, political, moral or lifestyle orientation (ibid.: 21). For my work, I only consider empirical and methodological transnationalism, i.e., the field of empirical research on transnational phenomena and appropriate research designs and methods.

3. This is not to say that only the investigation of social networks has had an impact on a transnational approach. In particular, Marcus's concept of a 'multi-sited ethnography' (1995) has influenced 'transnational thinking' (cf. Schmidt-Lauber 2007: 19).

4. Moreover, there is Appadurai's concept of 'global ethnoscapes' (1998), which posits a postnational unbounded space, and thus might be seen as the most postmodern and most radical of all concepts that seek to conceptualize society beyond the nation state (for a critique see Nieswand 2007: 37–40).

5. Network analysts (e.g., Mitchell 1974) have been criticized by anthropologists for maintaining a mechanistic and deterministic view of people's behaviour, for overestimating the role of social networks and for neglecting other crucial aspects of social life. In reaction to such criticism, some network analysts have tried to integrate other 'independent variables' into their explanations for people's actions. For instance, Emirbayer and Goodwin (1994), who followed White's plea (1992) for the inclusion of cognitive data, state that current meanings in a social network have the same explanatory weight as its structure. This, then, also means that the researcher must consider the importance people attach to certain relations, and what such relations mean to them personally.

6. Furthermore, the 'push-pull model' has been criticized for presupposing a sedentary world, which in an 'age of migration' no longer holds true. However, this critique dates back to Petersen's migration typology in which he also criticizes the 'universal sedentary quality' of 'the familiar push-pull polarity' (1958: 258). Moreover, one should certainly keep in mind that at the time of Petersen's writing, shortly after the Second World War, the number of migrants and refugees was enormous, though he is largely referring to mass emigration from Europe to the New World. Thus, as it has often been remarked (especially by historians, e.g., Gungwu 2005), the movement of people through space is hardly a new phenomenon, but rather one of humanity's fundamental characteristics.

Chapter 5
Relations in the Locality
Ethnic Mixing and Missing Kazakhs

People in Kazakhstan often emphasize that their country is home to more than a hundred ethnic groups, and that they have friends among many of them. It was not unusual for Germans or Russians, in particular younger ones, to show me photographs of them dancing or at a barbecue with friends, upon which I was told the details of their friends' ethnic belongings, be they Tatar, Ukrainian, Chechen, Korean and so on. However, the majority group, the Kazakhs, were often missing. It appeared that many Germans were not aware of the implicit contradiction in making a point of how welcoming they were to people of so many nationalities, and yet often not counting Kazakhs among them.

This chapter explores the significance of ethnic belonging with respect to social relations in a locality that has experienced extensive out-migration. To this end, people's personal networks and genealogies (Fischer 1996) are investigated. In light of this study's earlier discussion of the mental schema 'nationality', I also pay attention to the interrelatedness of cognitive representations with regard to questions of 'who is close' and 'who is not' in people's social environments. Moreover, the extent to which different identity types (presented in Chapter 2) are congruent with people's relationships will be examined. The final section takes up Brubaker's criticism (2004) of the notion of 'ethnic group' and explores the question of a German community in Taldykorgan. Across all sections, this chapter pays particular attention to individual variation and shows the substantial variability of Kazakhstani Germans' networks and social power.

The Relevance of Nationality in Personal Networks

The analysis of personal networks is a subfield of network analysis. According to Wellman (2007: 350): 'Personal network analysts use the essence of the network paradigm itself: a focus on relationships, wherever situated, rather than assuming that the world is built on solidary, bounded groups'. The analysis of personal networks today is largely a sociological concern and associated with large-scale surveys, but it also has its roots in anthropological case studies (e.g., Boissevain 1974; Bott 1957) and neighbourhood studies by urban anthropologists (e.g., Mitchell 1969; Sanjek 1982).

A personal (or ego-centred) network is defined as the relations of a single person (cf. Schweizer 1996: 241). The analysis of personal networks produces information about their size, composition and the kinds of social interactions within the networks (ibid.: 249). Usually researchers investigate the types of people in such networks and analyse what kind of support flows through different kinds of networks; e.g., whether friends provide more emotional support than kin (Wellman 2007: 349). Though studies of personal networks, and in particular those studies by urban anthropologists, investigate dense and multiplex relationships at the local level, Wellman (ibid.: 350) stresses that personal network analyses help to 'identify ties wherever they lead' and ultimately also help 'reconceptualizing – and documenting – communities as networks rather than as neighborhoods' (cf. also Berzborn et al. 1998: 18). For this study both are relevant: that is, to investigate multiplex local networks and to see how many and what kind of relations extend beyond the locality.

Determining people's networks is usually done by means of 'name generators'.[1] Questionnaires ask respondents to mention all persons they rely upon for different kinds of support and/or those persons they meet in different types of encounters.[2] I used a slightly altered version of the network questionnaire employed by Berzborn et al. (1998: 3–5) in the social support survey of the International Social Survey Programme (ISSP). The questionnaire comprises twelve hypothetical questions and focuses on social, economic and emotional support, with the last question asking about anybody else who is important to the respondent.[3] It should, however, be noted that the questionnaire mainly gives information about the inner core of someone's personal network, for it tends to disregard 'weak ties' (Granovetter 1973).

On the basis of the network questionnaire, I interviewed thirty Germans, all of whom lived in the city of Taldykorgan. The interviewees cannot be considered a random sample, since they were deliberately chosen to reflect the diversity of Kazakhstani Germans in terms of age, sex, educational background and professional life.[4] Ten of the interviewees were employed as school teachers, journalists, drivers or office clerks. Seven ran their own businesses, such as kiosks, construction companies or photo shops, or directed a hospital. Two were university students, two were housewives, and two received disability benefits and gained additional income by doing various kinds of jobs. The remaining seven persons were retired.

In the following, I will detail the thirty networks by focusing on their ethnic composition. With regard to the twelve support questions (and the additional question 'Who else is important to you?'), the interviewees mentioned, in total,

Table 5.1 Nationality of respondents' relations

	Total	Respondent's age			Respondent's sex	
		18–39	40–59	Above 60	Female	Male
Russian	200	83	70	47	80	120
	40,6%	42,8%	35,0%	47,5%	32,1%	49,2%
German	146	64	52	30	88	58
	29,6%	33,0%	26,0%	30,3%	35,3%	23,8%
Kazakh	78	24	41	13	35	43
	15,8%	12,4%	20,5%	13,1%	14,1%	17,6%
Korean	18	11	7	0	10	8
	3,7%	5,7%	3,5%		4,0%	3,3%
Tatar	14	2	10	2	6	8
	2,8%	1,0%	5,0%	2,0%	2,4%	3,3%
Ukrainian	12	3	7	2	9	3
	2,4%	1,5%	3,5%	2,0%	3,6%	1,2%
Other	15	3	8	4	12	3
	3%	1,5%	4,0%	4,0%	4,8%	1,2%
Unknown	7	3	4	0	6	1
	1,4%	1,5%	2,0%		2,4%	0,4%
Unclear	3	1	1	1	3	0
	0,6%	0,5%	0,5%	1,0%	1,2%	
Total	493	194	200	99	249	244

493 persons with whom they discuss their personal problems, spend their spare time and/or from whom they receive help economically.[5] Table 5.1 displays the ethnic categories of all respondents' relations. About forty per cent are Russian, a little less than a third are German, and only about fifteen per cent are Kazakh. The network size does not vary between men and women, nor between young and middle-aged persons; only elderly people mentioned fewer relations on average.[6] I will highlight two features: women mention more relations with Germans than men do, and middle-aged persons have the most relations with Kazakhs. However, the small size of the sample does not allow for any systematic comparison among the subgroups.

One interesting feature of personal networks is the presence of different kinds of social roles. Table 5.2 reports on the social roles and nationality categories of respondents' relations. In the overall sample, only about a third of relations are kin ties.[7] Furthermore, the categories 'friend' (*drug*) and 'acquaintance' ((*khoroshyj*) *znakomyj*) seem problematic with regard to their unequal application. Men and elderly people tend to use 'acquaintance', whereas younger people and women prefer 'friend'. Since the applied network questionnaire focuses on someone's core network, it is very unlikely that those who mentioned 'acquaintances' are referring to unimportant persons that they hardly know. If one, therefore, collapses the two categories, ties to friends and acquaintances by far outnumber relations with relatives.

Table 5.2 Nationality and social roles

	Family member	Friend	Acquaintance	Neighbour	Colleague
Russian	55 32,9%	74 46,0%	32 41%	28 51,9%	11 33,3%
German	100 59,9%	18 11,2%	18 23,1%	5 9,3%	5 15,2%
Kazakh	4 2,4%	33 20,5%	18 23,1%	13 24,1%	10 30,3%
Korean	0	12 7,5%	1 1,3%	0	5 15,2%
Tatar	2 1,2%	5 3,1%	4 5,1%	2 3,7%	1 3,0%
Ukrainian	0	7 4,3%	2 2,6%	2 3,7%	1 3,0%
Other	4 2,4%	9 5,6%	0	2 3,7%	0
Unknown	0	2 1,2%	3 3,8%	2 3,7%	0
Unclear	2 1,2%	1 0,6%	0	0	0
Total	167	161	78	54	33

Ties to Russians, apart from kin ties, with respect to all social roles are most important, followed by ties to Kazakhs. In other words, on average Germans have more Russian and Kazakh friends, acquaintances, neighbours and colleagues in their core networks than German ones. Thus, one might conclude that an ethnic German community is rather unlikely to exist. On the other hand, it is worth noting that on average about fifteen per cent of their friends, acquaintances, neighbours and colleagues are German, whereas Germans make up only about one per cent of the town's population.[8] I will return to the issue of a German community in the last section of the chapter.

Another basic descriptive aspect of personal networks concerns the kind of support provided by different categories of people. Table 5.3 displays the correlations of different types of support with different ethnic categories. Emotional support and lending money are given in equal shares by Russians and Germans, whereas social and everyday support is provided mostly by Russians. In this respect, the sample reflects what has been documented in several studies (see Belotti 2008: 320–21): friends offer companionship, while emotional and material support is most often provided by relatives. However, though this pattern is clearly visible, some Kazakhstani Germans also rely on Kazakh and Russian friends for both money and emotional support. Furthermore, it is worth noting that there are forty-three ties to Germans who do not provide any support but who were mentioned in answer to the last question, 'Who else is important to

Table 5.3 Nationality and kind of support

	Everyday support	Emotional support	Social support	Lending money	No support
Russian	73	63	81	25	24
	50,3%	39,9%	47,6%	36,8%	27,9%
German	26	62	35	24	43
	17,9%	39,2%	20,6%	35,3%	50,0%
Kazakh	26	16	28	7	11
	17,9%	10,1%	16,5%	10,3%	12,8%
Korean	3	2	14	4	2
	2,1%	1,3%	8,2%	5,9%	2,3%
Tatar	4	3	4	0	3
	2,8%	1,9%	2,4%		3,5%
Ukrainian	6	3	3	4	0
	4,1%	1,9%	1,8%	5,9%	
Other	4	5	3	2	2
	2,7%	3,2%	1,8%	2,9%	2,3%
Unknown	2	2	2	0	1
	1,4%	1,3%	1,2%		1,2%
Unclear	1	2	0	2	0
	0,7%	1,3%		2,9%	
Total	145	158	170	68	86

Note: The table's numbers do not add up to the 493 support ties because some persons provide several kinds of support. As for the last column, 'no support', those persons were only mentioned in answer to the last question 'Who else is important to you?'

you?' Since most of these ties refer to persons living in Germany, their role will be explored in the next chapter on transnational relations.

Research on interethnic relations in Kazakhstan has hardly ever touched on actual relations between Kazakhs and Russians, but the overall impression provided through macro analysis is one of a divide between 'Kazakh' and 'other people' (Dave 2007; Diener 2004; see also Chapter 1). This divide is seen as being 'deeply embedded in semi-official, academic, journalistic and popular references' (Dave 2007: 135), which is why 'Kazakhstan's claims to being an "oasis of stability and ethnic harmony"' is questioned by Dave (ibid.: 139). The separation between 'Kazakhs' and 'others' in state and other discourses is generally reflected in the actual relationships investigated here, since more than two thirds of all ties are to Russians or Germans, and only fifteen per cent to Kazakhs. However, a closer look at the individual networks reveals that such general statements on interethnic relations and the implementation of interethnic harmony do not exhaust the complexity of social relationships.

Firstly, respondents' networks differ remarkably in size. The average size of networks is 16.4 relationships, but eight persons mentioned more than twenty relationships whereas six persons mentioned only between five and ten relationships. Table 5.4 displays individual variation as to the number of relationships.

Table 5.4 Number of relationships

How many relationships did the interviewed Germans mention?				
5–10	11–15	16–20	21–25	More than 25
6 respondents	10 respondents	6 respondents	4 respondents	4 respondents

Table 5.5 Number of relationships to Kazakhs

How many Kazakh relationships did the interviewed Germans mention?			
0	1–2	3–4	5 and more
7 respondents	12 respondents	3 respondents	8 respondents

Most of those Germans who have a small network are either elderly and/or have virtually no contact with their relatives, all of them having left for Germany or Russia and cut off ties. Moreover, one grew up as an orphan, and her son emigrated together with his wife and their children to Israel.

The massive out-migration has impacted on social networks in yet another way: people with small networks tend to complain about their rapidly changing social environment in Taldykorgan. Due to mobility their neighbours have often changed several times over the last fifteen years, and many respondents stated that they simply gave up trying to establish any new contacts. However, most often, it is not only that those Germans with a small network have abandoned making new contacts; most of them also did not mention a single tie to a Kazakh.

Table 5.5 reports on individual variation with regard to the number of relationships to Kazakhs. Seven Germans did not mention even a single Kazakh relationship, and another twelve had only up to two such relationships. Eight Germans, however, had between five and nine Kazakh friends, acquaintances, colleagues and neighbours. Thus, the above-mentioned average of fifteen per cent of relationships with Kazakhs (or 2.5 relations) is misleading,[9] since Germans seem to have either few or no relationships with Kazakhs (and if they have only one or two relationships, those are most likely with neighbours) or quite a few. The networks' size surely accounts for this notable difference, but it does not answer why some have established contacts with Kazakhs while others have not.

Germans with many Kazakh contacts might best be characterized as professionally successful: half of them run their own business, three others are employed and hold a good position, and only one of them is retired, who, however, is fluent in Kazakh since she grew up in a Kazakh settlement. Furthermore, most of them are middle-aged.[10] However, it is important to note that the 'successful Germans' for the most part did not mention ties to particularly influential Kazakhs, for example in the administration. The point is rather that most of them grew up in Taldykorgan, and they usually have already known their Kazakh friends and acquaintances for a very long time. Moreover, they feel at home in Taldykorgan and in Kazakhstan in general, and they refer to themselves as Kazakhstani Germans or as Germans in Kazakhstan. However, a large and diverse network might be seen as decisive for all kinds of self-help systems and for reciprocal favours or *blat* that were particularly important after the Soviet Union's collapse (see Ledeneva 1998 on the importance of *blat* in Russia). Though social capital in general is sometimes assumed to have diminished in the course of transition (ibid.), in the case of people in Taldykorgan, it rather seems that inequalities in terms of social (and economic) capital have become strengthened in recent years, or as Wallace (2003: 21) puts it: 'Social networks can be a way of reinforcing existing social inequalities'.

Those Germans who have few or no ties to Kazakhs cannot easily be placed into a single category. Some of them are openly prejudiced against Kazakhs, and perceive themselves as 'excluded Russians'. For instance, one respondent does not look to his neighbours for daily support but contacts his fairly distant living relatives instead. When asked why, he responded by asking how he could be expected to approach his neighbours, since they are Kazakhs. However, as has been explored in this study's earlier discussion on the concept of nationality and its normative implications, it is widely perceived as unacceptable to categorize and stigmatize people according to their ethnic belonging. In this spirit, most interviewed Germans did not specifically state that they disliked Kazakhs. On the contrary, many stressed during the taped interview that they have Kazakh friends, though they did not mention them in the network questionnaire that had been conducted on a different day.

The point here is not that people are being dishonest. Instead, it appears to reflect a rather generalized sensibility, in which one says he or she has friends belonging to all nationalities (and in particular Kazakh ones), which is a statement more in accordance with the state concept of 'interethnic harmony' than it is an accurate depiction of one's 'real friends'. This is reinforced in the network questionnaire, which tended to generate normative answers.[11] Thus, if a person in general supports the idea of interethnic harmony but does not report any Kazakh relationships in the questionnaire, it is reasonable to conclude that they do not actually have any Kazakh friends or acquaintances.

It is not surprising that Kazakhs are missing or noticeably under-represented in most German social networks. As for the youngest generation, which has the fewest relationships with Kazakhs (see also Table 5.1),[12] the Kazakh language appears to be decisive. In Taldykorgan, Kazakhs below the age of twenty-five speak mostly Kazakh, and non-Kazakhs usually lack proficiency in Kazakh; therefore, social networks are often divided along linguistic lines. On the one hand, non-Kazakh speakers feel excluded when people switch to Kazakh, and on the other, young Kazakhs in particular tend to prefer an exclusively Kazakh environment because they are aware that speaking Kazakh is not appreciated, as well as not fully understood, by non-Kazakhs. This difficulty is less present in older generations since almost all of them speak primarily Russian, and most of them speak only Russian.[13]

On the whole, Kazakhstani-German networks are quite varied. The age and status of respondents appear to exert major influences. Middle-aged persons with high occupational prestige generally have the most relationships, and also the most relationships with Kazakhs. Elderly Germans who do not speak Kazakh generally have small networks, whereas most young people have comparatively large networks with remarkably few Kazakh contacts. The differences in their social environment correspond to the identity types outlined in Chapter 2: those Germans who identify themselves with Kazakhstan and in particular those who do not view German as a subtype of being Russian do indeed have fewer contacts with Russians and more with Kazakhs. Most Germans, however, seem to live ethnically segregated from Kazakhs. Almost all of their ties are to Russians, Germans and other non-Muslim minority groups. This pattern remarkably resembles the mental representation of the arrangement of 'nationality groups' (see Chapter 3). Those with whom most Germans interact are seen as belonging to their category (the 'Russian category'), whereas Kazakhs, Kyrgyz, Uzbeks and other Turkic and/or Muslim categories are conceptualized as different and distant, and indeed ties to them are virtually non-existent. Thus, for most Germans, shared cognitive representation and actual relationships coincide and reinforce one another.

Since people with diverse social relationships usually share this view of the 'ethnic landscape', there is certainly no easy one-to-one representation of cognitive schemas and behaviour. A young German woman in her late twenties told me that most of her friends are Kazakh and not Russian. She said that she has very close Kazakh friends whom she could even phone at night, and she added that those friends were actually not 'very Kazakh' because they are *kulturnie* (well educated). I then asked her whom she would consider closer to Germans: Russians or Kazakhs. She thought about the question for a while before finally answering that Russians remain closer to Germans because both of them are Europeans. But also others perceive that their actual relationships with Kazakhs are better and closer than their relationships with Russians; one of them is Kolya:

> I think that Germans get along better with Kazakhs; the relationship to Russians is not that way. Anyhow, they are to one another as if they're strangers. Why this is the case – nobody ever talked about it openly, but one could always notice that. Even among the children it was noticeable that Kazakhs talked more with Germans, and that the Russians, well, it was just different. Although, that was something nobody mentioned. (Kolya, 48 years old)

Kolya's remark that people did not mention that German-Kazakh relations are (in his view) closer than those between Russians and Germans is suggestive that this view is seen to contradict the shared schema on nationality with its division between 'Christian European' and 'Muslim Central Asian' groups, as has been outlined earlier in this work. But his statement also shows that people's relations and how they evaluate them does not have to be in line with their concept of nationality. If, however, the networks of most people change in the future, it is reasonable to assume that their view of how nationality groups are organized will change as well.

The Relevance of Nationality in Marriages

This section explores the marriage patterns of Kazakhstani Germans, primarily relying on the genealogies of the same thirty persons whose networks are presented above. With respect to the genealogies, one should keep in mind that several waves of forced and intentional migrations make it very difficult for most interviewees to give detailed information, even about their close kin, since their relatives are very often spread over a huge territory, from Tashkent to Berlin. Therefore, most of them focused on their closest kin, usually only providing information about kinship up to two grades and going back, when they could at all, only as far as the period before the Second World War in which their parents or grandparents lived.[14]

On average, respondents gave information about forty-nine relatives; however, there is a remarkable variation between six and 102. On average, thirty of the forty-nine mentioned relatives are German and fifteen Russian, and altogether the interviewees mentioned only six Kazakh relatives. Table 5.6 displays the total figures of the relatives' nationality.

Table 5.6 Relatives' nationalities

	To which nationality do the relatives belong?
German	890
	60,7%
Russian	441
	30,1%
Ukrainian	15
	1%
Kazakh	6
	0,4%
Other	24
	1,6%
Unknown	89
	6%
Total	1465

As to individual variation, one should note that while there is no single 'pure' German genealogy, only four persons indicate more Russian than German relatives. All of them are above the age of sixty, and themselves have only German ancestors, but are married to Russians. Their children and grandchildren are Russian, which is also characteristic of the nationality of their brothers' and sisters' offspring, if they are also married to Russians. Thus, opting for a Russian nationality for one's children is typical for this generation.[15]

Table 5.7 reports on interethnic marriages. All in all, the interviewed persons gave information about 487 marriages. Marriages between Germans and between Russians and Germans appear in roughly equal shares (36–37 per cent), while marriages between Russians are at thirteen per cent. Thus, one might question the source of the Table 5.6 figure showing the number of German relatives at sixty per cent. This high percentage of German relatives partly derives from the fact that marriages between Germans are more likely in older generations to have produced more children. Moreover, one has to keep in mind that, since the 1980s, children from interethnic marriages between Germans and Russians are more likely to become German than Russian.

As for the situation in present-day Taldykorgan, by far most Germans are married to Russians; however, their children are also very likely to become German. Most of the reported marriages between Germans are either among those who live in Germany and/or involve their parents' and grandparents' generation.

Marriages between Kazakhs and Germans are the most uncommon, and since friendship between young Germans (as well as Russians) and Kazakhs is not very widespread, it is unlikely there will be an increase in such marriages in the future. One major obstacle to a Kazakh-German friendship and marriage is, as has been

Table 5.7 Spouses' nationalities

German-German	180
	36,9%
Russian-German	174
	35,7%
Russian-Russian	66
	13,5%
German-Ukrainian	10
	2%
German-Kazakh	6
	1,2%
Other	21
	4,3%
Unknown	30
	6,1%
Total	487

mentioned earlier, the increasing language divide. Furthermore, marriage plans in particular are linked most often to future plans, and many young Germans are considering migrating to Germany or Russia. Although in most cases this is only one plan for the future among others, a Kazakh spouse would most likely preclude such an option because it is assumed that a Kazakh wife, and in particular a Kazakh husband, would prefer to stay with their family in Kazakhstan.

When asked directly why there are so few Kazakh-German alliances, people tend to cite cultural distinctiveness. The Kazakh way of living is assumed to differ too much from the habits of Russians and Germans. Very often, this is exemplified by the very different wedding ceremonies – if the wedding itself would cause so many difficulties, then how could two such different persons live together successfully? Therefore, alliances between Germans and Russians seem to be the main marriage pattern for the upcoming generation of Germans. But many young Germans also mentioned that their favourite choice would be a German spouse. The earlier exploration in this study of discourses on nationality suggested that ethnic affiliations are not, or should no longer be, important in 'real life', i.e., beyond practices such as distinct traditional cuisines. However, friendships, and in particular marriage patterns, clearly indicate the opposite.

Is There a 'German Community' in Taldykorgan?

The notion that when the term 'ethnic group' is used, there is an accompanying assumption that a community of such people actually exists, has been the subject of criticism (Brubaker 2004). But while people who belong to one ethnically defined category are certainly not expected to all know each other, it can nonetheless be investigated as to what extent their social networks are ethnically homogeneous, or for which social roles or what kind of support ethnicity might be relevant.

The low number of German neighbours in the reported networks has already indicated that a compact German settlement is very unlikely to exist in Taldykorgan. Furthermore, social networks do not appear to be ethnically homogeneous since, on average, Germans have only five ties to other Germans (approximately three to relatives, and two to friends, acquaintances, colleagues or neighbours; see also Table 5.2). But again individual variation is significant; Table 5.8 displays the number of ties to Germans.

Table 5.8 Number of relationships to Germans

How many ties to Germans did respondents mention?				
0	1–2	3–5	6–10	10 and more
1 respondent	5 respondents	17 respondents	4 respondents	3 respondents

Most of the respondents mentioned between three and five ties to Germans, but three had more than ten, and six had no more than two. Generally, I did not have the impression that most Germans attach great importance to their friends or acquaintances being Russian or German. However, those Germans who share the identity type of Peter (see Chapter 2), and who feel discriminated against by Russians, not only have more ties to Kazakhs, as has been indicated above, but often tend to perceive relationships to Germans as more reliable:

> Just even the fact that someone is German and I'm German creates a kind of trust. With others relations are, of course [also trusting], but not so much. Why this is so – I don't know. Well, with Germans it's easier because you know that you're German and he's German, that's why you think that he's never going to cheat on you, and you're never going to cheat on him. With other nationalities, there's fraud. There is a kind of distrust because of someone's national belonging. This is so but generally I have friends of all nationalities.
> *RS: As you get to know someone, when does it become important to which nationality that person belongs?*
> This is not extraordinarily important but, of course, I prefer when someone is German. But generally it is not very important. But there's something, maybe it comes from the soul, from childhood, or whatever, that a German for whatever reason seems to be a person that is more honest than other people. This is how it is seen. (Kolya, 48 years old)

However, the identity type of Rosa (see Chapter 2), for whom a German identity is equally important as it is for Peter, cannot be identified by a particular network structure with more connections to Germans. Rosa herself, for instance, indicated only three ties to Germans. This, certainly, is no surprise since it has been argued that being German became important for her precisely because all of her relatives, and by far most of her German friends with whom she grew up in the German village, have emigrated to Germany. Thus, the number of ties to Germans only partly corresponds to someone's self-perception or, in other words, to the relevance someone attaches to a German identity.

Those persons with the most ties to Germans are the above specified 'successful businesspeople', who also have the most ties to Kazakhs. Often their German relatives work together with them, and the fact that their business is successful appears to play a role in preventing emigration (see also the case of Edik in Chapter 2). Moreover, those Germans who run their own businesses, and other Germans who are economically and/or politically influential, are inclined to know and help each other, and in this context I had the impression that it eventually makes a difference whether someone is German or Russian in such networks. There are quite a few Germans who hold important positions in Taldykorgan (but not all of them are part of this sample): the head of a hospital, a bank director, the head of an influential sports club, and others who have construction companies. Only by chance was I present when credits were granted and work contracts allocated, one of which was several times affirmed by saying that 'Germans should ultimately always help each other'. But when directly asked about the significance of a German ethnic identity in Taldykorgan, most Germans make a point of supporting the concept of interethnic harmony, which they interpret as diminishing the relevance of someone's ethnic belonging.

Furthermore, the German Rebirth organization and its financial potential, as well as personal contacts with others in Germany, account for the status of Germans in Taldykorgan. The impact of transnational ties with Germany is the topic of the following chapter; the role of the Rebirth organization as a 'transnational institution' will be explored in Part IV.

Summary

The social relations of Kazakhstani Germans generally reveal contradictions with regard to the nationality concept: while statements concerning (international) friends appear to promote the 'friendship of peoples', actual networks tend to highlight the national binarism between Kazakhs (and other Muslim Central Asians) and Russians (and other European Christians). Again, this supports Herzfeld's (2005) assertion that binarism is a strategy that seeks to deny its own existence. But in investigating the genealogies and social networks of Germans in Taldykorgan, what is initially striking is the finding that, despite the envisioned ethnic mixing, it is above all ties to Kazakhs that are often absent. Moreover, actual relationships reveal remarkable individual variation that partly corresponds to the identity types discussed in Chapter 2. Those who have significantly more contacts with Kazakhs usually refer to themselves as Germans living in a Kazakhstani homeland, while those with few or no relations to Kazakhs primarily see themselves as 'excluded Russians'.

Furthermore, network analysis demonstrates the links between the composition of people's relations, the significance of nationality, and social as well as economic power. As has been shown earlier in this study, nationality is not necessarily expressed differently in conversation, but it is definitely lived in different ways, which has consequences with respect to a person's social and economic status. The condition of out-migration has increased differences related to an individual's social power, in particular because relationships to Kazakhs have consequently gained in importance. However, equally important are transnational ties, which will be explored in the next chapter.

Notes

1. A different approach is 'Boissevain's following people around' (Wellman 2007: 352). Such an approach, however, does not regard ties outside of one's locality.
2. Schweizer (1996: 245f) advises not to use predefined roles such as 'friend' and to ask someone to list all his 'friends', instead of asking for all persons upon whom he relies for various kinds of support – because roles are never clearly defined and they might not exhaust a person's network.
3. Firstly, the questionnaire generates a list of actual persons. In a second step, the respondent is asked to provide information about the listed persons: age, nationality, place of residence, profession, religious affiliation and role (whether the person is viewed, for example, as a friend, colleague or neighbour). Additional questions ask how often the two people see each other and talk to each other on the phone. For the version of the questionnaire that I used, see the Appendix.
4. It has been suggested that deliberately choosing respondents might be the best option during fieldwork (cf. Schweizer 1996: 243). I conducted the questionnaire towards the end of my fieldwork. With all of the interviewees, I had conducted life story interviews beforehand. The thirty are split equally with respect to gender. Eleven of the interviewed Germans are between the ages of 18 and 39, eleven between the ages of 40 and 59, and eight persons are above the age of 60. The two age clusters from 18–39 and 40–59 each consists of six male and five female respondents, whereas the cluster above the age of 60 consists of five female and three male respondents. This distribution reflects different life expectancies for women and men.
5. On average, the interviewees mentioned 16.4 relationships, whereby the total number of mentioned persons ranges from five to thirty-seven. For comparison, the average size of the personal networks reported by Berzborn et al. (1998: 6–8) in Cosa Mesa/California is 10.3.
6. Elderly people mentioned on average 12.4 relations, middle-aged persons 18.2, and younger respondents 17.6 relations.
7. For comparison, 48.3 per cent are kin ties in the personal networks reported by Berzborn et al. (1998: 6–8) in the presumably 'highly mobile' and 'atomistic' Cosa Mesa/California (ibid.: 1).
8. Almost all ties to German friends, acquaintances, colleagues and neighbours exist within Taldykorgan. In the overall sample, there is only one friend and two acquaintances in Germany.
9. The average size of a network is 16.4.
10. Five of the eight persons with more than five relationships to Kazakhs are in the 40–59 age range; of the remaining three, two are younger, one older. The person's sex does not seem to be relevant: five Germans with many ties to Kazakhs are female, but all in all they mention slightly fewer relationships with Kazakhs than male respondents (see also Table 5.1).
11. Firstly, the network questionnaire generates cognitive data, and people systematically simplify when confronted with cognitive tasks. Secondly, most questions are hypothetical and begin with 'Suppose you …', which 'might have caused the informants to think of whom one should report instead of whom they actually asked for support the last time they needed it' (Berzborn et al. 1998: 14).
12. Seven of the eleven interviewed Germans between the ages of 18 and 39 mentioned two or fewer ties to Kazakhs.

13. Fierman (2006: 103) suggests that the elimination of mixed schools with both Kazakh and Russian language classes results in a linguistic segregation that might create greater social tension. As for Taldykorgan, schools are either Kazakh-language-only schools or mixed.
14. Certainly, there are 'experts' among the Kazakhstani Germans who collect extensive information about their genealogies and who therefore know much more about their relatives and ancestors. However, they are the exception, and though their knowledge is valid as background information about migration and marriage patterns, my interest here is with the knowledge, and more importantly, the actual relationships that 'ordinary people' have.
15. In cases of interethnic marriage, people usually referred to the children's passport entry. In only six per cent of cases were respondents unsure about someone's nationality (see Table 5.6).

Chapter 6

Disruption in the Transnational Social Field

In Taldykorgan, a middle-aged woman confided to me that her sisters, living in Germany, had not informed her of their grandmother's death because they were afraid of being obligated to pay for flying her out for the funeral. She did not learn about the death until six months after the funeral. At the beginning of my fieldwork, most people tended to paint a picture of a relatively idyllic family world, but after spending a few months establishing a certain level of intimacy, I began to hear stories of disappointing relationships with relatives in Germany. Ties in Germany affect people's lives in Kazakhstan: not so much because of financial support that the latter might receive from the former; rather, the transnational condition provokes feelings of disruption and resentment among Kazakhstani Germans as well as pride at having stayed in one's hometown.

This chapter investigates the impact of the migratory process on the present-day relationships of Kazakhstani Germans with relatives and friends in Germany. It will be shown that leaving for the 'historic homeland' was a decisive act insofar as such relatives and friends left with no intention of returning. Furthermore, since emigrating was perceived as the socially acceptable choice in the early 1990s, those who remained behind were often denigrated as losers or 'abnormal persons', both by those who had left and by non-Germans in Taldykorgan. Therefore one had to have, or subsequently had to create, good reasons for staying.

The concepts of transnationalism (Basch et al. 1997; Pries 2008) and diaspora (R. Cohen 1997; Safran 1991) have helped me to assess the interplay of identities and networks. This chapter points out that ties to Germany have ultimately fostered a local Kazakhstani-German identity, insofar as Kazakhstani Germans today, more than ever before, distinguish themselves from Germany's Germans and even from the relatives who live there. However, it is primarily persons with substantial social capital, which typically implies a certain elevated status, who have the power to form such identities.

Relatives and Friends Abroad

This first section provides an account of the transnational ties of Kazakhstani Germans. The 'geographical spread' (Berzborn et al. 1998: 7f) of people's social ties is one of the basic descriptive features of personal social networks. I begin by exploring the thirty genealogies that were introduced in the previous chapter and analysed there with regard to interethnic relations. In the context of this chapter it is important to know where the relatives in the genealogies currently live, as shown in Table 6.1.

The vast majority of the interviewees' relatives live abroad, either in Germany or Russia, whereas only about one fifth have remained in Kazakhstan. As indicated in the previous chapter, most interviewees only mention their close relatives, in particular regarding their kin in Russia and Germany, since they often do not know whether, for example, their cousins living in Germany have children or not. One young German told me that only two months ago, when her relatives who had emigrated to Germany in 1991 came to visit them for the first time, did she discover that her uncle has two children; she could not communicate with them, however, because they do not know Russian.

Furthermore, almost two thirds of the interviewed Kazakhstani Germans have close kin – siblings, parents or children – who live in Germany or Russia.[1] For instance, Tanya's parents live in Germany while her son lives in Russia, and Igor's older brother lives with his family in Berlin while his younger sister lives in Omsk. However, while seven persons do not have any kinship ties to Germany,[2] only two are without relatives in Germany or Russia.[3] Therefore, the reported kinship networks are extraordinarily transnational, spanning from Kazakhstan to Russia and Germany, and in particular the large number of close relatives living

Table 6.1 Residence of kin

Germany	549
	43,4%
Russia	304
	24,1%
Taldykorgan	249
	19,7%
Kazakhstan (other)	63
	5,0%
Other	19
	1,5%
Unknown	80
	6,3%
Total	1264

Note: The genealogies gave information about 1465 kinship ties. However, 201 relatives are deceased and therefore not included in this table.

Table 6.2   Residence of supporting persons

	Total	Respondent's age			Respondent's sex	
		18–39	40–59	Above 60	Female	Male
Taldykorgan	383	145	152	86	197	186
	77,7%	74,7%	76,0%	86,9%	80,7%	74,7%
Germany	42	28	12	2	7	35
	8,5%	14,4%	6,0%	2,0%	2,9%	14,1%
Kazakhstan (far away)	24	8	12	4	15	9
	4,9%	4,1%	6,0%	4,0%	6,1%	3,6%
Kazakhstan (nearby)	22	7	13	2	13	9
	4,5%	3,6%	6,5%	2,0%	5,3%	3,6%
Russia	20	6	10	4	10	10
	4,1%	3,1%	5,0%	4,0%	4,1%	4,0%
China	1	0	1	0	1	0
	0,2%		0,5%		0,4%	
Israel	1	0	0	1	1	0
	0,2%			1,0%	0,4%	
Total	493	194	200	99	244	249

abroad suggests that transnational networks also provide support to those who have stayed in Taldykorgan. To that end, I now turn to the personal networks that have been explored in the previous chapter. To recap, the thirty interviewees mentioned 493 support ties.

Table 6.2 indicates that almost four out of five supporting persons live in Taldykorgan, with 8.5 per cent in Germany and only about five per cent in Russia.[4] However, the number of transnational support relations seems to be dependent on the respondent's sex and age. In particular, young male Germans rely much more on support from Germany than older persons and women. Though the sample size does not allow for a generalized statement, it is reasonable to assume that younger people keep in touch with their relatives abroad more easily by using the internet. At the time of my fieldwork in 2007, there were still a number of households that did not have a main telephone line, and phone calls from Kazakhstan to Germany were approximately twice as expensive as those from Germany to Kazakhstan and, thus, for many people, simply unaffordable or at the relatives' initiative. Furthermore, since a regular mail service has essentially broken down in Taldykorgan, the only safe way to mail letters and parcels is by paying for a special delivery service.

Personal networks also provide information about the kind of relationship, i.e., whether the persons addressed are relatives, friends, acquaintances, neighbours or colleagues, as shown in Table 6.3. With regard to transnational ties to Germany, one should notice that over ninety per cent of those mentioned are family members; friends and acquaintances are of little account. That the interviewees referred to eight friends in Russia suggests that migrating there is often

Table 6.3 Role of supporting persons and place of residence

	Taldykorgan	Germany	Kazakhstan (far away)	Kazakhstan (nearby)	Russia	Other
Family member	100	39	8	7	11	2
	26,1%	92,8%	33,3%	31,8%	55%	100%
Friend	128	1	13	11	8	0
	33,4%	2,4%	54,2%	50,0%	40,0%	
Acquaintance	69	2	3	3	1	0
	18%	4,8%	12,5%	13,6%	5%	
Neighbour	54	0	0	0	0	0
	14,1%					
Colleague	32	0	0	1	0	0
	8,4%			4,5%		
Total	383	42	24	22	20	2

Table 6.4 Place of residence and kind of support

	Everyday support	Emotional support	Social support	Lending money	Total
Taldykorgan	140	130	151	52	473
	96,6%	82,3%	88,8%	76,5%	87,4%
Kazakhstan (nearby)	4	6	8	5	23
	2,8%	3,8%	4,7%	7,4%	4,3%
Kazakhstan (far away)	1	10	4	5	20
	0,7%	6,3%	2,4%	7,4%	3,7%
Russia	0	6	5	4	15
		3,8%	2,9%	5,9%	2,8%
Germany	0	5	2	2	9
		3,2%	1,2%	2,9%	1,7%
China	0	1	0	0	1
		0,6%			0,2%
Total	145	158	170	68	541

Note: The table's numbers do not add up to the 493 support ties because some persons provide several kinds of support while others, who were only mentioned in answer to 'Who else is important to you?', provide no support.

considered temporary – at least initially – by young people, who have gone there to study. Therefore, it seems that friendships with those in Russia are not broken off as easily as friendships with persons who have emigrated to Germany. I will return to this point in the subsequent section.

Finally, I address the kind of support that is provided by relations in Taldykorgan, Germany and Russia, as can be seen in Table 6.4. Again, the table underlines the enormous importance of local relationships, with almost ninety per cent of all supporting persons living in Taldykorgan. Of further interest is that only nine of the forty-two relationships to Germany indicated in Table 6.2 actually provide some kind of support, whereas the other thirty-three persons were only mentioned in response to the final question, 'Who else is important to you?'

Table 6.5 Number of relationships to Germany

How many relationships to persons in Germany did the interviewed Germans mention?				
0	1–2	3–5	6–9	10 and more
19 respondents	6 respondents	3 respondents	0 respondents	2 respondents

Additionally, only two persons living in Germany would be asked for money, and only five persons in Germany are relied upon for emotional support, after which the questionnaire explicitly asks about the migration decision.[5] Although only twenty relations to persons in Russia were indicated, three quarters of them provide some level of actual support, a much more significant number than nine out of forty-two.

Consequently, transnational relationships to Germany appear to be fragile. Germans in Taldykorgan usually do not ask their relatives for help or advice, and close relatives in Germany are mostly not even mentioned in answer to 'Who else is important to you?' Table 6.5 shows that nineteen of the thirty respondents did not mention any relationship to Germany. Since I knew from the life story interviews and genealogies that most interviewees had close relatives in Germany, I asked them after we had finished the network questionnaire why they did not mention their son, sister or mother. Sometimes the respondents excused themselves for having forgotten them, and asked me to add them to their list because their relatives in Germany were 'of course important'.[6] Other responses, however, were marked by bitterness. In about half of the cases, people told me that most of their relatives had cut all ties, and many had never returned to Kazakhstan to visit them.[7]

Exodus to an 'Historic Homeland'

This section addresses the subject of 'lost relatives' by taking a closer look at the peculiarities of Kazakhstani Germans' out-migration, including how the exodus of relatives to the 'historic homeland' (*istoricheskaya rodina*) has complicated present-day relationships. In the 1980s, the opportunity to migrate to Germany depended on an invitation from a relative already living in Germany.[8] In some genealogies such persons were listed; often the first nuclear families emigrated in the late 1980s, while the rest, as many as ten families, followed them after the Soviet Union's dissolution in 1991 and 1992. Genealogies in which such an initiating person from Germany was beyond a particular Kazakhstani German's kinship typically have very diverse migration patterns, since applications for immigration were made at a later date.

Overwhelmed by the influx of immigrants from the USSR in the late 1980s, German politicians hastily passed new immigration laws. A June 1990 law demanded that applicants had to fill out the application form while in

Kazakhstan. In 1992 a quota of 200,000 immigrants per year was introduced, and in 1996 a language test was instituted (Eisfeld 1999: 188f). Such immigration restrictions resulted in applicants having to wait several years before finally learning whether their immigration request had been allowed or denied.[9] Many families, while awaiting a decision, opted for migrating to Russia, particularly during 1995–97 when the city's infrastructure was on the verge of collapse. Some of those emigrants have returned to Taldykorgan in recent years or finally managed to emigrate to Germany.

According to the genealogies I collected, migration to Russia is also triggered by personal connections and the spouse's nationality. It is often the case that a son or brother stayed in Russia after having completed his military service or having graduated from university. Moreover, the spouse's nationality often caused different migration trajectories: a brother or sister married to a German is very likely to live in Germany, while someone married to a Russian will live in either Germany, Russia or Taldykorgan. Marriages between Germans living in Russia are the most uncommon. As for the generation raised during the 1950s, the tendency appears to be that all siblings married only Russians or only Germans, and therefore all of them are very likely to live in either Germany or Russia.[10]

To illustrate the effects of migration on families, I begin with the example of Tamara (see Figure 6.1). Her father and mother were born in Ukraine in, respectively, 1910 and 1911. Three of her siblings were born before the Second World War. In 1941, Tamara's relatives were deported by the German Wehrmacht to Poland, and some of them farther west to Germany. Only her mother's youngest sister managed to stay in Germany; all the others were ultimately deported by the Soviet Army to Siberia. Her father lost all of his relatives; her mother's siblings and their families survived. Only in 1949 did her parents meet again, and in 1950, Tamara and her twin sister were born, still in Siberia. Eleven years later, her parents moved together with their children to Taldykorgan. Her mother's

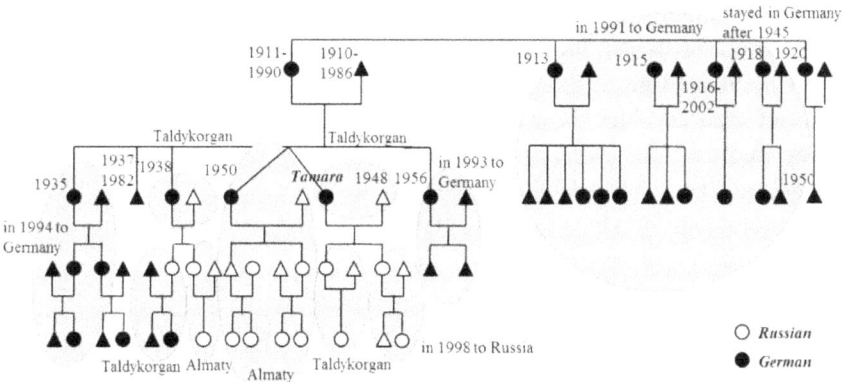

Figure 6.1 Genealogy of Tamara

sister had migrated to Almaty some years before and the other three siblings moved to the vicinity of Almaty in the following years.

Tamara says that her father had always been against emigrating to Germany because he had been there and he knew that the Germans would not accept them. Tamara's parents died before the Soviet Union collapsed, but her mother's sister, who has lived in Germany since 1941, invited her siblings with their families to immigrate to Germany. In 1991, all of them decided to leave Kazakhstan and immigrate to their 'historic homeland'. Since then, Tamara has not seen any of them. Finally, in 1993, her youngest sister, along with her family, moved to Germany; in 1994, her oldest sister followed. Both of them are married to Germans. Moreover, in 1998 her daughter moved together with her husband to Russia. Today only Tamara's older daughter and one of her sisters live in Taldykorgan, while another sister lives in Almaty. Tamara says that she is very happy in Taldykorgan and that she will always keep in mind what her father told her about Germany.

In the support questionnaire, Tamara did not mention any of her relatives in Germany. She does not have any contact with aunts, uncles or cousins living in Germany, for two reasons that have proved quite typical among Kazakhstani Germans with whom I interacted. Firstly, the time period in which emigration occurred is significant. For those who emigrated in the very early 1990s (which is the vast majority), contacts are most likely to be weak, simply because Kazakhstan's infrastructure almost collapsed during the 1990s. In particular, in the countryside, it was nearly impossible to make a phone call or send or receive a letter, not to mention that the internet was not yet available. Under these circumstances, many Kazakhstani Germans simply 'lost' their relatives, at least their distant relatives.

Secondly, the emigrants' motivation is important. Those who left Kazakhstan were mostly unsettled by the collapse of the Soviet Union, the changing economic system,[11] and the creation of a new nation state (cf. Brown 2005: 628; cf. Diener 2004: 33f, 89; cf. also Peyrouse 2007 for the out-migration of Kazakhstani Russians). Furthermore, many of the emigrants had long dreamed of living in the land of their ancestors, and once the opportunity arose, many did not even consider the possibility of ever coming back. They sold everything, and took their leave forever in order to start a new life in their 'historic homeland' (Ingenhorst 1997; Pfister-Heckmann 1998; Römhild 1998). This accounts in part for why most of them did not actively establish a 'transnational social field'.

This scenario, however, refers only to relations with relatives and friends in Germany; relations with those living in Russia seem to be more stable and, generally, less complicated. This again has to do with the time period and motivation: migration to Russia – as far as Kazakhstani Germans are concerned – mostly occurred later than migration to Germany; and I never heard anyone refer to

Figure 6.2 Letters and parcels are no longer delivered home (photo: R. Sanders, 2007).

Russia as a 'historic homeland'. Hence, for those who emigrated to Russia, the option to return to Kazakhstan was more important, and consequently, so is the need to keep in touch with one's relatives and friends in Kazakhstan.

Returning to the case of Tamara, who still is in touch with her sisters in Germany: she told me that her sisters, now living in Germany for almost fifteen years, are still 'close to her heart, somehow'. However, when they call her, Tamara says that they actually have nothing to talk about; they have their lives and she has hers, and, in a way, they have become strangers to one another. But Tamara also says that there were times when she was very angry with her sisters. In the difficult years of 1996 and 1997, Tamara's sisters came to visit her, but instead of offering to help her out financially, they expected her to host them for several weeks for free and even dared to show photographs of their new cars and furniture. Tamara says that, after having been humiliated by them once too often, she would never ask them for help.

Again, Tamara's story reflects the experience of many Kazakhstani Germans, as indicated above by the analysis of the network questionnaire. Most of them are still in touch with their very close kin living abroad, but the relationships are described as complicated. For instance, Anna, a 27-year-old journalist, told me that both she and her mother would find it extremely embarrassing to ask any of their numerous relatives in Germany for help. When they call her, she always simply says that they are doing well, regardless of their situation. Others told me that their relatives tried to cut all ties because they did not want to help them and were afraid of being asked for financial support.[12] Remarkably, it sometimes happened that a couple, whom I interviewed separately, responded to the question of supporting relatives in highly contradictory ways. While the women often told me that 'of course they help and everything is fine', it was usually the men who openly complained that the relatives were not helpful.

Feelings of shame and pride appear to be pivotal in this transnational field, relating mainly to how people expect a family to act. It is often stated (Dietz 1996: 127; Ingenhorst 1997: 172; Schieffer 2005; cf. also Römhild 1998: 202) that Russian Germans foster a densely interconnected web of kinship relations and hold family life in high esteem. Therefore, as indicated above, several related nuclear families often emigrated at the same time, while cases of individual persons migrating were an exception (cf. also Dietz 2006: 125). Separated families are generally perceived as a great misfortune, and blame is accorded depending on the circumstances; for example, those who deliberately stayed behind in Kazakhstan are considered to have acted in violation of what is expected of a family member, whereas those who left their previous homeland and subsequently cut all ties to those who remained are likewise accused of subverting family life.

Similarly, the case of Rosa, presented in Chapter 2, must be viewed against this background. Rosa emigrated to Germany twice, but each time found it too difficult to stay there. That she is the only one from her family who remains in Kazakhstan is a source of distress for her. She did not mention her relatives in the support questionnaire, explaining that she feels guilty for having left 'rich Germany', and that she has to prove to her relatives that she can live without their help. After her second attempt to live in Germany, there were months when she hardly had enough to eat, but she was so ashamed that she could not bring herself to ask any family members for help.

In particular those who were not permitted to immigrate expect their family in Germany to help them.[13] In order to explain their relatives' wrongdoing, which violates the unwritten rule of 'helping the family', many talk at length about how life in Germany has changed their relatives, as exemplified by Irma:

> Well, here they're this kind of people, but when they go to Germany, within one, two years, they are completely different – because there, it is not possible to live in another way. There, you have to live this way; you have to be energetic – but here, not very much. (Irma, 45 years old)

Most often their relatives in Germany are perceived as arrogant persons who now only think of making money. One man even told me that he hates Germany because of how the country has corrupted his relatives.

Indeed, in some cases family relationships were strained even before discussions about emigration, and in fact were part of the reason someone chose not to emigrate. Peter (see Chapter 2) is one such example:

> In Germany, I now only have my younger sister and my mother. I called her [his sister] several times, but I couldn't reach her. Why, I don't know. How is this possible? Well, she moved there from Russia. Right after school she went to Russia, but we still were in contact, we wrote each other, she came to visit us as long as my father was still alive. But the contact was not very intensive. And, of course, we have also changed: she became Russian, and I, Kazakh. You see, she is very different, her attitude to life, and this is how it is. (Peter, 56 years old)

Peter did not sustain a close relationship with his sister before she left for Germany, which is why they did not keep in touch after she finally moved to Germany. Though Kazakhstani Germans – and Russian Germans in general – are characterized as family oriented, the case of Peter is not a rare exception. Furthermore, many Kazakhstani Germans, who were deported from Ukraine or the Volga Republic to Siberia, decided – after the abolishment of *komandatura* – to move to the southern part of Kazakhstan or Kyrgyzstan because of the better climatic conditions. This migration wave split families, with some staying in Siberia while others left for Kazakhstan. Stoll (2007: 116f) emphasizes the importance of migratory networks in facilitating the logistics of emigration. For this reason Kazakhstani Germans such as Peter are unlikely to emigrate on their own because they lack the necessary social capital in Germany, i.e., access to information about immigrations laws, agencies, and so on.

It is important, however, to equally present a slightly different version of the migration story and its transnational implications, i.e., those Germans who have deliberately remained in Kazakhstan because they have achieved a good position or are running a successful business, mostly accomplished during years of waiting for immigration permission, and who usually have many supporting ties to Germany. Certainly, those connections help some of them to run their businesses, but it also appears that their success has facilitated good relationships with relatives in Germany, in part because any sense of anger and shame is much less of an issue.

Figure 6.3 Almost as in Germany: new houses in Taldykorgan (photo: R. Sanders 2007)

One such example is Olga, who decided to stay in Kazakhstan because of her job. She is the director of a bank branch in Taldykorgan, and describes her family situation as follows:

> In our family, I'm the eldest daughter. I have one brother who lives in Germany, and one sister who lives in Russia. Through the emergence of Perestroika, and when the Soviet Union fell apart, probably, people felt such panic – where to go? Interethnic questions came up. During Soviet times, somehow, we didn't pay much attention to interethnic questions. Well, in the beginning of the 1990s, the following happened: my brother and my sister went to Russia, and I stayed here. Several times they tried to convince me to go with them to Germany. But I, for instance, do not know the language, I know it very badly. But they didn't know it either. I think that you have to struggle everywhere. Germany also did not prepare any gifts for us. When someone is not needed in his home country, then, the more he will not be needed there [in Germany]. At that time, my daughter studied at university, and yes, they left. My brother couldn't immigrate to Germany without our mother; therefore, she left together with him, my sister stayed in Russia, and I here – though, until 1991, we all had lived together. This is of course such a tragedy in our family that we split up. Well, now I live together with my family here, I work here, and we visit each other.
>
> …
>
> You see, for us, for Germans, this problem [not being integrated into society] comes up everywhere.[14] For instance, my relatives who went

to Germany, they have so many problems in Germany. They say they do not get any good jobs, or whatever. But, this is not the problem; the main problem is the lack of language knowledge. Without the language, they're simply not able to do anything else. When I go there, they say to me, 'People offend us here'. But I say: 'Nobody offends you here. Your level of language proficiency simply does not allow for other work. If you knew German sufficiently, you could do the same work as they do. Why should people support you?' (Olga, 55 years old)

In particular, the 'successful' Kazakhstani Germans tend to criticize their relatives in Germany for not being active, for not sufficiently knowing the German language, and even for not being integrated. By flipping the argument in this way, it is no longer the Kazakhstani Germans who have to justify why they decided to stay in Kazakhstan, but those in Germany who must justify their decision for leaving.

Views on Germany

Kazakhstan's German minority is commonly referred to as a diaspora (Akiner 2005; Brown 2005; Diener 2004; Pohl 2008; see also Oh 2006 on the Korean 'diaspora' in Kazakhstan). The term 'diaspora', in its broadest sense, implies feelings of belonging to an imagined or real 'historic homeland'. But since it has most often been applied to the Jewish experience of diaspora, the term also connotes oppression and 'moral degradation' (Safran 1991: 83). Departing from the 'ideal type' of the Jewish diaspora, the notion of diaspora has been used as a descriptive typological tool for the analysis of transnational migration and ethnic relations. Robin Cohen (1997), for instance, developed a diaspora typology that comprises seven distinct types, in which only the first two are characterized by victimhood. But the expansion of the concept to include 'trade diasporas' and 'labour diasporas' (Cohen 1997) is also criticized. For instance, Anthias (1998: 557) remarks that diaspora is an 'over-used but under-theorized term' (cf. also Brubaker 2005).

A second interpretation of diaspora is concerned with 'diaspora experiences' (Hall 1990) and 'diaspora consciousness' (Clifford 1994). In this vein, Stuart Hall (1990: 235) claims that diaspora is a concept that avoids essentialism since 'the diaspora experience … is defined, not by essence or purity, but by the recognition of a necessary heterogeneity and diversity; by a conception of "identity" which lives with and through, not despite, difference; by *hybridity*'. Furthermore, the term is used to capture 'globalization from below' (Clifford 1994: 327), since 'diasporas' are assumed to 'think globally' but 'live locally', which is an interpretation that 'lies at the heart of much recent globalization theory' (Anthias 1998: 566). However, the postmodern version of the diaspora has been criticized for its essentialist connotation. Anthias (1998: 558) remarks that 'the concept of diaspora, whilst focusing on transnational processes and commonalities, does so by deploying a notion of ethnicity which privileges the point of "origin" in constructing identity and solidarity'. Thus, 'a notion of primordial bonding seems to lie at the heart of the "diaspora" notion' (ibid.: 563).

Certainly, the concept of diaspora at first glance seems applicable to Soviet Germans, who were forced to leave their homeland and to live in scattered settlements after 1941. However, one runs the risk of presupposing feelings of belonging to an 'historic homeland' which, in the case of Kazakhstani Germans, is further complicated by the fact that there is no single homeland: people might long to live in either Germany, the former Volga Republic, or previous German settlements in Ukraine. Moreover, the term's connotation of victimhood presumes this is how Kazakhstani Germans interpret their own history and perceive their contemporary situation. Rather, it should be determined empirically whether people construct their identity by referring to a real or imagined 'historic homeland', how they define their relation to it, and what it means to them (cf. also Hagendoorn and Poppe 2001 for a critique of the application of diaspora to Russians in the 'Near Abroad').

Views about Germany as the assumed 'historic homeland' are most significantly transmitted directly by the Kazakhstani Germans' relatives and friends who live there, or are based on Kazakhstani Germans' own experiences there, since quite a few have visited their family members in Germany at least once. Most often those trips were paid for by their relatives (cf. also Stoll 2007: 123) and, thus, presuppose good relations. But one should keep in mind that in recent times it seems to have become ever more difficult, in particular for young and unmarried persons, to obtain a tourist visa for Germany.[15]

There are also Kazakhstani Germans who have lived and even worked in Germany, Igor being one such person.[16] He did not legally immigrate to Germany, and therefore could only do unsanctioned work. But he told me that he had seen enough in Germany to know that even if he could live there legally, he would not have a future there. He says that in Taldykorgan he is respected, and only in Taldykorgan can he realize his career plans. Igor currently has his own business in the city, and his daughter also runs her own business.

Some Kazakhstani Germans stayed for several years in Germany, including Sasha, who lived for four years in Duisburg. Together with his parents, siblings and wife, Sasha moved to Germany in 2000. His parents were the last to emigrate of their siblings, who had all been living in Germany for several years at that time. But receiving social benefits without believing they would be able to land even a half-decent job convinced Sasha and his wife to return to Kazakhstan in 2004, where he had no such difficulty finding good employment. Sasha said he is very satisfied with his life in Taldykorgan, which he describes as far preferable to the terrible life he had in Duisburg. Based on current conditions, it seems likely that more than a few of Sasha's relatives also might return to Kazakhstan someday.[17]

But views about Germany might also derive from one's own or one's parents' experiences in Nazi Germany. One man born in Ukraine in 1926 first asked me what my grandparents did during the war. Then, he began to speak German and told me about his time in Germany during the war.[18] He repeatedly stressed that he had seen everything in Germany, that he hated everything German, and that he would never again set foot in such a 'disgusting country'.

Another man born in Taldykorgan in 1956 started purchasing cars in Germany in the early 1990s.[19] He has been to Germany many times and he spends most of his time there bargaining at German car markets. He also repeatedly told me how awful Germany is, how dislikeable the Germans are, and that he must have been crazy to seriously think about emigrating to such a 'stupid country'.

Those narratives about German car markets and the Second World War convey exceptionally negative attitudes towards Germany, but such comments are not unusual coming from those who have lived in Germany for even longer periods of time and then returned, and their stories and attitudes also influence the way others view Germany. Negative views on Germany were typically not voiced during taped interviews, but they were a favourite topic when several Germans and others sat together and discussed their relatives' stories or their own experiences in Germany.[20] One such discussion unfolded when I was invited to Svetlana's home for dinner:

> Svetlana, her husband, two of her adult sons, and I were just settling in around the table when one of her sons – whom I had not met before – began to speak of Germany. He started by mentioning the ugly landscape, and then said that one could not recover 'by being in nature' because everything there is privately owned and, therefore, access is denied. In particular, he mentioned the fact that one needs permission to fish. Furthermore, people in Germany are not hospitable, and only with a fixed appointment is one allowed to visit someone. His mother interrupted him and stressed that she likes Germany very much, in particular, its cleanliness, describing how even the central railway station in Cologne was clean. Her husband, however, replied that he did not like Remscheid at all – the town where his brother lives – because of all the old houses, the narrow streets and all the hills. (Field notes 04/10/2007)

This account exemplifies much of the stereotypical narrative about Germany, which comprises two main topics: 'nature and freedom' and the distinct 'German mentality'. Furthermore, it is very characteristic that women's perceptions of Germany are more positive than men's and/or that women were more hesitant to offend me. It is usually mentioned that Germany is more orderly than Kazakhstan; however, even this positive feature is often weakened by pointing out that the many Turks and Russians (i.e., Kazakhstani/Russian Germans) have brought 'their dirtiness' to Germany.

Many narratives, in particular those told by men, deal with nature and the perceived freedom in Kazakhstan, while describing Germany as a country where everything seems to be *verboten* (forbidden). During taped interviews, the beautiful landscape of Kazakhstan is depicted in detail and compared to Germany's landscape, as exemplified here:

> I like everything [in Germany], with the exception that it's not what we are used to, this vastness. I told you that I'm a fisherman. ... We just go [to fish], and we do not have to ask anybody. We have such a vastness, you travel and travel, maybe even 200 kilometres without seeing anybody, without seeing any village, any person, any car. You can even find places where up to now no single human being has set foot. (Sasha, 50 years old)

Differences with regard to nature and climate are also often mentioned when people are asked why they chose not to emigrate to Germany. On this subject, people stress that it would have been too difficult for them to adapt to a different climate. However, this is certainly not their only reason for staying in Kazakhstan. Furthermore, it seems that people who were denied permission to immigrate tend to later emphasize the difficulties of living in a foreign country. It happened several times that people told me that they did not want to emigrate to Germany, and only later did I discover that they in fact had not been given the opportunity.[21] Since being denied the chance to emigrate is often perceived as a failure, people either avoid the subject or provide reasons why emigration is not desirable, such as the difficulty of adapting to another climate.

Secondly, it is the 'mentality' (*mentalitet*) of Germans that Kazakhstani Germans refer to when they talk about the country or explain why they did not emigrate to Germany. Generally, people in Germany are seen as being very different from them and are usually characterized as egotistical, individualistic rather than family-oriented, reserved and sometimes hostile, while people in Kazakhstan (irrespective of nationality) are regarded as hospitable and family-oriented. Differences in 'mentality' are evident in Sonya's statement:

> But for me it seems that living in Germany is difficult because the mentality is different. This was noticeable – in the German House there were guys who emigrated to Germany, and we are in touch with them, we write to each other. And they write that it is difficult to settle down. Why? Because somehow the mentality of the people [she uses the term

narod] is completely different. There were kind of different historical objectives, right? Today people have completely different objectives. For example, our Kazakhstani man [*Kazakhstantskij chelovek*] has his own mentality. He has his own ideas. He has – how to say – other values. In Germany, the Germans have other [values]. Anyhow, people are different. (Sonya, 23 years old)

As exemplified by the quote above, Kazakhstani Germans are hesitant to make negative comments on the 'mentality' of Germans in Germany. However, the fact that they insist on stressing the difference can imply a negative attitude. One narrative on Germans is widely held:

As far as I understood, you can only live there [in Germany] as long as you only visit someone.
RS: Could you explain that?
Well, because we did not grow up like that. We grew up like, how to explain – around us is so much liberty, yes. The streets are wide, and you can go wherever you want to. You can go into the forest, in the mountains. There, this is not possible, there, everywhere is private property. … She [his mother] is doing fine there [in Germany], but life is boring for her. Our people are used to visiting each other, to talking to each other while sitting outside. There, life is different. There, in any case, you have to inform others about your visit in good time. This is called '*Termine*' [German for appointments]?
RS: Yes, 'Termine'.
So you have to make a '*Termin*'. But here, for example, you just go to your neighbours, at any time. But there you have to say exactly when you intend to come. She is not used to that. Therefore, she is bored there, and she often calls me. (Nikolai, 47 years old)

The idea that one needs a fixed appointment to visit someone in Germany is the story told most often by Kazakhstani Germans in Taldykorgan. When mentioning this feature of life in Germany, people also refer to the difficulties many of their relatives and acquaintances have had in making friends in Germany (cf. Sanders 2013b: 87–89).

On the whole, only in exceptional cases do views about Germany suit the notion of diaspora. Only rarely do Kazakhstani Germans refer to Germany as their 'historic homeland'; rather it is the depiction of Kazakhstan's beautiful landscape and the country's freedom that embodies the notion of homeland. Thus, in present-day Kazakhstan most Germans do *not* have 'an idealized vision of a better life in the distant kin-state of Germany', as pointed out by Diener (2006: 222). Furthermore, by referring to 'mentality' Kazakhstani Germans stress the difference between them and the Germans in Germany, hence any primordial reference to an all-inclusive category is absent. Therefore, the perception of Germany as a country that gives a home to all Germans, which was certainly present in an earlier time, appears to be on the wane.

Networks and Identity

Ideas, experiences and feelings of belonging, which are transnationally negotiated, contribute not only to Kazakhstanis' views on Germany, but also play a significant role in how they construct their own identities. In order to understand this process, one should keep in mind several aspects: the situation of Kazakhstani/Russian Germans in Germany; what these people communicate about their life to relatives and friends living in Kazakhstan; and how Kazakhstani Germans react to such information.

A number of studies (Boll 1996; Dietz 2006; Eder et al. 2004; Graudenz and Römhild 1996; Kühnel and Strobl 2000; Römhild 1998, 2007; cf. also Becker 2001 for Russian Jews in Germany) about Russian Germans (*russlanddeutsche Aussiedler/Spätaussiedler*) deal with their 'complicated integration' into German society. The desire to live as a German among Germans held by many who came to Germany in the late 1980s or early 1990s is often seen as an obstacle to integration. The fact that the native population in Germany largely does not accept this view of ethnic belonging has led to frustration and disenchantment (cf. Graudenz and Römhild 1996: 37–52). Eder et al. (2004: 267) identify a *contradictio in adjecto* for Russian Germans who perceive themselves as assimilated in terms of their ethnic identity but marginalized with regard to their economic situation. This is particularly problematic for most Russian Germans, who regard employment and career making as very important (ibid.: 265–67). Further, several studies have shown that many are employed below the level of formal qualification they had attained in the Soviet Union or one of its follower states, and the unemployment rate in Germany for Russian Germans is significantly higher than the national average. Lack of German language proficiency and non-recognition of Soviet or post-Soviet degrees and certification are regarded as the primary reasons for the difficult economic integration of Russian Germans (Dietz 2006: 128f). In addition, one should also keep in mind that immigrants are generally not appreciated by the native German population (Schmidt-Lauber 2007: 10).

Pichler and Schmidtke (2004) have investigated the portrayal of several immigrant groups in various German newspapers, finding that Russian Germans are predominantly seen as a threat to, and an economic burden on, the German welfare state.[22] Moreover, they are described as 'culturally foreign' and denied legitimacy as Germans (ibid.: 61).[23] In reaction to being denied acceptance into the German category, many Russian Germans have had to renegotiate their identity (Salein 2005; Schmidt 2005). Dietz (2006: 129–34) observes 'processes of segregation' in that many Russian Germans no longer even intend to become part of German society. Furthermore, Römhild (2007: 168f) states that Russian Germans most often identify themselves as Russian in present-day Germany. In particular young Russian Germans use the inclusive category 'Russian' in order to establish contacts with other immigrants from the former Soviet Union. In doing so, they also strengthen the position of this newly created category 'Russian' against Turks and other immigrant groups in Germany.

As for the Germans in Kazakhstan, it is noteworthy that their narratives about their relatives' situations focus on the same themes as the literature does: the difficulties in the labour market and complicated relationships with native inhabitants, which are in part explained by their distinct 'mentality', as has been explored in the previous section. On this note, Germany's Germans are often criticized for being hostile towards the migrants, though the latter are also sometimes criticized for not making adequate efforts to integrate into society. This ambivalent position is exemplified by Lena, who works as a bank manager in Taldykorgan:

> My mother has always been saying that she doesn't want to go there [to Germany] and that, only if you have many relatives, can you go there – because they [Kazakhstani Germans in Germany] only deal with one another. I have a colleague who went to Karlsruhe [city in southern Germany] last year for a wedding party of his cousin. There were something like 150 guests – and they have lived in Germany for about ten or fifteen years – and this wedding was conducted in Russian, with a Russian toastmaster. So they really only associate with one another – also, because the other people are not interested in them. And that would also concern me. Who knows me there, and who needs me there? (Lena, 48 years old)

Lena expresses her astonishment that the wedding celebration is in Russian, even though the migrants had been living in Germany for at least ten years. However, she not only criticizes Kazakhstani Germans for their failure to make more effort to associate with Germans, but also the local population for being dismissive towards them. Since most people did not want to offend me, this was usually expressed indirectly, as Lena does above. According to her, it is not advisable to emigrate to Germany when you do not have many relatives there; otherwise, you will be alone, considering the unlikelihood of making new acquaintances.

The flow of information from migrants across great distances has long been the subject of investigation (e.g., Thomas and Znaniecki 1958 for Polish peasants in the United States). In this context, it is important to recall Levitt and Glick Schiller (2007: 188): 'Individuals who have such direct connections with migrants may connect with others who have not'. Thus, many more people than only those having direct transnational ties are embedded in a transnational social field. For instance, knowledge about Germany spreads easily because 'life in Germany' is a favourite topic among Kazakhstani Germans.[24]

In light of such conversations, it is widely known that Kazakhstani Germans are perceived as Russians in Germany, and not surprising that many Kazakhstani Germans know several vulgar German terms for Russians. One young Kazakhstani German told me that even some Kazakhs in Taldykorgan are now familiar with such words, and she was deeply shocked and offended when one young Kazakh recently addressed her by using one of them.

The relatives' often difficult employment situation is also widely discussed in Taldykorgan. For example, the above-mentioned Olga, who directs a branch bank, reacted with astonishment when I asked her why she did not emigrate to Germany, first by saying did I really think she wants to '*putzen*' (i.e., work as a cleaning woman) in Germany, like the other members of her family living there (cf. also Liberona 2005). In this regard, it is also revealing that the 'popular' term in Germany for social benefits – *Hartz IV* – has become part of Kazakhstani Germans' everyday speech.

At first glance, it does not seem that Kazakhstani Germans depict the lives of their relatives in Germany in an extraordinarily negative way merely to reaffirm that they made the right decision by staying in Kazakhstan, since the overall impression of their relatives' situation is by and large confirmed by research studies on Russian Germans in Germany. However, the above-cited studies are open to criticism for their insistence on viewing Russian Germans as a problematic group. In doing so, the studies give the impression that almost all Russian Germans are unemployed and/or are unsatisfied with their professional career and their life in Germany in general, which is certainly not true (see also Eder et al. 2004). Thus, the fact that largely negative narratives about life in Germany are told in Kazakhstan does not fully mirror their relatives' situation in Germany and might also stem from complicated transnational relations.

Levitt and Glick Schiller (2007: 189) distinguish between 'ways of being' – individuals embedded in a transnational social field though they do not identify themselves with it – and 'ways of belonging' – individuals with a conscious connection to a particular transnational group. With regard to Kazakhstani Germans, the question is not so much whether people are conscious of their connections to Germany (since all of them are to some degree), but rather how they evaluate and feel about those connections. Paradoxically, the fact that contact with their 'historic homeland' has been possible during recent years has strengthened references to the local and national and, therefore, has ultimately fostered a Kazakhstani-German identity. Or, relying on Levitt and Glick Schiller, the established transnational 'ways of being' have meant that 'ways of belonging' are consciously drifting apart.

There is evidence that reference to a Kazakhstani-*German* identity has been strengthened in recent years. Germans in Kazakhstan certainly do not perceive themselves as more Russian because their relatives in Germany are categorized as such, above all because they are aware that being identified as Russian in Germany is not well intentioned. Moreover, and more importantly, their German identity is simply not challenged by Kazakhs. Kazakhstani Germans are, through their (assumed) relations to Germany, today even more associated with Germany and being German. In this context, one should keep in mind that Kazakhs often do not draw a firm line between Germans here and Germans there and that their perception of a German identity and the country is predominantly positive (see Chapter 3). This also illustrates the ethnically fragmented nature of local networks, which is why the more recent informational 'flows' from Germany have so far not reached most Kazakhs. Furthermore, Germans continue to profit from the Kazakhs' positive perception of 'their country', which might prevent some of them from saying anything to the contrary to alter that perception.

Finally, since information about and conceptions of Germany are mostly generated in local networks in Taldykorgan, their internal structure should be considered. As has been shown above, those who have the most contact with Germany also have the most contact with Kazakhs and generally have the largest networks. These Germans are typically middle-aged, and often run their own business or occupy a high-ranking position. Thus, they not only have the most social capital, but often the most economic capital. Since most of them made a deliberate decision to stay in Kazakhstan, none of them dream of living in the 'historic homeland' Germany. But most of them also profit from identifying as German. It is this group who have the greatest influence with regard to coining and promoting views on Germany as well as the above-discussed Kazakhstani-German identity. The few who hold to a mythical vision of Germany as a homeland are, based on the findings of my sample, always marginalized. Their networks are significantly smaller, and they rarely have any contact with Germany or with Kazakhs. For this reason, their view of 'Germanness' is not widespread, but the fact that they do not have much social capital in Taldykorgan might foster the wish to emigrate and to project their idealized vision of an 'historic homeland' onto a foreign country that most of them barely know.

Summary

This chapter has explored the interconnectedness of transnational relations and feelings of belonging. Stoll (2007) states that the migratory process of Kazakhstani Germans is in a transitional phase that is leading from an ethnically defined immigration to a transnational one. It is certainly true that many current applicants do not meet the legal criteria for being an ethnic German and, thus, opt for other ways of migrating to Germany. However, the present-day situation of Kazakhstani Germans is less characterized by continuous out-migration than by the fact that almost every Kazakhstani German has relatives in Germany who immigrated as ethnic Germans seeking their 'historic homeland'. The particular circumstances of Kazakhstani Germans' out-migration – the large numbers, the specific point in time, the immigrants' motivation, and that it occurred on a family basis – shape present-day transnational relations. Many Kazakhstani Germans still feel left behind, and many blame their relatives for having forgotten them after they left for Germany. Some feel ashamed to admit that their relatives do not help them; others feel ashamed because they refused to live together with their family in Germany. Kinship ties have often been cut, and friendships dissolved. Therefore, the case of Kazakhstani Germans is unusual, because many did not actively strive for inclusion in their country of origin Kazakhstan once they had left it, as is elsewhere often observed in migratory processes.

Thanks to Kazakhstan's rapidly growing economy in recent years, some Kazakhstani Germans have prospered, and the shrinking gap in economic terms has also had an effect on relations with relatives in Germany. Those who stayed cannot so easily be perceived as 'losers' who were not brave enough and/or clever enough to immigrate to Germany. Furthermore, many Kazakhstani Germans previously thought that their relatives had gone to live among their own kind, in their 'historic homeland', whereas they had remained behind (whether willingly or unwillingly) in the alien nation state of the newly established Kazakhstan. But the present-day situation appears to be perceived as having partially reversed itself, in that it is their relatives who must deal with a range of difficulties in a foreign country while they have stayed in their homeland Kazakhstan where prospects are improving.

As for the process of strengthening a Kazakhstani-German identity, the 'successful' Germans who possess the most social and economic capital appear to be in the best position to encourage and promote such an identity. Personal links to Germany have stimulated localized identities that exclude both Germans in Germany and their relatives living in Germany. This also could have resulted because Kazakhstani Germans have had to rescue and even defend their German identity, since their relatives in Germany are categorized as Russian. Thus, not only official community leaders – who are the topic of the subsequent part – should be considered when analysing people's unequal capacities to alter identities, but also the power that generally derives from social relationships.

Notes

1. Twelve persons have parents, children or siblings living in Russia, and twelve have parents, children or siblings living in Germany. Five have parents, siblings or children in both Germany and Russia.

2. Four of the seven persons actually have relatives in Germany, whom they have never met and about whom they could not say anything beyond the fact that they exist; for example, the offspring of an uncle who remained in Germany after 1945, or relatives who immigrated to Germany from distant places such as Moscow and with whom they had not been in touch prior to their immigration.
3. One of them is an orphan whose son lives in Israel.
4. For comparison, in the social networks reported by Berzborn et al. (1998: 7f) for Cosa Mesa/California, 48.1 per cent of all ties exist within Cosa Mesa and an additional 24.1 per cent in the wider area of Orange County. Thus, the Kazakhstani Germans' networks explored here are slightly more local and less transnational than those reported in California.
5. It is question five of the personal network questionnaire: Suppose you need advice with a major change in your life, for instance changing jobs, or emigrating. Who would you ask for advice if such a major change occurred in your life?
6. I did not add those relatives to the list.
7. Other statistically informed research has resulted in similar findings, namely 'that involvement in transnational activities was exceptional [as to a representative survey of Latin American immigrants in the United States], with less than 15 per cent of immigrant family heads taking part in them on a regular basis' (Portes and DeWind 2007: 10).
8. Under Gorbachev, a new law on emigration was introduced in 1987. Only then were Germans allowed to immigrate without being invited by family members in Germany. As a result, immigration numbers drastically increased: from 753 immigrating persons from the USSR in 1986 to 14,488 in 1987 (47,572 in 1988; 98,134 in 1989; 147,950 in 1990; 147,320 in 1991; and 195,576 in 1992) (Eisfeld 1999: 188).
9. Stoll (2007: 123) states that during the 1990s people often had to wait for as long as five years.
10. Immigration to Russia was generally easier since 'all former residents of the Soviet Union, regardless of their ethnicity, were entitled to Russian citizenship under the 1992 Law on Citizenship, which remained in force until May 2002' (Flynn 2007: 465). However, in practice government policy was more restrictive towards immigrants since they were also seen as 'a vital component of an emerging Russian national identity stretching beyond the borders of the Russian state' (ibid.). In 2000, this view changed slightly with Putin's initiative to solve Russia's demographic question by encouraging immigration (ibid.). However, a repatriation programme was only decided on in 2006. Thus, 'the lack of interest of post-Soviet Russia for its diaspora has surprised and shocked many' (Peyrouse 2007: 496). Immigrating to Russia is not currently popular among Kazakhstani Germans. Living standards in rural areas are assumed to be even worse than in Kazakhstan, while the costs of living in urban centres are prohibitive. Furthermore, the 'Russian mentality' is usually depicted as quite different; the general picture is that 'all of Russia drinks' and that Russians do not welcome newcomers (cf. Flynn 2007; cf. Peyrouse 2007: 497).
11. After the Soviet Union's collapse, Kazakhstan's economy and its standard of living drastically worsened within a few years: whereas in 1989 only five per cent of the population lived below the poverty line, in 1994 this grew to more than fifty per cent. In addition, hundreds of hospitals and schools closed and many diseases such as tuberculosis reappeared (Peyrouse 2007: 482).
12. Certainly, such narratives can be viewed as fairly one-sided. Their relatives in Germany may have very different opinions about the relationship and their level of support, but such perspective is beyond the scope of this book. To provide a brief example, I was

told by Victoria, a middle-aged woman who runs a small kiosk, that no one helps her financially. However, when talking to her brother, who emigrated to Germany about seventeen years ago and was visiting Victoria with his wife and children for several weeks, I learned that he regularly sent her about a hundred euros a month. Victoria later confirmed that, but said the money was not for her but for her mother, with whom she lives.

13. Many of them tried to pass the necessary German language exam several times, which also means that they had to spend a lot of money.
14. Previously she had brought up the subject of the integration of Kazakhstani Germans in Kazakhstan.
15. Stoll (2007: 120, 156) notes that the German embassy was the subject of a media campaign in Kazakhstan in July 2002, which asserted that it was nearly futile for Kazakhstani Germans to apply for a tourist visa, in light of the embassy's cancellation of its relationship with several travel agencies in 2001 which, among others, were accused of faking documents. But according to an employee of the German embassy in 2002, ninety-five per cent of all applicants (i.e., Germans, Russians, Kazakhs or others) still received a tourist visa. Nevertheless, I should point out that I heard about several cases of Kazakhstani Germans who were denied a tourist visa, in particular those who were unmarried.
16. Return migration has not been the subject of extensive theoretical or 'on the ground' investigation; among the exceptions are Cassarino (2004), Christou (2006) and Currle (2006). Russian/Kazakhstani-German return migration has been investigated only very recently (Fenicia 2015; Mattock 2015; Schönhuth and Kaiser 2015; Suppes 2015).
17. On the other hand, because he has German citizenship, Sasha and his wife could move back to Germany at any time.
18. Those Germans in the German Wehrmacht-occupied areas of Ukraine after the battle of Stalingrad in 1942/43 were chaotically resettled by the Wehrmacht to western areas of Poland and Germany. Most of them were settled in the Warthegau (see Chapter 1). However, young men above the age of sixteen were also recruited for the Waffen SS, and though the above-cited man did not say it explicitly, I assume that he had been affected by these events (cf. Römhild 1998: 122–24; cf. Brake 1998: 66, 184f; cf. Riek 2000: 43).
19. In particular during the 1990s, many Kazakhstanis were engaged in trade activities. In 2001 alone, the German embassy issued about 85,000 visas, most for purposes of small trade (Stoll 2007: 108).
20. Certainly, my presence may often have provoked discussions of Germany. But I had the impression that people were not generally telling their stories for the first time, and had not 'invented' them for me.
21. Between 2000 and 2003, about fifty per cent of all applications for immigration were denied (Stoll 2007: 103). Insufficient German language skills, missing documents, a previous Russian nationality, and a high-ranking position in the USSR are the main reasons given for denials (cf. also ibid.: 134, 137, 179).
22. They compared the portrayal of Polish, Russian-German and Turkish immigrants between 1996 and 1999 in the following newspapers: *Berliner Zeitung, Taz, Süddeutsche Zeitung, Die Welt, Frankfurter Allgemeine* and *Focus* (Pichler and Schmidtke 2004: 50f).
23. In comparison to Turks and Poles, Russian Germans are seen as particularly problematic (Pichler and Schmidtke 2004: 61). Thus, paradoxically it seems the very fact that Russian Germans claim to belong to the German ethnic category (primarily because their immigration is ethnically defined) causes German society to exclude them.

24. I do not have the impression that media is a primary source with respect to how people in Taldykorgan obtain information about Germany. First of all, most of them do not understand German and thus cannot read German websites or newspapers or watch German television. Certainly, there are websites in Russian (usually written by Russian/Kazakhstani Germans living in Germany) about life in Germany, and people can chat on the internet in Russian with people living in Germany. But use of the internet, at least in Taldykorgan, is for the most part confined to young people, and, secondly, personal stories by Russian/Kazakhstani Germans remain the main way in which information is transmitted to people in Kazakhstan. Furthermore, 'first-hand information' directly provided by relatives living in Germany appears to be more highly valued than what people might have read about Germany.

Part IV
The Effect of Two States' Policies of 'Germanness' on Kazakhstani Germans

This part investigates the nexus of minority group, 'host-state' and homeland (Brubaker 1999: 44) and explores the organization of the German minority in Kazakhstan and how it is linked to the nationality and minority policies of Kazakhstan and Germany. It will be shown not only how people cope with contradictory state policies, but also how they creatively use state-mandated conditions for their own purposes. Although Kazakhstani Germans, at first glance, appear to comply with the ascribed role of being a minority within Kazakhstan, their activities often run contrary to the intended outcomes of the two states' policies.

It has often been asserted (e.g., Cummings 2005; Diener 2004; Holm-Hansen 1999) that, during the course of the Kazakh nation-building process, ethnic identity has increased in importance. In this process, Nazarbayev is described as a 'protector' of the smaller ethnic groups (Holm-Hansen 1999: 212). He founded the Assembly of the People of Kazakhstan in 1995; as the president's consultative body, the assembly unites pro-regime ethnic movements, one of them being the German Rebirth organization (*Wiedergeburt*). The German minority organization was actually founded by political activists in 1989, with the goal of re-establishing the Volga Republic (Römhild 1998: 128–30). But in present-day Kazakhstan, the Rebirth organization has *de facto* become a national cultural centre; hence, the assembly supervises it in conjunction with Kazakhstan's president. Furthermore, the Rebirth organization is still partially funded by Germany and is thus shaped in part by German state policies.

The situation of Kazakhstani Germans is, therefore, likely to be heavily influenced by the policies of the two states, their concepts of ethnic belonging, and their means of implementing them. The ensuing chapter depicts various activities of the Rebirth organization in Taldykorgan, investigates their significance in constructing (Kazakhstani) German identities and stimulating group solidarity, and explores how they are linked to the desired outcomes of the two states' policies.

Chapter 7
Changing Transnational Institutions

Before arriving in Taldykorgan for the first time, I had already heard about one of their transnational institutions, namely the local branch of the Rebirth organization. Employees of other institutions in Almaty, such as the Friedrich-Ebert Foundation and the GTZ (German Organization for Technical Cooperation),[1] praised the Rebirth organization for its numerous activities, which were further hailed as being relevant and forward-looking in contemporary Kazakhstan. This commendation certainly implied that the organization in Taldykorgan collaborates well with institutions in Germany and, thus, appears to be effectively integrated into a transnational institutional web.

The other organization presented in this chapter is the so-called 'German parish', which is actually a Lutheran parish. Only two decades ago, the congregation comprised several hundred members, most of them Germans. Today, however, the church is attended by no more than a few families. Furthermore, the priest clearly downplays the parish's German past, probably in the hope of attracting a wider range of possible new members. Therefore, I was not surprised when many Germans told me that the 'German parish' would eventually cease to exist.

In presenting these two organizations as they function in Taldykorgan, this chapter focuses on their different approaches – whether by choice or by necessity – to new transnational demands following the fall of the Iron Curtain. I will show how those in charge of them, and their employees and followers, deal with their transnational counterparts in Germany, how they react towards new requirements coming from Germany and how they creatively transform such requirements to conform them to their own needs and beliefs.

The 'German House'

In Taldykorgan, there is a local branch of the Rebirth organization founded in 1992 that people simply refer to as the 'German House' (*Deutsches Haus*).

Figure 7.1 The German House in Taldykorgan (photo: R. Sanders, 2007)

Today's director of the German House regards German language courses as one of the centre's main activities.[2] Every person working in the German House asserts that by means of teaching the 'mother tongue', the German House can make a contribution to the 'preservation and development' of the 'German national culture', and indeed a range of language courses are offered.[3] In addition to the Sunday school for children and several evening courses for adults, there are various language camps for teenagers and children during the summer. Apart from the summer camps, German language courses are not particularly crowded, so generally anyone interested in learning the language has the opportunity to do so. Language courses are free; only the language camps, which usually take place in the mountains, charge a fee, which is affordable for most people in Taldykorgan.

Funding of the Rebirth organization has changed over time, and the GTZ has reduced the amount of money transferred directly to the Rebirth organization and its local German Houses.[4] Now each German House must apply for funding on the basis of individual projects, for example, the establishment of a language camp. This new funding approach has led to a change in focus, away from purely linguistic training and towards, in particular, ecological topics, which appeared to be viewed more favourably by the GTZ in 2006/2007.[5] In this spirit, one summer camp in 2007 was even accompanied by an Austrian ornithologist.

Another change in focus has resulted from the Kazakh state's language policies that also require every language camp to include the Kazakh language. In addition, Nazarbayev, in 2007, declared that every Kazakhstani should speak English as well. Therefore, the German House could only receive permission for the realization of their language camp by teaching Kazakh and English in addition to German.[6]

Figure 7.2 The Sunday school in the German House in Taldykorgan (photo: R. Sanders, 2006)

As part of the Sunday school, along with German language training, children can attend classes in dancing, music and handicrafts (*basteln*). Most of the approximately twenty-five children spend their entire Sunday morning in the German House. All classes focus on something specifically German. Songs and dances must represent 'German culture', and very often whole mornings are given over to such topics as the Advent season (*Adventszeit*) or the harvest festival (*Erntedankfest*).

In addition to the aforementioned classes, the German House offers two weekly meetings, one for teenagers (*Jugendclub*) and one for elderly people (*Seniorenclub*). Both clubs are guided by someone who is responsible for the club's programme. Though those meetings are not organized like classes, they usually relate to major annual German festivities, on which subject the club's heads prepare an entertaining game or some kind of quiz. However, to a much greater degree than in the Sunday school for children, both clubs also consider Kazakh and even Soviet festivities in their weekly programme. While most meetings revolve around games as a way of learning about various cultural celebrations, they also serve as convivial gatherings where people sit together, drinking tea or dancing.

Another aim of German House activities, especially at the youth club and the Sunday school, is to prepare for performances of German dances and songs for special occasions, such as the town's day, the First of May, Independence Day, and *Nauriz*, the 'Kazakh new year'. As major festivities approach, members of the youth club and the Sunday school often meet more than once a week for rehearsals.

A further concern of the German House is to provide various goods and services. There is a translation service, primarily for documents required for immigration to Germany. Basic medicine is offered for those in need, and a stay of one or two weeks in a sanatorium is offered annually to elderly persons.[7] In recent years the German House has also provided goods such as coal, flour and sugar to some Germans. Members of the *Seniorenclub* are from time to time given toothpaste, watches, suncream and clothes that have been sent from Germany. Sometimes the club's members receive them as prizes for winning one of the above-mentioned games.

Altogether, the German House in Taldykorgan is currently involved in three main areas: allocation of goods and services, organization of group activities and public performances celebrating 'German culture'. I will explore these activities separately by looking at how they are organized, how they are evaluated, in what way they affect people's ideas of what it means to be German, and how all of this might have an impact on the actions of people in Taldykorgan. The third activity – the public celebrations of 'German culture' – will be dealt with in the subsequent chapter on the policies of the Kazakh and German states.

Support from Germany

The allocation of goods and services is above all considered as 'help from Germany', and most of those who have received such 'help' believe that Germany is obligated to provide them with such assistance. These goods and services are primarily given to elderly persons and, according to the head of the GTZ for Central Asia in 2007, are intended to recompense Kazakhstani Germans for their suffering during and after the Second World War. Though financial support from Germany through the GTZ is decreasing, the local Rebirth centres still receive a certain amount of money for different kinds of aid. How then is the disbursement of such aid organized by the German House in Taldykorgan?

First of all, the German House does not simply dole out aid to all Germans in Taldykorgan, although this – at least theoretically – would be possible, since each German could be identified through the nationality registered in his or her passport. However, only those who have established some kind of relationship with the German House, and are therefore on one of the German House lists, are eligible to benefit from German support. Because the lists are a crucial means of allocating the provided goods and services, it is worth taking a closer look at them.[8] First, such lists are expected to be the 'correct' length;[9] that is, long enough to prove to the GTZ, which is officially responsible for monitoring the lists, that there are a sufficient number of people in need, and short enough so as not to overburden the German House and overstrain its resources, and so as to allow for a reserve to be maintained in the event of future worthwhile purposes.[10] From the perspective of the recipient, too many people on the lists means an over-division of available resources. While the allocation of goods and services by means of such lists is generally accepted by people who work in the German House and by those who profit from them, disbursement practices continue to be discussed and debated.

How then does the German House go about constructing lists that are ideal in length? In actuality, the lists usually start out too long; for example, the person responsible for sanatorium stays might have to choose twenty-five persons from a list of forty potential candidates. This procedure, however, should be in line with a legitimate category system. Among the Germans in Taldykorgan, when such a winnowing process is necessary, the largely accepted approach appears to be, first and foremost, the exclusion of Russians. Russians are found on almost every list, mostly as relatives or friends of Germans on the same lists.

Peaceful coexistence with other nationalities is mostly praised (see also Part II). This is especially the case with Russians, considering that most Germans perceive themselves as both German and Russian, and in some situations as more Russian than German. In the discussion of the German category in Part II, it was pointed out that the category's boundaries are ultimately not sharply delineated, and thus people are able to identify as German and/or Russian depending on the context. But whether one identifies as German or Russian becomes an issue when the 'help from Germany' is at stake. The disbursement of donations triggers fundamental debates about who is German and who is not, which often take place in an emotionally charged atmosphere in the *Seniorenclub*. People who regularly profit from the German House are vigilant in their observance of who is chosen for particular benefits, and decisions perceived as unjust are discussed and debated, sometimes for several months afterwards. In particular the fact that persons without German ancestors receive a portion of the support is the subject of widespread criticism.

In order to identify the deserving persons for 'help from Germany', people take into account German ancestry, German language proficiency, experiences of suffering due to being German, and a person's proper (i.e., German) way of living. Some factors are considered more decisive than others, and how decisive they are depends on who is doing the deciding. For instance, someone with only a German mother but who is able to speak a little German is perceived by those who also know German to be more German than someone who has German ancestors but no language proficiency. In every case, however, some German ancestry is the minimum criterion; without it, being German is not possible.

Some members of the *Seniorenclub* are Russian. Since being a member of that club implies being towards the top of many lists, including for the sanatorium, for clothes and for various lesser items, this is perceived by many Germans as a core problem. The head of the *Seniorenclub* told me she is aware that many German members criticize her and the German House in general for allowing Russians to take part in the club. She expressed sympathy for such a position, explaining that in the past Russians had oppressed Germans, and only now, when they can get something from the Germans, do they sit peacefully with them around the table. However, as she explained further, it is necessary that German House's policy be generally open to all nationalities.

One Russian member of the *Seniorenclub* told me that she likes the 'German atmosphere' in the German House and 'German culture' in general, having started attending with a German friend a couple of years ago. She was one of the few members who at first declined to be interviewed, although after several months she changed her mind and finally invited me to her home. She prepared an extraordinarily well-appointed table and was obviously eager to prove that Russians are at least as orderly as Germans. She did not mention that she does not feel welcomed by everybody in the *Seniorenclub*, which I only heard from her German friend:

> In the German House, [Germans complain] that also Russians go there. I say to them 'calm down'. Well, and also Russians helped us; those Russians who are decent. And all nations, right? Well, in our *Seniorenclub* we have Valentina, she's Russian. Well, she has some German ancestors, her grandmother, hasn't she?[11] [I said that I don't know.] Well, she told me …, and she even started to cry. I told her: 'Don't cry, you should keep coming to us'. Russians and Germans – we should support each other. They [the members of the *Seniorenclub*] create such a split which is frightening. (Anna, 79 years old)

Some months after the interview, I attended Valentina's birthday party in the German House. It is conventional that the club's members celebrate their birthdays in the *Seniorenclub*. On such occasions dishes are shared as well as bottles of vodka and cognac. These parties are officially opened by the *Seniorenclub*'s head, who expresses her congratulations, and rather lengthy toasts by each guest typically follow. However, Valentina's birthday party was different, in that noticeably fewer people attended and less than half of them offered a toast. During the party one man beckoned me over to confide in German that Valentina was an evil woman (*böse Frau*). But since I could not find out anything 'evil' she had done, and since I assume I would eventually have learned about such behaviour if she had actually done anything 'evil', it seems likely that the man was referring in large part to her being non-German.

Furthermore, members of the *Seniorenclub* often gossip about Russian habits. The most prominent narrative involves the 'greedy Russians'. Many Germans told me that they have had to resist the Russians' greed or there would be nothing left for them, and stories of Russians sneaking away with food while attending a birthday party in the German House are often retold. On several occasions things disappeared from the German House, such as soap or utensils, and the Germans always believed the Russians to be guilty of the thefts. Other narratives reinforcing the idea of the 'greedy Russians' mention how Russians attempt to ingratiate themselves with the head of the *Seniorenclub* and the head of the German House, presumably to improve their situation when goods or services are to be disbursed.

An obvious question arises: Why are there any Russians in the *Seniorenclub* or on any of the lists, and in the latter case, why are the lists not completely filled by Germans, considering that there are more than fifteen hundred Germans in Taldykorgan? The simple answer: being German does not mean that a person is guaranteed access to the lists. First, one has to establish some kind of connection to the German House. As a start, one might send one's children to the Sunday school to learn German. Having established this initial link, then one must volunteer for an activity, such as baking a cake for one of the festivities or sewing costumes. Furthermore, the less 'Germanness' one is able to claim, the more one must offer their volunteer services in order to become an accepted member of the German House. This could be one reason why Germans tend to allow at least some Russians, simply because the latter have to contribute more time and effort to be accepted.

It is also important to stress that the majority of Germans in Taldykorgan have never been to the German House, above all, because they do not need the offered services. While, to be fair, the German House does more than simply provide goods and services, elderly Germans in particular believe that the German House was built primarily to help them. I also had the impression that many if not most participate in order to be on one of the lists; even the head of the *Seniorenclub* complained about the 'club's participants' mentality'. She said that a lot of people only attend the weekly meeting of the *Seniorenclub* shortly before the bigger festivities such as Christmas, just to show that they are still an active member who should not be forgotten when it comes to the distribution of Christmas gifts.

Thus, the 'help from Germany' has in effect led to a narrowing of the German category, so as to exclude as many as possible from the distributed goods. Consequently, in the context of benefits, a distinction is made between Germans and Russians that is otherwise rarely clear-cut. Above all, the negative stereotyping of Russian habits that is common among *Seniorenclub* members is in fact not common among Taldykorgan Germans outside the German House. The next section shifts to younger Germans, exploring the effects of group activities on group solidarity and on an awareness of being German.

Socializing with Other Germans

The following is a description of a Valentine's Day celebration at the German House's *Jugendclub*:

> A week before Valentine's Day, I was invited to a programme at the *Jugendclub*. The following Sunday, I arrived at the basement of the German House, where the party was to take place. Although it was the announced five o'clock starting time, only two break-dancers were

present, working on their moves; since they more or less ignored me and the music was too loud to talk anyway, I went outside, where I met the *Jugendclub*'s head, who confirmed that the party would start soon. Together with her and another boy, I went back to the basement. As soon as we entered the room the third boy began to dance, whereupon one of the others said between tracks: 'Look, a German came and immediately started to work', and the youth club's head told me that 'their guys' came third in a town-wide break-dancing competition in 2006.

Eventually about twenty other teenagers arrived, chatting and watching the dancers. Finally, around half-past six, the day's official master of ceremonies asked everyone to take a seat. She welcomed them and read a brief speech to an attentive audience about the history and idea behind Valentine's Day. Afterwards she explained the first in a series of games on today's topic – 'love'. Everyone seemed quite eager to take part in the games, kissing others and dancing in the dark. Watching the kissing and dancing, I began to understand what the *Jugendclub* is about, first and foremost. Eventually, the disco started and most of the teenagers danced to American hip hop, Russian pop, Rammstein and Tokio Hotel.[12] (Field notes 11/02/2007)

During subsequent months, as I came to know some of the teenagers better, I realized that many relationships had gotten their start in the *Jugendclub*, which was founded in 2000. Also, I learned from persons in their mid-twenties that they had met their husband or wife in the German House and that both the youth club and the summer camps are the best places to find a German spouse. However, not only Germans attend the *Jugendclub*, as explained by its head:

> Sixty per cent of those who come to the *Jugendclub* are German. But the thing is, we have many mixed marriages, for instance, marriages between Germans and Russians, or Germans and Koreans. That's why those who come to our club are not pure Germans; however, to a certain extent, German blood does exist. But we also have members who are not German; we have Kazakhs, Koreans and Tatars. Though they're not Germans, they're interested in our activities. They're active members who help us.[13] So why shouldn't they come to us? – even more so because we have some passive German members. (Natalya Shenknecht, head of the *Jugendclub*)

Her description of the youth club's ethnic composition matched my observations for the most part, except that I came across only one Kazakh girl in the ten or so meetings I attended. Most *Jugendclub* members prefer having a boyfriend or girlfriend with German ancestors, but would not mind connecting with a Russian or Korean boy or girl (for marriage patterns in general, see Chapter 5). Moreover, and in contrast to the attitudes of the *Seniorenclub*'s members, young Germans do not clearly distinguish between the German and Russian categories, perhaps because most of them have both German and Russian ancestors. In addition, there seemed to be no need to exclude anyone, for two main reasons: there was no 'help from Germany' to be distributed, and everyone seemed quite proud that the German national minority centre had one of the largest and most active youth clubs.[14] That being said, while most of them identified as German and Russian, many at the same time made a point of mentioning that they were 'fifty or seventy-five per cent German'.

Such pride and awareness of one's German identity is definitely encouraged by the various joint activities in the German House. Children and teenagers who attend the Sunday school, summer camps or youth club receive information about German culture, traditions, festivities, dishes and so on. The idea is promoted that an essential 'Germanness' exists, beyond time and space; it is a part of them, and therefore omnipresent. Furthermore, most of these narratives regarding a German identity imply a normative dimension – for example, children are told how to behave properly, i.e., according to how Germans are expected to behave.

The website of the German House aptly describes its overall philosophy, beginning with a quote by Karsten Packeiser stating that 'punctuality, benevolence, intelligence, unbelievable work-ethic, orderliness, and respect towards other people are the main characteristics of the German national character'.[15] The text continues: 'The German people, who endowed the world with excellent scientists and composers, philosophers and authors, have been living in Kazakhstan for a long time'. The text then touches briefly on the history of Germans in Kazakhstan, mentioning Catherine the Great and the deportation by Stalin, and pointing out that the German people had suffered as many other peoples did. The opening paragraph concludes with the affirmation that the German people were not destroyed and 'went on to work honestly in the new territory'.[16] It is exactly this view of a German identity that is taught in many of the German House classes. This is certainly not to say that such an education in 'Germanness' always succeeds, and indeed many teachers complained about pupils who arrived late and did not apply themselves in class. Nonetheless, how to be a proper German is not only taught to the children but even in the *Seniorenclub* as well. For instance, someone who arrived late by even a few minutes usually had to sing a song on their own to 'atone' for their mistake.

Despite the occasional unmotivated pupil, many children at the German House are proud of and like to talk about German culture, and the fact that they are taught to join in the 'great German culture' helps them foster emotional attachments to it. Interestingly, young people identify themselves much more with a German identity than the elderly do, and feelings of belonging to a group of people who are exclusively German is most often found among teenagers. Thus, the German House is quite successful in inspiring young people to embrace German culture, especially the summer camps in the mountains, which they regard as an exciting adventure and which came about because of their German connection, have helped to reinforce this aim.

In contrast, among the elderly Germans of the *Seniorenclub*, feelings of belonging to a group are rarely emphasized. As discussed above, most members first of all expect the institution to support them. There were several incidents where the *Seniorenclub*'s head had proposed some kind of group activity, for example on the occasion of Easter, but because members were expected to contribute money to subsidize the proposed excursion (with those who were better off financially expected to pay more than those who were not), many complaints arose and cancellation followed. The head of the *Seniorenclub* explained that this behaviour, revealing a lack of solidarity among Germans, was result of their having been oppressed for so long.

Together with the *Seniorenclub* head and another employee of the German House I attended a festivity – *Sabantui* – celebrated by the Tatar national minority centre. The place was crowded an hour before the event was supposed to start, and all of the approximately two hundred waiting guests were served ice cream. The German House representatives admired the festivity's organization, and added that such an event would not succeed in the German House because of the lack of solidarity among the Germans. Whenever they arranged a celebration, only the organized groups showed up, in particular the *Jugendclub* and the *Seniorenclub*, and certainly not half of the Germans of Taldykorgan, as was the case for the Tatars and *Sabantui*. How and for whom the German House organizes festivities will be discussed in the subsequent chapter.

A Parish in Transition from 'German' to 'Lutheran'

Aside from the German House, the other institution in Taldykorgan labelled 'German' by many is the Lutheran parish. The parish in Taldykorgan dates back to 1979, when various communities united to buy the house where members still gather today. Before that time the different Lutheran communities met in several private houses. In 1989 the house was rebuilt and converted into a church, but it only began to attract a greater following after independence in 1991. However, at the same time the vast majority of its German members were preparing to emigrate. While about three hundred people attended Sunday mass at the beginning of the 1990s, that number has steadily declined during the last fifteen years, until only about forty people were attending in 2007. About a third of the parishioners were Germans above the age of sixty-five. The parish's younger members are German, Russian and Kazakh, and belong to only three families: the family of

Figure 7.3 Sunday mass in the 'German parish' (photo: R. Sanders, 2007)

the Russian priest, whose wife is also Russian; the family of a Kazakh friar, also married to a Russian woman; and the family of a German friar, whose German wife is deceased. The first two families have many children, and the third has two children. Thus, apart from the elderly members, each family holds an official position in the parish.

In contrast to the other parishes in town – two Orthodox and two Baptist parishes, a Presbyterian parish, the Jehovah's Witnesses parish, and two Catholic parishes – which all have more members, the Lutheran congregation does not appear particularly eager to attract new members. Consequently, many Germans do not know where the parish is situated, or even doubt that it exists at all. In contrast to minority centres, parishes do not have an official role in the state's implementation of interethnic harmony, and thus they are not asked to participate in any official festivities. However, the various parishes are tolerated, and Kazakh state officials from time to time point out that they have spent a lot of money on the renovation of Orthodox churches.[17]

Furthermore, there are no institutionalized links between the German House and the German parish, and they do not cooperate with regard to financial support by German charity organizations such as the Red Cross. On the contrary, the support from Germany seems to be a contentious issue. For instance, I was present when the priest at a meeting with the other officials of the parish complained heavily about the attitudes and practices of the German House with regard to support by the Red Cross.

The Lutheran faith arrived in Central Asia during the Second World War due to the influx of deported Germans. During Soviet times most Lutheran communities were not officially registered, preserving their religious and ethnic specificities in isolation, and – unlike most Protestants – not actively proselytizing (Peyrouse 2004: 655). A special connection forged between religious and ethnic belonging has often been asserted with regard to the Soviet era. For instance, Pelkmans (2007: 883) states, 'the [Soviet] regime encoded religious identities through its nationality politics'. After independence, some scholars contend that the link between religious and ethnic identity has further tightened. As Peyrouse (2004: 658) writes: 'The national vector has thus become a key element in religious affirmation, even more so than in Soviet times'. Moreover, Peyrouse (ibid.: 652) views the condition of out-migration as a key factor in religious revival:

> For exogenous nationalities, individuals who have refused to or could not emigrate, religion can constitute one of the possible – as much spiritual as cultural – compensations: the Orthodox Church for Russians, the Catholic Church for Poles or again Protestant prayer houses for Germans are then a place of spiritual as well as cultural-national communion.

However, the priest of the Lutheran parish in Taldykorgan, which is referred to as the 'German parish' by outsiders, does not connect his religious message to anything particularly German, and one is left with the impression that the German inscriptions on all of the church's images now appear out of place. The only reference to the parish's German past made by the priest during mass came before the praying of the 'Our Father', when he said that those who did not know the prayer in Russian should recite it in German.

The priest of the Lutheran parish describes himself as Russian. He was born in Taldykorgan in 1972, and began his ministry in 2001. His parents, according to him, were not believers, but he recalls that his mother told him not to say that God did not exist. He fell in love with a classmate who regularly attended the Lutheran parish, and at the beginning of the 1990s he also became a member of the Lutheran community (although the classmate was preparing to migrate to Germany). At that time he was the only non-German member. In the mid-1990s he was first asked to work with the children during Sunday school, and then asked to lead the Lutheran community when the German priest also decided to emigrate. To prepare, he attended a seminary in Ukraine, then returned to assume his duties in 2001.

In the late 1990s, the Lutheran parish faced a severe crisis, with most of its former members having emigrated to Germany. The remaining members, weary of the emotional farewells, began to distance themselves from the parish. The priest explained to me that the parish needed a new beginning, and that by introducing Russian into the services they could attract new members. Until 2006, some prayers were still spoken in German, but because it appeared to split the community, it was decided to abandon the language during services. In ethnic terms the parish's younger members designate themselves as Russian, Kazakh or German, or some combination of the three. But most of them also contend that their ethnic belonging is basically irrelevant, and thus the Lutheran parish appears to have not only overcome its previous German identity but any ethnically defined attachment. The priest explained the ethnic-religious relationship as follows:

> Today we are open for everyone [because they now conduct all services in Russian]. I mean we have always been open to everyone. The thing is just when people cannot understand anything, it is difficult for them to stay. And if for whatever reason all of a sudden many Kazakhs come to us, it will be possible to conduct some services in Kazakh. This will come. This is not all connected to culture; though it is close to it, but it is not the same thing. We do not strive to support old traditions, but to bring people close to God. We will not uphold any traditions if they are not helpful in strengthening people's faith. (Priest of the Lutheran parish in Taldykorgan)

Thus, the priest is generally open to attracting new members, but he views the detachment of the Lutheran faith from ethnic belonging as a prerequisite. The priest also told me that he has difficulties with his relatives living in Germany, who cannot understand his faith, so it cannot be discounted that these troubled personal relationships may be in part responsible for the parish's break with its German past, which also implies a break from previous members who emigrated to Germany and who rarely return to visit the parish. In any event, the refusal to associate religious belief with ethnicity suggests that the priest and other church officials have had to recreate their own cultural backdrop for the faith.

Pelkmans, investigating the interconnectedness of religious and ethnic belonging, has shown that missionaries in Kyrgyzstan first managed to separate Christianity from Russian culture by stating that religious faith had nothing to do with ethnic belonging, but then ultimately joined it to Kyrgyz lifestyle and values by incorporating Kyrgyz dances and music and referring to national symbols. Therefore, Pelkmans (2007: 887) concludes, 'the kind of culture that evangelicals promoted was Kyrgyz in form and Christian in content'. And this in part explains their success.

In the case of the Lutheran community in Taldykorgan, it is far from clear what cultural form can be drawn upon if not a reference to a Kazakhstani-German past. This cultural vacuum arises, for instance, during the Bible class that follows Sunday mass when the congregation meets in the basement for tea. While the younger women clean the dishes, the elderly and male members prepare for the class. A few questions on the week's Bible passage, each written on a single sheet of paper, are distributed. In turn, everyone is expected to answer all of the questions, whereupon some are harshly reprimanded for their lack of knowledge by one of the church officials. This Bible class, which moreover appears to be socially mandatory, seemed likely to frighten away potential new members. Furthermore, the Bible lessons, arising out of no clearly established cultural context, create a feeling of both uncertainty and exclusivity. The parish neither presents a universalist message nor relies upon Kazakhstani/Soviet cultural practices such as toasting, singing or dancing. Rather, the officials appear intent on building a local, independent, autochthonous community.

The German House in Transition

The era of vast out-migration has ended. During the year I spent in Taldykorgan, I only knew of one person preparing to emigrate to Germany. Thus, the German House is no longer concerned with giving advice on the most efficient and cost-effective way to obtain immigration documents. Furthermore, the fact that out-migration essentially came to a halt in Taldykorgan in 2006/2007 also reduced the number of German language participants and, thus, the financial support of the GTZ. Therefore, the German House had to seek out other money-making opportunities, such as engaging in other business.

The head of the German House, like every other businessman with whom I talked, is proud of knowing many people who are ready to help him:

> Many businessmen help us … [He mentioned the name of a businessman who recently helped the German House financially] He also helped. It was no big amount of money, but this also helps. Generally, I think that whenever we approach somebody, wherever we knock on somebody's door, it'll be opened to us. And we have a saying: *Under a lying stone the water won't run*. Therefore, we don't lie still but strive to be active and knocking on people's doors. (Vladimir Molodtsov, head of the German House)

The fact that the German House still receives some external support, and maintains a certain level of financial wherewithal, provides the opportunity to run other businesses. To that end, the German House established contacts with other businessmen, who until recently had no involvement with the institution. In present-day Taldykorgan, the German House offers them the opportunity to profit from its positive image, as well as its transnational networks.

The German House is often visited by official delegations, such as the Red Cross, the GTZ, a Russian-German association, the Catholic Church in Poland,

and the German embassy. Thus, it has become well connected to individuals working in other (state) institutions and companies in Kazakhstan and beyond. Furthermore, once such personal contacts are established, they have their own specific impacts on the implementations of policies and the work of the German House in general.

To give an example of these efforts to branch out, the German House currently runs a tourism enterprise. With the help of 'friends', the head of the German House succeeded in acquiring leasing rights to one of Kazakhstan's most scenic areas around the nation's highest waterfall, located about two hundred kilometres east of Taldykorgan. In 2007, the area was used for the first time to conduct one of the two ecological camps for teenagers. In subsequent years, the German House planned to attract tourists from Germany, for example, by advertising horseback riding and hiking in one of the world's most remote areas. One of the 'friends', a Kazakhstani-German businessman, leased the neighbouring valley, having similar, but complementary, plans in mind. A GTZ delegation, brought to the mountainous region by helicopter, expressed their support and generally praised the German House's proactive spirit. The (German) helicopter pilot – yet another 'friend' – brought others, in addition to the GTZ delegation, to view the area. While the head of the German House uses his positive relationship with the GTZ and his other connections to promote his own business interests, the fact that he is active and successful also helps the German House. His projects serve to widen the social network of the German House, which in turn can be useful in creating future projects (Sanders 2009: 44).

These 'friends' of the German House head, who have only recently become involved in the organization's business activities, are primarily Germans for whom a German identity has not been important. In fact, most of them have been critical of German state policies, and Germany and Germans in general. However, now that they are profiting from the positive image of the German House, and that their networks are bound together by something German related, many cultivate an appreciation for the usefulness of a German identity. Furthermore, it is now considered respectable among them to send one's children to the German House. Consequently, a Kazakhstani-German identity is constructed that breaks its connection to a past of suffering, focusing instead on the economic success of Kazakhstani Germans built upon the reputation of its hard-working people. This newly formed Kazakhstani-German identity, though it makes some references to a 'German spirit', does not emphasize any affiliation with the German nation, but rather has been shaped in the local context, and it is within the local context that boundaries are drawn, and people are included or excluded.

Elwert (2002: 41) states that political entrepreneurs and the emergence of leadership are central to the process of collective switching, which is directly applicable to the role of the German House in Taldykorgan. It is these entrepreneurs and leaders who coin the new identities and who expand boundaries in order to include as many people as possible into the German category, in sharp contrast to the largely exclusionary practices that take place in the *Seniorenclub*. In light of the above discussion, it is not surprising that any efforts by the *Seniorenclub* members to narrow the German category are not supported by the head of the German House.

Summary

It is primarily elderly Germans who expect the German House first and foremost to help them financially and to guarantee an equitable distribution of benefits. Against this background, the *Seniorenclub* provides an arena where an understanding of who is German is publicly discussed. Most of the club's members seek to narrow the ethnic category's boundaries. However, the *Seniorenclub*'s participants' grandchildren, who attend the youth club, do not explicitly distinguish between Russians and Germans, and they are proud of the club's increasing size. That being said, those among the *Jugendclub* who can claim German ancestry are equally proud of being a part of 'German culture', which is an omnipresent element in all of the German House's classes.

In contrast to the German House and its focus on things German, the Lutheran parish is eager to overcome its German past. The parish does not profit from transnational links nor from a positive German image. For them a German identity is connected above all to the massive decline in membership due to the 1990s out-migration. By focusing on the religious message, they seek to attract new members and to ensure the parish's survival which, however, does not seem assured.

The German House, on the other hand, benefits from its omnipresent link to a German identity although they actually have even fewer German-speaking members than the Lutheran parish. But by drawing on the widely shared stereotype of the 'typical German characteristics' as well as by establishing transnational networks, people succeed in opening up other businesses. Thus, the existence of minority organizations, and their institutionalized relationships with other organizations, gives people the opportunity to creatively use such existing ties for purposes that go beyond the role of a cultural minority centre. Since their activities stimulate social relations to other Germans in Kazakhstan and Germany, an awareness of being Kazakhstani German might become stronger. However, a business network of mostly Germans is certainly not the aim of Nazarbayev's nationality policies, the foremost objective of which is to recognize ethnicity while at the same time diluting any real significance that might be attached to it. The roles of the Kazakh and German states will be discussed in the next chapter.

Notes

1. In 2011, the GTZ as such was dissolved and formed, together with the DED (German Organization for Development) and Inwent (International Training and Development), the GiZ (Organization for International Cooperation).
2. The current director obtained his position in 1999. Many people in Taldykorgan affirmed that only at this time did the German House become active and known to a wider circle of people.
3. According to the official German House website, they started twenty-nine German language courses in 2008 (http:/www.mank-taldyk.kz/rus/assembly/centers/german/data/tpl-print/, retrieved 07 July 2008).
4. The GTZ is in charge of deciding the allocation of funds to the Eastern Europe and Central Asia Rebirth organizations, as well as actually disbursing them.
5. During an interview Annegret Westphal, the head of the GTZ in Central Asia in 2007, positively remarked upon the dedication to ecological themes exhibited by the German House in Taldykorgan and its director, and confirmed that summer camps with such a focus are highly valued since, according to her, environmental protection is one of the most pressing future concerns of Kazakhstan.
6. The German House now offers German, Kazakh and English in the weekly language courses.
7. A two-week stay was provided in 2006, but only a single week in 2007, a source of discontent among the affected elderly persons.
8. Among them are, for example, lists for the children's summer camp, for medicine and for clothes. New lists are opened when new services are provided, such as the quite crowded Kazakh language course.
9. The idea of the 'correct' length can be viewed in accordance with ideal group size (Schlee 2008: 26). Rational choice theorists 'seek to predict the conditions under which ethnic collective action will arise' (Hechter 1996: 92). According to them, members of any kind of group will only engage in collective action when they believe that they will receive a net benefit from acting collectively (ibid.). Further, the relevant organization itself is a crucial factor with regard to stimulating or discouraging any kind of group activity. The organization should be able to control information, to monitor activities and to distribute the collective benefits in an equitable way. If the organization does so, group activities are likely to occur. Moreover, one needs the ideal number of members in order to perform the collective action as efficiently as possible. Any additional member means, of course, yet another person with whom benefits must be shared.
10. The GTZ does not pay the salaries of local Rebirth employees, which should be considered when practices of putting money aside for one's own purposes are discussed.
11. This seems to be invented, since Valentina herself did not mention any German ancestors in the interview, which presumably she would have made a point of doing. Thus, it appears that her German friend felt the need to justify her inclusion into the *Seniorenclub* by devising German ancestry.
12. The German bands Rammstein and in particular Tokio Hotel are very popular in Kazakhstan.
13. The head of the youth club also stressed that every non-German is welcome as long as he or she 'wants to help'.
14. Many of the minority centres in Taldykorgan have a youth club.

15. Karsten Packeiser is a German journalist, but based on his other writings, it is doubtful that he is quoted accurately here.
16. www.mank-taldyk.kz/rus/assembly/centers/german/data/tpl-print/ (retrieved 07 July 2008)
17. This was, for instance, brought to my attention by the head of the Assembly of the People of Kazakhstan of the Almaty oblast and by the person responsible for 'language and culture' in the town hall of Taldykorgan.

Chapter 8

The Divergent Ethnic Policies of Kazakhstan and Germany

The effects of 'Kazakhization', most importantly with regard to language policies, have been explored in Chapter 4. It was argued that the policies of 'Kazakhization' have pushed Kazakhstani Germans into a 'Russian' category which, while no longer associated with the folkloristic sphere of a Soviet-style nationality, encompasses most non-Kazakhs and can be seen as a form of exclusion from the Kazakh nation state. At first glance this does not appear to be reconciled with the nationality policy of the Kazakh state that aims at the opposite, namely the harmonious coexistence of the one hundred declared nationalities. The Assembly of the People of Kazakhstan is promoted as a major instrument dedicated to the achievement of this objective by institutionalizing the existence of distinct groups. However, by over-representing the smaller groups, the Kazakh state in effect under-represents the Russians (Peyrouse 2007: 484).[1] On the occasion of Kazakhstan's many festivities, each of these nationality groups, organized in minority centres that operate under the umbrella of the assembly, is expected to present their distinct 'culture' to the public. Thus these festivities can be seen as one means of implementing nationality policy, or more precisely, categorizing people.

The role of the state in the endeavour to build and rebuild identities has been controversial in anthropology and beyond. The modernists' assumption of states constructing people's national identities has been challenged by such postmodern concepts as the plural society and transnationalism. Vertovec (2007: 162f), however, remarks that the power of nation states need not be diminished by transnationalism and globalization, but perhaps only restructured (cf. Darieva 2007: 84). Ferguson (2006) generally criticizes the dichotomization of 'people' and 'state', which is often expressed in the vertical concept of the 'local', the 'regional' and the 'state' level of analysis, whereby the local is associated with 'the authentic', with grassroots movements 'from below' that struggle against a repressive state 'from above' (ibid.: 90). Instead, he advocates, firstly, that global/transnational connections should not be overlooked and, secondly, for 'an approach to the state that would treat its verticality and encompassment not as taken-for-granted fact, but as precarious achievement – and as an ethnographic problem' (ibid.: 95).

In the German House in Taldykorgan all possible vertical layers coincide. It is, above all, a local institution that is supposed to act for people living in the city, but the German House is, moreover, part of a network of Rebirth organizations on the territory of the former USSR. Furthermore, it is shaped by two states' nationality and minority policies, and thus it must be addressed as a transnational institution (Pries 2008), though it was once founded as a kind of grassroots movement from below. The following sections investigate the states' encompassment as an ethnographic problem.

The Kazakh State's Official Promotion of Interethnic Harmony

According to the head of the German House, its primary goal is to promote German skills and traditions, which, at the same time, is its official duty as a Kazakh state minority centre. All minority centres are directed by the Assembly of the People of Kazakhstan, whose top official defines the institution's main objective as the preservation of the 'unity of peoples' (*edinstvo narodov*) through which the 'friendship of the peoples' (*druzhba narodov*) can be ensured. One important means for the fulfilment of this aim, in his opinion, is for minority groups to present their culture to the public, so that others can learn about their traditions, religion, cuisine and so on. Such a statement resembles the Soviet idea of equal nationalities that could and should learn from one another, since Soviet culture was understood as the result of each nationality's individual development (cf. Hirsch 2005: 316; cf. Slezkine 1994: 414).

In the following, the assembly official describes how they attracted publicity with their first minority festivities in the mid-1990s:

> From Almaty and other towns came prominent authors and representatives of broadcasting companies. They started to show which nations we have that were – during a time of repression under Stalin – forcibly deported to Kazakhstan. Today they live here, prosper and preserve their habits, culture and traditions. In order that they're able to preserve and develop all this, we conducted these common events, we learned from one another since we had no experience at that time. ... This is how we united the people, so that there's a unity, that the people don't grow apart from one another, that there won't be any phobia. But, on the contrary, that people come closer to one another; get to know better the other's culture, traditions and religion. (Ghabit Tursynbay, head of the Assembly of the People of Kazakhstan of the Almaty oblast)

The Divergent Ethnic Policies of Kazakhstan and Germany   209

Figure 8.1 The *Jugendclub* of the German House presenting a polka during *Nauriz* (photo: R. Sanders, 2007)

This view is shared by the administrative officer responsible for 'language and culture' in the *akimat* (town hall) of Taldykorgan, who stresses the importance of presenting different 'cultures' during various festivities. In this context, he critically noted that the German minority centre – unlike the Russian and the Korean centres – had not yet managed to erect its own temporary exhibition booth (*domik*) on the festival's main grounds. He emphasized the relevance of 'cultural items', asserting that it would be interesting for people outside of Taldykorgan, where there are no Germans, to see what a 'pure German house' would look like (Sanders 2009: 40).

In support of this goal, the assembly allots to each minority centre a certain amount of money, which must be spent on the realization of a typical national festivity once a year. The Tatar minority centre's *Sabantui*, discussed in Chapter 7, was one such celebration. The German centre celebrated *Ostern* (Easter) in 2006 and prepared a language festival for November 2007. Official representatives from each minority centre and from the assembly must be invited to such festivities, where they are served traditional food and drink. In addition, all minority centres are officially requested to actively participate in other national and non-national festivities.

Those working in the German House are well aware of the role they are expected to play. For instance, the head of the *Jugendclub* describes the club's main purpose as follows:

> Our club has several tasks. But the most important thing is, of course, to acquaint the teenagers with German culture, the German language, traditions and so on. This is first of all done in that we celebrate all kinds of German festivities, among which are Christmas, Easter and so on. All

upcoming festivities we honour. Further, we have a couple of festivities in town when the youth club performs its national music and dances. … We have a national dancing troupe. Its members dance national dances and perform on the occasion of every festivity where they demonstrate their proficiency. These beautiful dances show the spectators how interesting this all is and it will encourage new people who will also engage in it. (Natalya Shenknecht, head of the *Jugendclub*)

In the following description based on my field notes, I depict one particular festivity – *Nauriz* – by highlighting the German House's role. *Nauriz* was introduced in the late Soviet period as a concession to the non-Russian population. *Nauriz* is Iranian, but its origins date back to a pre-Islamic past and it plays upon nomadic symbolism (cf. Eitzen 1999: 75f). Furthermore, Eitzen (ibid.: 74) stresses that in particular *Nauriz* has been used to support the idea of interethnic harmony for 'Nauwriz commemorates the meeting of opposites', thus, the meeting of different (opposing) ethnic groups:

> *Nauriz*, the 'Kazakh new year', as it is widely known, is celebrated on the twenty-first of March. The main road – the independence road – leading to the *akimat* had been closed the day before to allow the construction of many booths for the upcoming event. On the following day, at nine o'clock, I was supposed to be at the stand of the German minority centre. On my way to it, I passed about forty other booths, most of which were actually yurts, representing university departments, banks and companies as well as concession stands. In between the booths were several stages for dance and music performances to be held by school and university groups. The booths closest to the *akimat* were the ones set up by minority centres opposite the largest one for 'Nur-Otan', the president's party. The nine minority stands were still busy with the arrangement of dishes, handicrafts and information posters when I arrived.[2] The German stand exhibited various wool handicrafts as well as sausages, meatballs, a streusel cake and deep-fried bread. Furthermore, there were posters informing the visitors about the Kazakhstani Germans' history and the minority centre's current activities. In addition, two dancing troupes and one singer were dressed in German costumes, but none of the German House's employees were dressed in such costumes. The head of the German House wore a suit, whereas the representatives of all the other minority centres were dressed in their traditional costumes, or at least were identifiable by known ethnic markers such as hats or caps.
>
> At exactly ten o'clock, at the event's official beginning, the German House's head made sure that the first dancing troupe started its

performance. All in all, their repertoire consisted of four dances, one of which was performed to an English song and three to German music, and two singing acts, one in German, the other in Kazakh. The audience formed a circle around them and applauded politely, particularly after the Kazakh song, which was presented in 'pure Kazakh', as one of the spectators informed me. However, most of the spectators did not linger for more than a couple of minutes and were moved onward by the mass of people. Only a very few approached the exhibition stand, or talked to the German House's representatives.

At about half-past twelve, when the twenty-five performing children and teenagers were already quite tired, the event reached its peak for the German House. The mayor (*akim*) of the city of Taldykorgan and a high-ranking representative of the oblast came to visit each of the minority stands. They were accompanied by an entourage of administrators and bodyguards. Seeing that they were about to leave the neighbouring Tatar stand, everybody at the German stand became slightly nervous as the streusel cake was hastily cut into pieces and the dancers were directed to stand in line in order to begin their performance. They performed a 'German polka' as both officials embraced first the representative of the club for elderly people (*Seniorenclub*) – an elderly woman – and then shook hands with the centre's head and all the others. After partaking of the offered German cake and beer, the officials complimented German cuisine in flowery language, called German beer the best in the world, and praised the present state of German-Kazakh relations.[3] Once they left, the head of the German House expressed his satisfaction by saying that it was a very good sign that they had drunk the offered beer and stayed much longer at the German stand than at any other, which was true at least compared to the neighbouring Tatar and Kurdish stands. Soon afterwards, minority centres appeared eager to pack up as quickly as possible and, within two hours, the event of *Nauriz* had basically shut down except for the performances on the big stage. The Germans of the German House, however, continued to celebrate in their minority centre, the teenagers of the *Jugendclub* gathered for their disco, and the staff met on the first floor for drinking tea and vodka. (Sanders 2009: 40f; field notes 22/03/2007)

During the year, I attended a few other festivities – the First of May, the town's day, and the day of the cultures – all of which were aimed at demonstrating interethnic harmony. These public performances have become a decisive manifestation of Kazakhstan's nationality policy. As Eitzen (1999: 74) contends: 'by providing occasions that emphasize eclecticism and promote multi-ethnicity, the concerns of many groups are intermittently addressed. Mass public events as a tangible means of exploring consensus literally and figuratively can set the stage for public policy'.

For the festivities, the minority centres are asked to exhibit their particular traditions and demonstrate a variety of practices, most of which are virtually non-existent in everyday life. For instance, outside the German House, I never witnessed Germans dancing the polka, and since no one knew how to bake a 'traditional German apple pie', and I was often asked to do so, I finally looked up a recipe on the internet and baked the pie for one of the festivities. This view of ethnicity, focusing on handicrafts, dances, music and dishes, places the attribution of ethnicity in a rather circumstantial realm and, at least for the German minority, refers to cultural expressions that are largely absent from daily life (cf. Sanders 2013b: 83).

Thus, by means of such festivities, the Kazakh state is able to demonstrate its liberal position towards minority groups while at the same time diminishing the political significance of ethnic belonging. Consistent with the Soviet understanding of ethnicity, Nazarbayev intends for nationalities to be 'cultural', not political, entities. The national minority centres are chiefly concerned with the performance of their cultures, an undertaking in which 'culture is constructed in a folkloristic sense, with fixed meaning and insignias, devoid of a subjective identity dimension', as Dave (2007: 130) argues. Therefore, the German House seems to perfectly support the president's view of ethnic belonging as a folkloristic expression and does not appear to transgress the allowed depoliticized role of ethnicity.

That being said, the fact that those 'traditions' are only ritually expressed during such festivities might still accord them significance (Sanders 2009: 42). Many studies on ritual expressions have explored the interconnectedness of performance, identity formation and 'ultimate truth'. For instance, Kaschuba (2001: 22) remarks that ritual forms of cultural expression bestow their messages with ultimate truth and give their spectators ontological security exactly because they are detached from daily life (cf. Giddens 1993). Furthermore, Köpping et al. (2006: 21) argue for viewing performances as a means of 'making "culture" real as a mode of existence'. Keeping this in mind, ritualized forms of cultural expression are not devoid of a subjective identity dimension. On the contrary, the performances of culture appear to support, in the context of present-day Kazakhstan, the assumption of inherited ethnic identities, which are set beyond the realm of the rationale and of individual experience. But, certainly, for the anthropologist the question remains: How do Kazakhstani Germans themselves see the role they are expected to play?

I should mention at the outset that almost everyone in the German House and beyond stressed the positive effects of the assembly. Many people were proud of being part of a state that has an institution which supports all nationalities. As explored in Chapter 4, the knowledge of traditional customs and the fact that the

The Divergent Ethnic Policies of Kazakhstan and Germany   213

Figure 8.2 The German stand serving 'traditional' food at the 'day of the town' (photo: R. Sanders, 2007)

president himself makes sure everyone has the opportunity to express themselves culturally, even in public during the state's most important festivities, is generally appreciated.[4]

Moreover, the concept of culture that the German House pursues and how the German category is outlined matches views about Germans expressed by Kazakh state representatives, such as in this excerpt from an interview with the head of the assembly for the Almaty oblast:

> Well, first of all, what characterizes all Germans is punctuality. When they say that they'll come at twelve o'clock, they'll come at twelve. Secondly, religion – Russians are Orthodox, Germans Catholic. Thirdly, for the most part, Germans were deported here. Almost all in our settlement – who were forcibly settled here in Kazakhstan – as far as I know, during my childhood when I was a little boy, were Germans and all of them spoke Kazakh. Since that time many Russians don't know Kazakh because here – what happened was that under the Soviet regime the Russian people were like the great elder brother and the Russian language was everywhere, like the state language. Therefore, they knew that they didn't have to learn and know Kazakh particularly well. There was such an attitude. But Germans were always on good terms with the local population because at the time they were brought here, they were hungry, they had no clothes, nothing. When they were brought here during the war, many lived in Kazakh families, in Kazakh houses. That way they survived. They respected the Kazakhs' culture and traditions, and

they wanted to know Kazakh. I think this might also make a difference. (Ghabit Tursynbay, head of the Assembly of the People of Kazakhstan of the Almaty oblast)

He not only stresses positive German characteristics but also highlights the fact that Germans are much more likely to speak Kazakh than Russians are. By doing so, he makes a distinction between Russians and Germans and invokes the oft-mentioned German-Kazakh bond that also specifically excludes Russians. Thus, in receiving such a favourable official acknowledgement, it is little wonder that Germans generally appreciate the assembly and understand the role that the German House, as a part of the assembly, is expected to play.

At the same time, however, many Germans in Taldykorgan are aware that they are supposed to take part in representing ethnic diversity and, in this way, expressing their loyalty towards the Kazakh state. For instance, on the occasion of the first of May, which now bears the theme of 'the unity of the people of Kazakhstan' (*edinstvo naroda Kazakhstana*), I accompanied some German businessmen. In 2007, a procession was organized for the first time, in which universities, schools and companies were asked to participate. While waving Kazakh flags, most of those with whom I walked complained that the idea of the procession was ridiculous, saying that they did not have the time for such insipid events but that they felt obliged to be there. The roughly two-kilometres-long procession ended in front of the *akimat*, where the *akim* and other officials were seated at a dais. Each company or university department was announced through a loudspeaker as they passed, while spectators cheered. The German businessmen also disparaged the new motto, adding that Nazarbayev never missed an opportunity to promote his vision of interethnic harmony. Nonetheless, all of them generally appreciated his policies (cf. Sanders 2013b: 77).

The same holds true for the German House. Of course, some employees complained about the sometimes absurd performances, for instance, when they had to wait for the president's visit in front of the party building, dressed in their ethnic costumes and standing in the sun for several hours in the middle of August. Moreover, some members of the German House admitted that they only join in those performances for the *akim* to prove that they have 'done their homework'. But this is not to say that they are not generally in accord with the Kazakh state's policies towards interethnic harmony. Though many people in Taldykorgan do not take the festivities about the 'people of Kazakhstan' seriously and, furthermore, are well aware of the political intent behind them, those cultural representations are still likely to have an effect. The festivities as well as the numerous ethnic competitions in which, for instance, pupils or university students sing different ethnic songs, repeatedly demonstrate both the existence and – thanks to Nazarbayev – the harmonious coexistence of distinct ethnic groups.

In this respect, as has been mentioned above, the minority centres certainly aid the president in spreading his views with regard to the 'people of Kazakhstan' and ensuring interethnic harmony. However, other activities of the German House and how they are implemented might be seen as running contrary to that aim. Above all, it is almost exclusively non-Kazakhs who take part in the German House's activities, and thus feelings of being excluded from the Kazakh state – despite all the proclamations of interethnic harmony – might more easily take hold and the gap between Kazakhs and other Kazakhstanis widen. Many activities in fact intensify the feeling of being non-Kazakh. This feeling can be explored, for example, through a discussion of the German House's Kazakh language course.

Quite recently, the German House started to offer free Kazakh language courses, conducted in the evenings by a young Kazakh woman who works during the day as a school teacher of Kazakh and who impressed me as a good instructor. She explained to me that she wants pupils to speak the language and not simply learn grammatical rules and poems, which until recently was the primary method of teaching Kazakh. For example, she asked her students to play out a scene in a shop. Most pupils only knew a few phrases by heart and found it difficult to use them correctly, even though by that time they had received about six months of language training at the German House (not to mention Kazakh language training in regular school).[5] For instance, some of them confused a question about the price with the shopkeeper's question 'How much do you want?'

The main point of interest here, however, is how Kazakhs themselves were discussed. After I had attended the language course for several weeks, I realized that above all these pupils needed to learn by interacting with native speakers. It was striking, however, that the students talked about Kazakhs and the Kazakh language as something quite distinct from them. One could make the argument that it would be better to organize *any* kind of common activity with Kazakh language speakers rather than conducting a language course where conversations are so obviously contrived. First, such contrived conversations in class basically served to convince the students that they were not capable of speaking Kazakh in public and left them instead joking about not knowing the language, at times with a sense of pride and at other times with a sense of frustration, not to mention the jokes about the sound of the Kazakh language itself. Thus, for the most part, the course confirmed feelings of being non-Kazakh and a non-Kazakh speaker instead of inspiring pupils to improve at the Kazakh language and to lose some of their self-consciousness at trying to speak it in public, and in doing so increase their meaningful contacts with Kazakhs.

In short, based on my observations, while the German House operates in accordance with Nazarbayev's nationality policy and is eager to continue complying with it, the ascription of fixed ethnic identities and the factual exclusion of Kazakhs might, nonetheless, impede identification with the Kazakh state.

The German State's Contradictory Policies

Official statements about Kazakhstan by German politicians are often inspired by the idea of the German minority as a bridge linking Germany and Kazakhstan, as can be seen in this statement by German Chancellor Angela Merkel on the occasion of President Nazarbayev's visit to Germany in January 2007:

> We have human relations. We have a German minority in Kazakhstan which in a way serves as a bridge. One representative of the German minority, who is today here, even bears my surname. Thus, we are definitely in various ways connected.[6]

However, the last two decades of ethnically defined immigration policies have severely weakened this envisioned bridge between the two countries now that more than eighty per cent of Kazakhstan's previous German minority resides in Germany. Overwhelmed with this large influx of immigrants, German law has changed several times since the early 1990s in order to monitor and reduce the number of immigrants, but the underlying assumption of the *Volksdeutsche* category, who belong to the German nation by descent and thus are entitled to German citizenship, has not been challenged.[7]

The fundamental contradiction in policy – shifting between inviting people to reside as German citizens in Germany and encouraging them to stay where they were born – has shaped the work of the GTZ (German Organization for Technical Cooperation) and the German Rebirth organizations that must implement it. Since 1990 the GTZ has been charged with carrying out a programme for German minorities in Eastern Europe and Central Asia to improve their circumstances and, in the case of Kazakhstani Germans, to strengthen their desire to remain in Kazakhstan.[8] The GTZ aspires to fulfil this objective through five main activities: involvement in gathering places such as local Rebirth organizations (the German Houses), German language courses, work with children and teenagers, educational training, and humanitarian and social aid. The GTZ website contends that their activities (together with the improved economic situation in many of the concerned countries) have resulted in less out-migration to Germany and thus have achieved the aim of the GTZ.[9]

It is hardly controversial to counter that this is not true, and even the head of the GTZ for Central Asia conceded that their activities have at least partially fuelled the desire for out-migration. In particular the free German language courses, financed by the GTZ, have provided many with the opportunity to pass the language exam that is a prerequisite for immigrating to Germany.

It has often been discussed to what extent German state immigration policies influence people's concept of an ethnic German identity (Brake 1998; Moore 2000; Römhild 1998; Stoll 2007). To begin with, according to the

Bundesvertriebenengesetz (federal law on refugees) of 1955/56, section 6, being German is defined by descent, language, education and culture and requires a person to have professed her or his German identity.¹⁰ The law further demands that a person intending to immigrate 'as a German' has to prove their German descent through documentation (such as birth certificates), and only those who are approved by the federal administrative office (*Bundesverwaltungsamt*) will be invited to take a German language test in which also their German education and culture will be confirmed.¹¹

Römhild (1998) explores the difficulties Kazakhstani and Russian Germans have to face when confronted with being categorized in ethnic terms that often diverge from their perception of who they are. Brake (1998: 338–51) points out that most of his interviewees, during the process of immigration, began to frame their own experiences of hardship in a different way by referring more often to a collective memory of Russian-German history. Stoll (2007: 114f), however, rightly underlines that their findings, which derive from interviews with Russian/Kazakhstani Germans who mostly emigrated to Germany in the early 1990s, cannot be so easily transferred to those who did not emigrate. Stoll (ibid.: 115) states that Kazakhstani Germans are more concerned about practical matters related to how to immigrate most easily than about their ethnic identities. Finally, Moore (2000), who analyses German language tests conducted by officials of Germany's federal administration in Kazakhstan, argues that the German state's immigration policies communicate the existence of measurable fixed ethnic identities, in particular along linguistic lines.

Certainly the German state communicates fixed ethnic identities whereby the German language, most likely because it is the easiest to test, plays a decisive role. But how do Kazakhstani Germans deal with this definition of being German? The German language with respect to its potential as an ethnic boundary marker has been explored in Chapter 3, where it was asserted that German language skills only serve as boundary markers for the oldest generation. Furthermore, it was pointed out that most people consider learning German only because it is necessary for immigration to Germany. It is important to add here that those who did not pass the language exam, based on my interviews, neither felt less German than before nor saw their ethnic German identity as being challenged. Usually people held to the belief that their ethnic identity was inherited and thus could not be contested, and explained their lack of knowledge about German customs and language by referring to experiences of discrimination against Germans during childhood. Moreover, people complained about the 'unjust' language test since they knew of 'pure Germans' who failed to pass it.

Many people who work in the German House or who attend one of the clubs are generally critical of Germany's immigration policy. For instance, on the occasion of a birthday party of one of the members of the *Seniorenclub*, someone proposed a toast to the GTZ and German state policies in general (I had the impression that this was done solely for my sake), but was immediately challenged by another member who claimed that Germany would only betray them in the end. This criticism met with general approval, and the toast was not made.

Perceptions of Germany have been discussed at length in Chapter 6. Here it should be added that Germany's immigration policies contribute to the predominantly negative picture of an often assumed 'historic homeland'.[12] Attitudes towards immigration policy fall into two camps and depend largely on whether or not a person desires to immigrate. Those who desire to stay in Kazakhstan tend to criticize German politicians for having allowed Kazakhstani Germans to immigrate to Germany, even though Germans in Germany did not welcome them and jobs were not provided. The out-migration triggered by the German state is further held responsible for splitting up families (sometimes even compared to the deportations of 1941) and for having destroyed German life in Kazakhstan. Those who intended to immigrate or still intend to do so argue that Germany is right to allow all Germans to return to their 'historic homeland', but that German politicians (former Chancellor Gerhard Schröder was mentioned most often in this regard) were guilty of the ill-conceived reversal of those policies at a time that led to the splitting up of families and even the rejection of 'pure Germans'.

Thus, German state immigration policies are widely criticized, and the German state is not viewed as a legitimate authority for defining a German identity in Kazakhstan. Therefore, Stoll (2007) is correct when contending that Kazakhstani Germans are less concerned about being a proper German according to German law than about learning the most advantageous way to fill out immigration application forms. That being said, most Germans in Taldykorgan are not much concerned about either matter, but the fact that some of them have been denied immigration certainly contributes to the generally negative attitude towards German state policies.

Finally, it is important to note that, until recently, what has guaranteed the continued existence of most local Rebirth branches is the aim of German state policies to give Germans in Kazakhstan the opportunity to learn their 'mother tongue', which is why German language courses have been financed in Kazakhstan since 1996.[13] For local Rebirth branches this funding is often essential, which is why the lists of language course participants might sometimes be padded (cf. also Stoll 2007: 207). Furthermore, many Rebirth branches offer a translation service, which is second only to language classes as a source of funds. Often, those who translate the necessary immigration documents from Russian into German provide additional 'tips' on how to fill in the forms, which has brought them into conflict with the German embassy (cf. ibid.: 122f). Although the Rebirth organization is not officially allowed to advise people with regard to immigration matters (according to an agreement with the German embassy), in practice people are most often offered exactly that by the translation services (ibid.: 221). Thus, it is not the German state's minority programme but rather its regulations for immigration (above all the language test) that have shaped the work of German organizations in Kazakhstan. On the whole, German Houses in Kazakhstan profit from German state policies, but many who work there are also frustrated by the contradictory nature of the policies, which, while seeking to revive German life in the local context, also make it more likely that those who are 'trained' in the German language and customs can leave the country.

I now turn to Germany's minority policy, which has recently aimed at projecting a 'modern' image of Germany and which runs contrary to the state's ethnically defined immigration policy. The work of the German House in Taldykorgan and its promoted concept of 'Germanness' have been described in the previous chapter: it was argued that older people tend to expect the institution first of all to support them materially, while younger Germans profit from the German House by making friends there and learning about 'German culture'. The intended and unintended effects of the German House's practices have been a narrowing of the German category with regard to older Germans and the creation of feelings of ethnic belonging among younger Germans. Moreover, it was said that the performance of ethnic customs is in line with both the German House's declared mission and the purpose ascribed to it by Kazakhstani politicians.

In part, German state institutions strive to promote a cosmopolitan view of the country, and so the German House regularly receives informational material about Germany that is provided by the GTZ or the Goethe-Institut. A map of Germany, used by the head of the *Seniorenclub* to decorate the room in the recreation home where a couple of elderly Germans recuperated for a week, was subtitled '*Lebendigkeit, Witz und Vielfalt*' (liveliness, wit and diversity). I was asked what it meant and found it hard to explain how such a caption could be relevant to a conception of Germany as a state. While it is true that younger people are more open-minded and curious about Germany, there is not much for them to learn at the *Jugendclub* about contemporary German issues, and I sensed that wherever the map of Germany might be placed, it would serve to do little more than add colour to a wall.

So why do people in the German House persist in presenting, and accepting, an unrealistic picture of Germans and Germany? Most of the lessons in the German House make no real attempt to teach about the Germany of today; instead, children learn the story of *Sankt Nikolaus* or how to string an Advent wreath, or they learn about German philosophers and composers and German songs and dishes. However, it is not necessarily fair to attempt to determine right and wrong with regard to the subject matter taught in classes, since German traditions and customs in the German House are widely assumed to exist beyond time and space and, therefore, aim at an essentialized notion of 'Germanness'. Although teachers in the German House might agree that Germans in Germany do not dance the polka, they also believe that a type of

'German spirit' (*nemetskiy dukh*) nevertheless exists and should be culturally expressed. Thus, Germany remains the point of reference through which people in the German House define their ethnic belonging; however, how they conceptualize a German identity is not connected to most of present-day German state discourses (cf. Sanders 2009: 43f).

The lessons in the German House might be better understood if one regards them as performances and the imparted knowledge as more ritual than informative. Humphrey and Laidlaw (1994) argue that ritual action differs from other modes of action insofar as actors do not intend to communicate meaningful messages. Belliger and Krieger (2013: 26, 30) expand on this idea by adding that the ritual mode of communication does not imply that people learn something new. Instead, ritual knowledge entails acting in the 'right way', thereby renouncing agency. Ritual acting seeks to preserve the identity of culture and ultimately to establish social identities, draw profound boundaries and declare truth. Viewed in this manner, ritual knowledge becomes invulnerable to challenge on the basis of argument and reason.

The ritual nature of knowledge with regard to a German identity implies a process of authentication. Such knowledge provides Kazakhstani German children and teenagers with something at hand with which to directly identify as Germans in the local context. By knowing about *Sankt Nikolaus* they are able to 'prove' to other children that they are really Germans. Likewise, many German parents send their children to the German House because they want them to know the 'traditional customs' – i.e., their roots. These customs are accepted as how one lives as a proper German, even though they do not have much in common with how Germans in Taldykorgan actually live and – as far as I can judge – they have not been incorporated into their daily lives. Moreover, in present-day Kazakhstan, people no longer attend courses in German culture to prepare for a new life in Germany, as was pointed out during the 1990s (e.g., Römhild 1998: 260).

Interestingly, Germany and 'German culture' are perceived for the most part as distinctly different entities, which also explains why an image of present-day Germany is not prioritized by the German House – its representatives focus on imparting 'German culture' and, more importantly, Germans in Taldykorgan have other sources for learning about Germany (see Chapter 6). Nonetheless, the customs and habits taught in the German House are widely accepted as being 'authentically German', which is best summarized by the aforementioned concept of an essentialized 'German spirit'. The assumed existence of a 'German spirit' might also explain why I never came across a reference to a Russian or Kazakhstani-German culture. Paradoxically, or at least so it seems, by creating a 'German spirit' they draw a firm line between Germans in Germany and themselves, although without making any claim to being more authentically German than people in Germany.

It is important here to keep in mind that many employees of the German House have deliberately chosen to stay in Kazakhstan, and that most of them have been to Germany several times. Their reasons for staying in Kazakhstan are partially due to their negative perception of Germany, so it is not surprising that some of them are not motivated to inspire people about a country that they themselves do not particularly like. This helps to explain why they stick to their own version of German habits and customs, which do not attempt to explore any of Germany's '*Lebendigkeit, Witz und Vielfalt*'.

Most non-Germans, as has been discussed, generally lump together everything they have heard about Germany, Germans, German state policies and the work of the German House into the German category. Thus, non-Germans often perceive the German House as 'little Germany', and thereby the predominantly positive image of the German House is transferred to Germany itself. What is most commonly mentioned by non-Germans is the fact that the German House has by far the most abundant financial means of all minority centres in Taldykorgan and Kazakhstan in general (Stoll 2007: 40).

It is often argued (Brown 2005; Diener 2004: 133f) that the financial support from Germany is not welcomed by all Kazakhstani Germans because it singles them out as German and can in effect stigmatize them for being German. However, this attitude does not hold true for the Germans I met in Taldykorgan. Though the majority of Taldykorgan Germans do not avail themselves of the German House, and many of them do not need any assistance from it, none of them criticized on principle the aim of the German House to support Kazakhstani Germans. I never came across the argument that such help, exclusively for Germans, might be perceived as a negative categorization and/or that it had provoked envy from those who do not profit from it. Likewise, Kazakhs and Russians did not complain about the German House supporting only Germans. This might seem surprising, but it demonstrates that ethnic belonging in Kazakhstan is basically seen as something positive and thus it would be viewed as logical that Germans first of all help other Germans (Sanders 2009: 42). In fact, many people in Taldykorgan, irrespective of their ethnic belonging, appreciated the work of the German House and, with it, the attitude of the German state. The German House is generally seen as a reliable institution that seriously pursues its goals, and sometimes even the town's prominent Kazakh businessmen rely upon it.[14] The fact that such a German institution is generally held in high regard can first of all be seen as symbolically valuable. Thus, the financial means provided by the German state and how they are used by the German House have strengthened the position of Germans in Taldykorgan – not because many Taldykorgan Germans directly profit from the assistance, but because the good reputation of the German House supports positive stereotypes of Germans.

All in all, the effects of German state policies on the lives of Germans in Taldykorgan are mixed. It is obvious that the objective to strengthen people's wish to stay in Kazakhstan failed, especially during the 1990s. Furthermore, the above-discussed outcomes such as the narrowing of the concept of 'Germanness' and the reference to a 'German spirit', which in effect have led to a feeling of separation from the present-day reality of Germany, are not intended by the GTZ. While it would be misguided to state that all or even most of the intended and unintended effects of German state policies actually harm people in Taldykorgan, the preceding discussion has shown that policies by a state, particularly one as physically far removed as Germany, are likely to have unexpected outcomes, not least because they are shaped by the policies of another state, in this case Kazakhstan.

Summary

The Rebirth organization was founded on the eve of the Soviet Union's collapse with the aim of strengthening the position of German minorities and acting on their behalf, even when in opposition to the home state of those minorities. This erstwhile initiative 'from below' rose to the level of a state institution, when the formation of the Assembly for the People of Kazakhstan in 1995 led to an incorporation of all local Rebirth organizations, which became the assembly's minority centres. The Rebirth organization continues to receive financial support from the GTZ, however, and thus continues to be shaped in part by German state policies.

Kazakhs and many Russians attribute their mostly positive image of Germans and the German House to the German state. The Germans themselves, and in particular those involved with the German House, maintain a more critical stance towards Germany. That helps to explain why the German House employees are not particularly concerned with propagating information about Germany, and instead focus their efforts on promoting German habits and culture; moreover, this is perfectly in step with what is expected of them by the Kazakh state – that is, the public performance of traditional 'culture' aligns with the president's liberal stance towards ethnic minorities.

Two states with somewhat contradictory visions of ethnic belonging and different means of implementing those visions still leave enough space for Kazakhstani Germans to define their ethnic belonging (outside of German state influence) and to use their ethnicity for diverse activities (which aligns only partly with what the Kazakhs state wants them to do). Certainly, states do not have full control over the outcomes of their policies, and it is often the unexpected results that play the most decisive roles. In this case, it is the ethnically defined network around the German House and its positive image that have triggered unexpected activities.

The German House in Taldykorgan can be seen as a 'transnational organization' (Pries 2008) that effects transnational social networks and accounts for the inclusion of its members into two nation states. However, as far as Kazakhstani

Germans are concerned, it does not hold true that 'engagement between kin-states and dispersed communities inherently catalyzes cultural revival and a "re-imagining" of the co-ethnic groups as "diasporic"' (Diener 2006: 218). Germany's engagement has triggered ambivalent feelings towards it among Kazakhstani Germans, and has in fact stimulated an awareness of being culturally different from, and of ultimately not belonging to, the German nation.

Notes

1. The assembly consists of twenty-six per cent Kazakhs, fifteen per cent Russians and 6.5 per cent each of Koreans, Germans and Tatars. The other minorities are less represented (Peyrouse 2007: 484).
2. The nine stands represented the following minority centres: Tatar, German, Kurdish, Chechen, Jewish, Korean, Polish, Uighur and Russian.
3. I did not participate in the conversation, having been told by the German House's deputy to take as many photographs as possible. Obviously, at that time I was perceived rather as an employee than as a special guest.
4. In addition to festivities, there are other official ways of expressing a nationality's culture in the media. As for 'German culture', since 1958 there has been a German radio programme in Kazakhstan. In 1966 the German newspaper *Freundschaft* (Friendship) was founded, later renamed *Deutsche Allgemeine Zeitung*; it is currently financed by the Kazakh state and the association of Germans in Kazakhstan (*Assoziation der gesellschaftlichen Vereinigungen der Deutschen Kasachstans*). Furthermore, since 1989, there is a German-speaking programme on TV, which is broadcast weekly (Stoll 2007: 186f). All in all, however, German-speaking media are not very popular in Kazakhstan, and in fact most people in Taldykorgan, and also most Germans, are not aware of them.
5. Most of the fifteen or so pupils in the language course of the German House were around the age of ten and, therefore, had already received four years of Kazakh language training at school.
6. The translation is provided by the author; the original text in German is as follows: *Wir haben menschliche Beziehungen. Wir haben eine deutsche Minderheit in Kasachstan, die so etwas wie eine Brückenfunktion ist. Ein Abgeordneter der deutschen Minderheit ist heute dabei, der sogar den gleichen Nachnamen trägt wie ich. Man hat also durchaus vielerlei Verbindungen.*
7. The new law on immigration, passed in 2005, states that immigrating *Spätaussiedler* must provide proof of German parents (for passport entry) and not solely German grandparents (Stoll 2007: 149).
8. The programme operates on behalf of the *Bundesministerium des Inneren* (Ministry of the Interior) and the *Bundesverwaltungsamt* (Federal Administrative Office), which also articulates the German minorities' legal position. All other GTZ programmes that operate abroad work on behalf of the Ministry of Foreign Affairs.
9. http://www.gtz.de/de/weltweit/europa-kaukasus-zentralasien/regionale-themen/11394.htm (retrieved 16 July 2008)
10. The legislative text in German is as follows: '*Deutscher Volkszugehörige im Sinne dieses Gesetztes ist, wer sich in seiner Heimat zum deutschen Volkstum bekannt hat, sofern dieses Bekenntnis durch bestimmte Merkmale wie Abstammung, Sprache, Erziehung, Kultur bestätigt wird*' (cited in Stoll 2007: 133f).

11. There are two different types of language test: one for those who intend to acquire German citizenship (i.e., acquire the status of *Spätaussiedler* according to section 4 of the *Gesetz über die Angelegenheit der Vertriebenen und Flüchtlinge* [BVFG], which was implemented in 1996); and another for all non-German family members that was implemented by Germany's new immigration law. The first is not so much a test as it is aimed at assessing one's 'true Germanness' – during an ordinary conversation (usually also touching on the issue of German customs) one must demonstrate that they have spoken German within the family, which is above all determined by a person's knowledge of German dialects. If the person fails, both they (and their family) will ultimately be denied immigration. Only for the second type of language test – that is, for non-German family members – is a second chance permitted (cf. Stoll 2007: 113, 140–49).
12. A negative perception of Germany is also found among Russian-German authors. For instance, Wormsbecher writes that German state policies have inflicted more damage on Russian Germans than Soviet policies (in *Novoe vremya*, 17 January 1995; cited in Eisfeld 1999: 192).
13. In 2002, there were about 1,200 GTZ-funded German language courses with about 24,000 participants in Kazakhstan. To receive financial support from the GTZ, sixty per cent of the participants in a class must be German (Stoll 2007: 202).
14. This is not to deny that there are complaints about the German House's activities, primarily around issues of financial support provided by the German state, which some claim has been used by German House officials for private purposes. But their criticism does not influence the general perception of the German House in Taldykorgan.

Conclusion
Germans at Home in Kazakhstan

In the final years of the Soviet Union, Gorbachev's policies of *glasnost* enabled hundreds of thousands of Soviet Germans to head west. As for Kazakhstan, independent since 1991, fewer than one fifth of its once one million Germans have remained. Those who emigrated to Germany often did so to live 'among their own kind'. The idea of an 'historic homeland' formed the basis for assuming common German traits, and thus a common German identity. This research study, however, has dealt with those Germans who stayed in Kazakhstan and who, therefore, live apart from most of their relatives and friends, previous classmates and former neighbours. Their situation is shaped by the fact that they have been left behind, by their struggle to decide whether to leave or stay, and by their often complicated relationships with relatives and friends abroad.

This study has explored how people identify themselves and categorize others in their day-to-day lives, and how this is linked to their past experiences and their future strategies. It has been argued that, as a general principle, people use their ethnic belonging in order to pursue their goals, and that they have sufficient agency, but unequal power, to gradually rebuild identities if necessary. However, each individual is constrained to varying degrees by his or her emotional attachment to identities. Furthermore, it has been shown that identities and people's identifications mutually influence one another. Thus, people might alter the boundaries of ethnic belonging through their identifications, which in the long run changes the mental schemas of identities and, in turn, impacts the process of future identifications. This dialectical process is shaped by people's social relations – which include, in the case of Kazakhstani Germans, transnational relations – and by how identities are evaluated – which includes, but is not limited to, 'official evaluations' in state discourse and through state policies.

Identity and Memories

Part One has shown that identities draw on specific memories of the past. Those memories are themselves the result of an ongoing interpretation of past events. The history of Kazakhstani (Soviet and Russian) Germans tells the story of both prosperous German settlements in the Volga and on the Black Sea Coast and the hardship of deportation to Siberia and Central Asia. In the course of potential emigration from the Soviet Union in the 1980s, the Soviet German memory became associated with victimhood, which was seen as a precondition for having the right to abandon one's home for the sake of living in an imagined 'historic homeland' where justice was to be found. Thus, it is this collective memory of suffering and unjust treatment during and after the Second World War that Soviet and, later, Kazakhstani/Russian Germans referred to when applying for immigration to Germany. This interpretation of past events was, furthermore, reinforced by German state immigration policies that promoted precisely this view of Soviet-German history.

Those Kazakhstani Germans who did not emigrate for various reasons tend to highlight the positive aspects of Russian- and Soviet-German history, focusing on the formerly prosperous German settlements as the ultimate evidence of typical German characteristics, above all the working ethos. This is particularly relevant for younger generations who, on those grounds, are proud of their ethnic identity, but it is also supported by those elderly Germans who resist being depicted as victims. Therefore, it is misguided to simply contend (as per Diener 2004; Stoll 2007) that those who did not emigrate to Germany displayed the least ethnic awareness. Rather, a German identity in present-day Kazakhstan refers to a positively reconstituted German memory, wherein a German identity becomes an ever more attractive one. This, however, also entails that the boundaries for the process of ethnic identification have been changing to allow more people to identify themselves as German.

Identities and Identifications

As has been discussed in this study, although Kazakhstani Germans have very diverse biographies that have resulted in varying attitudes towards 'being German', they share, for the most part, a common perception of a German identity. This identity is widely viewed as being based on common ancestry that also entails the inheritance of positive German traits such as reliability and orderliness. German language proficiency, once seen as a fundamental prerequisite for claiming a German identity (Dorlin 2005; Stricker 2000), is, along with religion, no longer perceived as a defining feature of a German identity in present-day Kazakhstan. The vast majority of Kazakhstani Germans do not speak German and do not belong to a so-called 'German parish' (usually a Lutheran one).

The group's dramatic decrease in size appears to have shifted the boundaries of ethnic identifications. In this context, it makes sense to allow as many others as possible to identify themselves as Germans so that the number of Germans in Kazakhstan does not continue to decline, and so that Kazakhstani Germans are not reduced to irrelevance in the public arena and their (positive) stereotypes forgotten (Schlee 2008). But this inclusion of ever more people into the German category is only possible against the background of Kazakhstan's nationality policies and Kazakhs' views on ethnic belonging: that is, ethnic identifications and cultural expressions of all non-Russians are generally appreciated, both in the state discourse on nationalities and by most Kazakhs. It is important to add that a significant intention behind the ostensible policies of minority rights in Kazakhstan is to weaken the Russian category.

Russian and Kazakh perceptions of ethnic identities differ markedly. Often Kazakhstani Russians deny the existence of an ethnicity based solely on ancestry; hence, if 'Germans' do not speak German, they are generally seen as Russian. The inclusion of most non-Kazakhs into the Russian category is not a new phenomenon and dates back to Soviet times, but with the foundation of the Kazakh state and the (envisioned) reversal of the positions of Kazakhs and Russians within it, being Russian connotes the loss of cultural, political and language hegemony and, thus, feelings of exclusion from the Kazakh state. Moreover, the number of Kazakhstani Russians has also dramatically decreased during the last two decades. Kazakhstan's demographic figures are a major topic of discussion in the country, since a Kazakh majority is seen as fundamental to the legitimacy of the Kazakhstan state, while conversely a high percentage of Russians is viewed as a significant obstacle to such legitimacy. Understandably, many Russians reject the president's intention to break up the Russian category into categories thought to more accurately reflect people's 'true' ethnic identities, which were suppressed during Soviet (in the sense of Russian) rule. Therefore, cultural traits are not the reason for ethnic differences, but serve only to legitimate ethnic difference.

The 'cultural stuff' (Barth 1969) – in this case how German identity is defined by people – remains relevant to the process of ethnic identifications. First, shared concepts of identities set the framework for which identities might be plausibly presentable to others; second, the connotations of identities make them, depending on the interlocutor, more or less attractive; and third, defining features such as language skills or ancestry impact identifications since some features are more flexible than others and/or easier to hide. Hence, it is decisive that most Kazakhstani Germans do not have indisputable cultural boundary markers such as language skills. Consequently, they are usually categorized in day-to-day life as Russian, the default category for all European-looking people, and they themselves might flexibly identify as either Russian or German. However, a German identity is largely built on ancestry and thus on the ancestors' past and related memories, which are still to a certain extent about a complicated relationship between Russians and Germans. It is also for this reason that some Germans refrain from identifying themselves as German in the presence of Russians. But towards Kazakhs, it is usually favourable to present oneself as German, since Kazakhs are more inclined to appreciate a German identity. As demographic figures and the status of Kazakhs and Russians continue to change in the Kazakh nation state, a Kazakhstani-German identity might become more important in the future.

Individual biographies and diverse personal attitudes towards identities also shape the process of ethnic identifications. Though people share the common schema of a German identity, how they actually identify themselves and categorize others in day-to-day life is also the result of individual life experience. It has been shown in Parts One and Two that the status of Kazakhstani Germans in present-day Taldykorgan, as well as individual feelings of abandonment and experiences of discrimination, influences how people evaluate ethnic identities and how they identify themselves in various encounters. First, those who perceive their lives as deeply impacted by their German identity tend to attach more significance to ethnic identities and are less flexible as to ethnic identifications. Second, some conceptualize a German identity as a subtype of being Russian, while others deny this interpretation by stressing a specific Kazakh-German bond. Such diverse interpretations affect how people identify themselves and categorize others, and since identities are also the result of people's identifications, individual life experiences matter not only in regard to the process of identification itself. However, it is certainly not the case that all identifications have the same weight. It has been explicated that Kazakhstani Germans differ significantly with regard to their social and economic resources, and that those who have achieved the highest status are the most influential in fashioning a German identity. These individuals usually profit from positive German stereotypes, though they personally do not attach much significance to ethnicity in general. Moreover, most of them feel at home in Kazakhstan. It is also for this reason that a *Kazakhstani* German identity has become stronger in recent years.

Friendship of the Peoples?

The development of official views on the concept of nationality during Soviet times, and in the states that gained independence upon the dissolution of the USSR, has been outlined in Chapter 1. The Soviet state's discourse was marked by an inherent contradiction: on the one hand, celebrating ethnic diversity, promoted as 'internationalism', and on the other, celebrating the merging of nationalities into the overarching idea of a Soviet people. Moreover, controversy persisted with regard to whether ethnic identities might be objectively ascribed by a catalogue of features or whether someone's self-ascription should be decisive.

It is usually asserted (such as in Dave 2007) that Kazakh state rhetoric is largely a continuation of the Soviet nationality discourse, but this is only partly the case. Kazakhstan's President Nazarbayev does not envision any merging. The notion of the Soviet man has not been replaced by a Kazakhstani one, as is often assumed. The country's very foundation is in fact the opposite. The Soviet Union, at least in its rhetoric, strove to support all non-Russians who were to be freed of Tsarist Russian oppression, whereas official discourse in Kazakhstan conveys the imperative to support the titular population. Consequently, the promotion of the Kazakh language is not meant to 'civilize' others (as was the case with Russian during Soviet times), but to guarantee the Kazakhs' own cultural survival. Since, at least for now, this remains the state's main task, ethnic merging can only be perceived as a major threat. Thus a Kazakhstani identity serves only to invite non-Kazakhs to identify themselves with the (above all others, Kazakh) homeland. Moreover, the ethnic concepts of Kazakh and Russian are different in that becoming Kazakh – in contrast to becoming Russian – is conceptually impossible (Finke 2004). But Kazakhstan's nationality policies are aptly not characterized as 'multiple re-ethnification' (Holm-Hansen 1999); the folkloristic outlook of the state's policies is not new, but rather a continuation of Soviet policies such as *korenizatsiya* (indigenization).

This study has not limited its focus to state-sponsored concepts and attitudes towards ethnicity; rather, it has elaborated on how those concepts are seen by people and how state concepts influence people's behaviour. It has been shown in Chapter 3 that Kazakhs, Russians and Germans share a common schema of nationality, and that this schema can be traced back to the oft-cited definition given by Stalin. Thus, nationalities are widely seen as groups of people who share a common (origin) territory, language, religion, customs and habits. Remarkably, Kazakhstan's ethnic and cultural variety is generally appreciated, even though the 'groups' comprising that variety are unlikely to fulfil those criteria. For instance, Kazakhstani Germans, as well as Kazakhstani Koreans and Poles for example, rarely speak their 'native' language, do not belong to specific religious communities, and do not practise any particular ethnic customs or habits in their daily lives.

The normative concepts of internationalism and friendship of the peoples are widely shared, but many people struggle with the inherent contradictions, as did the creators of such concepts. This is above all the contradiction between the envisioned merging of all nationalities and concurrently stressing that each nationality has the duty to 'develop its culture', which accounts for seemingly antithetical statements by the current Kazakhstan state concerning the role and status of nationalities. On the one hand, people seem proud to live in a country that actively addresses minority issues, while at the same time they find themselves emphasizing that someone's nationality should not have any relevance since people are all the same. Consequently, this ambivalence leaves room for very different actions by the state, and equally the interpretations of those schemas by individuals guide their behaviour.

Furthermore, almost everyone is proud to say that his or her friends are drawn from among many nationalities, though this is very often no more than a nod to the 'friendship of the peoples' and has little or nothing to do with actual relationships. Such discourses on nationalities are repeatedly voiced, but limited in their power to guide interaction. Interestingly, although the state's relatively recent independence has resulted in a reversal in status of almost all people and has effected new actions, the nationality discourse of the past has persisted; however, it would be misleading to assume that because the old vocabulary persists, nothing has changed in how people behave.

The example of Kazakhstani Germans is particularly illuminating because it shows which dimension of ethnic belonging matters under which circumstances. Since most perceive themselves as both Russian and German, it can be explored as to when the state-sponsored view of over a hundred different ethnic groups living peacefully together impacts people's behaviour and when it does not. First of all, it is important to recognize that ethnicity matters in Kazakhstan. Whether one is Kazakh or Russian is perceived by many people as decisive in areas of career planning, job opportunities, place of living, marriage and, last but not least, emigrating versus not emigrating. However, whether someone is, for example, German, Ukrainian, Polish or Korean is mostly seen as irrelevant in those areas. This is why being German is generally regarded as a private matter, while being Russian is important, even crucial, with respect to public perception. As Chapter 3 has shown, cognitive tests have confirmed the hierarchical nesting of ethnic belonging and revealed, furthermore, that many people hold to a black-white binarism between Kazakhs (and other Central Asians and sometimes all Muslim people) and Russians (and other European-looking people). Therefore, one might conclude that ethnic belonging is much more conceptualized in terms of fixed dichotomies than ever before.

Moreover, the gap between the 'European group' and the 'Central Asian group' is not only present in people's representations of Kazakhstani nationalities but also in their actual relationships, and this especially concerns the younger generation. In addition, it is very likely that Kazakhstani Russians today feel freer to utter negative stereotypes about Kazakhs than during Soviet times, since Kazakhs are now seen to occupy a position of unjustified (in the minds of most Kazakhstani Russians) superiority. This is particularly relevant in a city such as Taldykorgan that primarily offers jobs in administration, most of which are, for all practical purposes, inaccessible to non-Kazakhs. Furthermore, it is the increasing split of social networks along linguistic lines that results in a separation of Kazakh speakers from non-Kazakh speakers and fosters ethnic stereotyping. Thus, the state-sponsored concept of 'friendship of the peoples' seems to be of little importance with regard to people's concerns about their future prospects in Kazakhstan.

The case of Kazakhstani Germans demonstrates, however, that people in certain situations continue to rely on the highly accessible concepts of nationality promoted by the state. The fact that ethnic folklore is pervasive – through festivals, on television and in almost every speech by a politician – consistently upholds the idea that something essentially ethnic exists beyond time, and in the case of Germans, it is the idea of a 'German spirit' that differentiates them from other nationalities. Moreover, the state-sponsored ethnic performances further reinforce Germans connecting with their German identity as a way of avoiding the feeling of exclusion that can accompany defining oneself as 'Russian' in Kazakhstani society. How people define their ethnic belonging and its assumed relevance is an important component to consider when attempting to explain their behaviour, but it is equally important to consider how people's current status in Kazakhstan impacts their evaluation of their own ethnic identity and ethnicity in general.

Exclusion through Inclusion: The Role of Personal and Institutional Links to Germany

Kazakhstani Germans are usually referred to as a diaspora, which is problematic for several reasons. First, the concept of diaspora presupposes feelings of belonging to an 'historic homeland' which, in the case of Germans in Kazakhstan, is at best a crude oversimplification. Second, it connotes victimhood, which might apply to those who emigrated to Germany years ago, but which contradicts the positively reformulated memory of those who have stayed in Kazakhstan. Third, diaspora does not account for the 'double inclusion' of Kazakhstani Germans – i.e., that their ancestors had come from a place to which many of their relatives have recently decided to return; in other words, the concept does not encompass factual transnational social relations. This latter phenomenon is usually investigated in the framework of transnationalism, but applying the concept of transnationalism risks losing sight of features that run contrary to its implicit assumptions. While advocating to overcome the nation state container view is of merit, often this methodological approach overreaches by assuming empirical facts, namely the existence and relevance of transnational ties and communities.

As has been shown in Chapter 6, most Kazakhstani Germans have close relatives among recent immigrants to Germany. However, the analysis of people's networks has also revealed that those transnational ties are barely relevant in the context of emotional, social and/or economic support. One should keep in mind here that the concept of transnationalism has been built largely on findings derived from labour migration, whereas in the case of Kazakhstani Germans, most emigrated with no intention of returning to Kazakhstan. Moreover, although concepts such as transnationalism, diaspora and, more generally, globalization give the impression that every corner of the world is connected with every other corner of the world, the situation in Kazakhstan during the 1990s was different. A rapidly collapsing infrastructure after independence complicated even a simple phone call, and for the rural population it was often technically impossible to keep in contact with their relatives in Germany. Though this has gradually changed in recent years, both their relatives' motives for emigrating and Kazakhstan's weak infrastructure meant that the ties between those who left and those who stayed were under duress from the outset.

Furthermore, the out-migration of Kazakhstani Germans typically occurred on a family basis. Thus, most of those who stayed were either not well integrated in their families before emigration, which accounts for their weak ties to Germany, or they violated the rule of acting together as a single family, which helps to explain their complicated relationships with their relatives in Germany. Often people feel ashamed to admit that they have a disordered or dysfunctional family life, and at the same time feel uncomfortable disclosing that their relatives have not helped them economically, or that they have broken all ties with them. Some Kazakhstani Germans stayed, however, because they held a good position, or had opened their own business. They tend to have better relations with relatives in Germany because they do not expect their relatives to help them and they can afford to visit Germany. This explains why they usually know the most about life in Germany and about the difficult situations that some of their relatives are experiencing there. Thus, it is also the status of people in Kazakhstan that can be decisive with regard to the quality of personal ties to Germany. Consequently, all of the above aspects help in understanding how transnational flows operate in local contexts: quantity and quality of actual relationships with people in Germany; what is transmitted through such ties; how people feel about their connections; and who – in terms of economic and political power – has what kind of relations, in the local, national and transnational arenas.

The fact that many Kazakhstani Germans have complicated relations with relatives in Germany because they decided against emigrating has played a significant role in how they justify their decision for staying. This is mostly done by praising Kazakhstan's natural beauty and relative freedom, and in cases where Kazakhstani Germans are economically well off, by referring to their success. Many of them have even developed a kind of pride for having stayed in their homeland Kazakhstan, and accordingly distinguish themselves positively from those who left the country. They have also heard from Kazakhstani Germans in Germany about the shortcomings of the German social benefits system as well as the vulgar German words directed at immigrant Russians (and thus directed at immigrant Kazakhstani Germans as well, who are widely regarded as Russian). However, it can also be asserted that Kazakhstani Germans tend to focus on the negative aspects of their relatives' situation in Germany in order to reaffirm their decision to stay (or to reconcile themselves with having been denied permission to immigrate). As a result, the picture of Germany and Germans has become by and large negative. Often, this negative evaluation applies even to one's own relatives, for they are said to have adapted to the way of life of Germany's Germans. Therefore, it does not come as a surprise that most Kazakhstani Germans no longer refer to the country as an 'historic homeland'; that is to say, among those who regarded it in that way in the first place. They usually see themselves as having nothing in common with Germany's population, and further distance themselves from their relatives in Germany who are regarded as Russians in order to reinforce their own (Kazakhstani) German identity, which is respected and helpful in the local and national context in Kazakhstan.

Along those lines, social power, and the power to influence identities, plays a key role in Kazakhstani-German attitudes. Those Germans who are successful in Kazakhstan also have the most contacts both locally (including with Kazakhs) and transnationally. Their large networks put them in the position to spread their information about Germany and to promote their interpretation of a German identity. The ambivalent and often negative perception of Germany, which has stimulated a *Kazakhstani*-German identity, is thus more powerful because its strongest advocates have the most social capital, whereas the vision of Germany as an 'historic homeland' is increasingly marginalized because it is shared, for the most part, by those with generally small social networks.

Following the earlier discussion of personal ties, Part Four elaborated upon institutional connections to Germany. It has been shown that the Rebirth organization is currently in a transitional phase. Until recently, its main tasks have been related to helping with emigration issues and offering German language classes. In light of the diminished focus on emigration and language, however, the institution, though still partially financed by the Kazakh and German states, has had to reorganize to find new ways of making money. In doing so, the head of the German House – a local branch of the Rebirth organization – makes use of the institution's economic and social potential. But the fact that he and other members of the German House establish and, in turn, rely upon contacts with Germany does not entail that a transnational social field is under construction.

First of all, those who work in the German House are fully aware of the German state's contradictory policies, namely (legally) inviting people to immigrate while at the same time wanting them to stay where they are. Second, the German state is not seen as the legitimate authority with regard to telling people in Kazakhstan who they are or what 'German' means. This attitude towards the German state also concerns immigration tests, which are commonly referred to as ridiculous and unfair. Third, the Kazakh state is perceived as the more legitimate authority as for supporting people's ethnic belonging, and it is for that reason that people refer to a 'German spirit' which transcends time and space. Thus, the Kazakhstani Germans' situation is certainly influenced by transnational flows, be they information about Germany or actual business contacts, but this does not create a homogenous social field since those flows are interpreted and evaluated by people who orient their behaviour primarily towards a local context.

Consequently, despite the apparent continuing institutional and personal inclusion of 'ancestral' Germans into the German nation, feelings of exclusion among Kazakhstani Germans have deepened. Transnationally transmitted knowledge about Germany and the Germans has served to widen the gap separating Kazakhstani Germans from Germany, and German state legislation and policies, although they partially aim at including Kazakhstani Germans, have nonetheless contributed to a sense of 'not belonging' to a previously assumed 'historic homeland'.

This research has drawn on different methods in order to grasp the shifting significance of ethnic belonging in the Kazakh nation state. The combination of narrative life stories, cognitive tests and personal networks has proven fruitful in order to better understand how people conceive, use and live ethnicity. Additionally, the historic dimension of identities has been gauged by analysing memories of the past. However, only by exploring people's routines in their daily lives and through the intimate knowledge gained during long-term fieldwork can such findings about ethnicity and the effects of the past be adequately evaluated.

With regard to the Germans of Kazakhstan, identities develop in engagement with an individual's social environment, which includes her or his family and the people who live nearby, but also those who were previously close but who have left to start a new life in another country. Since identities are built through interactions with others, people usually know or can guess what is known and expected by others. This is the intermediate level of shared schemata that are, however, constantly changing because of people's new experiences, new interpretations and new evaluations in a changing world. Kazakhstani Germans hold different views on ethnicity and feel differently about ethnic belonging, but they share a common perception of who is German and how such a person ought to act. This idea of what it means to be German has developed through many generations of Russian, Soviet and Kazakhstani Germans, and it is relatively stable since, in the first place, it is transmitted from parent to child and, furthermore, because it has been mostly shared by non-German neighbours, colleagues and friends. But the potential for change remains, and people, some more powerful than others, might bend this idea of what it means to be German to better suit their own needs. While identities can only be legitimized through people's shared memories, they lose their power if they do not appear, at least for some people, to fulfil their future hopes and plans. For the time being, Kazakhstani Germans seek to maintain a German identity that they hope will make their lives more liveable at home in Kazakhstan.

References

Abashin, S. 2007. *Natsionalizmy v Crednej Azii. V Poiskakh Identichnosti.* St Petersburg: Aletejya.
———. 2008. 'Sovetskaya teoriya etnoca: o genealogii kontseptsii'. Paper presented at the Martin Luther University Halle-Wittenberg, Halle (Saale), Germany.
Akiner, S. 2005. 'Towards a Typology of Diasporas in Kazakhstan', in T. Atabaki and S. Mehendale (eds), *Central Asia and the Caucasus: Transnationalism and Diaspora.* London: Routledge, pp. 21–65.
Al-Ali, N., and K. Koser. 2002. 'Transnationalism, International Migration and Home', in N. Al-Ali and K. Koser (eds), *New Approaches to Migration? Transnational Communities and the Transformation of Home.* London: Routledge, pp. 1–14.
Alexander, C. 2007. 'Rationality and Contingency: Rhetoric, Practice and Legitimation in Almaty, Kazakhstan', in J. Edwards, P. Harvey and P. Wade (eds), *Anthropology and Science: Epistemologies in Practice.* Oxford: Berg, pp. 58–74.
Allworth, E. 1989. *Central Asia: 120 Years of Russian Rule.* Durham: Duke University Press.
Anderson, B.R. 1983. *Imagined Communities: Reflections on the Origin and Spread of Nationalism.* London: Verso.
Anthias, F. 1998. 'Evaluating "Diaspora": Beyond Ethnicity?', *Sociology* 32(3): 557–80.
Appadurai, A. 1988. 'How to Make a National Cuisine: Cookbooks in Contemporary India', *Comparative Studies in Society and History* 30(1): 3–24.
———. 1998. 'Globale ethnische Räume: Bemerkungen und Fragen zur Entwicklung einer transnationalen Anthropologie', in U. Beck (ed.), *Perspektiven der Weltgesellschaft.* Frankfurt/M.: Suhrkamp, pp. 11–40.
Assmann, J. 1995. 'Collective Memory and Cultural Identity', *New German Critique* 65 (Spring–Summer): 125–33.
Aydıngün, A. 2008. 'State Symbols and National Identity Construction in Kazakhstan', in I. Bellér-Hann (ed.), *The Past as Resource in the Turkic Speaking World.* Würzburg: Ergon, pp. 139–58.
Barth, F. 1969. 'Introduction', in F. Barth (ed.), *Ethnic Groups and Boundaries: The Social Organization of Culture Difference.* Bergen, Oslo: Universitetsforlaget, pp. 9–38.
———. 1996 [1969]. 'Ethnic Groups and Boundaries', in J. Hutchinson and A.D. Smith (eds), *Ethnicity.* Oxford: Oxford University Press, pp. 75–82.
———. 2000. 'Enduring and Emerging Issues in the Analysis of Ethnicity', in H. Vermeulen and C. Govers (eds), *The Anthropology of Ethnicity: Beyond 'Ethnic Groups and Boundaries'.* Amsterdam: Het Spinhuis, pp. 11–32.
Basch, L., N. Glick Schiller and C. Szanton Blanc. 1997. *Nations Unbound: Transnational Projects, Postcolonial Predicaments, and Deterritorialized Nation-States.* Amsterdam: Gordon and Breach.
Bausinger, H. 1987. 'Das Problem der Flüchtlinge und Vertriebenen in den Forschungen zur Kultur der unteren Schichten', in R. Schulze, D. von der Brelie-Lewien and H. Grebing (eds), *Flüchtlinge und Vertriebene in der westdeutschen Nachkriegsgeschichte.* Hildesheim: August Lax, pp. 180–95.

Becker, F. 2001. *Ankommen in Deutschland. Einwanderungspolitik als biographische Erfahrung im Migrationsprozeß russischer Juden*. Berlin: Reimer.
Beissinger, M.R. 1992. 'Elites and Ethnic Identities in Soviet and Post-Soviet Politics', in A.J. Motyl (ed.), *The Post-Soviet Nations: Perspectives on the Demise of the USSR*. New York: Columbia University Press, pp. 141–69.
Belliger, A., and D. Krieger. 2013. 'Ritual und Ritualforschung', in A. Belliger and D. Krieger (eds), *Ritualtheorien. Ein einführendes Handbuch*. Wiesbaden: Springer, pp. 7–34.
Belotti, E. 2008. 'What are Friends for? Elective Communities of Single People', *Social Networks* 30(4): 318–29.
Bernard, H.R. 1995. *Research Methods in Anthropology: Qualitative and Quantitative Approaches*. Walnut Creek: AltaMira Press.
Berzborn, S., T. Schweizer and M. Schnegg. 1998. 'Personal Networks and Social Support in a Multiethnic Community of Southern California', *Social Networks* 20(1): 1–21.
Beyer, J. 2006. 'Rhetoric of "Transformation": The Case of the Kyrgyz Constitutional Reform', in A. Berg and A. Kreikemeyer (eds), *Realities of Transformation: Democratization Policies in Central Asia Revisited*. Baden-Baden: Nomos, pp. 43–62.
———. 2011. 'Settling Descent: Place Making and Genealogy in Talas, Kyrgyzstan', *Central Asian Survey* 30(3–4): 455–68.
Bloch, M. 1998. *How We Think They Think: Anthropological Approaches to Cognition, Memory, and Literacy*. Boulder: Westview Press.
Boissevain, J. 1974. *Friends of Friends: Networks, Manipulators and Coalitions*. Oxford: Blackwell.
Boll, K. 1996. 'Akkulturationsprozesse rußlanddeutscher Aussiedler in der ehemaligen Sowjetunion und in der Bundesrepublik Deutschland. Zusammenfassende Ergebnisse einer empirischen Studie', in I. Graudenz and R. Römhild (eds), *Forschungsfeld Aussiedler. Ansichten aus Deutschland*. Frankfurt/M.: Europäischer Verlag der Wissenschaften, pp. 69–84.
Bonnenfant, I.K. 2012. 'Constructing the Homeland: Kazakhstan's Discourse and Policies Surrounding Its Ethnic Return-Migration Policy', *Central Asian Survey* 31(1): 31–44.
Bott, E. 1957. *Family and Social Network: Roles, Norms, and External Relationships in Ordinary Urban Families*. London: Travistock.
Bourdieu, P. 1977. *Outline of a Theory of Practice*. Cambridge, New York: Cambridge University Press.
Boyd, M. 1989. 'Family and Personal Networks in International Migration: Recent Developments and New Agendas', *International Migration Review* 23(3): 638–71.
Brake, K. 1998. *Lebenserinnerungen rußlanddeutscher Einwanderer. Zeitgeschichte und Narrativik*. Berlin: Reimer.
Brandes, D. 1996. 'Die Wolgarepublik. Eigenstaatlichkeit oder nationales Gouvernement?' in H. Rothe (ed.), *Deutsche in Rußland. Studien zum Deutschtum im Osten*. Cologne: Böhlau, pp. 103–30.
———. 1997. 'Von der Verfolgung im Ersten Weltkrieg bis zur Deportation', in G. Stricker (ed.), *Deutsche Geschichte im Osten Europas: Rußland*. Berlin: Siedler, pp. 131–212.
Brass, P.R. 1985. *Ethnic Groups and the State*. London: Croom Helm.
———. 1996. 'Ethnic Groups and Ethnic Identity Formation', in J. Hutchinson and A.D. Smith (eds), *Ethnicity*. Oxford: Oxford University Press, pp. 85–90.
Bremmer, I.A., and R. Taras. 1993. *Nation and Politics in the Soviet Successor States*. Cambridge: Cambridge University Press.

Brown, A.J. 2005. 'The Germans of Germany and the Germans of Kazakhstan: A Eurasian Volk in the Twilight of Diaspora', *Europe-Asia Studies* 57(4): 625–34.
Brubaker, R. 1992. *Citizenship and Nationhood in France and Germany*. Cambridge, MA: Harvard University Press.
———. 1999. *Nationalism Reframed: Nationhood and the National Question in the New Europe*. Cambridge: Cambridge University Press.
———. 2004. *Ethnicity without Groups*. Cambridge, MA: Harvard University Press.
———. 2005. 'The "Diaspora" Diaspora', *Ethnic and Racial Studies* 28(1): 1–20.
Bunn, S. 2011. 'Moving People and the Fabric of Society: The Power of Felt through Time and Place', *Central Asian Survey* 30(3–4): 503–20.
Carrère d'Encausse, H. 1995. *The Nationality Question in the Soviet Union and Russia*. Oslo: Scandinavian University Press.
Casey, E.S. 2000. *Remembering: A Phenomenological Study*. Bloomington: Indiana University Press.
Cassarino, J.-P. 2004. 'Theorising Return Migration: The Conceptual Approach to Return Migrants Revisited', *International Journal on Multicultural Societies* 6(2): 253–79.
Casteel, J. 2008. 'The Politics of Diaspora: Russian German Émigré Activists in Interwar Germany', in M. Schulze, J.M. Skidmore, D.G. John, G. Liebscher and S. Siebel-Achenbach (eds), *German Diasporic Experiences: Identity, Migration, and Loss*. Waterloo: Wilfrid Laurier University Press, pp. 117–30.
Castles, S., and M.J. Miller. 1993. *The Age of Migration: International Population Movements in the Modern World*. Basingstoke: Palgrave Macmillan.
Chanfrault-Duchet, M.-F. 1991. 'Narrative Structures, Social Models, and Symbolic Representation in the Life Story', in S.B. Gluck (ed.), *Women's Words: The Feminist Practice of Oral History*. New York: Routledge, pp. 77–92.
Charmaz, K., and R.G. Mitchell. 2001. 'Grounded Theory in Ethnography', in P. Atkinson, A.J. Coffey, S. Deramont, J. Lofland and L.H. Lofland (eds), *Handbook of Ethnography*. London: Sage, 160–74.
Chikadze, E., and V. Voronkov. 2003. 'Different Generations of Leningrad Jews in the Context of Public/Private Division: Paradoxes of Ethnicity', in R. Humphrey, R. Miller and E. Zdravomyslova (eds), *Biographical Research in Eastern Europe: Altered Lives and Broken Biographies*. Aldershot: Ashgate, pp. 239–62.
Chinn, J., and R. Kaiser. 1996. *Russians as the New Minority: Ethnicity and Nationalism in the Soviet Successor States*. Boulder: Westview.
Christou, A. 2006. *Narratives of Place, Culture and Identity: Second-Generation Greek-Americans Return 'Home'*. Amsterdam: Amsterdam University Press.
Clifford, J. 1994. 'Diasporas', *Cultural Anthropology* 9(3): 302–38.
Cohen, A. 1996 [1969]. 'Ethnicity and Politics', in J. Hutchinson and A.D. Smith (eds), *Ethnicity*. Oxford: Oxford University Press, pp. 83–84.
Cohen, A.P. 2000a. 'Introduction: Discriminating Relations – Identity, Boundary and Authenticity', in A.P. Cohen (ed.), *Signifying Identities: Anthropological Perspectives on Boundaries and Contested Values*. London: Routledge, pp. 1–13.
———. 2000b. 'Boundaries of Consciousness, Consciousness of Boundaries: Critical Questions for Anthropology', in H. Vermeulen and C. Govers (eds), *The Anthropology of Ethnicity: Beyond 'Ethnic Groups and Boundaries'*. Amsterdam: Het Spinhuis, pp. 59–80.
Cohen, R. 1997. *Global Diasporas: An Introduction*. Seattle: University of Washington Press.

Cortazzi, M. 2001. 'Narrative Analysis in Ethnography', P. Atkinson, A.J. Coffey, S. Deramont, J. Lofland and L.H. Lofland (eds), *Handbook of Ethnography*. London: Sage, pp. 384–94.

Crowe, D.M. 1998. 'The Kazakhs and Kazakhstan: The Struggle for Ethnic Identity and Nationhood', *Nationalities Papers* 26(3): 395–419.

Cummings, S.N. 2005. *Kazakhstan: Power and the Elite*. London: Tauris.

———. 2006. 'Legitimation and Identification in Kazakhstan', *Nationalism and Ethnic Politics* 12(2): 177–204.

Currle, E. 2006. 'Theorieansätze zur Erklärung von Rückkehr und Remigration', *soFid Migration und ethnische Minderheiten* 2: 7–23.

D'Andrade, R.G. 1996. *The Development of Cognitive Anthropology*. Cambridge: Cambridge University Press.

———. 1997. 'Cultural Meaning Systems', in R.A. Shweder and R.A. LeVine (eds), *Culture Theory: Essays on Mind, Self, and Emotion*. Cambridge: Cambridge University Press, pp. 88–122.

Darieva, T. 2007. 'Migrationsforschung in der Ethnologie', in B. Schmidt-Lauber (ed.), *Ethnizität und Migration: Einführung in Wissenschaft und Arbeitsfelder*. Berlin: Reimer, pp. 69–93.

Dave, B. 2004. 'A Shrinking Reach of the State? Language Policy and Implementation in Kazakhstan and Kyrgyzstan', in P. Jones Luong (ed.), *The Transformation of Central Asia: States and Societies from Soviet Rule to Independence*. Ithaca: Cornell University Press, pp. 120–55.

———. 2007. *Kazakhstan: Ethnicity, Language and Power*. London: Routledge.

Davies, C.A. 1999. *Reflexive Anthropology: A Guide to Researching Selves and Others*. London: Routledge.

Davis, S., and S. Sabol. 1998. 'The Importance of Being Ethnic: Minorities in Post-Soviet States – The Case of Russians in Kazakstan', *Nationalities Papers* 26(3): 473–91.

Diener, A.C. 2004. *Homeland Conceptions and Ethnic Integration among Kazakhstan's Germans and Koreans*. Lewiston: E. Mellen Press.

———. 2006. 'Homeland as Social Construct: Territorialization among Kazakhstan's Germans and Koreans', *Nationalities Papers* 34(2): 201–35.

———. 2009a. 'Diasporic Stances: Comparing the Historical Geographic Antecedents of Korean and German Migration Decisions in Kazakhstan', *Geopolitics* 14(3): 462–87.

———. 2009b. *One Homeland or Two? The Nationalization and Transnationalization of Mongolia's Kazakhs*. Palo Alto, CA: Stanford University Press.

Dietz, B. 1996. 'Rückwanderung in eine fremde Gesellschaft. Zur sozialen Integration rußlanddeutscher Aussiedler in der Bundesrepublik Deutschland', in I. Graudenz and R. Römhild (eds), *Forschungsfeld Aussiedler. Ansichten aus Deutschland*. Frankfurt/M.: Peter Lang, pp. 123–37.

———. 2006. '*Aussiedler* in Germany: From Smooth Adaptation to Tough Integration', in L. Lucassen, D. Feldman and J. Oltmer (eds), *Immigrant Integration in Western Europe, Then and Now*. Amsterdam: Amsterdam University Press, pp. 116–36.

Dorlin, S. 2005. *Histoire culturelle des allemands au Kazakhstan de la Seconde Guerre mondiale à nos jours. Des efforts d'enracinement aux perspectives de retour*. Paris: Connaissances et savoirs.

Dubuisson, E.-M., and A. Genina. 2011. 'Claiming an Ancestral Homeland: Kazakh Pilgrimage and Migration in Inner Asia', *Central Asian Survey* 30(3–4): 469–85.

Durkheim, E., and M. Mauss. 1970. *Primitive Classification*. London: Cohen and West.

Easthope, H. 2004. 'A Place Called Home', *Housing, Theory and Society* 21(3):128–38.

Eder, K., V. Rauer and O. Schmidtke. 2004. *Die Einhegung des Anderen. Türkische, polnische und russlanddeutsche Einwanderer in Deutschland.* Wiesbaden: Verlag für Sozialwissenschaften.
Edgar, A.L. 2007. 'Marriage, Modernity, and the "Friendship of Nations": Interethnic Intimacy in Post-War Central Asia in Comparative Perspective', *Central Asian Survey* 26(4): 581–600.
Eisfeld, A. 1999. *Die Russlanddeutschen.* Munich: Langen München.
Eitzen, H.C. 1999. 'Nawriz in Kazakstan: Scenarios for Managing Diversity', in I. Svanberg (ed.), *Contemporary Kazaks: Cultural and Social Perspectives.* Richmond: Curzon, pp. 73–101.
Elwert, G. 2002. 'Switching Identity Discourses: Primordial Emotions and the Social Construction of We-Groups', in G. Schlee (ed.), *Imagined Differences: Hatred and the Construction of Identity.* Münster: Lit, pp. 33–54.
Emirbayer, M., and J. Goodwin. 1994. 'Network Analysis, Culture, and the Problem of Agency', *American Journal of Sociology* 99(6): 1411–54.
Eriksen, T.H. 1993. 'Ethnicity and Nationalism: Definitions and Critical Reflections', in H. Lindholm (ed.), *Ethnicity and Nationalism: Formation of Identity and Dynamics of Conflict in the 1990s.* Göteborg: Nordnes, pp. 40–50.
Erikson, E.H. 1959. *Identity and the Life Cycle: Selected Papers.* New York: International Universities Press.
Féaux de la Croix, J. 2011. 'Moving Metaphors We Live by: Water and Flow in the Social Sciences and around Hydroelectric Dams in Kyrgyzstan', *Central Asian Survey* 30(3–4): 487–502.
Fenicia, T. 2015. 'Rückkehrentscheidung aus Genderperspektive. Remigrierte (Spät-)Aussiedlerfamilien in Westsibirien', in M. Kaiser and M. Schönhuth (eds), *Zuhause? Fremd? Migrations- und Beheimatungsstrategien zwischen Deutschland und Eurasien.* Bielefeld: transcript, pp. 239–73.
Ferguson, J.G. 2006. 'Transnational Topographies of Power. Beyond "the State" and "Civil Society" in the Study of African Politics', in B. Maurer and G. Schwab (eds), *Accelerating Possession: Global Futures of Property and Personhood.* New York: Columbia University Press, pp. 76–98.
Fierman, W. 1991. *Soviet Central Asia: The Failed Transformation.* Boulder: Westview Press.
———. 1998. 'Language and Identity in Kazakhstan: Formulations in Policy Documents 1987–1997', *Communist and Post-Communist Studies* 31(2): 171–86.
———. 2006. 'Language and Education in Post-Soviet Kazakhstan: Kazakh-Medium Instruction in Urban Schools', *The Russian Review* 65(1): 98–116.
Finke, P. 2004. *Nomaden im Transformationsprozess. Kasachen in der post-sozialistischen Mongolei.* Münster: Lit.
———. 2013. 'Historical Homelands and Transnational Ties: The Case of the Mongolian Kazaks', *Zeitschrift für Ethnologie* 138(2): 175–93.
———. 2014. *Variations on Uzbek Identity: Strategic Choices, Cognitive Schemas and Political Constraints in Identification Processes.* Oxford, New York: Berghahn.
Finke, P., and M. Sancak. 2005. 'Migration and Risk Taking: A Case Study from Kazakstan', in L. Trager (ed.), *Migration and Economy: Global and Local Dynamics.* Walnut Creek: AltaMira Press, pp. 127–62.
———. 2007. 'Konstitutsiya buzildi! Gender relations in Kazakstan and Uzbekistan', in J. Sahadeo and R. Zanca (eds), *Everyday Life in Central Asia: Past and Present.* Bloomington: Indiana University Press, pp. 160–77.

Finke, P., R. Sanders and R. Zanca. 2013. 'Mobility and Identity in Central Asia: An Introduction', *Zeitschrift für Ethnologie* 138(2): 129–37.
Fischer, H. 1996. *Lehrbuch der genealogischen Methode*. Berlin: Reimer.
Flynn, M. 2007. 'Reconstructing "Home/lands" in the Russian Federation: Migrant-Centred Perspectives of Displacement and Resettlement', *Journal of Ethnic and Migration Studies* 33(3): 461–81.
Frotscher Kramer, M. 2008. 'The Nationalization Campaign and the Rewriting of History: The Case of Blumenau', in M. Schulze, J.M. Skidmore, D.G. John, G. Liebscher and S. Siebel-Achenbach (eds), *German Diasporic Experiences: Identity, Migration, and Loss*. Waterloo: Wilfrid Laurier University Press, pp. 419–30.
Fuller, J.M. 2008. 'Language and Identity in the German Diaspora', in M. Schulze, J.M. Skidmore, D.G. John, G. Liebscher and S. Siebel-Achenbach (eds), *German Diasporic Experiences: Identity, Migration, and Loss*. Waterloo: Wilfrid Laurier University Press, pp. 3–20.
Geertz, C. 1963. 'The Integrative Revolution: Primordial Sentiments and Civil Politics in the New States', in C. Geertz (ed.), *Old Societies and New States: The Quest for Modernity in Asia and Africa*. New York: Free Press, pp. 105–57.
Gellner, E. 1983. *Nations and Nationalism*. Oxford: Blackwell.
Gentile, M., and T. Tammaru. 2006. 'Housing and Ethnicity in the Post-Soviet City: Ust'-Kamenogorsk, Kazakhstan', *Urban Studies* 43(10): 1757–78.
Giddens, A. 1993. 'Tradition in der post-traditionalen Gesellschaft', *Soziale Welt* 44(4): 445–85.
Giordano, C. 2003. 'Studying Networks Nowadays: On the Utility of a Notion', in D. Torsello and M. Pappová (eds), *Social Networks in Movement: Time, Interaction and Interethnic Spaces in Central Eastern Europe*. Šamorín: Forum Minority Research Institute, pp. 9–14.
Golofast, V. 2003. 'Three Dimensions of Biographical Narratives', in R. Humphrey, R. Miller and E. Zdravomyslova (eds), *Biographical Research in Eastern Europe: Altered Lives and Broken Biographies*. Aldershot: Ashgate, pp. 53–67.
Goodenough, W.H. 1968. 'Componential Analysis and the Study of Meaning', in P. Bohannan and J. Middleton (eds), *Kinship and Social Organization*. Garden City: Natural History Press, pp. 93–124.
Goody, J. 1987. *The Interface between the Written and the Oral*. Cambridge: Cambridge University Press.
Granovetter, M.S. 1973. 'The Strength of Weak Ties', *The American Journal of Sociology* 78(6): 1360–80.
Graudenz, I., and R. Römhild. 1996. 'Grenzerfahrungen: Deutschstämmige Migranten aus Polen und der ehemaligen Sowjetunion im Vergleich', in I. Graudenz and R. Römhild (eds), *Forschungsfeld Aussiedler: Ansichten aus Deutschland*. Frankfurt/M.: Europäischer Verlag der Wissenschaften, pp. 29–68.
Gumppenberg, M.-C. 2004. 'Nation- and State-Building in Kazakhstan between Ethnic and Social Conflict', in G. Rasuly-Paleczek and J. Katschnig (eds), *Central Asia on Display: Proceedings of the VII. Conference of the European Society for Central Asian Studies*. Vienna: Lit, pp. 77–82.
Gungwu, W. 2005. 'Migration and its Enemies', in B. Mazlish and A. Iriye (eds), *The Global History Reader*. New York: Routledge, pp. 104–13.
Gupta, A., and J. Ferguson. 1992. 'Beyond "Culture": Space, Identity, and the Politics of Difference', *Cultural Anthropology* 7: 6–23.

Hagendoorn, L., and E. Poppe. 2001. 'Types of Identification among Russians in the "Near Abroad"', *Europe-Asia Studies* 53(1): 57–71.

Halbwachs, M. 1925. *Les cadres sociaux de la mémoire*. Paris: Félix Alcan.

Hall, S. 1990. 'Cultural Identity and Diaspora', in J. Rutherford (ed.), *Identity: Community, Culture, Difference*. London: Lawrence and Wishart, pp. 222–37.

———. 1998. 'Introduction: Who Needs "Identity"?' in S. Hall (ed.), *Questions of Cultural Identity*. London: Sage, pp. 1–17.

Hannerz, U. 2007 [1996]. 'Das Lokale und das Globale: Kontinuität und Wandel', in B. Schmidt-Lauber (ed.), *Ethnizität und Migration: Einführung in Wissenschaft und Arbeitsfelder*. Berlin: Reimer, pp. 95–113.

Hechter, M. 1988. *Principles of Group Solidarity*. Berkeley: University of California Press.

———. 1996. 'Ethnicity and Rational Choice Theory', in J. Hutchinson and A.D. Smith (eds), *Ethnicity*. Oxford: Oxford University Press, pp. 90–98.

Herzfeld, M. 2005. *Cultural Intimacy: Social Poetics in the Nation-State*. New York, London: Routledge.

Hilkes, P. 1996. 'Die Rußlanddeutschen in der Sowjetunion und ihren Nachfolgestaaten', in H. Rothe (ed.), *Deutsche in Rußland: Studien zum Deutschtum im Osten*. Cologne: Böhlau, pp. 151–69.

Hirsch, F. 2005. *Empire of Nations: Ethnographic Knowledge and the Making of the Soviet Union*. Ithaca: Cornell University Press.

Hobsbawm, E.J. 1990. *Nations and Nationalism since 1780: Programme, Myth, Reality*. Cambridge: Cambridge University Press.

Hobsbawm, E.J., and T.O. Ranger (eds) 1983. *The Invention of Tradition*. Cambridge: Cambridge University Press.

Holm-Hansen, J. 1999. 'Political Integration in Kazakstan', in P. Kolstø (ed.), *Nation-Building and Ethnic Integration in Post-Soviet Societies: An Investigation of Latvia and Kazakstan*. Boulder: Westview Press, pp. 153–226.

Humphrey, C., and J. Laidlaw. 1994. *The Archetypal Actions of Ritual: A Theory of Ritual Illustrated by the Jain Rite of Worship*. Oxford: Clarendon.

Humphrey, R., R. Miller and E. Zdravomyslova. 2003. 'Introduction: Biographical Research and Historical Watersheds', in R. Humphrey, R. Miller and E. Zdravomyslova (eds), *Biographical Research in Eastern Europe: Altered Lives and Broken Biographies*. Aldershot: Ashgate, pp. 1–23.

Hyman, A. 1996. 'Volga Germans', in G. Smith (ed.), *The Nationalities Question in the Post-Soviet States*. London: Longman, pp. 462–76.

Ilkhamov, A. 2013. 'Labour Migration and the Ritual Economy of the Uzbek Extended Family', *Zeitschrift für Ethnologie* 138(2): 259–84.

Info-Dienst Deutsche Aussiedler. 2001. *Zahlen, Daten, Fakten*. Bundesministerium des Inneren, Vol. 110.

Ingenhorst, H. 1997. *Die Rußlanddeutschen zwischen Tradtition und Moderne*. Frankfurt/M.: Campus.

Isabaeva, E. 2011. 'Leaving to Enable Others to Remain: Remittances and New Moral Economies of Migration in Southern Kyrgyzstan', *Central Asian Survey* 30(3–4): 541–54.

Jenkins, R. 1996. *Social Identity*. London: Routledge.

———. 1997. *Rethinking Ethnicity: Arguments and Explorations*. London: Sage.

Jones Luong, P. 2004a. 'Introduction: Politics in the Periphery. Competing Views of Central Asian States and Societies', in P. Jones Luong (ed.), *The Transformation of Central Asia:*

States and Societies from Soviet Rule to Independence. Ithaca: Cornell University Press, pp. 1–26.

―――― . 2004b. 'Economic "Decentralization" in Kazakhstan: Causes and Consequences', in P. Jones Luong (ed.), *The Transformation of Central Asia: States and Societies from Soviet Rule to Independence*. Ithaca: Cornell University Press, pp. 182–210.

Kalshev, A.B. 1998. 'Struktura i tipy semi u nemtsev Semirechya', in I. Erofeeva and Yu. Romanov (eds), *Istoriya Nemtsev Tsentralnoj Asii: Materialy Mezhdunarodnoj Haychnoj Konferentsii*. Almaty: Kompleks, pp. 165–70.

Kaschuba, W. 2001. 'Geschichtspolitik und Identitätspolitik: Nationale und ethnische Diskurse im Vergleich', in B. Binder, W. Kaschuba and P. Niedermüller (eds), *Inszenierung des Nationalen: Geschichte, Kultur und die Politik der Identitäten am Ende des 20. Jahrhunderts*. Cologne: Böhlau, pp. 19–42.

Kehl-Bodrogi, K. 2008. *'Religion is Not so Strong Here': Muslim Religious Life in Khorezm after Socialism*. Münster: Lit.

Kennedy, P., and V. Roudometof. 2002. 'Transnationalism in a Global Age', in P. Kennedy and V. Roudometof (eds), *Communities across Borders: New Immigrants and Transnational Cultures*. London: Routledge, pp. 1–26.

Khagram, S., and P. Levitt. 2008. 'Constructing Transnational Studies', in L. Pries (ed.), *Rethinking Transnationalism: The Meso-Link of Organisations*. London: Routledge, pp. 21–39.

Khazanov, A.M. 1995. 'The Ethnic Problems of Contemporary Kazakhstan', *Central Asian Survey* 14(2): 243–64.

Knight, N. 2000. 'Ethnicity, Nationality and the Masses: Narodnost and Modernity in Imperial Russia', in D.L. Hoffmann and Y. Kotsonis (eds), *Russian Modernity: Politics, Knowledge, Practices*. New York: St. Martin's Press, pp. 41–64.

Kolstø, P. 1999. 'Bipolar Societies?' in P. Kolstø (ed.), *Nation-Building and Ethnic Integration in Post-Soviet Societies: An Investigation of Latvia and Kazakstan*. Boulder: Westview Press, pp. 15–43.

Köpping, K.P., B. Leistle and M. Rudolph. 2006. 'Introduction', in K.P. Köpping, B. Leistle and M. Rudolph (eds), *Ritual and Identity: Performative Practices as Effective Transformations of Social Reality*. Münster: Lit, pp. 9–32.

Krieger, V. 2006. *Iz ictorii nemtsev tsentralnoy Azii*. Almaty: Dajk-Press.

Kühnel, W., and R. Strobl. 2000. *Dazugehörig und ausgegrenzt: Analysen zu Integrationschancen junger Aussiedler*. Weinheim: Juventa-Verlag.

Kuzio, T. 2005. 'Western Multicultural Theory and Practice and its Application to the Post-Soviet States', *Journal of Contemporary European Studies* 13(2): 221–37.

Laszczkowski, M. 2016. *'City of the Future': Built Space, Modernity and Urban Change in Astana*. Oxford, New York: Berghahn.

Landa, J.T. 1998. *Trust, Ethnicity, and Identity: Beyond the New Institutional Economics of Ethnic Trading Networks, Contract Law, and Gift-Exchange*. Ann Arbor: University of Michigan Press.

Ledeneva, A. 1998. *Russia's Economy of Favours*. Cambridge: Cambridge University Press.

Lemberg, H. 2008. 'Reasons and Conditions of Population Transfer: The Expulsion of Germans from East and Central Europe and Their Integration in Germany and Abroad after World War II', in M. Schulze, J.M. Skidmore, D.G. John, G. Liebscher and S. Siebel-Achenbach (eds), *German Diasporic Experiences: Identity, Migration, and Loss*. Waterloo: Wilfrid Laurier University Press, pp. 359–78.

Lemon, A. 2002. 'Without a "Concept"? Race as Discursive Practice', *Slavic Review* 61(1): 54–61.
Lévi-Strauss, C. 1969. *The Elementary Structures of Kinship*. Boston: Beacon Press.
Levitt, P., and N. Glick Schiller. 2004. 'Conceptualizing Simultaneity: A Transnational Social Field Perspective on Society', *International Migration Review* 38(3): 1002–39.
———. 2007. 'Conceptualizing Simultaneity: A Transnational Social Field Perspective on Society', in A. Portes and J. DeWind (eds), *Rethinking Migration: New Theoretical and Emperical Perspectives*. Oxford, New York: Berghahn, pp. 181–218.
Liberona, A. 2005. '"Egal ob es Akademikerinnen sind oder Professor oder wie auch immer, Prokuristen, Maschinisten, Melkerinnen, die fangen hier alle in Deutschland mit Putzen an": Niedriglohndienstleistungssektor und russischsprachige Migrantinnen', *Anthropolitan* 12: 65–72.
Linde, C. 1993. *Life Stories: The Creation of Coherence*. New York: Oxford University Press.
Lounsbury, F.G. 1968. 'The Structural Analysis of Kinship Semantics', in P. Bohannan and J. Middleton (eds), *Kinship and Social Organization*. Garden City: Natural History Press, pp. 125–48.
McBrien, J. 2006. 'Extreme Conversations: Secularism, Religious Pluralism, and the Rhetoric of Islamic Extremism in Southern Kyrgyzstan', in C. Hann (ed.), *The Postsocialist Religious Question: Faith and Power in Central Asia and East-Central Europe*. Berlin: Lit, pp. 47–73.
Malkki, L. 1992. 'National Geographic: The Rooting of Peoples and the Territorialization of National Identity among Scholars and Refugees', *Cultural Anthropology* 7(1):24–44.
Marcus, G.E. 1995. 'Ethnography in/of the World System: The Emergence of Multi-Sited Ethnography', *Annual Review of Anthropology* 24: 95–117.
Martin, T.D. 1998. 'The Origins of Soviet Ethnic Cleansing', *The Journal of Modern History* 70(4): 813–61.
———. 2001. *The Affirmative Action Empire: Nations and Nationalism in the Soviet Union, 1923–1939*. Ithaca: Cornell University Press.
Masanov, N. 1999. 'Migratsionnye metamorfozy Kazachstana', in N. Kosmarskaya, A. Vyatkin and S. Panarin (eds), *V dvizhenii dobrovol'nom i vynuzhdennom*. Moscow: Natalic.
Massey, D. 1995. 'The Conceptualization of Place', in D. Massey and P. Jess (eds), *A Place in the World? Places, Cultures and Globalization*. Oxford: Oxford University Press, pp. 45–85.
Mattock, V. 2015. 'Rückwanderung von (Spät-)Aussiedlern nach Russland: Annäherung an ein schwer fassbares Phänomen', in M. Kaiser and M. Schönhuth (eds), *Zuhause? Fremd? Migrations- und Beheimatungsstrategien zwischen Deutschland und Eurasien*. Bielefeld: transcript, pp. 171–91.
May, S. 2001. *Language and Minority Rights: Ethnicity, Nationalism and the Politics of Language*. Harlow: Longman.
———. 2004. *Ethnicity, Nationalism and Minority Rights*. Cambridge: Cambridge University Press.
Miller, J.C. 1980. 'Introduction: Listening for the African Past', in J.C. Miller (ed.), *The African Past Speaks: Essays on Oral Tradition and History*. Folkestone: Dawson, pp. 1–60.
Miller, R.L. 2000. *Researching Life Stories and Family Histories*. London: Sage.
Mitchell, J.C. 1969. 'The Concept and Use of Social Networks', in J.C. Mitchell (ed.), *Social Networks in Urban Situations: Analyses of Personal Relationships in Central African Towns*. Manchester: Manchester University Press, pp. 1–50.
———. 1974. 'Social Networks', *Annual Review of Anthropology* 3: 279–99.
Moore, D.S. 2000. 'Germany's Repatriation Policies and Nationality Tests in Russia: An Ethnography of Immigration Policy', in B. Agozino (ed.), *Theoretical and Methodological*

Issues in Migration Research: Interdisciplinary, Intergenerational and International Perspectives. Aldershot: Ashgate, pp. 167–79.
Morley, D., and K. Robins. 1990. 'No Place like *Heimat*: Images of Home(land) in European Culture', *New Formations* 12: 1–23.
Morley, D. 2000. *Home Territories: Media, Mobility and Identity*. London: Routledge.
Naumkin, V. 1994. *Central Asia and Transcaucasia: Ethnicity and Conflict*. Westport: Greenwood Press.
Nieswand, B. 2007. 'Ghanaian Migrants in Germany and the Status Paradox of Migration: A Multi-Sited Ethnography of Transnational Pathways of Migrant Inclusion', Ph.D. dissertation. Halle (Saale): Martin Luther University Halle-Wittenberg, Philosophical Faculty I.
Niethammer, L., and W. Trapp. 1985. 'Einführung', in L. Niethammer and W. Trapp (eds), *Lebenserfahrung und kollektives Gedächtnis: Die Praxis der 'Oral History'*. Frankfurt/M.: Suhrkamp, pp. 7–33.
Nolte, H.-H. 1996. 'Deutsche Fachleute in Rußland – gefürchtete Gäste?' in A. von Saldern, H. Bley and H.-H. Nolte (eds), *Deutsche Migrationen*. Münster: Lit, pp. 77–88.
Oh, C.J. 2006. 'Diaspora Nationalism: The Case of Ethnic Korean Minority in Kazakhstan and its Lessons from the Crimean Tatars in Turkey', *Nationalities Papers* 34(2): 111–29.
Oka, N. 2006. 'The "Triadic Nexus" in Kazakhstan: A Comparative Study of Russians, Uighurs, and Koreans', in O. Leda (ed.), *Beyond Sovereignty: From Status Law to Transnational Citizenship?* Sapporo: Hokkaido University, Slavic Research Center, pp. 359–80.
Olcott, M.B. 1981. 'The Collectivization Drive in Kazakhstan', *Russian Review* 40(2): 122–42.
———. 1997. 'Kazakhstan: Pushing for Eurasia', in I. Bremmer (ed.), *New States, New Politics: Building the Post-Soviet Nations*. Cambridge: Cambridge University Press, pp. 547–70.
———. 2002. *Kazakhstan: Unfulfilled Promise*. Washington: Carnegie Endowment for International Peace.
Oltmer, J. 2006. '"To Live as Germans among Germans": Immigration and Integration of "Ethnic Germans" in the German Empire and the Weimar Republic', in L. Lucassen, D. Feldman and J. Oltmer (eds), *Immigrant Integration in Western Europe, Then and Now*. Amsterdam: Amsterdam University Press, pp. 98–115.
Otarbaeva, B. 1998. 'A Brief History of the Kazak People', *Nationalities Papers* 26(3): 421–32.
Passerini, L. 1992. 'Introduction', in L. Passerini (ed.), *Memory and Totalitarianism*. Oxford: Oxford University Press, pp. 1–20.
Patten, A. 2001. 'Political Theory and Language Policy', *Political Theory* 29(5): 691–715.
Pelkmans, M. 2007. '"Culture" as a Tool and an Obstacle: Missionary Encounters in Post-Soviet Kyrgyzstan', *Royal Anthropological Institute of Great Britain and Ireland: The Journal of the Royal Anthropological Institute* 13(4): 881–99.
Petersen, W. 1958. 'A General Typology of Migration', *American Sociological Review* 23(3): 256–66.
Peyrouse, S. 2004. 'Christianity and Nationality in Soviet and Post-Soviet Central Asia: Mutual Intrusions and Instrumentalizations', *Nationalities Papers* 32(3): 651–74.
———. 2007. 'Nationhood and the Minority Question in Central Asia: The Russians in Kazakhstan', *Europe-Asia Studies* 59(3): 481–501.
———. 2008. 'The "Imperial Minority": An Interpretative Framework of the Russians in Kazakhstan in the 1990s', *Nationalities Papers* 36(1): 105–23.
Pfister-Heckmann, H. 1998. *Sehnsucht Heimat? Die Rußlanddeutschen im niedersächsischen Landkreis Cloppenburg*. Münster: Waxmann.

Pichler, E., and O. Schmidtke. 2004. 'Migranten im Spiegel des deutschen Mediendiskurses: "Bereicherung" oder "Belastung"?', in K. Eder, V. Rauer and O. Schmidtke (eds), *Die Einhegung des Anderen: Türkische, polnische und russlanddeutsche Einwanderer in Deutschland*. Wiesbaden: Verlag für Sozialwissenschaften, pp. 49–76.

Pine, F., D. Kaneff and H. Haukanes. 2004. 'Introduction: Memory, Politics and Religion: A Perspective on Europe', in F. Pine, D. Kaneff and H. Haukanes (eds), *Memory, Politics and Religion: The Past Meets the Present in Europe*. Münster: Lit, pp. 1–30.

Plummer, K. 2001. 'The Call of Life Stories in Ethnographic Research', in P. Atkinson, A.J. Coffey, S. Deramont, J. Lofland and L.H. Lofland (eds), *Handbook of Ethnography*. London: Sage, pp. 395–406.

Pohl, J.O. 2008. 'Suffering in a Province of Asia: The Russian German Diaspora in Kazakhstan', in M. Schulze, J.M. Skidmore, D.G. John, G. Liebscher and S. Siebel-Achenbach (eds), *German Diasporic Experiences: Identity, Migration, and Loss*. Waterloo: Wilfrid Laurier University Press, pp. 405–18.

Portes, A., and J. DeWind. 2007. 'A Cross-Atlantic Dialogue: The Progress of Research and Theory in the Study of International Migration', in A. Portes and J. DeWind (eds), *Rethinking Migration: New Theoretical and Empirical Perspectives*. Oxford, New York: Berghahn, pp. 3–28.

Pries, L. 2008. 'Transnational Societal Spaces: Which Units of Analysis, Reference, and Measurement?' in L. Pries (ed.), *Rethinking Transnationalism: The Meso-Link of Organisations*. London: Routledge, pp. 1–20.

Radenbach, N., and G. Rosenthal. 2015. '"Ich versteh das immer noch nicht": Belastende Vergangenheiten und brüchige Zugehörigkeiten von Deutschen aus der ehemaligen Sowjetunion', in M. Kaiser and M. Schönhuth (eds), *Zuhause? Fremd? Migrations- und Beheimatungsstrategien zwischen Deutschland und Eurasien*. Bielefeld: transcript, pp. 27–52.

Reeves, M. 2007. 'Unstable Objects: Corpses, Checkpoints and "Chessboard Borders" in the Ferghana Valley', *Anthropology of East Europe Review* 25(1): 72–84.

———. 2010 'Migrations, masculinité et transformations de l'espace social dans la vallée de Sokh', in M. Laruelle (ed.), *Dynamiques migratoires et changements sociétaux en Asie Centrale*. Paris: Editions Petra, pp. 131–47.

———. 2011a. 'Staying Put? Towards a Relational Politics of Mobility at a Time of Migration', *Central Asian Survey* 30(3–4): 555–76.

———. 2011b. 'Introduction: Contested Trajectories and a Dynamic Approach to Place', *Central Asian Survey* 30(3–4): 307–30.

———. 2014. *Border Work: Culture and Society after Socialism*. Ithaca, NY: Cornell University Press.

Riek, G.-A. 2000. *Die Migrationsmotive der Rußlanddeutschen: Eine Studie über die sozial-integrative, politische und ökonomische Lage in Rußland*. Stuttgart: Ibidem.

Roberts, S.R. 2007. 'Everyday Negotiations of Islam in Central Asia: Practicing Religion in the Uyghur Neighborhood of Zarya Vostoka in Almaty, Kazakhstan', in J. Sahadeo and R. Zanca (eds), *Everyday Life in Central Asia: Past and Present*. Bloomington: Indiana University Press, pp. 339–54.

Robertson, R. 1998. 'Glokalisierung: Homogenität und Heterogenität in Raum und Zeit', in U. Beck (ed.), *Perspektiven der Weltgesellschaft*. Frankfurt/M.: Suhrkamp, pp. 192–220.

Römhild, R. 1998. *Die Macht des Ethnischen: Grenzfall Rußlanddeutsche. Perspektiven einer politischen Anthropologie*. Frankfurt/M.: Lang.

———. 2007. 'Fremdzuschreibungen – Selbstpositionierungen. Die Praxis der Ethnisierung im Alltag der Einwanderungsgesellschaft', in B. Schmidt-Lauber (ed.), *Ethnizität und Migration: Einführung in Wissenschaft und Arbeitsfelder*. Berlin: Reimer, pp. 157–77.
Rosenthal, G. (ed.) 1998. *The Holocaust in Three Generations: Families of Victims and Perpetrators of the Nazi Regime*. London: Kassel.
Roy, O. 2000. *The New Central Asia: The Creation of Nations*. London: Tauris.
Sabol, S. 2003. *Russian Colonization and the Genesis of Kazak National Consciousness*. Basingstoke: Palgrave Macmillan.
Safran, W. 1991. 'Diasporas in Modern Societies: Myth of Homeland and Return', *Diaspora* 1(1): 83–99.
Sahadeo, J. 2007. 'Druzhba Narodov or Second-Class Citizenship? Soviet Asian Migrants in a Post-Colonial World', *Central Asian Survey* 26(4): 559–79.
Sakenova, K.A. 1998. 'Kharakternye osobennosti etnokulturnogo oblika selskikh nemtsev Kasakhstana v mestakh dispersnogo rasseleniya (na meterialakh etnosotsiologicheskogo obsledovaniya Almatinskoj oblasti)', in I. Erofeeva and Yu. Romanov (eds), *Istoriya Nemtsev Tsentralnoj Asii: Materialy Mezhdunarodnoj Haychnoj Konferentsii*. Almaty: Kompleks, pp. 171–86.
Salein, K. 2005. 'Was heißt russisch?', *Anthropolitan* 12: 5–12.
Sancak, M. 2007. 'Contested Identity: Encounters with Kazak Diaspora Returning to Kazakstan', *The Anthropology of East Europe Review: Central Europe, Eastern Europe and Eurasia* 25(1): 85–94.
Sanders, R. 2009. 'In the Twilight of Two States: The German House in Tekmok, Kazakhstan', *Anthropological Notebooks* 15(1): 37–47.
———. 2013a. 'Deutsche im ländlichen Kasachstan: Das Streben nach besseren Lebensumständen und die Rolle von Ethnizität', *Zeitschrift für Ethnologie* 138(2): 195–216.
———. 2013b. 'Cosmopolitanism in Kazakhstan: Sociability, Memory and Diasporic Disorder', in U. Ziemer and S.P. Roberts (eds), *East European Diasporas, Migration and Cosmopolitanism*. New York: Routledge, pp. 77–91.
———. 2015. 'Zwischen transnationaler Verstörung und Entzauberung. Kasachstandeutsche Heimatkonzepte', in M. Kaiser and M. Schönhuth (eds), *Zuhause? Fremd? Migrations- und Beheimatungsstrategien zwischen Deutschland und Eurasien*. Bielefeld: transcript, pp. 293–314.
Sanjek, R. 1982. 'The Organization of Households in Adabraka: Toward a Wider Comparative Perspective', *Comparative Studies in Society and History* 24(1): 57–103.
Sarsembayev, A. 1999. 'Imagined Communities: Kazak Nationalism and Kazakification in the 1990s', *Central Asian Survey* 18(3): 319–46.
Savoskul, M. 2015. 'Transnationale Beziehungen hochqualifizierter Migranten aus Russland und der Ukraine in Frankfurt am Main', in M. Kaiser and M. Schönhuth (eds), *Zuhause? Fremd? Migrations- und Beheimatungsstrategien zwischen Deutschland und Eurasien*. Bielefeld: transcript, pp. 379–407.
Schatz, E. 2000. 'The Politics of Multiple Identities: Lineage and Ethnicity in Kazakhstan', *Europe-Asia Studies* 52(3): 489–506.
———. 2004. *Modern Clan Politics: The Power of 'Blood' in Kazakhstan and Beyond*. Seattle: University of Washington Press.
Schieffer, J. 2005. '"Zu Hause ist dort, wo die Familie ist": Eine deutsche Familie aus Russland', *Anthropolitan* 12: 73–88.
Schlee, G. 1989. *Identities on the Move: Clanship and Pastoralism in Northern Kenya*. Manchester: Manchester University Press for the International African Institute.

———. 2001. 'Einleitung', in A. Horstmann and G. Schlee (eds), *Integration durch Verschiedenheit: Lokale und globale Formen interkultureller Kommunikation*. Bielefeld: transcript, pp.17–46.

———. 2006. *Wie Feindbilder entstehen: Eine Theorie religiöser und ethnischer Konflikte*. Munich: Beck.

———. 2008. *How Enemies are Made: Towards a Theory of Ethnic and Religious Conflicts*. Oxford, New York: Berghahn.

Schlee, G., B. Donahoe, J. Eidson, D. Feyissa, V. Fuest, M.V. Höhne, B. Nieswand and O. Zenker. 2009. 'The Formation and Mobilization of Collective Identities in Situations of Conflict and Integration', *Max Planck Institute for Social Anthropology Working Papers No°116*. Halle (Saale): Max Planck Institute for Social Anthropology.

Schmidt, B. 2005. '"Jeder will Respekt haben in seinem Leben": Junge Spätaussiedler in der Ambivalenz transnationaler Dynamiken', *Anthropolitan* 12: 89–106.

Schmidt-Lauber, B. 2007. 'Ethnizität und Migration als ethnologische Forschungs- und Praxisfelder: Eine Einführung', in B. Schmidt-Lauber (ed.), *Ethnizität und Migration*. Berlin: Reimer, pp. 7–27.

Schröder, P. 2013. 'Ainuras Amerikanische Karriere – Räumliche und soziale Mobilität einer jungen Kirgisin', *Zeitschrift für Ethnologie* 138(2): 235–58.

Schoeberlein, J.S. 1994. 'Identity in Central Asia: Construction and Contention in the Conceptions of "Ozbek", "Tajik", "Muslim", "Samarkandi" and Other Groups', Ph.D. dissertation. Harvard University.

Schönhuth, M., and M. Kaiser. 2015. 'Einmal Deutschland und wieder zurück. Umkehrstrategien von (Spät-)Aussiedlern im Kontext sich wandelnder Migrationsregime', in M. Kaiser and M. Schönhuth (eds), *Zuhause? Fremd? Migrations- und Beheimatungsstrategien zwischen Deutschland und Eurasien*. Bielefeld: transcript, pp. 275–90.

Schweizer, T. 1996. *Muster sozialer Ordnung. Netzwerkanalyse als Fundament der Sozialethnologie*. Berlin: Reimer.

Seifert, E. 2006. 'Pesnya rossijskikh nemtsev: k opytu klassifikatsii', in E.G. Boos (ed.), *Trudy: V. Konferentsii Naychnogo Obedineniya Nemtsev Kasakhstana*. Almaty.

Sherbakova, I. 1992a. 'The Gulag in Memory', in L. Passerini (ed.), *Memory and Totalitarianism*. Oxford: Oxford University Press, pp. 103–16.

———. 1992b. 'Voices from the Choir: Reflections on the Development of Oral History in Russia', in L. Passerini (ed.), *Memory and Totalitarianism*. Oxford: Oxford University Press, pp. 188–91.

Sienkiewicz, J.J. 2015. 'Informelle (trans-)nationale soziale Sicherung von Kasachstandeutschen in Deutschland', in M. Kaiser and M. Schönhuth (eds), *Zuhause? Fremd? Migrations- und Beheimatungsstrategien zwischen Deutschland und Eurasien*. Bielefeld: transcript, pp. 355–78.

Slezkine, Y. 1994. 'The USSR as a Communal Apartment, or How a Socialist State Promoted Ethnic Particularism', *Slavic Review* 53(2): 414–52.

Slocum, J.W. 1998. 'Who, and When, Were the *Inorodtsy*? The Evolution of the Category of "Aliens" in Imperial Russia', *The Russian Review* 57(2): 173–90.

Smith, A.D. 1994. 'The Origins of Nations', in J. Hutchinson and A.D. Smith (eds), *Nationalism*. Oxford: Oxford University Press, pp. 147–53.

———. 1996. 'Chosen Peoples', in J. Hutchinson and A.D. Smith (eds), *Ethnicity*. Oxford: Oxford University Press, pp. 189–97.

Smith, G. 1996. 'The Soviet State and Nationalities Policy', in G. Smith (ed.), *The Nationalities Question in the Post-Soviet States*. London: Longman, pp. 2–22.

Sökefeld, M. 2007. 'Problematische Begriffe: "Ethnizität", "Rasse", "Kultur", "Minderheit"', in B. Schmidt-Lauber (ed.), *Ethnizität und Migration: Einführung in Wissenschaft und Arbeitsfelder*. Berlin: Reimer, pp. 31–50.

Spradley, J.P. 2005. *Participant Observation*. South Melbourne: Wadsworth, Thomson Learning.

Stoll, F. 2007. *Kasachstandeutsche: Migrationsstrategien Kasachstandeutscher im Übergang von ethnischer zu transnationaler Migration – aus der Sicht von Kasachstan*. Kisslegg: STOLLVerlag.

Strauss, C., and N. Quinn. 1997. *A Cognitive Theory of Cultural Meaning*. Cambridge: Cambridge University Press.

Stricker, G. 2000. 'Ethnic Germans in Russia and the Former Soviet Union', in S. Wolff (ed.), *German Minorities in Europe: Ethnic Identity and Cultural Belonging*. Oxford, New York: Berghahn, pp. 165–79.

Strutz, A. 2008. '"Memories from Afar": Aspects of Memories Spanning Several Generations in Families of Austrian Jewish Refugees', in M. Schulze, J.M. Skidmore, D.G. John, G. Liebscher and S. Siebel-Achenbach (eds), *German Diasporic Experiences: Identity, Migration, and Loss*. Waterloo: Wilfrid Laurier University Press, pp. 83–94.

Suppes, G. 2015. 'Geförderte Rückkehr von Spätaussiedlern in ihre Herkunftsregionen: Die Arbeit des Projektes "Heimatgarten"', in M. Kaiser and M. Schönhuth (eds), *Zuhause? Fremd? Migrations- und Beheimatungsstrategien zwischen Deutschland und Eurasien*. Bielefeld: transcript, pp. 193–204.

Surucu, C. 2002. 'Modernity, Nationalism, Resistance: Identity Politics in Post-Soviet Kazakhstan', *Central Asian Survey* 21(4): 385–402.

Svanberg, I. 1996. 'Kazakhstan and the Kazakhs', in G. Smith (ed.), *The Nationalities Question in the Post-Soviet States*. London: Longman, pp. 318–33.

Szporluk, R. 1994. *National Identity and Ethnicity in Russia and the New States of Eurasia*. Armonk: Sharpe.

Tauschwitz, Y.-O. 2015. 'Nicht geboren zum im Deutschland leben: Eine Interviewstudie zu den Motiven Russlanddeutscher, in Russland zu verbleiben', in M. Kaiser and M. Schönhuth (eds), *Zuhause? Fremd? Migrations- und Beheimatungsstrategien zwischen Deutschland und Eurasien*. Bielefeld: transcript, pp. 149–70.

Thomas, W.I., and F. Znaniecki. 1958. *The Polish Peasant in Europe and America*. New York: Dover.

Tishkov, V. 1997. *Ethnicity, Nationalism and Conflict in and after the Soviet Union: The Mind Aflame*. London: Sage.

van den Berghe, P.L. 1981. *The Ethnic Phenomenon*. New York: Elsevier.

van Meurs, W. 2001. 'Die sowjetische Ethnographie: Jäger oder Sammler?' in B. Binder, W. Kaschuba and P. Niedermüller (eds), *Inszenierung des Nationalen: Geschichte, Kultur und die Politik der Identitäten am Ende des 20. Jahrhunderts*. Cologne: Böhlau, pp. 107–35.

Vansina, J. 1985. *Oral Tradition as History*. Madison: University of Wisconsin Press.

Verdery, K. 2000. 'Ethnicity, Nationalism, and State-Making', in H. Vermeulen and C. Govers (eds), *The Anthropology of Ethnicity: Beyond 'Ethnic Groups and Boundaries'*. Amsterdam: Het Spinhuis, pp. 33–58.

Vertovec, S. 2007. 'Migrant Transnationalism and Modes of Transformation', in A. Portes and J. DeWind (eds), *Rethinking Migration: New Theoretical and Empirical Perspectives*. Oxford, New York: Berghahn, pp. 149–80.

Wallace, C. 2003. 'Social Networks and Social Capital', in D. Torsello and M. Pappová (eds), *Social Networks in Movement: Time, Interaction and Interethnic Spaces in Central Eastern Europe*. Šamorín: Forum Minority Research Institute, pp. 15–25.

Weber, M. 1996 [1922]. 'The Origins of Ethnic Groups', in J. Hutchinson and A.D. Smith (eds), *Ethnicity*. Oxford: Oxford University Press, pp. 35–40.
Weitz, E.D. 2002. 'Racial Politics without the Concept of Race: Reevaluating Soviet Ethnic and National Purges', *Slavic Review* 61(1): 1–29.
Weller, S.C., and A.K. Romney. 1998. *Systematic Data Collection*. Newbury Park: Sage.
Wellman, B. 2007. 'The Network is Personal: Introduction to a Special Issue of Social Networks', *Social Networks* 29(3): 349–56.
Wensel, S. 1998. 'Muzykalno-pesennoe tvorchestvo i teatralnoe iskusstvo nemtsev Kazakhstana (50-80-e gg.)', in I. Erofeeva and Yu. Romanov (eds), *Istoriya Nemtsev Tsentralnoj Asii: Materialy Mezhdunarodnoj Naychnoj Konferentsii*. Almaty: Kompleks, pp. 154–64.
———. 2006. 'Nemetskij teatr kak faktor vliyaniya na protsessy natsionalnoj kultury (ot idei sozdaniya do protsessa razrusheniya)', in E.G. Boos (ed.), *Trudy: V. Konferentsii Naychnogo Obedineniya Nemtsev Kasakhstana*. Almaty, pp. 233–57.
Werner, C.A. 1997. *Household Networks, Ritual Exchange and Economic Change in Rural Kazakhstan*. Bloomington: Indiana University Press.
White, H.C. 1992. *Identity and Control: A Structural Theory of Action*. Princeton: Princeton University Press.
Wolfe, T.C. 2000. 'Cultures and Communities in the Anthropology of Eastern Europe and the Former Soviet Union', *Annual Review of Anthropology* 29: 195–216.
Yessenova, S. 1996. 'The Outflow of Minorities from the Post-Soviet State: The Case of Kazakhstan', *Nationalities Papers* 24(4): 691–707.
———. 2005. '"Routes and Roots" of Kazakh Identity: Urban Migration in Postsocialist Kazakhstan', *The Russian Review* 64(4): 661–79.
Yessenova, S., and W.D. Dobson. 2000. *Changing Patterns of Livestock, Meat, and Dairy Marketing in Post-Communist Kazakhstan*. Madison: University of Wisconsin Press.
Zanca, R.G. 1999. *The Repeasantization of an Uzbek Kolkhoz: An Ethnographic Account of Postsocialism*. Urbana, Illinois: University of Illinois Press.

Appendix

Personal Network Questionnaire

1. Suppose you need eggs or something like that and the shops are closed, or you need a piece of equipment, for instance a hammer. Who would you ask to lend you that sort of thing?
2. Suppose you need help with jobs in or around the house, for instance you have to move a heavy cupboard. Who would you ask for this kind of help?
3. Suppose you have problems with filling in forms. Who would you ask for help with such problems?
4. Most people discuss important matters from time to time. Looking back over the last six months, who are the people with whom you discussed matters that were important to you?
5. Suppose you need advice with a major change in your life, for instance changing jobs, or emigrating. Who would you ask for advice if such a major change occurred in your life?
6. Suppose you have the flu and must stay in bed for a couple of days. Who would you ask to take care of you or to do some shopping?
7. Suppose you need to borrow a large sum of money. Who would you ask?
8. Suppose you have serious problems with your partner, or your children. With whom would you talk about such problems?
9. Suppose you are feeling depressed and you want to talk to someone about it. With whom would you talk about such problems?
10. With whom do you go out once in a while, for instance for a walk, to a café or a restaurant?
11. With whom do you have contact at least once a month, by visiting each other for a chat, or a cup of tea?
12. Is there anybody else who is important to you, not mentioned so far? For instance, relatives or colleagues?

Index

A

Agency, 9, 11, 14, 220, 225
akimat, akim, 46, 209, 210, 211, 214
Alexander I, 33
'Allrussischer Verband', 38
ancestry, 98, 99–100, 121n16, 193, 204, 205n11, 226, 227
Anderson, Benedict, 10
Assembly of the People of Kazakhstan, 47, 187, 207, 208, 213–14
assimilation, 43, 97
Astana, 47, 82–83, 90n24

B

Baltic Germans, 33, 34, 57n53
Barth, Fredrik, 7, 12, 19nn5–6, 95, 97, 133, 227
binarism, 95, 106, 108, 110, 159, 230
'black', 106, 107, 109, 114, 119, 133, 230
biography, 23, 61, 62, 63
Black Sea Germans, 33
blat, 73, 90n18, 153
'blood', 1, 19n5, 79, 98–100, 101, 121n10, 127n27, 198
boundaries, 47, 50, 93, 95, 102, 193, 203–204, 220
    ethnic, 7, 12–15, 128, 134, 225, 226–27
Brubaker, Rogers, 5, 6, 11, 13–14, 35, 38, 52, 58n74, 147, 157, 173, 187

C

capital
    economic, 153, 181, 182
    social, 153, 162, 171, 181, 233
categorization, 6, 8, 9–11, 12, 13, 14, 62–63, 107, 122n23, 221
Catherine the Great, 31, 32, 33, 54n25, 76, 197
Caucasus, Caucasians, 57n56, 98, 107, 108, 109, 120n6
Central Asia, 2, 3, 5–6, 19n2, 24, 32, 39, 41, 42, 44, 58n71, 96, 108, 120n6, 192, 200, 205nn4–5, 216, 226
China, 79, 97, 124, 139, 164, 165

Chinese, 40, 98, 107, 120n6, 122n23
Christmas, 13, 58, 75–76, 77–78, 195, 209
citizenship, 3, 51, 58n70, 58n74, 122n27, 124, 183n10, 184n17, 216, 224n11
classification, 10, 12–13, 14, 36, 108, 121n19
cognitive representations, 9, 147
cognitive tests, 97, 230, 234
Cohen, Abner, 8, 9, 11–12, 19n6
collective identity, 6, 117
collective switching, 203–204
collectivization, 40–41, 42, 56n46, 56n49
colonialism, 8
commonality, 6
'complicated integration', 178
connectedness, 6, 113
    interconnectedness, 17–18, 51, 144, 145, 181, 201, 212
connectionists, 13
constructionism, 110–16
cultural differences, 7, 8
cultural domain analysis, 97
'cultural revolution', 40–41
'cultural stuff', 7, 95, 106, 133–34, 227

D

D'Andrade, Roy G., 12–13, 15, 19nn9–10, 94, 117, 118
deportation, 3, 24–26, 41–42, 53n3, 53nn6–7, 57nn52–53, 60, 63, 64, 66, 70, 72, 81, 90n21, 105, 136, 197, 218, 226
deported, 16, 21, 25, 41–42, 57nn52–54, 63, 167, 171, 200, 208, 213
diaspora, 3, 5–6, 96, 103, 113, 127, 128, 138, 144–45, 145nn1–2, 162, 173–74, 177, 183n10, 231
'diaspora nationality', 41, 96
dichotomization, 144, 207
discrimination, 3, 24, 25, 26–28, 43, 53n14, 60, 65, 70, 77, 78, 86, 87, 88, 89n9, 89n11, 116, 135, 217, 228
dominant discourse, 11, 17, 94, 95
'double inclusion', 231

252　*Index*

E
Elwert, Georg, 8, 203–204
emotions, 12, 119, 133–37
essentialism, 95, 173
ethnic belonging, 1, 3, 5, 8, 11, 12, 15,
    19n5, 46, 53n14, 60, 70, 71, 76, 86,
    87, 88n1, 93, 98–100, 102, 103, 110,
    111, 114, 117, 118–19, 122nn27–28,
    127–32, 141n2, 147, 153, 159, 178,
    187, 200, 201, 212, 219, 220, 221,
    222, 225, 227, 230, 231, 233, 234
ethnic conflict, 5, 39
ethnic differences, 5, 227
ethnic group, 1, 2, 7–8, 12, 28, 36, 47, 49,
    58n69, 76, 85, 87, 93, 96, 103, 111,
    114, 116, 121n19, 122n21, 122n26,
    128, 139, 147, 157, 187, 210, 214,
    223, 230
'ethnic harmony', 2, 49, 151
ethnic identity, 8, 17, 19n5, 25, 29, 47, 52,
    53n14, 76–77, 82, 96, 97, 110, 124,
    140, 159, 178, 187, 200, 217, 226,
    231
ethnic minority, 10, 106
ethnic turmoil, 2, 5, 51
ethnic uprising, 5
ethnicity, 3, 4, 17, 19nn5–7, 39, 44, 53n14,
    74, 76, 88, 96, 99, 120n3, 122n21,
    124, 128, 133, 137, 140, 157, 183n10,
    201, 204, 211, 212, 222, 227, 228,
    230, 231, 234
    as a resource, 5, 8–9, 10
    concept of, 6–15, 111, 174, 229
ethnicization, 14, 70
'Eurasia', 50
European Kazakhstanis, 87
'evil Germans'(conception of), 70

F
family, 1
    separated, 63–66, 79–80, 163–72
    values of, 52, 77–78, 81, 170
'fascist', 26, 27, 64, 71, 77, 83, 85, 105,
    136
feature analysis, 12–13
festivities, 191, 195, 197, 198, 199, 207,
    208, 209–10, 212–13, 214, 223n4
First World War, 3, 35
'flows of support', 3
'folk traditions', 119
free list, 97, 107, 108

'friendship of the peoples' (*druzhba
    narodov*), 17, 43, 57n60, 124–30, 208,
    228–31

G
Gellner, Ernest, 10
Gemeinschaft, 7
genealogy, 156, 167
German celebrations, 63, 75, 78
'German characteristics', 29–30, 104, 105,
    111, 112, 115–16, 204, 214, 226
German community, 33, 147, 150, 157–59
German culture, 18n1, 77, 96, 127, 191,
    194, 197–98, 204, 209, 219, 220,
    223n4
    public performance of, 192
German dishes, 78, 117
'German enemy nation', 4
'German House', 100–101, 104, 112,
    121n13, 123, 127, 176, 189–99,
    202–204, 205nn2–3, 205nn5–6,
    208–17, 219–22, 223n3, 223n5,
    224n14, 233
    Jugendclub, 100, 191, 195–96, 198, 204,
        209, 210, 211, 219
    Seniorenclub, 101, 191, 192, 193–95,
        197, 198, 204, 205n11, 211, 217, 219
German identity, 2, 3, 4, 12, 17, 18, 25,
    26, 33, 60–61, 63, 65, 71, 76, 77, 79,
    81, 82–83, 87–88, 90n20, 96, 97,
    100–103, 105, 111, 112, 114, 116,
    118, 121n16, 124, 127, 130, 134, 136,
    137, 139–40, 158, 181, 182, 197–98,
    201, 203, 204, 216–18, 220, 225–28,
    231, 233, 234
German-Kazakh relations, 81, 155, 211
German *kolkhoz*, 104, 112
German language, 18n1, 26, 35, 38–39, 43,
    57n59, 70, 78, 89n9, 96–97, 100–102,
    103, 114, 121n11, 133, 173, 178,
    184n21, 193, 202, 209, 217, 219, 226
    courses, 190–91, 205n3, 216, 218,
        223n5, 224n13, 233
    tests, 52, 59n75, 184n13, 217
German memories, 24–30, 133
German parish, 67, 102, 134, 189,
    199–200, 226
    Lutheran parish, 102–103, 121n14, 189,
        198–202, 204, 226
German Rebirth organization, 47, 100, 159,
    187, 216

German Reich, 35, 41–42
'German spirit' (*nemetskiy dukh*), 203, 220, 222, 231, 234
German state, 2, 33, 52, 58n74, 187, 203, 216–22, 224n12, 224n14, 226, 233–34
German success stories, 4
'Germanness', 1, 41, 53n13, 63, 96, 101, 181, 195, 197, 219, 222, 224n11
Germany
   help from, 192–95, 197
   life in, 1, 82, 143, 170–71, 177, 180, 185n24, 220, 232
   views about, 3, 50, 174, 175, 177
Germany's Germans, 2, 4, 24, 162, 179, 233
Germany's minority policy, 219
Goffman, Erving, 9, 19n6
globalization, 144, 145, 173, 207, 231
'good German products', 4
Gorbachev, Mikhail, 43–44, 183n8, 225
Great Patriotic War, 89n11
group size, 205n9
groupism, 12
groupness, 6, 52n1
GTZ (German Organization for Technical Cooperation), 189, 190, 192, 202–203, 205n1, 205nn4–5, 205n10, 216–17, 219, 222, 223n8, 224n13

H
'*Heimat*', 138
Herzfeld, Michael, 10–11, 15, 93–94, 95, 98, 103, 110, 119, 133, 140, 159
'historic homeland', 1, 2, 3, 4, 51, 73, 82, 131, 139, 144, 162, 166–73, 174, 177, 180, 181, 182, 218, 225, 226, 231, 233, 234
Hobsbawm, Eric, 10
homeland, 1, 3, 41, 42, 50, 51, 59n76, 70, 72, 73, 76, 85–86, 90n13, 112, 120n1, 122n27, 127, 131, 137–40, 159, 170, 174, 177, 181, 182, 187, 229, 232

I
identification, 6, 17, 21, 52, 90n24, 94, 103, 133–40, 215, 225, 226–28
   ethnic, 4, 8, 18, 103, 137, 226–28
   process, 4, 7, 9, 49, 88, 120, 135
identity (as analytical tool), 5, 6, 7, 10, 14, 15, 52, 62–87, 95, 147, 154, 158, 159, 173

identity politics, 5, 52
immigration, 2, 3, 4, 32, 33, 42, 54n21, 54n26, 101, 102, 181, 183n2
   application, 53n13, 59n75, 166, 184n21, 191, 202, 218, 226
   policies, 34, 51, 52, 53n13, 59n75, 87, 90n22, 167, 171, 183n8, 183n10, 216, 217–19, 223n7, 224n11, 226, 233
inclusion, 182, 205n11, 222, 227
inclusion and exclusion, 2, 9, 231–34
in-migration, 124
inorodtsy, 31, 32, 114
institutions, 2, 8, 14, 23, 41, 45, 46, 47, 52, 88n2, 189, 203, 219
instrumentalism, 8–9, 19n5
integration, 47, 178
interaction, 7, 8, 9, 10, 13, 14, 19n10, 23, 52n1, 55n34, 112, 134, 148, 230, 234
interethnic harmony, 76, 124–25, 126, 151, 153, 159, 199, 208–15
interethnic marriage, 47, 55n35, 74, 75, 76, 96, 97, 156, 161n15
'internationalism', 38, 42, 43, 50, 56n50, 128–29, 140, 228, 229

J
Jenkins, Richard, 8, 9–10, 11, 12, 19nn5–8, 62, 95
Jugendclub, *see* 'German House'

K
'Kazakh characteristics', 81
Kazakh diaspora, 5–6
Kazakh kinship, 1, 111
Kazakh SSR, 42–45, 48, 53n11, 57n54, 84
Kazakh state, 4–5, 46, 61, 72, 76, 81, 120n1, 121n19, 126, 130, 137, 140, 190, 199, 207, 212, 213, 214, 215, 222, 223n4, 227, 229, 233
'Kazakhization', 46–48, 52, 207
Kazakhstan's nationality policies, 4, 227, 229
Kazakhstani identity, 4, 17, 49–50, 71–76, 124, 139–40, 229
Khan of the *Kishi Zhuz*, 31
kinship, 1, 12, 155, 163, 166, 170, 182
kin ties, 149, 150, 160n7
Kirghiz Autonomous Soviet Socialist Republic, 37
komandatura, 16, 20n13, 42, 53n6, 67, 70, 171

Koreans, 75, 93, 98, 106, 107, 120n1, 120n6, 121n19, 122n23, 129, 141n2, 196, 223n1, 229
korenizatsiya, 39, 43, 44, 229
kultura, 37
kulturnie, 154
Kyrgyz, 75, 109, 120n6, 154, 201
Kyrgyzstan, 5, 171, 201

L

landscape, 17, 154, 175, 176, 177
language, 7–8, 14, 35– 37, 39, 41, 43, 46, 48–49, 53n3, 55n36, 58nn66–67, 73, 85, 86, 95, 96, 97–106, 110, 112, 114, 119, 122n26, 124, 126, 130–33, 134, 136, 137, 140, 141n3, 157, 173, 190, 201, 207, 209, 213, 217, 227, 229
  German, 18n1, 25, 26, 35, 38–39, 43, 52, 57n59, 59n75, 67, 68, 70, 73, 74, 75, 77, 78, 83, 87, 89nn9–10, 91n26, 96, 97, 100–103, 114, 121n11, 133, 134, 173, 175, 178, 184n13, 184n21, 190–91, 193, 200, 201, 202, 205n3, 209, 216, 217, 218, 219, 223n4, 224n13, 226, 232, 233
  Kazakh, 39, 48, 49, 76, 58nn67–68, 73, 74, 83, 85, 86, 91n26, 100, 112–13, 125, 126, 129, 130, 131, 132, 133, 134, 135, 136, 137, 139, 141n7, 153–54, 161n13, 190, 201, 205n6, 211, 213–14, 215, 223n5, 229, 230
  Russian, 43, 48, 49, 55n36, 57n59, 58n68, 68, 73, 76, 83, 85, 87, 89n5, 99, 100, 110, 123, 126, 130, 132, 133, 135, 136, 141n5, 161n13, 163, 179, 185n24, 200, 201, 213
language of interethnic communication, 48, 49, 126
language policies, 48–49, 76, 124, 131, 137, 139, 140, 141n3, 190, 207
Lenin, Vladimir, 35, 36, 55n37, 56n38, 56n42
life experience, 11–12, 13, 17, 228
life story, 15, 21, 23–26, 28, 30, 53n4, 60, 62–64, 69–71, 76, 77, 78, 82, 86, 88, 89n5, 90n25, 105, 135, 136, 141n2, 160n4, 166
local networks/relationships, 18, 145, 148, 165, 181
locality, 144, 147, 148, 160n1

M

marriages, 155–57, 167
  interethnic, 47, 55n35, 96, 156, 196
  patterns, 155, 157, 161n14, 197
Marxism, 35
'Marxism and the National Question', 35, 55n32, 97
memories of the past, 4, 23–30, 226, 234
'memory of deportation', 25–26, 53nn6–7
'mentality', 1, 79, 86, 95, 97–106, 109, 110, 111, 119, 175–79, 183n10, 195
'micro-interaction', 10
migration, 5, 6, 30, 32, 42, 51, 55n30, 122n27, 123, 132, 134, 138, 143, 144–45, 146n6, 161n14, 166, 167, 168, 171, 173, 231; *see also* out-migration
  labour migrants, 4, 145
  refugees, 4, 53n7, 145n1, 146n6, 217
  return, 174–75, 184n16
  rural migrants, 132
minority centres, 126, 199, 205n14, 207–12, 215, 221, 222, 223n2
minority nationality, 4, 18
minority policies, 4, 47, 52, 126, 187, 208
modernity, 10, 46
mother tongue, 58n68, 67, 73, 85, 89n10, 100, 101, 102, 106, 121n12, 126, 190, 218
Muslim, 97, 102, 103, 107, 108, 109, 119, 122nn22–23, 154, 155, 159, 230

N

NKVD (Narodnyi Komissariat Vnutrennikh Del), 41, 71, 90n16
narodnost, narodnosti, 36
national binarism, 95, 106, 108, 159
national categories, 97, 119
national delineation, 38–40
national dichotomies, 106–10
nationalism, 10, 19n7, 44, 46
  disguised nationalism, 46
  ethnic nationalism, 137
  Kazakh nationalism, 39, 46
nationality policies, 4, 18, 23, 37–45, 55n34, 56n38, 89n10, 140, 204, 227, 229
nation-building, 45, 52, 187

nation state, 4, 5, 14, 17, 140, 144, 146n4, 182, 207, 222, 231
  rise of, 10, 45–52, 168
nature, 78, 109, 110, 139, 175, 176, 181
Nauriz, 191, 209, 210, 211
Nazarbayev, Nursultan (president), 2, 45, 47, 49–50, 58nn62–63, 58n71, 70, 76, 125–26, 130, 140, 141n3, 187, 190, 204, 212, 214, 215, 216, 229
norms, 7, 8, 14, 118

O

oral history, 88n2
out-migration, 4, 59n76, 124, 131, 144, 147, 152, 159, 166, 168, 182, 200, 202, 204, 216, 218, 232

P

passport system, 41–42, 56n50, 57n51
personal networks, 90n18, 145, 147–55, 160n5, 160n7, 164, 234
Peter the Great, 31, 32, 33
pile sort, 97, 107–109, 110, 114
postsocialism, 45
power, 5, 8, 9–11, 13, 14, 15, 19n2, 37, 45, 46, 47, 52n1, 53n8, 93–94, 118, 120, 140, 147, 159, 162, 182, 207, 225, 230, 232, 233, 234
primordialism, 19n5, 110–16
Protestants, 102, 121n14, 200
'pure Germans', 2, 100, 196, 217, 218

R

racism, 10, 19n7, 98, 110
  racist, 98, 109, 110, 133
rational choice, 8, 9, 205n9
rebirth organizations, *see* German Rebirth organization.
relationships to Germany, 165–66
relatives in Germany, 51, 82, 124, 162, 163, 166, 168, 170, 171, 173, 180, 181, 182, 183n2, 183n12, 232–33
religion, 7–8, 14, 53n3, 54n24, 95, 97–106, 107, 110, 119, 200, 208, 213, 226, 229
Reliktkultur, 6
repatriation (of the Kazakh diaspora), 5–6, 183n10
ritual, 212, 220
Ruf der Heimat, 3
'ruralization', 132

Russian Empire, 11, 30–35, 55n31
Russian Germans, 1, 6, 19n5, 23, 24–26, 34, 35, 53n3, 53n7, 53n10, 54n25, 63, 76, 84, 89n11, 90n21, 170, 171, 176, 178–80, 184n23, 217, 224, 226
Russians, 2, 16, 26, 27, 28, 29, 31, 32, 34, 39, 40, 47, 48, 50, 53n14, 55n28, 55n36, 60, 65, 66–67, 69, 70, 75–76, 80, 81, 82, 83, 84, 85, 86, 87, 90n19, 93, 95, 96, 97, 102, 103, 104, 105, 107, 108–16, 118–19, 120n6, 121nn18–19, 122nn23–24, 122nn26–27, 123, 124, 125, 126, 129, 130, 131–37, 139, 141n3, 141n6, 147, 150, 151, 153, 154–59, 167, 176, 180, 183n10, 193, 194–95, 200, 204, 207, 213, 214, 221, 222, 223n1, 227–28, 229, 230, 232, 233
Russification, 32, 34, 57n59, 100

S

schema, schema theory, 13–14, 17–18, 94, 95, 110, 117, 119, 124, 147, 154, 155, 225, 228, 229, 230
Schlee, Günther, 7, 8, 9, 15, 94, 116–17, 139, 205n9, 228
Second World War, 3, 6, 16, 24, 25, 26, 27, 30, 42, 53n10, 65, 70, 84, 86, 89n3, 96, 105, 112, 116, 133, 145, 146n6, 155, 167, 175, 192, 200, 226
self-identification, 9, 14, 18, 62, 97, 133
self-understanding, 6, 14
Seniorenclub; *see* German Rebirth organization.
sense of self, 10, 12, 61
Siberia, 3, 16, 21, 24, 32, 42, 55n30, 57n53, 57n56, 63, 64, 115, 167, 171, 226
Sibiriendeutschtum, 6
situational switching, 8
sliyanie, 36
social categorizations, 10
social identities, 9, 10, 12, 220
socialism, 30, 35, 37, 40, 55n37, 56n42, 56n50
Soviet people, 35, 36, 41, 49, 71, 93, 122n28, 228
Soviet policies, 39, 224n12
Soviet racism, 98
Soviet regime, 6, 132, 200, 213
Soviet Russians, 86

Soviet Union, 2, 3, 5, 11, 17, 21, 23, 27, 28, 30, 35–54, 55nn35–36, 56n50, 57n51, 58n61, 58n74, 59n75, 61, 62, 63, 67, 69, 70, 71, 76, 79, 80, 82, 84, 86, 87, 90n12, 90n16, 96, 100, 103, 111, 121n11, 131, 138, 143, 153, 166, 168, 172, 178, 179, 183nn10–11, 222, 225, 226, 229
'sovietology', 6
Stalin, Joseph, 21, 24, 27, 35, 36, 37, 40, 44, 55n32, 55n35, 56n38, 56n45, 86, 97, 197, 208, 229
stereotypes, 10–11, 17, 93–94, 103, 106, 109, 110, 112, 116, 118–19, 121n18, 122n30, 132, 133, 140, 221, 227, 228, 230; *see also* Herzfeld, Michael

T
Tajiks, 75, 97
Taldykorgan, 15–18, 21, 26, 27, 47, 63, 64, 71, 72, 77, 79, 80, 85, 89n5, 97, 100, 102–104, 111, 114, 116, 117, 120, 121n14, 123, 124, 125, 127, 129, 131, 132, 141n1, 141n5, 143, 147, 148, 152, 153, 156, 157–59, 160n8, 161n13, 162–68, 172, 174–75, 177, 179, 180, 181, 185n24, 187, 189–93, 195, 198, 200, 201, 202, 203, 204, 205n2, 205n5, 205n14, 208, 209, 211, 214, 218, 219, 220, 221–22, 223n4, 224n14, 228, 230
territorialization, 51, 59n76
   de-territorialized, 51
   re-territorialization, 51
territory, 35, 38, 39, 41, 42, 47, 48, 49, 57n55, 58n70, 84, 90n13, 95, 97, 98, 105, 114, 119, 122n27, 139, 144, 155, 197, 208, 229

the Bolsheviks, 35–38
'top-down' process, 5
'transition process', 5
'transnational organization', 222
transnational relations, 145, 151, 180, 181, 182, 225
transnationalism, 3, 4, 144–45, 145nn1–2, 162, 207, 231
trudarmya, 42, 53n6, 68, 70, 78, 105

U
Ukraine, 3, 20n13, 24, 39, 40, 42, 55n31, 56n45, 57nn52–53, 78, 82, 101, 112, 122n26, 167, 171, 174, 175, 184n18, 200
unilineal descent system, 99
USSR, 3, 11, 14, 35, 38, 41, 44, 51, 56n49, 62, 70, 90n13, 122n28, 166, 183n8, 184n21, 208, 228

V
Vaterland, 117, 118
Verdery, Katherine, 9, 10
Vertriebenenvolkskunde, 6
victimhood, 21, 30, 173, 174, 226, 231
victims, 6, 11, 30, 61, 62, 226
'Virgin Lands Programme', 42
Volga Germans, 34, 39, 54n27, 57n54
Volga Republic, 20n13, 21, 24, 26, 39, 42, 56n42, 63, 64, 171, 174, 187
Volksdeutsche, 58n74, 216

W
Weber, Max, 7, 8
'white', 106–107, 109, 114, 115, 119, 133
Wolgadeutschtum, 6
working ethos, 105, 112, 226

www.ingramcontent.com/pod-product-compliance
Lightning Source LLC
Chambersburg PA
CBHW070916030426
42336CB00014BA/2432